Mary Lyon.

THE POWER

OF

CHRISTIAN BENEVOLENCE

ILLUSTRATED IN THE

LIFE AND LABORS

OF

MARY LYON.

COMPILED BY

EDWARD HITCHCOCK, D. D., LL. D.,

PRESIDENT OF AMHERST COLLEGE;

WITH THE ASSISTANCE OF OTHERS.

THIRD EDITION.

NORTHAMPTON:

HOPKINS, BRIDGMAN, AND COMPANY.

PHILADELPHIA: THOMAS, COWPERTHWAIT, & CO.

1852.

STEREOTYPED AT THE
BOSTON STEREOTYPE FOUNDRY.

PREFACE.

THE following memoir ought earlier to have been presented to the public. But it has not been in my power. It was not till several months after Miss Lyon's decease that I reluctantly consented to take charge of its compilation. I say reluctantly, not because I thought it an unimportant matter to bring out the private history of such a woman, but because my hands were already too full, and my health too poor. The result was, that before much progress had been made in the work, I sailed for Europe; not, however, until I had requested the trustees of the seminary to put the work into other hands. But on my return I found it still upon me, and I have urged it forward as rapidly as the pressure of other duties has permitted.

When I consented to undertake this work, at the request of the trustees, I had the hope and the prospect of acting merely as the arranger of materials prepared by others. Four ladies were still living who had been associated with Miss Lyon in all the important portions of her life — personal and confidential friends, indeed, who had an intimate knowledge of her character. They were Mrs. Z. P. G. Banister, (formerly Miss Grant,) of Newburyport, Miss Hannah White, of Ashfield, Mrs. Eunice Cowles, (formerly Miss Caldwell,) of Ipswich, and Mrs. M. C. Eddy, of Fall River, (formerly Miss Whitman,) a teacher for many years in the Mount Holyoke Female Seminary, and Miss Lyon's successor as principal. These all consented to give an account of those portions of Miss Lyon's life in which they had been most intimately associated with her; except that Mrs. Banister, on account of her state of health, could not engage to furnish original matter for that portion assigned to her. But Miss Whitman's health so entirely failed her, that she was compelled to abandon her part of the work, which embraced the twelve years of the new seminary before Miss Lyon's death.

The final result of this plan has been, that Part I. of the memoir, which I denominate "The Preparatory Discipline," embracing the first thirty-seven years of Miss Lyon's life, and extending to the time when she left the school at Ipswich, in October, 1834, has been prepared by the joint labors of Miss White and Mrs. Banister. Part II., embracing the next three years, when the effort was made to found and endow the new seminary, and which I denominate "The Great Struggle," has been prepared by Mrs.

Cowles. Part III., entitled "The Victory gained and secured," I have prepared myself, though assisted by the materials accumulated by Miss Whitman which she put into my hands. As compiler of the work, I do, indeed, feel responsible for the whole; and yet I have found it necessary to make but few alterations in Parts I. and II., and those chiefly omissions of epistolary correspondence, in order to keep the work within reasonable limits.

I consider it peculiarly fortunate that I have been able to bring forward this memoir as the work of several authors rather than one. By such a method, indeed, it is difficult to avoid some repetition; but it has the advantage of presenting Miss Lyon's character as it appeared to several of those well acquainted with her, and the average of the whole will be more apt to be right than if all the materials had passed through only one crucible.

The materials for developing Miss Lyon's character have been found more abundant than we supposed accessible. Having been intimately acquainted with her for thirty years, I had imagined that I was well acquainted with her character; but the documents presented in the following pages have developed new traits, and given me a more exalted opinion of her than I ever before entertained. I shall be surprised if the details that follow do not exert a salutary influence upon the cause of education and religion. And I feel that much responsibility rests upon me in attempting to present the outlines of a character so eminent for piety and usefulness. I regret that my part of the work has been necessarily done in too much haste, and under the pressure of too many cares. But personally I feel truly thankful that I have been called to examine and scrutinize a character so worthy of imitation. If I am not made better by it, the fault is my own. Rarely, if ever, has any other private uninspired history made me feel so much the defects of my own motives and actions, or made the retrospect of life appear so meagre and unsatisfactory. May God's blessing accompany the work, so that many others may feel the like influence, and see *the power of Christian benevolence illustrated in the life and labors of Mary Lyon.*

AMHERST COLLEGE, July 1, 1851.

LIST OF ENGRAVINGS.

CONTENTS.

PART I.

THE PREPARATORY DISCIPLINE.

Section I.

Section II.

Section III.

PART II.

THE GREAT STRUGGLE.

Section I.

Section II.

Section III.

Section IV.

Section V.

Section VI.

PART III.

THE VICTORY GAINED AND SECURED.

Section I.

Section II.

Section III.

Section IV.

PART I.

THE PREPARATORY DISCIPLINE.

SECTION I.

From Miss Lyon's Birth, in 1797, to 1821, when she went to Byfield.

MARY LYON was born in Buckland, Franklin county, Massachusetts, February 28, 1797. Her ancestors were among the first settlers of Ashfield, a town adjoining Buckland, in the same county. As far back as they can be traced, they lived, with one or two exceptions, to a very advanced age, were remarkable for the discharge of filial duties, and were of irreproachable character. All were followers of Christ.

Deacon Isaac Shepard, her maternal grandfather, was an eminently pious man. His six children all became Christians in early life, and were blessings to society around them. His father and his son bore the name of Isaac, and each held the office of deacon, thus making three deacons in succession of the same name in the family. A letter from her maternal grandmother is preserved among Miss Lyon's papers, written with the tremulous hand of extreme old age, in which she says it is more than seventy years since she "'listed a soldier for Jesus." She was the daughter of Chileab Smith, a man of ardent piety, whose prayers for his "posterity to the latest generation" are still remembered by those who heard them.

There being no Baptist meeting in the vicinity, and Mr. Smith having a preference for that denomination, he opened his house for public worship, and was instrumental in organizing a small church from the borders of three adjoining townships, Conway, Ashfield, and Buckland. Of this church Mr. Smith was the first leader and instructor. Two of his sons became preachers in the Baptist denomination. One of them succeeded his father in the care of this little church; a good man, who long and steadfastly resisted the current of error and immorality which at times threatened to overwhelm that community. This church still exists, a blessing to the neighborhood.

Aaron Lyon and Jemima Shepard, the parents of Mary, were both members of this church. Their residence was in Buckland, within half a mile of the Ashfield line, and about one mile and a half from the parents of each, and from the place of worship. They therefore continued to worship with their fathers. These and other circumstances led Mary often to say, playfully, that she belonged to both towns.

Her father was remarkable for the uniformity of his temper. He was never known to speak an angry word. Kind and obliging in his manners, he was greatly beloved by his acquaintance, and often was sent for to pray with the sick and dying. Her mother was a person of strong mind and active piety. Her praise is in the churches, and it is enough to say of her here, that Mary was emphatically in her mother's own image. These parents were united in honoring the institution of the Sabbath, and in training their children to make preparation for entering on holy time at an early hour Saturday evening.

Under such influences, "the germ of Mary's character received the culture that decided its future form and growth." It is not known how many of her excellences or principles of action are to be attributed to early and judicious *parental* training; for often "the descending stream of influence owes its salubrity to the salt some pious hand cast into it at a point so high that it has ceased to be acknowledged or known."

Mary was the fifth of seven children, only one of whom, the son, still lives. Her parents, though in comfortable circumstances, were not among the rich of this world. With industry and economy, they were enabled to meet all the *necessary* wants of their rising family. A small farm, that yields a competence to such a family when tilled by a judicious father, and its avails managed by a frugal mother, will, when divided, give but a small portion to each of the children. On the death of their father, in 1802, at the age of forty-five, they were left to depend mostly on their own exertions.

But this loved and rock-bound farm was for a while kept together by the superintendence and frugality of the mother; the only son being then but thirteen years of age.

Let us learn their situation from Mary's own words in the "Missionary Offering," a small book written by her in 1843. After speaking of a want of correspondence between the dress and contributions of a widow and her daughter, who were supported by the widow's needle, she says, "I was strongly reminded by contrast of another widow, whom I knew and loved forty years ago, and of her 'mountain home.' She was not rich in the treasures of earth. Her little farm was surely not more to her, in providing for her seven, than was that skilful needle in providing for the one. But want, at that 'mountain home,' was made to walk so fairly and so gracefully within that circle of limited means, that there was always room enough and to spare for a more restricted neighbor. I can now see that loved widow, just as I did in the days of my childhood. She is less than forty years of age, and her complexion is as fair and her forehead as noble and as lofty as on her bridal day. Now she is in that sweet garden which needs only to be seen to be loved. Now she is surveying the work of the hired man and her young son on that wild, romantic farm; made, one would think, more to feast the soul than to feed the body. But almost always she was to be found busy, both early and late, amid her household cares, and in the culture of the olive plants around her table. In that domain, nothing was left to take its own way. Every thing was made to yield to her faithful and diligent hand. It was no mistake of that good-hearted neighbor, who came in one day, begging the privilege of setting a plant of rare virtue in a corner of her garden, because, as he said, there it could never die. The roses, the pinks, and the peonies, those old-fashioned flowers, which keep time with Old Hundred, could nowhere grow so fresh and so sweet as in that little garden. Nowhere else have I ever seen wild strawberries in such profusion and richness as were gathered near by. Never were rareripes so large and so yellow, and never were peaches so delicious and so fair, as grew on the trees of that favored farm. The apples, too, contrived to ripen before all others, so as to meet in sweet fellowship with peaches and plums, to entertain the aunts and cousins.

"I can now see that 'mountain home,' with its sweet rivulet, finding its way among rocks, and cliffs, and hillocks, and deep, craggy dells. Then just beyond the precincts of the family domain was the 'top of the hill,' crowned by its high, rolling rock, ever inviting the enterprise of each aspiring heart. Every one was amply repaid who would climb that steep hill, and ascend that high rock. There might be seen the far-off mountains, in all their grandeur, and the deep valleys and widely-extended plains, and, more than all, that village below, containing only a very few white houses, but more than some young eyes had previously seen. But, sweetest of all, the length of a mile or more, to the village church, was that wild, winding way, traversed each Sabbath morning by that orderly group, while the family pony gave the mother her horseback ride. There, too, in winter, was that sleigh, packed so snugly and gliding so gently over that same winding way to that same small church.

"At that 'mountain home' every want was promptly and abundantly met by the bounties of summer and the provident care for winter. The autumnal stores, so nicely sorted and arranged, always travelled hand in hand through the long winter, like the barrel of meal and cruse of oil. The apples came out fresh in the spring, and the maple sugar, that most important grocery of the neighborhood, was never known to fail before the warm sun, on the sparkling snow, gave delightful indication that sugar days were near. When gathered around that simple table, no one desired a richer supply than was furnished by the hand of that dear mother. The simple school-day dress, too, so neat and so clean, and amply sufficient in the view of those young minds, should not be forgotten; while the rare gift of the Sunday suit, kept expressly for the occasion, formed an important era in the life of the possessor, and was remembered with grateful smiles for many days afterwards. The children of that household, thus abundantly supplied, never thought of being dependent or depressed. They felt that their father had laid up for them a rich store in grateful hearts, and among the treasures which will never decay; and that their mother, who was considered in all that neighborhood a sort of presiding angel of good works, was continually adding to those stores. I can now remember just the appearance of that neighbor who had a numerous household to clothe, as she said, one day, 'How is it that the widow can do more for me than any one else?'

"But I remember the sorrows, as well as the joys and the labors, of that loved widow, that dearest friend of my young heart. On the 21st of last December, about noon, the days of forty long years were just numbered and finished since death came to that 'mountain home,' and took away that affectionate husband, that kindest of fathers. The dying scene, in that retired 'north room,' I can never forget. How mournful was the contrast between the clear midday sun and those sorrowing hearts, those bursting sighs, and those flowing tears! Those last faltering words, 'My dear children, — what shall I say to you, my children? — God bless you, my children,' have not yet died away on my ear. Then came the funeral, which gathered all the neighborhood around that mourning circle. Gently was it whispered by one and another, 'We have all lost a friend; the peacemaker is gone.' How deep were those weeds of mourning, shrouding that family! Even the plaintive tones of the little one, but just able to lisp her father's name, were oft and long repeated by kind-hearted neighbors. Then came that first cold winter of widowhood. How mournfully did the cheerful fire blaze on the domestic hearth, as we gathered around that bereaved family altar! What child of that household could ever forget those extraordinary prayers of the sorrowing mother for the salvation of her fatherless children, as they were offered up, day by day, through all the long, cold winter? Before that mourning day came, the eldest, while yet a child, professed to love the God of her fathers. As the remaining six were gathered in, one by one, and all before they had passed the years of their youth, the mother failed not to refer to her own agonizing prayers, during that first winter of her widowhood. But the mother is gone, and most of the seven are gone. Together they are gathered to their peaceful rest. Only a remnant is left to talk of that sweet 'mountain home,' of that bereaving December, and of those never-to-be-forgotten prayers." *

* A Sketch of the "Mountain Home," from the pencil of Miss Hannah White, will be found at the end of the first part of this memoir. — E. H.

Previous to the time here described, little is known of Mary. We learn from her friends and acquaintance that she early exhibited marks of a reflecting mind. They relate little events of her childhood, which, though not uncommon at her age, show her inclination to philosophize on subjects as they passed before her. For instance, when she was quite a child, a cousin, who was visiting at her father's, recollects that she left the task her mother had given her to perform, and climbed up by a chair to the hour-glass. Her mother, coming in at the time, inquired what she was doing. She replied, that she had been studying upon it, and believed she had thought of a way by which she could *make more time.*

From all the sources left us, it appears that from childhood to womanhood she was remarkable for a solidity of mind and sobriety of deportment rarely found in the volatile season of youth. With teachableness, energy, frankness, and warmth of heart, were combined elasticity of spirits and an ardent desire to do something to augment the happiness of her friends. To this were added a keen perception of the ludicrous, and a power of humorous description, which rendered her a very enlivening companion.

In early life, her opportunities for education were limited; but being one of the youngest of a family which is known to have excelled in intelligence and scholarship, she undoubtedly received much instruction at home. Until she was six or seven years of age, there was a district school within a mile of her mother's residence. From the time that she was old enough to walk that distance, she attended it regularly when it was in operation. It was then removed two miles from them, and she attended but occasionally. Sometimes she lived with her relatives in Ashfield, sometimes near a school in Buckland, assisting the families into which she was received, as a remuneration for her board.

She was early noticed for her uncommon progress in

study. One of her teachers said, "I should like to see what she would make if she could be sent to college."

She had some peculiarities as a scholar which should be noticed. She committed to memory with unusual facility, and recited with verbal accuracy; yet she did not fail to get a clear understanding of the meaning of her lessons. The teacher is now living with whom she studied Alexander's Grammar; and he says that, in four days, she learned all that scholars were accustomed to commit, and repeated it with correctness at one recitation. Her progress in arithmetic was equally rapid, and she understood clearly and at once the reasons for every operation. But instead of depending on genius, as minds less gifted are prone to do, she believed that her school lessons were to be mastered only by hard study, and applied herself to them with great assiduity and perseverance. She could not express her thoughts in so few words as many do, who have fewer thoughts to express; and her enunciation was so rapid as sometimes to be painful to the listener. She is remembered, even when quite young, to have been particularly attentive to religious instruction. As has been intimated, she was accustomed to worship with her father in the old Baptist meeting-house in Ashfield. There were then no Sabbath schools; and when the weather would permit, it was customary, during the interval of public worship, for the congregation to resort to the cool grove, or the burying-place of the dead. As a necessary consequence, especially where young people are thus grouped together, levity, and conversation unsuited to the Sabbath, would prevail. Mary is remembered as withdrawing herself from those circles, and expressing surprise to her associates that any one could indulge in such things on God's holy day.

The old beech-tree is still remembered, which stood behind a school-house in Ashfield, on whose crooked trunk, in a season of religious interest, she used to sit during the school intermissions, and tell those who gathered around her of the way of salvation, as she had been taught it by her parents, though she had not then herself begun to tread in it.

It is not known that she has left any record of her mental conflict while under religious conviction. Some of her early friends know that the first exercises of her mind, which she was led afterwards to look upon as indicative of a saving change, were in 1816, under the plain, simple explanations of Bible truth from Elder Enos Smith, the brother of her grandmother, to whom reference has already been made. The day which she afterwards regarded as probably the one on which her heart was renewed by the Holy Spirit was the Sabbath. The sermon to which she had been listening was on the character of God; and as she walked through the fields on her return home, reflecting on his glorious attributes, her mind was filled with a sweet sense of his love, and her affections seemed, for the first time, to flow out towards that Being whom she had reverenced, and whose character she had approved from her earliest recollection. But, as will hereafter be seen, her feelings were not then so marked in their character as to lead her to speak of them to others, or to give her much confidence that she was accepted of God.

But let us return to the inmates of "the mountain home." The three sisters older than herself, at a suitable age, entered into the married state. One was settled in Ashfield, one in Buckland, and the oldest resided, first at New Marlborough, Massachusetts, then a few years in Ohio, and finally in Chatauque county, New York. In 1810, her mother married again, and removed to Ashfield, taking with her the two younger sisters. Mary, with her only brother, remained at the homestead. For a year previous to the marriage of this brother, in 1812, being about fifteen years of age, she took the charge of housekeeping, and rendered herself so useful, that he paid her one dollar a week for her services, to aid her in the prosecution of her studies. From this time until

1819, when he removed to the State of New York, her home continued to be in his family.

The removal of her brother, to whom she was tenderly attached, was a great trial to her. She felt that, for the second time, she was made an orphan. Not only must she leave the spot that gave her birth, but she must also be separated from the family so dear to her heart. Yet, while distressed at the separation, with characteristic composure she handed these lines, from an old familiar song, to her brother's wife: —

> "Not one sigh shall tell my story,
> Not one tear my cheek shall stain;
> Silent grief shall be my glory,
> Grief that stoops not to complain."

But those dear children, whose "little hands cling closest to the heart," how did she grieve for them! Her friends that remained with her well remember her grief as they were borne away. For months afterwards, whenever that brother was spoken of in her presence, her tears would flow, and her silent and subdued feelings did not hinder her friends from seeing how deeply and tenderly she loved him. Little did she then imagine that, in process of time, those daughters were to return, to receive instruction from her lips in a seminary founded by her instrumentality; and, being better fitted to perform the duties of life, were to go forth, some to labor as teachers in our own country, and one to teach the benighted heathen under the shadow of a Chinese pagoda.

We now return from this digression.

From her brother's marriage until 1817, little is known of her, except that she occasionally attended school, and commenced her career as teacher near Shelburne Falls, Massachusetts, receiving as compensation, at first, seventy-five cents per week with board.

It was in the autumn of 1817 that she first entered Sanderson Academy, at Ashfield, between four and five miles from her birthplace. She was then emphatically nature's child. Those who knew her only at Ipswich or South Hadley, can realize but little of the Mary Lyon of those days. One remarked of her then, "She is all intellect; she does not know that she has a body to care for." But a warm and true heart soon gained the love and confidence of her associates. Her whole appearance at that time was so unique, her progress in study so unprecedented, her broad, intelligent face so inviting, that no one who was a member of the academy at that time will ever forget her; nor how the scholars used to lay aside their books when she commenced her recitation. Here she found friends to encourage and assist her in her search for knowledge. In the rough specimen, they could see a diamond of uncommon brilliancy, and knew that it needed only to be polished to shine with peculiar lustre.

The slender means which she had collected by services to her brother, by spinning, weaving, teaching, &c., were soon expended. She was about to return to her old employments, when the trustees of the academy gave her the free use of all its advantages. It is supposed that this was the time when she resolved to prepare herself particularly for teaching. She collected her bedding, table linen, &c., constituting the full amount of her household treasures, and exchanged the whole at a boarding-house for a room and a seat at the table. Nothing could exceed the eagerness with which she engaged in the prosecution of her studies. It was judged by the family where she boarded, that she slept, on an average, not more than four hours in the twenty-four; and all her waking moments, except the time occupied by her hurried meals, were spent in study. The academy in Ashfield, although it may, at times, have enjoyed more prosperity, yet never has had collected within its walls, at any other time, minds more fitted to bless the world by their influence. But distinguished as some of them have been for talents and acquirements, no one was able to keep up with Mary in her recitations; and one additional study after another was given her by her teacher, partly as a clog, to keep her within reciting distance of her classes. But all proved insufficient for the purpose. The more her powers were taxed, the more she seemed capable of performing. At last her teacher gave her Adam's Latin Grammar, directing her to omit her extra lessons while committing it to memory, only keeping up with her regular classes in their studies. This, he supposed, would employ her for some time. But within *three days* she had committed and recited all those portions which students then commonly learned when first going over the work. Her teacher* preceded her to the spirit world; but he was frequently heard to say, that he never knew the Latin Grammar more accurately recited; and there are many now living who heard the recitations, and can bear the same testimony.

Her services as a teacher soon began to be eagerly sought, and wherever she could find an opportunity to improve herself and others, she would take a class of pupils. When she had thus obtained sufficient means to justify it, she would go to some place and receive instruction on particular subjects, in which she found herself deficient. No one was more ready to set about and accomplish an improvement in any respect, *when convinced it was necessary.*

At one time, she might be found in a family school in Buckland, teaching all the variety of studies necessary or desirable for an intelligent group of sons and daughters. At another time, she resided for a season in the family of Rev. Edward Hitchcock, then pastor of a church in Conway, (now Dr. Hitchcock, President of Amherst College,) learning from him the principles of natural science, and from his wife the

* E. H. Burritt, author of the "Geography of the Heavens."

arts of drawing and painting. In that place also she taught a select school with much ability and success. Then we find her for one term in Amherst Academy, when, for the first time, she encroached on the small patrimony left her by her father.

At this period of her history, a love for spiritual things did not prominently appear, and she studiously avoided any allusion to her own exercises of mind.

About two years after first entering the academy at Ashfield, being desirous of improving her handwriting, she placed herself under the instruction of one whose name has long been associated with education in that vicinity, and who was known to excel in the art of penmanship. From him we have the following testimony as to her character and appearance at that time: —

" About the year 1819, I was engaged as usual in instructing a district winter school. After I had taught a few weeks, as I went one morning into the school-room, I saw there a stranger seated with my first class. They immediately introduced her, stating that she wished to attend a while, and devote her time especially to penmanship. With that unassuming manner which ever characterized her, she took her place among the common scholars, until, by their request, she was furnished with a chair and a place at the table, there being no desk in the house. Here she patiently sat from day to day, affording assistance in instructing the younger classes as she found she was needed, until she had acquired the elementary principles of the art. After beginning to combine those principles, she handed me her book for a caption or subject, which I was accustomed to furnish for my first class. I wrote hers in Latin. She returned her book, requesting that she might have it in English, remarking that she feared those who might review her book would think her to be *wiser than she was*. I mention this circumstance merely to show that it was a prominent trait in her character *never to appear better than she was.* She was naturally unostentatious, willing to be taught, thankful for favors in any form, especially those which related to the mind.

"While a member of my school, she always appeared delighted with its religious exercises, both at commencement and close, never seeming weary of any thing which related to the welfare of the soul ; and I doubt not she is still Mary Lyon now that she is in heaven, bowing with the redeemed, and engaged in the exalted worship of sainted spirits in the world of glory."

SECTION II.

At Ashfield, *Buckland*, *and Derry*, 1821 *to* 1828.

We have now traced Miss Lyon's course until 1821, when, with the avails of her labor and the remnant of her patrimony, she went to attend the Rev. Joseph Emerson's school, in Byfield, Massachusetts.

Extracts from a letter written since the death of Miss Lyon by the friend* who influenced her to avail herself of Mr. Emerson's instructions will show some of her traits of character at this period.

"Your request to furnish some particulars of dear Mary, at that time, is one with which I would gladly comply ; but the scenes through which I have since passed are so many and so varied, that much which might be of interest has escaped my memory. My first acquaintance with her was at the time when she became a pupil in the academy at Ashfield. On returning from a religious lecture, we fell in company with each other, and we needed no formal intro-

* That friend was Amanda White, afterwards wife of Rev. Mr. Ferry, missionary at Mackinaw, on Lake Superior.

duction. Her frank, open countenance invited confidence, and a mutual interest was at once awakened. Our walk was a long one, and we conversed freely on various subjects. Learning that I was expecting to enter the school also, she expressed a wish that we might occupy the same desk. With this I readily complied; and I pursued the same branches of study that she did, so far as I could keep up with her. She was ever ready to lay aside her books, and lend a helping hand to those of weaker intellect. Though nearly thirty years have elapsed since then, I seem even now to see her cheerful, laughing face turned upon me, as I presented some Gordian knot in my studies for her to unravel. You know we occupied the same room at Byfield, and you are also aware that at that time she had many undesirable habits of person and manners. I felt, from my first acquaintance with her, that she was made for some important station; and that, unless various little things were corrected, they would greatly detract from her usefulness. Though conscious of my inferiority, I ever felt it my duty, while with her, to be faithful in helping her to *see*, *feel*, and *correct* these defects. But, O, my very heart aches now, as I review these tasks of friendship. Not that I have any reason to suppose she was unwilling to be improved. Far otherwise. Almost invariably, when I commenced speaking to her, she would come directly to me, and place a hand upon each shoulder, while her bright, beaming eyes and sunny face spoke the gratitude of her heart. 'O,' she would exclaim, 'was there ever a poor, erring mortal that had such kind friends!'

"I made it a point to attend to the nameless little duties necessary to our comfort in the room, leaving to her share such as she could not well overlook or omit. You know she then needed constant watchfulness as to her personal appearance, the care of her clothing, &c. Indeed, she did not devote sufficient thought and attention to the subject to know when she was suitably dressed to appear in company. Of course, she never went out without my inspection, to see that all was right; as she was very liable to leave off some article, or put one on the wrong side out. She was also one of the unfortunate ones whose wearing apparel seems doomed to receive the contents of every overturned inkstand or lamp; but she met every such accident with the same good humor and pleasantry that she manifested on every occasion."

At Byfield, her intellectual capacity was appreciated by the discerning. In speaking of her, years afterwards, Mr. Emerson remarked to Miss Grant, that he had instructed several ladies, whose minds were better disciplined than Miss Lyon's; but in mental *power*, he considered her superior to any other pupil he had ever had in his seminary. That she there exercised great application is shown by one of the letters of her room-mate, written at that period, wherein she says, "Mary sends love to all; but time with her is too precious to spend it in writing letters. She is gaining knowledge by handfuls."

From this friend we have also some account of the improvement in her religious character while at Byfield.

"Within two or three days after our term commenced, Mr. Emerson, having prepared the way by appropriate remarks, requested such of his pupils as were professors of religion, or hoped they had been renewed by divine grace, to remain in the seminary hall during the time of recess, that he might see them a few minutes by themselves. He then endeavored to show them their responsibility as the representatives of Christ in that school; the importance of their growing in grace while there; and the propriety of their exerting an influence in favor of the Redeemer and his cause upon their fellow-pupils. He then appointed a weekly prayer meeting, which he requested they would all uniformly attend. This caused Mary much agitation of mind; for she felt that here was a dividing line. She must now class herself with the children of God, or with those who knew him not. She said that she had too long denied Christ before men, while her conscience testified that the friends of God were her chosen companions. After much deliberation, she concluded to attend the meeting. She never regretted her decision, although, for some weeks after, she was so entirely absorbed in her studies as to neglect many Christian duties. To my reproof she would say, that her object was a laudable one; her means were so limited, and her time so precious, that it could not be wrong for her to employ her energies in gaining knowledge. You know there was unusual interest in religious subjects during that summer, and Mary's mind became deeply exercised. She said she had neglected duty, yielded to temptation, and that her unbounded thirst for knowledge had so absorbed every feeling, that there was no room left for a Savior's love. "O, my leanness, my leanness!" was her bitter cry. In the course of a few days, she became more calm. As there was no family worship under the roof where we boarded, she proposed that we should invite one of the young ladies of the family, who was serious, to unite with us in our evening devotions. From this time Mary was faithful in conversing with her and her sisters; and she seemed, in her daily pursuits, to do all heartily as unto the Lord.

"I sincerely thank you for the particulars of dear Mary's sickness and death. Her being taken away in the midst of her extensive usefulness reminds me of a remark she made when Mr. Evarts was called home: 'Perhaps such mighty ones are removed, that such weak, insignificant instruments as we are may have the privilege of doing more to promote the cause of Christ.'"

The following letters to her mother and sisters should here find a place:—

TO HER MOTHER.

"BYFIELD, May 13, 1821.

". . . . . . I feel that this summer is, or ought to be, peculiarly profitable to me. Much depends on it. Such a spirit of piety is mingled with all Mr. Emerson's instructions, that the one thing needful is daily impressed on our minds. From our scientific pursuits he is ever ready to draw practical and religious instruction. O my mother, I know you would be delighted to witness our devotional exercises, both morning and evening; to hear him read and explain the Scriptures, to hear such pious counsel from his lips, and to unite with him in his fervent prayers at the throne of grace in behalf of his scholars. He renders every recitation attractive. Never have I attended one, from which I might not gain valuable information, either scientific, moral, or religious. We have Sabbath lessons to recite Monday morning.

. . . . .

"You ask if I am contented, and if I am satisfied with my school. I am perfectly so. I can complain of nothing but myself."

TO THE SAME.

"July 21, 1821.

"Each passing day carries my heart home to you, my dear parent, and all my other friends, till I can no longer refrain from writing. Did you know how much my heart dwells on her who loves me with a mother's love, some of you, ere this, would have filled a sheet for my perusal. I long to see you; but I will suppress my tender emotions, while I have recourse to my slow, feeble pen, as a poor substitute for the rapid conversation at the meeting hour of a mother and daughter — conversation which stops not for thoughts. Recently I have thought more of you than ever, and there has been a *reason*. Dear mother, could you, in imagination, have visited Byfield this week, and have had presented to your view a true picture of the passing scene, methinks your heart would have risen in gratitude to Him who is able to soften the hardest heart, and arouse the most stupid mind. We have a female prayer meeting on Saturday evenings, termed 'the seminary concert,' for those members of the school who dare hope that they have an interest at the throne of grace; and these constitute about half our number. This has been regularly attended ever since the establishment of the seminary. Four or five weeks ago, it began to be an inquiry with many, what they should do for the salvation of their own souls and the souls of others. Even eight or nine weeks since, as I was conversing with Miss D., (a young lady whom I mentioned to you as designed for a mission to Jerusalem,) she expressed great anxiety for those who had no hope; observing that she thought Christians had much to do, and that their situation here as school associates gave them a peculiar advantage. Her observations made some impression on my mind, but on my heart I fear such impressions are mostly 'like the morning cloud and early dew.' With many other excellences, I believe she is eminently pious; and I hope she will be an instrument of much good in her anticipated situation. An increasing anxiety for a revival in the seminary began to prevail. I believe that in this respect Mr. Emerson has been highly blessed in his school. I cannot but think it has been owing, in a great measure, to his excellent instruction, together with the influence of his pupils, a great number of whom are pious. All, at this time, appeared to believe that it would be their fault if this stupidity and carelessness continued through the summer. Mr. Emerson's assistant expressed her feelings, at one of our meetings, in the most interesting and affecting manner. She feared that the Savior was here wounded in the house of his friends; that Christians in this school were grieving the Holy Spirit; that the state of their hearts presented obstacles to his special presence and work. The solemnity, affection, and tender solicitude with which she uttered these remarks, appeared to make a deep impression on every mind. Since that, a visible change has been in progress in the school. This week, especially, a deep solemnity has been depicted on every countenance. Sometimes, during devotional exercises, or while listening to Mr. E.'s instructions and solemn warnings, scarcely a heart has been able to refrain from sighs, or an eye from tears. Four express a faint hope that they have passed from death unto life; but they hope with trembling. They feel that there is great danger of being deceived; that they shall believe stupidity to be trust in God, and thus sink down in security, and finally plunge themselves in everlasting ruin. Such fears seem to me not unfavorable. Well may they fear, and well may we tremble for them, and for all those who are passing this critical period, this all-important moment of their lives. Should any cherish a false hope, should any lay their foundation in the sand, almost as easily might the dead be raised, as such be rescued from eternal destruction. May this not be the case with me?

"This attention is entirely confined to the seminary. Imagine to yourself a little circle of about forty females, almost excluded from the rest of the human family, all appearing solemn as eternity.

"*Monday Eve.* — We had a solemn time yesterday. Mr. E. is very solicitous for our spiritual, as well as temporal, welfare. This morning he made some remarks on the importance and manner of studying the Scriptures, and the importance of prayer. He daily gives us much good instruction. Friday morning was a solemn time. Mr. E. remarked upon the great importance of improving the present period to secure our salvation, observing that a little cloud had arisen, which was gently distilling a few drops on this favored spot. Though it was equally easy with God, yet it was not probable, when most of us should disperse and mingle with our friends and companions, that the cloud would follow us; but most likely that those who had not made their peace with God would gradually lose their impressions, and when they should return, the shower would be past. This school term closes to-morrow, and the vacation is two weeks. After earnestly and solemnly inviting, entreating, and warning us not to let the present moment pass, he closed by saying, 'What you do, do quickly.' There is great reason to fear that this cloud will pass by. It reminds me of the favorable appearance at Buckland last fall; but, alas! that passed away as the morning cloud and early dew. Will that be the case here? I cannot bear the thought. As we are about to separate, the members of the seminary concert met at our chamber after school for prayer. We had an impressive season. O my mother, will you not remember this meeting Saturday evening?"

"BYFIELD, July 30, 1821.

"DEAR SISTER ROSINA:

". . . . . I have been over to the seminary, and spent a part of the day in writing alone, for the purpose both of amusing myself during this lonesome vacation, and of improving my handwriting. As I mentioned amusement for vacation, perhaps you think I have nothing to do. Far otherwise. The vacation is almost half gone, and I have but just begun the business I designed to complete. Still I cannot say that I am not lonesome. You cannot imagine the contrast between this week and last. What think you my emotions were, when I saw my companions dispersing in all directions to embrace their parents, brothers, and sisters?

. . . . . .

"O that I could fly over the hills and pay you a visit. Friends know best the strength of their love when they are separated. If possible, I think more of you now than ever.

But should I fill a whole sheet in describing my desire to see you, and the delight which would be derived from an interview with you, it would be saying just nothing at all; therefore I shall leave all to be supplied by your imagination.

. . . . .

"A lady from Maine has just arrived to attend the seminary. Perhaps you will be surprised when I tell you that she is a minister's widow. I should judge she was more than thirty years of age. This would be remarked as uncommon in any school but Mr. Emerson's. Though no married ladies were here last term, yet there had been such in seasons past.

. . . . .

"You ask what proficiency I make in my studies. You know I always found difficulties, doubts, and inconsistencies in grammar; and the most I have done in that branch is to multiply these difficulties on every hand. But I must not be discouraged at this. Mr. E. remarked to us that nothing yet has been brought to perfection; and, as there are difficulties in every pursuit, if a person sees none, it argues his almost entire ignorance. Dr. Emmons observed once to Mr. E. that he often found it much harder to make a pupil discover a difficulty, than to remove it when discovered."

TO HER YOUNGEST SISTER.

"BYFIELD, August 11, 1821.

". . . . . I possess many facilities for improvement, but they only increase my obligation. I believe I have never before realized the solemnity of living, so much as I do this summer. I often think that, if possible, it is more solemn to live than to die. What important consequences may depend on a single word, or on the most trifling deed! With how much care and deliberation should we regulate all our conduct, and even our every thought! This requires the most vigorous exertion of all our faculties; nay, more, we need constant instruction from heaven, and the daily guidance of the Holy Spirit."

After Miss Lyon's return from Byfield, in the winter and spring of 1822, she was engaged to assist in the academy at Ashfield, then under the care of Mr. Abijah Cross, now settled in the ministry in West Haverhill, Massachusetts. There had also been a season of deep religious interest in that school; and coming into it so directly from Byfield, where her feelings had undergone a change, her religious character still gradually improved. She was not then inclined to speak to others of the things concerning their eternal welfare, nor did she acknowledge much religious enjoyment. But she always listened with the greatest deference and interest to any religious instruction; and it is the testimony of Mr. Cross that her influence was decidedly for Christ and his cause.

It should not be understood that she did not at this time converse with her pupils on what would generally be termed religious subjects. Her regard for the Bible was so fervent, and her reverence for it so profound, that she would dwell on its beauty and sublimity with deep interest. She would also talk with great delight of the principles of natural religion; and when instructing in natural philosophy, astronomy, &c., she never omitted an opportunity of impressing on the minds of her pupils the power, wisdom, and goodness of God, as displayed in his works. But she was not then in the habit of bringing Bible truth to bear on the minds of her pupils, and of leading them to feel personal responsibility in the great work of renovating the world. Indeed, the desire to labor for Christ had not then *fully* possessed her own heart. Still, her consciousness of reliance on him for salvation, and of her obligation to honor him by obeying his last command, led her openly to profess her faith in him by uniting herself with the Congregational church in Buckland in the spring of 1822.

She continued to instruct in the Sanderson Academy after Mr. Cross left it, and at one time was connected in teaching with Mr. Amasa Converse, now Dr. Converse, editor of the Philadelphia Christian Observer, which paper, after her death, contained an article from his pen in testimony of her talents and worth.

Moments often occur in the lives of individuals which give character to their whole future existence. There were two of these seasons in Miss Lyon's life, in which we cannot but admire and adore the wisdom of that Providence which led her in a path that she had not known. One was, when, principally for want of success, she seriously contemplated never again engaging in teaching. She has been heard to remark that the reasons for and against it were so nearly balanced, that the least circumstance on either side would have turned the scale. But she was guided by an unseen hand, and was induced again to make the attempt. The other was when she was invited by her brother, in 1822, to go to Chatauque county, New York, as a teacher. The question then before her was one which tried her exceedingly, and was not only one of the most difficult, but it was also one of the most important, of her life. On the one hand was her dear and only brother, who had come from a great distance, with all the anxiety he would naturally feel to secure her return with him; the consideration of his increasing family, in a comparatively destitute region, and her own personal affection for them. On the other hand were the friends who had encouraged and assisted her to fit herself for what they thought a more appropriate sphere than a new country, and their increasing esteem for her services in that sphere. For a long time, she vacillated, and seemed to find no relief in her perplexity, save in her flowing tears. But God opened to her mind the way she should choose.

For the better understanding of some parts of this narrative, it may be proper here to state that her sister R., the one next in age to herself, afterwards went to her brother's in Stockton, New York, and occupied a situation there as a teacher until her marriage in that place.

Go where she would, Miss Lyon never could have been an ordinary woman. She would have made the world better by having lived in it. Still, at that time she had many habits, both of person and mind, that, without the counteracting influence which was afterwards exerted upon her, must have been a great obstacle to her usefulness. Her character was then peculiar; it would have become distorted. It was like the unchiselled marble, which few can behold without perceiving that it is valuable; yet all desire that its worth and beauty may be drawn forth by the artist's hand.

Had she then gone to Western New York, she would, no doubt, have been useful; but there is no probability that she would ever have accomplished what she has for the world.

Soon after her decision not to go with her brother, she was invited to assist Miss Z. P. Grant* in the Adams Female Academy, at Londonderry, (now Derry,) New Hampshire. The acquaintance between these ladies commenced in 1821, Miss Lyon being a member of Mr. Emerson's seminary during the first term in which Miss Grant aided Mr. E. as a teacher.

The following letters will show the light in which the question of engaging in this academy was viewed by Miss L.: —

TO MISS G.

"ASHFIELD, December 1, 1823.

"I will not waste time in describing my feelings on receiving a letter from your own hand. I had received some indirect information respecting the academy at Londonderry before. From what I had learned of the general plan, I concluded it might be an eminent means of doing good. A

* Now Mrs. Banister, of Newburyport.

few days previous to the reception of your letter, a secret desire entered my heart that you might be connected with that institution. But I dismissed it as a romantic thought. After breaking the seal of your letter, and eagerly running over the contents, said I, 'Is this a dream, or a sober reality?'

"At least, my friend, I rejoice that taking the charge of this school has been submitted to your consideration. May the Lord direct you in the path of duty.

"But I must say something upon the great question before me; and, indeed, I know not what to say. The academy in which I am now engaged is an infant institution. The founder, Rev. Alvan Sanderson, the former pastor of this church, was governed by the purest motives; and I consider it a privilege to aid in carrying out his benevolent designs. Many of its present guardians are my friends, and from them I have frequently received favors. This is the school where I was principally educated, and to which I feel in no small degree indebted. This school has so far been a silent, retired, and powerful means of doing good. The number of pupils has usually been small; but I believe the church will hereafter count some able supporters which she would not have had if this school had never existed. Soon after I returned from Byfield, I entered this school as an assistant. No other female teacher has ever been employed by the trustees, and they earnestly desire to secure my labors as great a proportion of the time as their funds will permit. Besides, there have been circumstances which have led me to think that my usefulness might be more extensive here than in almost any other place of equal importance.

"Yet the inducements to accept your invitation are great. It seems to be a field especially adapted to my capacity. The systematic arrangement which you propose would be highly gratifying to me, as it perfectly meets my views. Finally, the pleasure of spending the time with you is truly inviting. If I am not deceived, I have taken some satisfaction in committing this subject to God. If that is not the place for me, may He give you some other one, who will be a useful assistant and a pleasant companion. I slept but little for one or two nights after I first heard from you; since that time, my mind has been remarkably calm. May the Lord direct our course. I cannot, I would not, choose for myself."

TO MISS G.

"ASHFIELD, December 30, 1823.

"By the last mail I received your letter. I am glad you have decided affirmatively respecting Derry. The new plan of that school will require some peculiar qualifications in those who are to take charge of it. I believe those qualifications, at least, are possessed by yourself in such a degree as will enable you, in the most important points, eminently to excel.

"The more I think of your plan, the more I approve it. I cannot but hope that that academy will yet be the means of much good. Should the plan succeed, the influence of example would be something. Public opinion in favor of systematic female education needs support. Every proof that system is practicable, would add its weight in the scale.

"Respecting myself, though the proposal did not strike my mind unfavorably at first, yet the more I think of it, the more I am inclined to decide affirmatively. The obstacles have seemed gradually to diminish, and the favorable circumstances rather to brighten by examination. In relation to my own *personal situation*, the prospect, since you first wrote me, has appeared sufficiently pleasant; indeed, I fear too pleasant. I tremble more than if the path appeared more rugged. The desire you have expressed that I should engage with you has been one means of inclining me to believe that my field of labor is with you. It did, however, lead me to much self-scrutiny. Expect not too much from me, I beseech you. I fear you will be disappointed. I have a strange, rebellious, wicked heart. When shall I be wholly devoted to God? I cannot trust myself. I find my best promises violated, my best resolutions broken. The half cannot be told."

At the close of another letter to the same friend, she writes, —

"January 15, 1823.

"Pray for me, that I may habitually know and feel my dependence on God. How safe it is to trust in God! How easily can he give counsel and assistance in all things, the smallest as well as the greatest! And how ready and willing is he always to assist! It would seem that I have too frequently tried my own strength, that I have experienced too many instances of the particular guardian care and protection of God, to doubt in whom I should place my trust. Alas! I have a treacherous heart. But our God is faithful. The unfaithfulness of his rebellious creatures cannot exceed his mercy and long-suffering. His mercy endures forever, and his promises never fail."

As the result of this correspondence, Miss Grant paid a visit to Miss Lyon at Ashfield. Miss L., having decided to go with her to Derry, attended Professor Eaton's lectures on chemistry and natural history at Amherst, Massachusetts, that she might be prepared to illustrate by experiments the science of chemistry.

As the plan adopted in the school at Derry was the commencement of that which was so successfully carried out at Ipswich, and afterwards at South Hadley, a few extracts will be made from her letters during the first summer she was at Derry, which will not only introduce us to the operations of that school, but will also exhibit her own personal feelings.

TO HER MOTHER.

"LONDONDERRY, June 5, 1824.

"I feel that I am almost worthy of blame that I have not yet written home since my arrival here; but I content myself, knowing that my friends are too well acquainted with my usual delays in writing to be very much disappointed.

"A letter arrived here before I did, stating the death of brother Moore. I expected it might contain some important intelligence, and almost feared to open it. It was pleasant to be greeted by the handwriting of my sisters L. and F., but mournful to be thus called to sympathize with dear sister E. *You* know, my dear mother, by experience, what her afflictions are; and probably you never before have so desired to see sister Moore as at the present time. But this cannot be, and may you be resigned to the will of God. . . . .

"My health has been much better since I came here than it was during the spring. My spirits, which commonly rise and sink with my health, are consequently very good. I hope I am thankful for health. We have a very pleasant school, over sixty in number. I find in Miss G. all I expected. There are two assistants besides myself, Mrs. R. and Miss C., and we all find enough to engage our whole time. I see nothing now but that I may pass the summer pleasantly; and I would hope that I may be in some measure useful in this institution. So many young ladies are collected together here from different places to gain knowledge and form habits, which they are to carry with them to their respective homes, that it is to us an interesting spot. How important that the minds and habits of these youth should be rightly formed!

"We hope a few of our pupils love the Lord Jesus Christ in sincerity. What cause of rejoicing, should others be added to the number! You will not cease to pray for us, my mother, that we may be blessed, and that we may be made a blessing in the world."

TO MISS H. W.

"LONDONDERRY, July 2, 1824.

". . . . . . The regulations of this school are such as to enable us to have much system and order. This regular system is calculated to give our pupils faithful, attentive habits. They feel that their course is marked out, and generally that whatever is assigned them must be accomplished. Composition, you know, is one of the most trying exercises. But even in this we have not had an instance yet in which any young lady has been in the least delinquent. In some respects, perhaps, this school meets our wishes more fully than any I have seen. I might mention particulars; but the beginning of all little evils in a school is whispering. Miss G. has adopted a plan to prevent this, which has been very successful. After leading her pupils to feel the importance of being truthful, and stating facts as they are, she requires each to bring in a weekly ticket with her name attached, stating whether she has, or has not, made any communication in school during the week, either by whispering, or by writing, or in any other way equally suited to divert the attention. We have some young ladies who have not made a communication of this kind since the commencement of our school; and probably none who have not passed some weeks without a failure on this point. Miss Grant, of course, would not adopt this plan unless the scholars evinced a conscience both enlightened and lively as to the distinction between truth and falsehood.

"The prospects of this school at present are very promising. The trustees take a deep interest in its prosperity. They place great confidence in the principal, and are ready to do every thing she requests. The location here not being favorable for a winter school, our academy is open only thirty weeks in a year; Miss G. devoting the winter, however, as well as the summer, to the interests of the institution.

. . . . .

"I shall spend my vacation with Rev. Mr. C. He is at length united to his beloved P. She appears to be just such a wife as he needs; uniformly cheerful, polite, and attentive to all. They passed one night with me on their marriage tour; and when he led in prayer in the family, his voice and manner were just as formerly. You can imagine how much it recalled past scenes in Ashfield Academy."

TO HER SISTER F.

"LONDONDERRY, July 7, 1824.

"Three weeks from to-day our vacation commences, and then I shall probably think much of home. Although I am pleasantly situated, and have no more cares and little daily trials than I should expect, yet it would be pleasant to spend an hour with one of my dear sisters, to whom I could tell all my heart. The fact that no two of our family, unless it be our brother and our sister Rosina, are spending this summer together, awakens emotions peculiar and rather gloomy. Ever since I heard of brother Moore's death, but more particularly for two days past, I have thought much of my brother and sisters. I have seemed to review twenty years in relation to ourselves. Change and revolution, uncertainty and disappointment, decay and death, are stamped on every object. I see this family, that about twenty years ago were prattling children, united and happy in the arms of their fond parents, now scattered over four different states of the Union, and some of them seven hundred miles apart. I see the eldest, in whom we all placed confidence as a counsellor and friend, and to whom we are in some degree indebted, separated from her friends, carried by Providence into the lonely wilderness, there to pass her days almost alone and unpitied, where no one of us can give her a cheerful smile or a word of consolation. I well remember how much animation and energy she possessed, when she used to spend her days in teaching. But over her head age has crept apace; ill health has worn down her spirits; and, to use her own language, 'sickness and trials have followed, till now this terrible blow is struck.' Where now are her buoyant spirits? Where her resolution?

"I see another sister, too, passing through different scenes, and now called to consign her oldest child to the silent tomb. . . . . . You wrote in somewhat of a gloomy strain, but I hope it was only momentary. You will do well to endeavor to gain the confidence of your pupils, and to make them see the reasons of your requirements. Do not say too much to them at one time. I think it best to devote some attention to their behavior, even if they do not study so much. If your older pupils should be disposed to trouble you, perhaps it may be beneficial to converse with each one out of school, and entirely alone. By taking such a method occasionally, you may operate upon their feelings, and lead them to a right determination when you otherwise could not. The good influence of every well-behaved pupil in school is great. Endeavor to lead them *always* to speak the truth, and then let them know that you depend on their word. If they *are* truthful, and have enlightened consciences, so that you can depend on their stating facts as they are, I would recommend to you a plan to prevent whispering. . . . .

"If you require it, you must see it faithfully performed; otherwise it will have a very bad influence on your school. If you adopt this plan, you would do well to begin at first individually with a few of the oldest.

"Let me hear not only from yourself, but also from my other friends. Separation does not lessen the interest I take in their welfare. When I think of the older members of our family, I also involuntarily think of their children. I have the same kind of interest in their prosperity that I have ever had for that of their parents. Sometimes I feel that it would be a privilege to live, if I could only render myself useful to the children of my brother and sisters."

TO HER ROOM-MATE WHEN AT SCHOOL.

"LONDONDERRY, September 26, 1824.

"I am now engaged in teaching in the 'Adams Female Academy,' Londonderry, N. H. This school commenced its operations in the spring. The plan may be called *Emersonian*, though considerably altered to meet our particular purpose. The care of the school is committed to Miss Grant. You know she is well fitted to guide, and I think she has improved very much since you knew her. She spent about six weeks here last winter, making arrangements with reference to the school. This was a very favorable circumstance. In every part of the plan I can see her design; consequently it is much more easily executed. Although, as you know, I have the highest opinion of the utility of Mr. Emerson's plan for young ladies of adult age, yet I never considered it fitted to carry a young lady through her whole course of school education; I mean, as conducted when we were at Byfield. It supposed too much previous improvement. The course was too rapid for ordinary minds, and also for such as were young, or but little improved. We have more classes, our course is slower, and the increased number of teachers will enable us to execute our plans thoroughly. We have three regular classes, denominated senior, middle, and junior. Certain defined qualifications are necessary to enter each of these classes. Members of the senior and middle classes can attend a course of drawing and painting if they choose. We have also as many preparatory classes as circumstances require. The young ladies are examined, and are placed where it is thought they will improve the most. They are classed, not at all according to the number of books they have studied, but according to the real knowledge they are found to possess. We have but very few under fifteen years of age who can enter the regular classes. We have this summer about sixty pupils, and we have sufficient employment. You know that Mr. E. attended to many little things in his school, which were not common in schools generally. Some, however, he was able only to recommend, and leave for the young ladies to accomplish, or not, as they thought proper. The design of Miss G. is to have every thing that is proposed for immediate attention pursued until it is accomplished; and the teachers see that it is done. This requires care and exertion. It is not a small task to instruct our young ladies in writing. Pen-making and the manner of holding the pen, I think, require one half the exertion in this department. Each is required to write with her own pen, and no one is allowed to request a pen to be made for her by any other young lady without permission. This we find not difficult. Though I should not enter into a particular detail, yet I believe you will think I have something to do. My friends, however, receive letters from me rather more frequently than when I was at Byfield; but I suppose they will even now complain.

"In several branches we use a method in some degree new, commenced in Mr. Emerson's school two years since, and by him termed the *topic system.* Subjects are selected from the lesson, which are first to be simply defined; and then more or less, or all, that the book contains, is to be learned and recited.

"Before coming to this place, Miss G. had tried the experiment, term after term, in her own private school, of having young ladies give daily attention to lessons from the Bible. She has great confidence in the study of this book for intellectual discipline, as well as for the guidance and control of the heart. Before she engaged to take charge of this academy, she gained the consent of the executive committee, that, in accordance with a deeply-cherished purpose, she should feel at liberty to employ one seventh part of the intellectual energies of her pupils upon what is contained in this storehouse of knowledge. While examining the classes at the commencement of the school, all were occupied in the daily study and recitation of Scripture history. Every week of the term, each pupil is expected to apply her mind closely, two hours or more, to the Scripture lesson given out early in the week, and recited the next Monday morning. This study has excited more deep and universal interest than any other. Some now feel the force of the truths they are learning; and many, I trust, will eventually be made wise unto salvation.

"In gaining a knowledge of the Scriptures, a variety of methods is useful. While I was pursuing the study on the topic system, I thought it might be profitable to older members of Sabbath schools, and I will annex a few of the topics from Genesis. Creation; the Sabbath; garden of Eden; tree of knowledge of good and evil; tree of life; the serpent; disobedience of our first parents; expulsion of our first parents from the garden of Eden; Adam; Eve; sacrifices; Cain; Abel; Enoch; wickedness of man; the flood; Noah's ark; the rainbow; Noah; Babel."

Self-knowledge was one of the distinguishing traits in Miss Lyon's earlier character. She knew where her superior strength lay, and she as well knew her own peculiar weaknesses. What she could do well in school she was ready to attempt, and what she could not do well she preferred not to do at all; unless it was something that *must* be done, and *could* be done by no one else. For several of the first years of her teaching young ladies, she would avoid mingling with them at recess, and when they were coming in and going out of school; for she said she could not do this, and command their respect sufficiently to maintain her influence over them. At the same time, she knew that she could excite the interest and command the attention of a class, and that on some subjects she could interest a large school. It was not uncommon for her to say, "*That* is one of the things which I cannot do; but I can do *this* very well, or so well that no one will suffer loss; and I want this for my part to-day." But rather than the school, or an individual, should suffer loss, especially in respect to moral habits, she would, with great self-command, put forth her best efforts, even when she thought it probable that she should, by the effort, lose a part of the confidence and respect which she had previously possessed. The estimation in which she might be held, important as it was in one view, was, in her judgment, a minor circumstance, compared with the good of those under her care.

The defects in her manners and style of conversation were felt in a considerable degree by herself, as well as by her friends.

For several years after entering upon her duties as teacher in the Adams Female Academy, she took great pains to correct her undesirable habits. Some of them she entirely overcame; others were modified; and of others, all that could be perceived, as the fruit of her endeavors, was that they did not essentially increase. She looked upon these defects, in things external, as totally different in character from such as have their seat in the understanding or in the heart. She felt that they were obstacles in the way of her usefulness; that they might, with comparative ease, have been corrected in her childhood or youth, but that after middle life, when her whole soul was absorbed with the wants of a race of immortal beings, she could not overcome many of these little things, without giving to the work so much thought and effort as essentially to diminish her capacity to labor for the good of others. Her uncommon success in correcting her early defective habits was truly praiseworthy, and eminently encouraging to others. Persons who knew her not in early life can form but little conception of her power of self-control, or her inherent strength. To give an idea of this, some particulars will be mentioned.

In the early part of her literary career, her habits, in every respect, were desultory. She would study, eat, and sleep, just when she could find the time, and would even sit up all night to study. But as soon as she was convinced that it was best, *if not for her*, yet for her influence, she entered into a methodical arrangement, and no one around her would be more systematic in her division of time. At the appointed hour she would retire, whatever might be left undone.

She always said, that her first attempts at teaching were unsuccessful, and that she essentially failed in government. How far she was unsuccessful in the view of others, we are not able to say; but it would appear that she exhibited no peculiar aptness for the employment, as she said that it was frequently remarked to her, "You will never equal your sister E. as a teacher." How much self-control she must have exercised to overcome these difficulties, let those judge who were associated with her the last few years of her life.

Which of her pupils or friends of later years would suspect, that naturally she was easily discouraged, and that from childhood to womanhood, if any of her plans failed, she would be so disheartened as not to know which way to turn for a substitute? Yet that this was the case, her early friends will bear witness.

Who that, in later life, saw her countenance, every day, serene as the summer's setting sun, would ever suspect that she formerly could not rise above disappointment, but would yield to great depression, and even depend on indulging in long seasons of weeping? A friend, in whose father's family she was then an inmate, well recollects that after she had been for a long time a teacher, she one evening inquired how long it would be before tea. On being informed, she expressed disappointment that it was to be so soon. She was told it could be delayed, if it would be an accommodation to her. With her accustomed cheerfulness she replied, "O, no; I was only wishing to have a good crying spell, and you could not give me time enough." She afterwards became convinced that such seasons of weeping were wrong; and a friend who occupied the same room with her for months together, and under the most trying circumstances, has known that she did not yield at all to depression, or indulge herself in the luxury of a single tear.

Though the same strong points in her character were obvious through life, she had not at this time that unity of object, or firmness of purpose, which she afterwards possessed.

She had naturally strong preferences and aversions, which would have been very detrimental to her usefulness as a teacher. But her large benevolence enabled her in a great measure to conquer this defect, and also to deny herself and to make any sacrifice for the good of others. She was quick to discover defects, but slow in devising remedies; she could see that pupils were wrong, but could not easily discover how they could be led to correct their errors. Indeed, she was equally slow in discerning what elements belong to a character of symmetrical excellence. At this time it was her great aim to make fine scholars. Her later pupils may be surprised to learn, that she would not have hesitated to borrow from the needful repose of her scholars, if she could but bring them up to her standard. She had acquired her own education by learning one thing after another, as opportunity offered, without any previous plan or system; and it is probable that she had not yet marked out in her own mind any course desirable to be pursued in order to form even a well-balanced intellectual character.

Some extracts from Miss Lyon's correspondence, scattered through several years, will now be given, which show her affection to her friends and relatives. They also show how she walked with God from day to day. They are not inserted as specimens of literary taste, or of vigorous thought. Her energy was expended on the minds around her, and in schemes for future action. When she unbent after the day's labors, she often refreshed herself by communion with absent friends, to whom she was accustomed, in personal converse, to open her heart without reserve. The repeated expression of the same desires, purposes, and emotions, as they flowed from her heart, may be valued by those readers who wish to learn the secret of her attaining views of divine truth, which were transforming in their influence on her own character, and on that of many of her pupils to whom these views were communicated.

TO MISS G.

"BUCKLAND, December 13, 1824.

" . . . . . I ought to be thankful that Providence has so ordered it that I do not spend the winter at Derry; because I think the privilege of seeing my friends, and enjoying more society, is favorable to my health and spirits, and conducive to my usefulness.

" Rev. Mr. Clark, the pastor of this church, has proposed my taking a school in this place, if pupils can be obtained, and I have concluded to do so. As the school will be small, I shall not have to make exertions that will injure my health, and thus be detrimental to my usefulness next summer. I shall board with Mr. C., and feel at home in his family."

This school in Buckland was the origin of a succession of winter schools in that place and in Ashfield. Many teachers of the common schools in that vicinity availed themselves of these advantages. They were the means of awakening a lively interest in the cause of education, and some efforts were made to retain her permanently. The influence of her school attracted the attention and secured the coöperation of the clergymen throughout that region; and the seed there sown is now bearing fruit a hundred fold.

To give some account of this school, and to show to young teachers her self-diffidence at this period of her life, the following letter, written to one of the teachers in the Adams Female Academy, is copied: —

TO MISS C.

"BUCKLAND, February 21, 1825.

"MY DEAR MISS C.:

". . . . . My school here consists of twenty-five young ladies. After so large a number had been admitted, I had some anxiety respecting it. I feared that I might attempt more uniformity about books, than, considering the circumstances, would be expedient. I expected, also, a cold winter, and my design was to have the scholars study in school. And as I possess not much natural dignity, I could foresee my scholars crowding around the fire, some whispering, some idle, &c. I remembered that, several years ago, I had a school of young ladies in this town, in which there was more whispering than in all the schools in which I have been engaged for the last three or four years. The fault then was mine, and I knew not but that the effects might be felt even now.

"I kept my school occupied on general subjects at first, and now I have about as much uniformity in books as we had at L. In teaching, I am constantly wishing for your or Miss G.'s advice. Indeed, I sometimes need your assistance more than words can express.

"At the commencement, I thought it best to assume as much artificial dignity as possible; so, to begin, I borrowed Miss Grant's plan to prevent whispering. All, with one exception, strictly complied; and that was one of the first young ladies in age and improvement. It appeared altogether probable that the termination of this affair would be a matter of considerable importance in relation to her, her father's family, and perhaps to the school generally. But after I had passed a few almost sleepless nights about it, a kind Providence directed the result in a manner which seemed the best calculated to promote the interests of the school; for at length she came cheerfully into the arrangement.

"A circumstance, in relation to the first set of compositions, was somewhat trying. One pupil refused entirely to write; but I was assisted in leading her to comply with the requirement. Some other things I *could* mention. Suffice it to say, that I have had just enough of such things to give me continual anxiety; but God, in his providence, has been very kind to me. Many events have terminated as I desired, when it seemed not at all in my power to control them. Perhaps I have generally been able to accomplish about what I have undertaken. My school, in many respects, is very pleasant. I have but two or three pupils under sixteen years of age. With the exception of two or three, they a very studious. On the whole, I think it the best school ever had; the best, because the most profitable to its members; I do not mean the best in which I have been engaged. I have an opportunity this winter to see the value of what I gained at Derry.

"I hope, my dear sister, you live near your Savior, while I am far from him, and walk on in darkness. I hope you enjoy the light of his countenance, and rejoice in the God of your salvation. I do not think it favorable to piety to have so much anxiety as I have had this winter; but I would not attribute my coldness to any outward circumstances; I would rather fear that I have never known the love of the Lord Jesus Christ."

After the close of her school in Buckland, she went to Troy, N. Y., and passed her vacation in the family of Professor Eaton, from which place she wrote to Miss Grant.

'April 1, 1825.

"I wrote to Professor E., stating my general success and difficulties in experiments in chemistry, last summer. He returned an answer, generously inviting me to his house, and saying that I should do well to come to Troy, even if I could stay only two or three weeks, as he could tell me m. things during that time which would be useful to me. A. first, I thought it would be altogether impracticable. I had just closed my school, and wished to spend some time with my friends; but I remembered well the difficulties attending some of my experiments last summer, and thought it possible that further instruction might aid me sufficiently to compensate for the fatigue and the expense of the journey. I thought my personal gratification seemed to require that I should stay with my friends, but my duty to the school at Derry might require that I should leave them, not to see them again until next fall. At length, after suffering some trials in my feelings on this subject, I decided in the affirmative; and accordingly I packed up all, as soon as possible, and arrived here this morning.

"I shall attend what lectures are given to the Rensselaer school, while I am here, — principally in chemistry and natural philosophy. I shall endeavor to review the most difficult and most important principles of chemistry, in order to avail myself of the opportunity to gain the information which I need. I do not intend to study hard."

TO HER MOTHER.

"LONDONDERRY, September 7, 1825.

"Since I last wrote you, we have been afflicted by the sickness of Miss Grant. She has had a regular course of bilious fever. She is now gaining slowly; but I fear the effects on her feeble constitution will remain a considerable time. The suspension of her labors greatly multiplies our cares and anxieties; but we have reason to be thankful that we have been able to consult her every day. I have been so well that I could do more, with the same effort and the same fatigue, since Miss G. has been sick, than at any other time.

"Our school continues prosperous and pleasant. We had one hundred scholars the first term; now we have ninety-two.

"We need the influence of the Holy Spirit more than any other blessing. Most of our scholars are probably without hope and without God in the world. We have here the children of many pious parents, whose prayers are daily offered up for them and us; we also have the prayers of many others. Several mothers, who have daughters here, devote a little time every Wednesday morning, between eight and nine o'clock, to supplicate the influence of the Spirit on this institution. Will not you, my mother, sometimes think of us at that hour? May we not hope for a blessing?"

TO THE SAME.

"September 25, 1825.

". . . . . . I have thought much more of you than usual, for a week or two past. Although my situation is necessarily rather different from what it was in childhood, yet you will not suppose that on this account I love my friends less. I sincerely desire that I may ever be saved from neglecting my early friends, especially my mother, to whom I am more indebted than to all others, except my Maker. When I think of my mother, I think of one who ardently and unceasingly desires my temporal and spiritual welfare; one to whom I owe much that I can never repay; one who never forgets me, and never forgets that I have an immortal soul; one the benefit of whose prayers I have long enjoyed, and whose desires, I trust, are now every day ascending to the throne of mercy in my behalf.

"I have thought considerably this day of the importance of being prepared to do the will of my heavenly Parent. What is more desirable than to have the privilege of doing those things which are well pleasing to God; to have such a frame of mind, that the habitual and uniform desire of the heart shall be, 'Lord, what wilt thou have me to do?' But I find a strange propensity to desire ardently those things which would seem to be a peculiar gratification to myself. I *would* desire to have such a frame of mind that I might be eve ready to say, 'Not my will, but thine, be done.' I would not desire any thing that would not be for the glory of God, and in accordance with the will of my Savior. Sometimes I almost *feel* that I am not my own, but I find my heart repeatedly desiring those things from which I had almost supposed it was forever separated.

"It seems as if you could not be so anxious to receive letters from me as I am to hear from my friends. Although my situation is far from being unpleasant, yet there is a kind of loneliness which is ever ready to oppress my spirits. You will remember, however, that we have now our cold, equinoctial storm. When this is over, much of the present gloom will be dispersed, and all our spirits will be more cheerful."

TO MISS GRANT.

"BUCKLAND, December 26, 1825.

"My school is larger than I expected, having about fifty scholars.

. . . . .

"My heart is pained to see so much important unaccomplished labor accumulating on my hands, and I have engaged an assistant.

"At present, there is a little more than usual religious attention in this town. The friends of Zion are hoping that the Lord is about to visit us. This circumstance produces in my mind some hopes and some fears. It adds, if possible, to my responsibility. The thought that some, who were beginning to think about their eternal interests, may here become so much absorbed in their studies, so much interested in the business of the school, as to exclude God from their hearts, is truly painful. I hope I may not be the instrument of hardening the hearts of those whom I tenderly love. My pupils appear very attentive to religious truth. Some are thoughtful, though I have no evidence that any are particularly serious, except those who profess to love the Savior. Two or three of the latter appear very well. That heart must be insensible, which could not feel on observing the general attention manifest when a sermon is reviewed, a Bible lesson recited, or any religious subject brought forward. Perhaps the Lord may visit us with his grace. In him is all our hope.

"For a long time, I have at intervals been anxious about my own state of mind. I have felt that, if I were ardently attached to the Savior, my desires to honor him would be more uniform and uninterrupted. I have hoped that the Lord would direct to means which would effectually move my soul, so that I could no longer sleep when reflecting on the cause of our dear Redeemer. I have thought that possibly Providence had brought me to this place for good, that this season might be profitable to my soul. But let me not depend on any means; let me depend on nothing short of God. I know, my dear friend, that you will pray for me. Pray that I may be altogether devoted to the Savior, that I may ever do his will, ever honor his name.

"Fourteen of my scholars board in the family with me. Before I came here, and for the first week after, I had much anxiety about the arrangements for these young ladies. We have finally become settled, so that every thing seems to go on well. The members of the school in the family have a table by themselves. As I was well aware that it would require more than an ordinary share of dignity to prevent too much, if not improper, conversation at meals, I thought it the safest to introduce some entertaining exercise. This requires an effort, on my part, which I had scarcely realized. But I find it pleasant indeed. I frequently think, 'How *could* Miss G. take care of so many last summer?' But I recollect hearing you say that your first schools were as much your all, as your one hundred pupils at Derry.

"My spirits have been unusually uniform for four weeks.

I do not recollect an hour of depression. I consider this a blessing for which I ought to be thankful."

TO MRS. A. W. F.

"BUCKLAND, February 20, 1826.

". . . . . I can scarcely believe I have written you so seldom since you have been away. The truth is, for two years past, my time has been so constantly occupied that I now understand what you mean, when you say that it is almost necessary to blind the eyes and harden the feelings against present and urgent calls, and calmly sit down to write letters of friendship. Besides, every thing which I could write, you will receive from other sources.

"Your sister H. assists me, and we have a pleasant school of about fifty members. I enjoy so much that I sometimes almost fear lest I may have all my good things in this life. We have eleven in our school professedly pious, and some of them appear very well. Some others are particularly attentive to religious truth. There is more religious attention in this town at present than usual. I have had a faint hope, through the winter, that this town and my school might be visited by the special influence of the Holy Spirit."

The hopes expressed in the foregoing letters were realized, and several under her care there commenced a religious life.

TO HER MOTHER.

"LONDONDERRY, May 20, 1826.

". . . . . I hope my friends will remember that I am interested in little things. It does my heart good to read a page filled with home, friends, and acquaintance. Especially am I interested in all that I can learn about my dear pupils, or, rather, those whom I called such last winter. My attachment to that school and to that spot I cannot well describe. I delight to dwell on some of the last weeks of that term. Those days must be numbered with the most precious of my life; and sometimes I can scarcely believe that all of those scenes were real.

"I do not number it among the least of my blessings that I am permitted *to do something.* Surely I ought to be thankful for an active life. I hope, however, not to be so attached to activity, that, if health should be taken away, all my enjoyment would be gone. I would rather so enjoy present favors, as coming from the hand of God, that, should the streams hereafter be cut off, the fountain might remain to me a never-failing source of enjoyment. I would desire ever to acquiesce in all the dispensations of Providence. I would fain have it my first desire to do those things which are well pleasing in the sight of God; and I believe I may safely leave all futurity in his hands. For this, my dear mother, I hope I have your daily prayers.

"We have a pleasant school of ninety pupils, thirty-nine of whom have been with us before the present year. They are very attentive and studious. Only a small proportion profess religion, or hope they are Christians. Nearly eighty are probably living without God in the world. At this period, when so many spiritual blessings are bestowed on literary institutions, may we not hope that ours will be among the favored number? Many Christians, parents and others, have been interested for this institution. We hope their prayers will be answered.

"The young ladies are so very attentive to Bible lessons, that I sometimes hope there are good things in store for us; but my own heart is so cold I have reason to fear. Surely there is no hope but in the mercy of God. Do pray for us, and especially that I may have a heart to seek the favor of God.

"The intelligence which we receive of the work of grace in Dartmouth College is refreshing. I hope the students from Ashfield share in the work."

TO HER SISTER F.

"LONDONDERRY, July 4, 1826.

"This day, you will recollect, completes half a century since the Declaration of our Independence. How interesting must be the reflections of those few who can remember that eventful day! And to every one, the events in our history must be an exciting theme. Who, on the face of the earth, fifty years ago, could have anticipated such results? It is true that Washington, and almost all Americans who lived in the days of Washington, hoped for independence. But did they look forward to this time, and anticipate such a nation as this? Must not all believe that 'promotion cometh neither from the east, nor from the west, nor from the south; but God is the judge; he putteth down one, and setteth up another'? Must not all exclaim, 'This is the finger of God'? We wonder why we are made to differ from others. Perhaps that same Being, that could with a glance look through the course of the Israelitish nation, from the selling of Joseph to the coming of the Messiah, has designs of mercy on all the nations of the earth, through the unparalleled blessings which he has bestowed on this great people. And have not his dealings with our beloved country some connection with the causes which will bring forward that happy day, to which all who love the Lord Jesus Christ are looking with earnest prayer?

"Considerable attention has been devoted to the celebration of the anniversary in this place; consequently we have not been able to continue the usual exercises of the school. We have had some anxiety for our young ladies, as the scenes of the day would, of course, be rather exhilarating. Perhaps you will wonder why there should be this anxiety. I will tell you, my sister. We believe the Holy Spirit is now with us by his special operations. It is now a very critical period. I think the school is in such a state as ours was last winter, about three weeks before its close. Seven or eight give more or less evidence of a change of heart. A few at the present time are deeply affected. Several others are in some degree solicitous, and perhaps nearly half the school occasionally inquire with interest what these things mean. This school is very different from our school last winter. We have about ninety pupils, of a great variety of character. A large number, we have no doubt, are yet thoughtless. Throughout the school, however, there is a propriety of conduct, and an interest in Scripture recitations; and when I look on their state, it seems as if 'the fields were white already to the harvest.'"

TO HER SISTER F.

"LONDONDERRY, July 30, 1826.

"I seem to hear you anxiously inquiring about our school. The showers of divine grace continued to descend after I wrote you, even to the close of the term. But to give you a just account of the work would be difficult. If you will look back to our school last winter, you will have a more correct view of our state than I can give you; as the scenes of a few weeks past have brought that season vividly before my mind. The attention cannot be considered so general here as it was in my school near its close last winter. This might naturally be expected in a school like this, where there is such a variety of character in the young ladies. Their habits, education, views, feelings, and principles are so entirely different, that it is to be expected that there will be a great number who will feel that it is all an idle tale; a great number who will have it in their hearts to ridicule, could they but find a favorable opportunity. I have no doubt that many left the school as thoughtless as when they entered. This painful conviction forces itself on our hearts. But on the other hand, we are encouraged. We have decisive evidence that the Spirit of God has been present with us. The hearts of several have apparently been humbled; hearts which the power of man could never have softened. When our term closed, about twenty had expressed hope; a few were anxious, while others were just beginning to ask their own hearts whether these things concerned themselves. In this state of things our pupils dispersed; and what will be the result we know not. Revivals in seminaries of learning generally terminate with the commencement of vacation. Yet there are some exceptions, and we do hope that our case will be one of these exceptions. For this, I believe many of our Christian friends are praying; and we hope their prayers may be heard and answered. Should the Spirit leave us now, it would be mournful indeed. Much the largest part of our school are still without God. At the commencement of the term, eleven indulged a hope that they loved the Savior, though they were not all professors; add to these the new plants, some of which, we trust, will bear fruit, and you will see how many are left in the gall of bitterness and in the bonds of iniquity.

"Do write to me immediately, and tell me all I want to know. Give a great deal of love to our dear mother, brothers, sisters, nephews, nieces, and all my friends."

During the next term, the religious interest was deep and extensive; but there is no record of the *number* who received the truth in love.

TO HER SISTER F.

"LONDONDERRY, October 25, 1826.

"We have a pleasant school, this term, of about eighty scholars. You can understand the happy effects of a system so long continued. I can see that the same labor accomplishes more than when I first came here. At present, I am deeply absorbed in grammar and arithmetic. We are conducting both the exercises on the monitorial plan. Grammar for this quarter has just commenced. Between forty and fifty now recite at the same time on this plan. We shall occupy about an hour in the recitation. I shall devote my time as I commonly do, when we have recitations in this way. We have regular monitors appointed for grammar from the senior class. These monitors study their lessons; and for the present, I shall devote about half an hour to them out of school. We have been attending to Adams's Arithmetic on the monitorial plan for a long time, with usual, or rather increasing success. We shall very soon lay it aside for the season. Between fifty and sixty have attended this exercise together, comprising all the regular classes except the senior class; and, indeed, most of this class have been engaged all the time as monitors. We have adopted the plan of having a regular monitor for every section, consisting of from five to twelve, according to the capacity of the monitors and of the students. Last spring, the school all attended to Colburn's Arithmetic. About a week since, seventy commenced a review. To this we devote an hour in school, our usual time for a recitation. As they are nearly together at present, I spend about half the time in asking questions to the whole, and then they are arranged in small monitorial classes. I pass from one class to another, assisting the monitors or listening to the recitations, as the case may require. This exercise is very pleasant. It is highly animating to observe seventy pupils, with the attention of all fixed on the same point at the same moment. I am fully persuaded that this is one of the best exercises to call and fix the attention of a great number. You see, I tell what I am doing, and let the rest go. As I have begun to be so egotistical, I will just say, that I have had a most delightful time in teaching Whelpley's History: we finished it a few weeks since. Part of the time, three classes attended together, making between thirty and forty. I had some anxiety about undertaking with so large a class; but the young ladies took up the study with so much interest and resolution, that I found it more pleasant than a smaller class, and perhaps equally profitable to them.

. . . . .

"The influence of the Holy Spirit on schools is indeed a great blessing. It should call forth the gratitude of Christians, that this blessing is more frequently and abundantly bestowed than in former days. I trust you will not forget my anticipated charge for next winter, in Sanderson Academy, and that you will pray that we may there receive a refreshing from the presence of the Lord. The school commences December 13. About the 20th of next month you may expect me.

"Give a great deal of love to my mother. I want she should share largely in this hasty letter."

TO MISS G.

"Ashfield, February 28, 1827.

". . . . . We have about fifty pupils. I find no difficulty in introducing the monitorial system. Pupils, parents, patrons, and trustees are all pleased with it. Many of my acquaintances in this region have requested permission to spend a half day in school, and witness the common exercises; and recollecting the readiness with which I was received into the schools in Boston, I could not well refuse. I believe it is the general opinion that the school this winter is better than it was last, and this is undoubtedly on account of the more systematic plan of mutual instruction. We have most of our exercises much shorter than we had them last winter, and more of them. In grammar, instead of one long recitation, we have two short ones in a day, on the same lesson; one to myself, the other to monitors. *My* recitation is taken up principally in general questions and remarks, and then I leave it to monitors the next half hour. In all my attempts to teach grammar, I think I can safely say that I never saw so much lively interest on the subject, among so many, as I now see from day to day. I have no difficulty in obtaining skilful and suitable monitors; there are so many pupils of judgment and discretion, who have either taught school, or are prepared to teach to good advantage.

"Colonel Leavitt, of Heath, is now here, designing to spend two or three days, with a view of seeing the school. I am told that no man in the county has devoted so much time to common schools as he. Indeed, he has spent almost the whole winter in this way.

"I have a pleasant school; but one thing is wanting, and when I think of this, my heart is sad. Amidst all my blessings, I feel that the frown of God rests upon me. Pray for me and for my dear pupils."

TO MISS G.

"ASHFIELD, March 13, 1827.

". . . . . . I must confess, were it not for my personal attachment to yourself, I believe I should feel an increasing inducement to devote my labors to the youth of my native hills; but as it is, I am not inclined in the least to give any encouragement of teaching here in the summer, before I shall have again seen you. There is an increasing interest on the subject of education in this vicinity. Indeed, there seems to be an enlivened, if not a new spirit extending itself respecting schools. The number prepared to teach is much greater this winter than last; and the demand from our common schools is so urgent, that I feel it to be a duty to endeavor to do something, at least *one winter* more. I have therefore made engagements to return here next autumn."

TO HER SISTER F.

"DERRY, August 22, 1827.

". . . . . . I love Miss G.'s society more than ever, and I believe we may love our friends very ardently, and love them according to the principles and spirit of the gospel. I also think we may love them in a manner displeasing in the sight of God. May I love in that manner which God will approve. I have been interested in the lovely and perfect example of Jesus Christ. Though he loved all his own, as the world loveth not, and though he laid down his life for his enemies, yet, as a man, we have reason to think he acknowledged some as his particular friends. It is said, emphatically, that Jesus loved Martha, and her sister, and Lazarus; and among the twelve was found 'that disciple whom Jesus loved.'

"My health is very good. I believe I have had more vigor of body and mind than usual, this summer."

When Miss Lyon left Derry, in the autumn of 1827, the question was then pending, whether the plan commenced in the Adams Female Academy should be carried on there, or in some other place.

After reaching Ashfield, she writes

TO MISS G.

"ASHFIELD, November 26, 1827.

". . . . . I do ardently desire to continue with you, if I can be useful; even though trials should beset us behind and before, on the right and on the left. My own trials from without have seemed to decrease with my distance from D., while the privilege of being with my dearest earthly friend has increased in my estimation. If I am ever permanently separated from you, I hope it will be by slow and cautious steps; and that I shall have clear evidence that I am deprived of this precious blessing by a direct dispensation of Providence.

"I have spent this evening in company with Mr. S., from Connecticut, a graduate of Williams College. He mentioned being acquainted with you, and the interest with which he should always remember some religious conversation you once had with him. I thought you would say it was characteristic of me, if I should tell you how readily I said to myself, 'Had it not been for that conversation, perhaps there had been one less servant of the Lord, and perhaps one less minister of the gospel.' You will be willing that I should enjoy your doing good, if I don't say much about it."

TO MISS G.

"ASHFIELD, December 10, 1827.

". . . . . . I ought to be humbled in view of my own ignorance, and to be led to depend more entirely on God. I know that I have been earthly and grovelling in my desires, that I have been far from the fountain of life, and that I have been inclined to trust the creature more than the Creator. Since I received your letter, I have deeply felt that I needed a heart conformed to the will of God, that I should place my affections on things above, and not on things on the earth; and I believe that my distance from the fountain of all consolation does not seem quite so great.

"If I should try to tell you how much I sympathize with you in your trials, how my heart bleeds when I think of you, and how I want to be with you, and share in your daily sorrows and joys, the attempt would be altogether in vain. I know I can do nothing but commit you to God. May I have a heart to do this daily. May I remember you as Paul did the Romans, (Rom. i. 9.)

"It is a sweet relief to my mind that you have a Father in heaven, and I do believe that all things will work together for your good, though the way in which this is to be effected may seem to us very undesirable. You may not be saved from trials, but I do believe you will be supported under them; and, after all, I trust you will find more enjoyment even in the present life than the worldling, who has no such support.

. . . . .

"When you supplicate the throne of mercy in my behalf, pray that I may love my dearest friends according to the spirit and precepts of the gospel; that I may so regard and improve my most precious blessings, that it shall not be necessary to take them from me, and that I may be like Him who, when on earth, was holy, harmless, and undefiled. You know I am prone to be earthly, and that I need the grace of God."

TO MISS G.

"ASHFIELD, December 26, 1827

". . . . . . I fear that I ask more for you that is temporal than I do that is spiritual. I have been led to inquire whether it is not very common for my prayers to centre on blessings which may end with this life. Three things I desire for you daily without an effort; and for these I have daily supplicated the Father of mercies; that you may have wisdom from above to direct you to the best measures; that you may daily trust in your Almighty Friend, and in him find immediate and continual support in every time of need; and that you may be saved from overwhelming trials.

"If you should leave D., my feelings and desires are all in favor of engaging with you summers. If, however, Providence should so direct that you should think it not my duty to be with you, probably a field of labor would be opened in this region. But I do not purpose to make any provision, even in my mind, for *summers*, at present; for I do not mean to be reconciled to parting with you, unless I see that I must. About the winter I am not so confident. When I reflect, I can see that I have gone on here, from winter to winter, in a regular and advancing course; and in scarcely any sphere can I expect to be so useful. I ought not wholly to give up this field without consideration; but I entreat you not to act on the idea that I cannot be with you winters.

"We have between forty and fifty pupils in school, and more are expected."

TO MISS G.

"ASHFIELD, December 28, 1827.

". . . . . The care I had at Derry of the conduct of two troublesome pupils in my classes caused me more anxiety than my whole school this winter. But our school is uncommonly good, in this respect, even for this place. It is several degrees better than my school last winter. I must confess that I have a strong partiality for pupils in this region; they are so easily guided. I ought to be very thankful that I have such a school, when in feebleness I must go on, without my best friend to advise, counsel, and comfort me."

TO THE SAME.

"ASHFIELD, January 6, 1828.

"For some time I have been endeavoring to examine my past life. The review is sad and mournful. It is now the twelfth year since the thought first entered my mind — 'Can these be the feelings of an unregenerate heart?' I remember the moment as well as if it were but yesterday; but since then there has been a period of clouds and thick darkness. What an immense loss I must suffer through life, on account of the misimprovement of so long a period of my existence! I humbly hope I shall finally be saved, although as by fire; but I have no reason to expect ever in this world all that spiritual enjoyment with which I might have been favored, if all these years had witnessed a regular advance in a life of faith and piety. Neither can I expect that satisfaction and success in laboring in the cause of the Savior which I might enjoy, if I had received that preparation which can be gained by no means but by a long course of active, faithful obedience. May I be enabled to improve the precious moments as they fly, realizing that when they are gone they can never be redeemed.

"It seems to me more and more important that the

professed followers of the Lamb should commence their Christian course, guided by the pure and perfect standard of truth. Is it not too true that many take their standard from those around them, and on that account live a life which leads others justly to inquire, 'What do ye more than others?' During all these years, I know not how many, just commencing a life of godliness, may have received an impression from me which will be felt all their lives. May I, in this, be saved from blood-guiltiness. But I tremble lest even this winter should bear witness against me. You know that I frequently feel that I can do little or nothing to aid Christians in a life of holiness. In this respect, my responsibility is greater than ever before; indeed, it is so great, that I know not what to do. Almost half of my pupils have more or less hope that they are the friends of the Redeemer. Several have indulged this hope but a few months; in some it is like the faint glimmering of a distant taper. But few can be considered established Christians; and of scarcely any have I much evidence that they possess deep feeling and a lively faith. Here we are; what shall we do? What can we do? The influence of these on each other, the influence from absorbing studies, and that which I may exert, may produce an impression which shall affect their whole lives. These precious souls have been sent here by the providence of God; but what to do I know not. I am weaker than weakness itself, and my wisdom is altogether folly. May I be more and more sensible of the preciousness of the direction, 'If any of you lack wisdom, let him ask of God.'"

TO MISS G.

"ASHFIELD, January 8, 1828.

"You fear lest the care of my school, and my solicitude for you, should in some measure exclude divine realities. I wonder not, my dear sister, that you thus fear. I feel that I am in danger on every hand. I know that almost every thing proves to me a snare. I do not think, however, that my solicitude for you is so great a temptation as many other things; there is so much to lead me to feel that help can come only from God. At times, it seems as though I could believe this in some degree, and that I do find sweet relief in committing the whole to that Friend who sticketh closer than a brother. It is true that I have an anxiety for you daily, which seems to enter more deeply into my heart than almost any thing else; but I have been saved almost altogether from a restless solicitude. It is true that I share with you in all your trials, in no common degree; but that I am thus permitted to share even in your sorrows, I consider a precious privilege; and though it might seem a little paradoxical, yet I do believe that my enjoyment, even for the present time, is very much increased by this participation.

"I hope you will never fear lest your letters should increase my solicitude; for the reverse is always the effect. The more definitely I know all about you, the less difficult I find it to avoid that restlessness which I always find so unprofitable. What you have written to me, from week to week, has been useful as well as gratifying. Sometimes, when I have been re-perusing your letters, sentence by sentence, to see if there was not some idea expressed or implied which I did not at first apprehend, I have thought it would be well for me to read my Bible with like care."

TO MISS G.

"ASHFIELD, January 19, 1828.

"I have told you that the trustees of this academy consider it undesirable to break the course of a regular school through the year, by having a school exclusively for females in the winter. I have, therefore, decided to leave Ashfield after the present winter, as it is not best I should continue longer, unless I stay through the summer.

"I find that this academy, where I have received so much

instruction, and where I have labored so much, from time to time, has taken a firmer hold of my affections than I had supposed. It seems like bidding an old friend farewell, whom I do not expect to meet again. But He who knows how to temper the wind to the shorn lamb, has ordered all the circumstances in much mercy."

TO MISS G.

"ASHFIELD, February 12, 1828.

". . . . . . I feel that there is one way, and only one, in which I can guard against this easily besetting sin, and that is, to seek daily the presence of Him who can turn the hearts of all as the rivers of water are turned. I have been too much inclined to seek to direct my own path. May I be saved from this. The Lord in great mercy has given me a field of labor; so that for several years I have not doubted about the path of duty. The privilege of laboring is to me more and more precious. I would not choose the spot. I would not choose the circumstances. To be able to do something, is a privilege of which I am altogether unworthy. Should I be laid aside, as a useless servant, it would be just. I would humbly seek that I may be permitted to labor faithfully and successfully, that I may be saved from those temptations which my feeble heart cannot withstand, and that I may be blessed with whatever may be desirable for health of body and health of mind, and for general usefulness. For little else of this world do I feel at present that I ought to ask. May I be the Lord's, spirit, and soul, and body."

TO THE SAME.

"ASHFIELD, February 25, Wednesday.

"Every time I have written to you, I have wanted to tell you something about my school, and about some plans you proposed, which I am endeavoring to execute; but I must leave it all for this time also, while I spend a few minutes on a subject more interesting to your heart, and, if I am not deceived, more so to mine. Before my last letter to you, I thought I had reason to believe that the Spirit of God was finding a resting-place in the hearts of some professors of religion in school. I did hope, too, that there was a secret, silent influence on the minds of some of the impenitent. This continued to increase, till not a doubt remained that the Lord was indeed among us. Since last Friday morning, our school-room has been a solemn place. During these five days, four have had a change of feeling, which has led them to hope they have passed from death unto life. About a week before, there was one instance of hopeful conversion. Several are now deeply anxious; some are inquiring with interest, and I know of only *one* entirely unaffected. I tell you all, for we need your prayers. Our state is most critical. I do not feel it to be the time for rejoicing; but for mourning, solemnity, and deep humiliation before God. I fear, first, lest *I* shall grieve the Spirit; and then I fear for the friends of the Redeemer here."

TO MISS G.

"ASHFIELD, March 18, 1828.

"I have this day parted with my dear pupils. Since I last wrote you, my labors have been greatly increased; but that they have been thus increased, I consider one of the greatest blessings I have ever enjoyed.

"When our school commenced, I had a faint hope that the Lord would visit us by his Holy Spirit. But on viewing my own heart, I felt that I had very little reason to expect it. There I found an apathy, chilling and distressing. It seemed almost as if the fallow ground could not be broken up. I felt that I was taking on myself a great responsibility; but what to do I scarcely knew; and the little that I did know I was very poorly prepared to perform.

"The first week I made a separation in the school after

the plan that you have generally practised. To my surprise, nearly twenty were found, who, in some form or other, indulged a hope that they were the friends of God. This affected my heart. The responsibility of attempting to do something for their spiritual improvement rested on my mind with an indescribable weight. It seemed to me that something must be done; but I felt that I could do little more than endeavor to ascertain something about them individually, and attempt to commit them to God. You know that this is a field of labor which I have generally avoided. I felt myself like a little child, without resolution, without strength, without experience, and without wisdom. During my life, I have done very little for the growth of Christians; but through the mercy of God, I humbly hope, that, during the present winter, I have been enabled to labor rather more in this field, and that I have labored more successfully.

"For several weeks, my desires for the impenitent were faint and few; and almost all I met, either in school or out, appeared to partake of the same spirit. I used to say to Miss W., that if the Lord should visit this school, we must always remember it as one of the more wonderful displays of his power, which he sometimes condescends to make. We would recount the scenes of Buckland, and contrast some, who, from the commencement of the term there, seemed to pray the prayer of faith, with those in this school who were the most interested for the salvation of souls; and we would say, 'There is no prospect of a revival, for this is not the way that God generally works;' and then my heart would sink within me. Thus I lived on, week after week, till more than half the term was gone. But while man looketh on the outward appearance, God judgeth righteous judgment. I now believe that the eye which saw seven thousand in Israel who had not bowed the knee to Baal, has seen the effectual prayer rising continually from some hearts in towns around us, though I knew it not at the time.

"The eighth week of the school, Rev. Mr. M., of H., called to take a daughter home on account of sickness in the family. A friend of mine, who is himself a clergyman, has remarked to me, that he considered it no disparagement to any of his ministerial brethren in this region to say, that he should prefer Mr. M. for *his* minister; though he cannot be said to excel in preaching. At the time he came for his daughter, I saw him only a moment. After expressing a great interest in the school on account of its influence on society, and on account of its containing so many teachers for district schools the ensuing summer, he said that he had been anxious for its *spiritual* prosperity. *He only said it*, but it found a resting-place in my heart, and there it has rested to the present time. I could read in his countenance and manner, that it was not an expression of common interest. It seemed suited at once to encourage and reprove me, and also to humble me in the dust. I have since learned, in more ways than one, that he has undoubtedly had great anxiety for souls here; and I believe some others have had a like spirit. It is worthy of notice that the attention commenced among the young ladies from Mr. M.'s parish, and was almost entirely confined to them for some time. It did seem that the prayers of this good man were answered. He has since said to me, that he had indeed been anxious for the school; but in the ardent desires of his heart, he had not been conscious of making any selection; even though he had a daughter here without God and without hope.

"This daughter returned after an absence of three weeks; but her father said he did not bring her depending on the school to give her a new heart. She found the influences in her room entirely changed. Her three companions, young ladies from the same town, were all rejoicing in hope. They had been ardently desiring her return, and now they could not see her willing to reject the Savior. She was immediately affected; but I did not dare to hope, for a while, that it was any thing but sympathy. Soon, however, her tears were exchanged for a solemn and distressed countenance, which bespoke deep, heartfelt sorrow. For a few days, her distress was great. Though generally very much inclined to converse, she would now pass the whole morning without scarcely speaking a word; and her companions, though possessing all the joy and ardor of young converts, were awed into silence; and like Job's friends, 'none spake a word.' In eight days after her return, she was brought to rejoice in hope of a blessed immortality.

"During the whole winter, Scripture recitations have been uncommonly impressive, compared with the means used to make them so. This interest was most manifest, when the subject was a solemn one, such as 'the mercy seat;' 'the thunderings of Mount Sinai,' &c. During some of these still and impressive exercises, it did seem that the effect must remain; but the first recess would carry it all away. It was not until about the middle of the term that I became sensible that professing Christians were more awake, and felt more deeply their responsibility. Sometimes we hoped that the mind of here and there one, among the impenitent, was not quite so indifferent as usual. The first of the tenth week I was convinced that the Holy Spirit was indeed among us. From this time, with a very few apparent interruptions, the work went forward with a regular and increasing advance, till the very last day. About twenty expressed hope in the Savior, six or seven left without hope, of whom two were not deeply affected. One of them tried to be interested, depending on her own efforts; but her efforts were in vain.

"The work was very still; so much so, that many in town knew scarcely any thing about it. Our school exercises were as usual. Many of our friends, who visited us, observed nothing to mark this as the place where the Spirit was operating so powerfully, except a general stillness, and here and there a deeply solemn countenance. But to us, connected with the school, the work has appeared great and wonderful. We have daily said to each other, 'Can this be true?' It has been carried on so independently of means, that we have frequently felt that our best hopes might easily be blasted, and as frequently that the Lord could work and none could hinder. We have all had the conviction daily, that this work is wholly of the Lord. The effect of this revival, on those who indulged a hope at the commencement of the school, has been favorable. Many of them seemed to leave the school with a much higher sense of their obligation to labor continually for the kingdom of Christ."

In reference to her future labors, she writes, —

TO MISS GRANT.

"ASHFIELD, April 3, 1828.

". . . . . . I am not indifferent to enjoyments. Your society seems to me a greater blessing than ever before. If I should enjoy it, may my heart be filled with gratitude to God; if, in his providence, he should deprive me of this, in a greater or less degree, may I never complain *in my heart* of Him who does all things well. The will of the Lord be done. My own strength is weakness. I am a sinner, a great sinner. I can have no hope but in the infinite mercy of God. Sometimes I do hope I depend on him. But O, my wicked heart! I dare not trust it. Still the Lord can give me pardoning mercy; he can give me strength; he can give me submission to his will, and a faithful, obedient heart. It may be he will do it. My daily desire for myself is, that I may know and do the will of God; that I may live by faith; that I may have a calm and quiet mind; that I may be a help to you; that I may be useful in your school; and that, in some way or other, I may be permitted to do something for the salvation of souls. I know I am remembered in your prayers."

SECTION III.

At Buckland and Ipswich, 1828 *to* 1834.

In the spring of 1828, Miss Grant removed from Derry to Ipswich, Massachusetts, where a large number of her pupils followed her. Miss Lyon, as before, coöperated personally with Miss G. in the summer, and kept up her winter school at Buckland the two following years. The school at Derry had not been open during the winter; at Ipswich, it was in operation through the year.

Near the close of her first summer in Ipswich, Miss L. was confined with a bilious fever, from which she had not entirely recovered, when she went to her friends in Franklin county. From thence she wrote to Miss Grant, —

"November 28, 1828.

"It seems to me more and more that we must expect afflictions in this world; but I think it appears to me more and more, too, that they are no cause for despondency. I feel that it is safe trusting in God, that he is a sure rock, which can never be removed. I believe that the blessings of this life are very great, and will continue to be so; and that trials are trials under all circumstances. But I think I can faintly see that there is a foundation for support, when this world is not made all in all.

"With the exception of sister Putnam's family, I find my friends well. The hand of affliction is now pressing sorely on that family. May I, and my family friends, be enabled to place our confidence in God, and cheerfully acquiesce in his government. I believe I mentioned to you that my sister and her husband were both sick. At first, her sickness appeared to be principally debility, produced by care and anxiety for her husband. But it resulted in a complication of diseases, which were baffled by the skill of physicians.

About the time I first heard she was sick, she had so far recovered as to leave her room. It was not long, however, before she became worse again. Her head was very much diseased, and at times her suffering was great. Soon her mind, at intervals, appeared to be affected; still it was hoped it would be nothing permanent. But all hope has failed; the result has been evident derangement, and by the advice of physicians and friends, she has been separated from her husband and children, and removed to the Insane Hospital at Hartford. She knew she was deranged, and was very urgent indeed to go to the hospital. Brother Putnam was not able to accompany his wife. Since she left, he has been much more unwell, and is at this time in a critical state. His physician tells me, that he fears more the loss of his limbs, than an *immediate* loss of life. Thus five little children, the oldest only in the eighth year of her age, are left, like orphans, while their father and mother are living.

"My sickness, and all its attendant consequences, seem to me a small trial, compared with what I am now called to experience on account of my sister's family."

The friend who was commissioned to communicate to Miss Lyon the intelligence of her sister's situation, well recollects the anguish of her heart on the occasion. For a long time, tears came not to her relief; but she walked the room in her agony, and remarked, that "the sickness of friends was trying; their death still more so; but their loss of reason more bitter than all." She also thanked God that this sister, while her powers of mind were under her own control, had chosen him for her everlasting portion.

Miss Lyon's benevolence was not all expended on public charities, as will appear by her remarks about her relatives and friends. The following letter was written soon after the death of Mr. Putnam, her sister's husband: —

TO MISS GRANT.

"BUCKLAND, February 2, 1829.

". . . . . . Among other cares, I am devoting many thoughts and some attention to sister Putnam's family. They are a little more than a mile from me. The whole care of the family, for several months, has rested on my youngest sister. I have been to see them often, and have known so much of their general concerns as to be able to consult with and advise sister F. I have felt it to be a great privilege that it was in my power to administer to the comfort of that afflicted, and to me very dear, family. Besides this, I have written to Hartford, almost or quite every week since my arrival in B.; but I shall have no more of this to do now, as my sister returned last week. She wishes very much to see me often, and says she does not mean to place much confidence in her own judgment at present. I have been to see her twice, and shall probably visit her at least once a week through the winter. Her mind is still weak, and in some respects she appears not quite the same as formerly; but, on the whole, she is to me exceedingly interesting. Her calmness, self-government, and settled resolution to go forward in the path of duty, under her present weakness of body and mind, and under all her complicated trials, considering her natural ardor of feeling, give me a very important lesson. It is a question yet to be settled whether sister, with her health, and under her circumstances, can keep her children together. I am exceedingly anxious that they should not be separated. There is no probability that they could be placed where their discipline, the formation of their minds and habits, and the regulation of their dispositions, could be nearly so favorable as under her care, if she regains the use of her mind. Now, my dear friend, I want your advice. If I should see that, by furnishing them yearly with what I am able to spare from my earnings, it would enable sister to keep her family together, would it not be a good time to cast my bread upon the waters?

. . . . .

"You remember that, after my sickness last summer, my hair came off by handfuls. For several weeks past, I have not lost any, so that I hope I shall continue to have enough to support my combs. For a while my head was very cold; but since I began to wear a turban, it has been quite comfortable.

. . . . .

"I hope you will be enabled to do as much this winter to correct the erroneous opinions of your teachers about schools, if they have any, as you have done to correct mine from year to year.

. . . . .

"Notwithstanding these sober hours, life seems to me more and more a blessing, on account of its labors, and not as a period of rest.

. . . . .

"For two or three weeks, I have been rather encouraged about the spiritual state of our school; but appearances this week are less favorable. Thus we go on between hope and fear. Do pray for us.

"I have seventy-four pupils, and Miss L. B. assists me this winter."

TO MISS GRANT.

"BUCKLAND, February 16, 1829.

"The past week has been an unusual time. My labors, cares, and anxieties have been greatly increased. It has been a solemn season — a trying time — a season of rejoicing, but of great mourning. I trust it has been a time when many hard hearts have been softened, and many a proud one brought low. I should be glad to tell *you* all, but I cannot describe the scenes I have witnessed. It is the Lord's doing, and it is marvellous in our eyes. It is proper to say to you, that I think the rapidity with which this work of grace has been carried forward, the week past, has never been equalled, where I have been permitted to be an eye-witness. It is now just a week since the first instance of conversion; and fifteen are now indulging a hope, though very feeble in some cases, that they know the grace of God in truth. I find it difficult to know how much to press study. I am satisfied, however, that it is not best to make much alteration from the usual course. On this point, I have had the advice of some of my judicious friends, and this is their opinion. On the whole, there is not much excitement in school, but all appears as usual, and in order. I consider it important that I should devote to them much individual attention. I have encouraged their coming to me frequently and familiarly. As my room is in the same building with the school, and as twenty-five of the pupils board here, my opportunities for private conversation are very good. I have had many interesting interviews with individuals, several since I have been writing this.

. . . . .

"I can have but a little more time, and I believe I must be *exceedingly* cautious not to encroach upon the time for sleep, not even to write to my dearest and best earthly friend."

TO MISS GRANT.

"BUCKLAND, March 2, 1829.

"As you have cast on me all the responsibility of deciding the place for my labors next winter, I have now only to tell you that the matter is settled. I have followed the course of Rev. Mr. W., when he could not decide whether to go to N. He did not *decide*, but continued where he was.

"In settling this question, I have looked at the situation of my sister's family, and the probability that my being here might enable me to render them some little service. I have looked at the marked providence that has led me along, since I have occupied this field, (Gen. xxxii. 10,) and especially have I reflected on the spiritual blessings bestowed on this school from time to time, notwithstanding my extreme unworthiness, base ingratitude, unbelief, hardness of heart, and blindness of mind. When I reflect on these things, I fear to forsake this field of labor.

. . . . .

"More than half the days since the term commenced, I have had more or less company in school, generally from out of town.

. . . . .

"There have been no new cases of seriousness in school recently. Still we have evidence that the Holy Spirit has not yet left us altogether. Do pray for us. Your niece Mary expresses some hope that she has commenced a religious life. I consider her case unusually interesting."

TO HER YOUNGEST SISTER.

"IPSWICH, September 11, 1829.

"Last week, I wrote a letter to Mr. Clark, of Buckland, stating some difficulties relating to my continuing to teach there, and some reasons in favor of my remaining here through the year. I hope I shall receive a line from him very soon, as I shall defer deciding this question till I hear from B."

TO HER MOTHER.

"IPSWICH, September 21, 1829.

"I have been considering, or rather reconsidering, the subject of my winter labors. I am more inclined to think that I ought to continue them here through the winter. My dear mother, what do you think about it? At first, it seems more like parting with my family friends, than the present arrangement. But, at second view, the subject appears rather differently. It is true that I have not generally favored visiting so much as to approve of the feelings and conduct of some, who seem to think that every thing *must* bend to this one object; that, however much self-denial they might practise in relation to others, if it is a mother or sister, every other object must yield. I would have all contented, wherever Providence may place them, whether or not they may be favored with the society of father or mother, brother or sister. And if duty should call, I would endeavor to be contented, though years should pass without my beholding the face of one near relative. With my present prospects, I have no need to anticipate this trial. By visiting my native place once a year, disencumbered of school affairs, I might in a few weeks enjoy quite as much of my friends as I now can. . . . . .

"The religious state of our school is interesting, and has been so for several weeks. The Spirit of God is evidently among us, operating on the hearts of our dear pupils. The work is silent and gradual, but the effects are certain; and that it is the work of God there can be no doubt. Eight or nine have indulged hope that they have found the Savior, and the state of many others is very encouraging. So far the work has been slow; but the way seems all prepared by the Holy Spirit for richer and more abundant displays of mercy. It does appear that the fields are white already to the harvest. The blessing seems just ready to descend upon us. If there is no Achan in the camp, if there is no stumbling-block in the way, if there is not a manifest and decided fault on the part of Christians, we shall probably see greater things than these. . . . . . Perhaps the Lord may put it into the heart of my dear mother to pray for these souls that prayer of faith, which God will hear in heaven, his holy dwelling-place, and answer on earth. The school is very attentive to general instruction on the subject of religion, but still there are many who think little or nothing on these things, and care as little as they think.

"Give my love to your family, especially to Mary. When I last parted with her, I supposed ere this she would probably be called to know the realities of eternity. May the Lord bless her.

The following letter to Mrs. A. W. F. will show her interest in *individual* scholars: —

"IPSWICH, October 1, 1829.

"MY VERY DEAR FRIEND:

". . . . . I know you feel a deep interest in ——, and that your first inquiries would be about her. She possesses a large share of our affection, and her welfare will continue to be a subject of anxious solicitude, and I hope of our faithful exertions. She is more than commonly engaging, and she requires more than common care. The ingenuousness with which she receives *new* ideas is very gratifying. This is particularly manifest in gaining instruction from the Bible, whether this instruction relates to historical facts, or to its doctrines and duties. She began to think of her own salvation nearly three months ago, just before vacation. During vacation she quite dismissed the subject, but soon after her return, she began to realize that in the giving up of seeking religion for the world she had greatly sinned, if in nothing else. Since that time, she has evidently experienced much of the strivings of the Holy Spirit. Her feelings have been variable, but her case has been very interesting, and for a few days particularly so. The result we must leave with God. When you remember yourself at the throne of grace, I know you will remember her.

"The religious state of our school is encouraging. Between ten and fifteen are indulging more or less hope. Several others seem near the kingdom of heaven, and in many there is an habitual solemnity.

"I am to teach in Buckland again next winter."

TO MISS GRANT.

"BUCKLAND, November 18, 1829.

"Though my school is such as to involve great and increasing responsibilities, yet some things are encouraging. I have quite as many of mature age in school as I have ever had, and I think quite as much improvement. Our present number is ninety-nine, and about forty indulge more or less hope that they love the Savior. Pray for us that these may not be dead, while they have a name to live."

TO THE SAME.

"BUCKLAND, November 30, 1829.

"I have just had an interview with Rev. Dr. P. of S. He waited on me to express the wish of the Franklin Association of ministers, that I would continue in this region. He took up the comparative importance of my labors here and with you. I did not succeed in my efforts to lead him to look directly at the two important points; one, the great difficulties of my laboring in two places, and the other, that I am pledged to you for summers. He brought no argument to prove that I ought to labor in both places, but, like many others, urged that I ought to labor here both winter and every summer."

TO THE SAME.

"BUCKLAND, December 21, 1829.

"My time is fully occupied. I am doing more than ever before for individuals, and especially for the more dull and less industrious. I want to be faithful to all, and to have every thing done well.

"My sister is no better, but worse. We are now consulting whether it is best to send her to Hartford. We hope first to try the effect of removing her several miles from her husband and children. My cares on her account are great. Sister F. scarcely knows how to have me away. I have spent part of to-day, and shall be gone all of to-morrow, on business for the family.

"The spiritual state of our school is rather encouraging. The minds of some professors, and of several among the impenitent, are tender. Three or four are deeply affected. One has expressed a change of feeling within a few days."

TO MISS GRANT.

"BUCKLAND, January 1, 1830.

"In dwelling on Matt. vi. 25, 26, 'Take no thought,' &c., in school, yesterday morning, I endeavored to point out that anxiety which is there prohibited. While I was speaking, I felt that I was condemning myself. I endeavor daily to avoid excessive emotions on any subject, but in no case do I find so much difficulty as in this.

. . . . .

"Our young ladies are deeply engaged in study; but I fear about our spiritual state. With the exception of two or three cases, we have remained just about the same for three weeks.

"My labors are indeed abundant, my cares almost overwhelming, and they continue to increase. I devote more attention to individuals than formerly. My pupils come to me with more freedom and more frequency. This I encourage. I consider it an important way of doing good, especially as this is my last winter with them. It is necessary to make such arrangements, that the school is never all together except when I am with them. It is always convenient to find some one whom I want to see, or some one who wants to see me; so that I have not a single half hour on which I can depend, from eight in the morning till nine in the evening. You will say that I need more aid, and I am happy to relieve your mind by informing you that the health of Miss W. is so far restored that I have engaged her for the remainder of the winter.

"It is late, and I have written this while half asleep in body; but my heart has been awake."

TO MISS GRANT.

"BUCKLAND, January 20, 1830.

"I want a few of your ideas on the fifth and sixth chapters of Upham's Philosophy very much, especially on the distinction between ideas of sensation and reflection, or those of internal and external origin. How much is to be included in the word *thinking*? (Page 85, sect. 62.) Is it not used in a vague sense? What is your opinion about our having two ideas in the mind at the same time?"

TO THE SAME.

"BUCKLAND, February 12, 1830.

"Since I wrote you, I have been laid aside by sickness; but Miss W. has communicated to you the state of our school. Good Mr. M. was in town Wednesday night, and came in the next morning, and opened the school. Perhaps my sickness is to lead me more fully to feel that the Lord can work without me. This week, it does seem as if we had nothing to do but to 'stand still and see the salvation of God.' As many as six or seven, within a few days, have expressed a change of feeling, which has either led them to hope for themselves, or led others to hope for them, that they have found the Savior. Among these are your niece E., and your cousin R. While I rejoice, I fear. 'He that endureth to the end shall be saved.'

"The school is very solemn, and marked by a deep, pervading stillness. When you pray for your own dear pupils, I am confident you will think of us."

TO HER SISTER ROSINA.

"BUCKLAND, March 9, 1830.

"It is now a week since I parted with my pupils. I should be glad to give you a description of this school, but it is impossible. Perhaps the thought of its being my last one in Franklin county has rendered it doubly dear. I believe that my schools have been more and more interesting every winter, and we all think this has been the most so of all. I have never witnessed such an improvement in moral character, in ardent desire to possess meekness, humility, patience, perseverance, &c. A spirit of benevolence has seemed to reign among us to such a degree, that selfishness has appeared to most of our little community somewhat in its own character. We have made it an object to gain enlarged and correct views, especially relating to our own country, its present state, its interesting character, its wants, its prospects, as to what needs to be done, what can be done, what ought to be done ; and, finally, as to what is our duty. Many intelligent, refined young ladies, who have been brought up in the lap of indulgence, thought they should be willing to go to the remotest corner of the world, and teach a school among the most degraded and ignorant, might it only be said of them by their Master, as it was said of one of old, 'She hath done what she could.' But, more than all, we have been visited by the influence of the Holy Spirit. Soon after the commencement of the school, the gentle dews began to descend, and continued to increase until the last week, when we were blessed with a plentiful and refreshing shower. More than thirty expressed some hope that they found the Savior precious to their souls. At the commencement of the term, more than forty indulged this hope. Among these there was evidently a great improvement in Christian character. It has seemed as if the effects of this work of the Spirit must continue."

TO HER MOTHER.

"IPSWICH, February 7, 1831.

". . . . . . Amidst all the trials of our family, I feel that we have many blessings. Whenever I see you, or hear from you, I feel it to be a very great comfort that you are supported under the various afflictions that have been sent upon you since my father's death. I often try to imagine how great the trial to me must be, if you were unreconciled, and without the consolations of religion. But I hope, my dear mother, that all your afflictions, by leading you to look at things unseen and eternal, will work out for you a far more exceeding and eternal weight of glory."

TO HER MOTHER.

"IPSWICH, April 9, 1831.

". . . . . . In great mercy, the Lord has been pleased again to visit our school by the influence of his Holy Spirit. There is seldom a time when some one belonging to the seminary is not apparently seeking the way of eternal life. During most of the winter, the school has been in an interesting state. For several of the last weeks it became much more so. Not far from twenty indulged a hope of having passed from death unto life. Our school will soon be together again. I trust you will pray for us, that we may again be visited by a refreshing from the presence of the Lord."

In the autumn of 1831, after Miss Lyon had been continuously with Miss Grant, in the Ipswich seminary, for a year and a half, the latter committed the charge of the school to Miss L., and sought the restoration of her health in a milder climate. Though unable to resume her active labors until the spring of 1833, the hope of a more speedy return led to a most copious correspondence between these ladies. In this Miss Lyon found her pastime, generally filling a sheet of folio post, weekly. From these letters a few extracts are here given.

"IPSWICH, October 22, 1831.

"MY DEAR MISS GRANT:

. . . . .

"*Sabbath Eve.* — I spent the time to-day, from one to two,

in trying to explain to our young ladies the subject of faith, from Rom. iii. After tea, they read some passages which they had selected on the same subject. I have seldom so highly prized the privilege of giving religious instruction. It seemed as if my stupid soul did possess a little latent feeling, which could on an important occasion be drawn out. This subject is suited to awaken the deepest interest. It brought vividly to my mind an expression which I have often heard fall from the lips of my dearest earthly friend, 'a more lively faith.'"

TO MISS GRANT.

"IPSWICH, October 24, 1831.

"Rev. Joseph Emerson was in school this morning. . . . . . I rejoice to have him take up the business of lecturing to popular assemblies. His spirit is so pure and so exalted, that, whatever may be his subject, I think he cannot fail to do something to purify the hearts of others, to raise the grovelling mind, and expand the contracted soul, though he may say some things which may be considered extravagant. O for a multitude of such souls as his! Could they be scattered all over the earth, this polluted and wretched world must soon become changed. The more I see of the rest of the world, the more I admire, the more I love such a spirit as his. What a delightful place will heaven be! Thanks be to God, that 'nothing shall enter there that defileth or maketh a lie'! Shall we, my dear sister, after passing through this wicked world, and having been so severely tried with our own evil hearts,—shall we, being washed and made white in the blood of the Lamb, be permitted, through rich, free, and wonderful grace, to sit down in that holy place, where there shall be no more pollution, no more pride, no more selfishness, no more disobedience to God; where we shall be no more distressed with our own sin, no more pained with the sins of others? May you, my dearest friend, be ripening more and more, continually, for that blessed home."

TO MISS GRANT.

"ASHFIELD, November 22, 1831.

. . . . .

"It is wonderful to me how the mind, after a state of doubt and difficulty, from which it seemed impossible to be extricated, can, without any new light, or new evidence, settle down into a state of calm and quiet decision."

After delineating a specific trial, she says, —

TO THE SAME.

"IPSWICH, December 3, 1831.

"I begin to hesitate whether I have done right to say all this to you, when you cannot help me. But I am not disheartened. Every thing will be right; and I doubt not that every thing will be for the best good of this beloved institution. It may be a pruning time this winter; but if so, I trust the goodly tree will take deeper root, and hereafter thrive more luxuriantly. Whatever temporary disappointment and hinderance in going forward we may experience, and with whatever worldly prosperity we may be called to part, O that this seminary may become more and more a successful instrument in advancing the Redeemer's kingdom! For this, I hope you will be enabled to offer up fervent supplication from day to day.

"I have only given you one side of my present situation. I could tell you of blessings great and many, of wonderfully kind interpositions of Providence. In my labors and cares the past week, I have had so many manifestations of the goodness and kindness of God, that it sometimes seems as if my cup was full and running over."

TO MISS GRANT.

"IPSWICH, December 28, 1831.

"For a few weeks I thought it might be a good plan to allow but a very little time for general instruction, except what is of immediate necessity to carry forward the business of the school properly. This was a reason, in connection with many others, for my taking a class in Watts on the Mind. I consider it a privilege to teach this book. I rejoice more and more that I have undertaken it. This exercise requires less care than I anticipated. I have not yet had time to study my lessons as I desire; but I have been able to read them over, and investigate so much, that I could meet my class with a good degree of freedom from embarrassment. I have as yet heard only three recitations. This, for the present, answers instead of general instruction for almost half the school."

TO THE SAME.

"IPSWICH, January 29, 1832.

"I am almost a stranger to lively faith and sensible communion with spiritual things. Subjects of great anxiety, I believe, I generally delight to commit to God; and I seem to have a reliance on him which casteth out fear. But most of these subjects are more or less connected with the world. In view of invisible and divine realities, my mind is darkened, my perceptions feeble, my heart cold and stupid. It seems as if such a low, grovelling worm of the dust could never be fitted for heaven. With men it is impossible, but with God all things are possible.

. . . . .

"Ever since vocal music was introduced into our seminary, I have had an increasing sense of its great practical importance. By our influence, and the influence of our pupils on this subject, probably hundreds may be benefited for a succession of generations. Those who have been able to sing from childhood, do not know by experience the feelings which *some* have who cannot sing. When passing near the music-room last summer, and thinking that a large part of the choir, probably, had no more of a natural voice than myself, I found it necessary to restrain, with firm determination, a rising murmur. I have sometimes felt, that I would have given six months of my time, when I was under twenty, and defrayed my expenses, difficult as it was to find time or money, could I have enjoyed the privileges for learning vocal music that some of our pupils enjoy."

TO MISS GRANT.

"IPSWICH, March 18, 1832.

"We are trying an exercise in connection with Grimshaw's Etymology. I wish some way could be contrived to have the English language studied with as much intensity as the Latin is. I have a few floating ideas upon this subject. I hope I shall do more next summer than ever before to enrich the minds of our pupils with a store of English words, associated with the ideas which they were designed to communicate. I do think that there is a deficiency on this point; but how to remedy it is the great question."

TO THE SAME.

"IPSWICH, June 21, 1832.

"The last evening I was with you, a little cloud of discouragement passed over me, such as I have scarcely before seen for several months. But it was soon gone. Even before I left you, future duties seemed pleasant. Whatever sphere or situation God may appoint, it is enough if I can see the path of duty. I doubt not you have learned, to a great extent, to depend on God day by day for your daily bread. This lesson I desire to learn. How sweet it is to be directed from hour to hour, with scarce a ray of light beyond! The darker the future, the brighter often is faith, and the more firmly do we rely on that arm which can never fail. I have often found myself attempting to preserve the manna till morning, but I have never succeeded. How wise is the economy of Providence, and the economy of grace! How should we rejoice that we cannot lay up stores for ourselves, either of wisdom or of faith!"

TO MISS GRANT.

"IPSWICH, July —, 1832.

"Last week my labors were unusually fatiguing, and of course I have had a headache generally in the morning, which has once or twice continued all day. I do not think it will be so this week. I had a few difficult cases, imperatively requiring much personal effort, besides some labors in school which necessarily demanded the last particle of my intellect and feeling, till I seemed to have but just physical strength enough left to bear me home, just intellect enough to think the very small thoughts of a little infant, and just emotion enough to tremble under the shock. I had been delaying some time, for a convenient opportunity to make as great an effort as I was capable of making, on the subject of conscientiousness in giving in accounts. I believe I have had some feeble desires, that in this and all other things every will should be bowed; that neither teachers nor scholars should have any way of their own, or *will* of their own, but that all might be swallowed up in the will of God. Pray for us, that in all these things God may be honored, and that it may be manifest to all that the will of God *is* done. For a few days, I have had a trying languor and stupidity, especially yesterday. How much of this I should attribute to the fatigue of last week, I know not; but I doubt not that much of it may be ascribed to my own barrenness of soul. On the whole, I have some reason to hope that I am becoming a little less worldly-minded. Pray that I may set my affections on things above.

"Sometimes my instruction in school is so barren, and so disconnected, that it distresses me all the day long. But perhaps, more frequently, I remember these seasons with some emotions of gratitude, that, in the midst of great weakness, infirmity, and sinfulness, the Lord is my strength and my Redeemer."

TO MISS GRANT.

"IPSWICH, August 17, 1832.

"O that my soul were in health as my body is! When my obtuse intellect and more obtuse heart can perceive the truths of the Bible, they seem exceedingly precious. The vagueness of my own mind is most trying, as connected with religious things. I often enjoy the anticipation of its not being thus in heaven. What a wonder of mercy, if I shall at last find a seat in that glorious world, where the will of God shall be known, and loved, and obeyed! If, amid so many deviations, so much lack in our services, the little seasons of conscious sincerity, when we desire for ourselves and others that we may do just what God sees to be exactly according to his will, are so precious, how glorious must heaven be! Did we know nothing more than that God is there, and that his will is done continually by all, it would be enough. Do you think it any proof of great holiness in those who shall live in the days of the millennium, that we are taught to pray that the will of God may be done on earth, as it is in heaven?"

TO MRS. H. C. B.

"IPSWICH, August 23, 1832.

". . . . . . I enjoyed my last visit at your house very much. My kind regards to your mother and to your husband. Much love to the dear little boys. May the family covenant, which I trust has been made in their behalf, be remembered in heaven. May these children of the church never break away from this covenant, so that God shall cast them off, as a branch violently broken from the vine. For this may you labor, and for this may you pray. Are not the promise and the revealed design of God, concerning the children of believers, suited to take fast hold of the soul, and to give to faith a peculiar power? Parental love is one of the strongest of the human affections; but how little this will accomplish, compared with what God can accomplish by the aid he has promised in the family covenant! During the past year, my interest in this subject has greatly increased. May you have wisdom and grace to guide these dear ones, whom the Lord has commanded you to train up for him."

TO MISS GRANT.

"IPSWICH, September 15, 1832.

"A letter arrived this morning, stating the death of my dear sister Ellsworth, — Rosina, you have heard me call her. She was a very dear sister to me.

. . . . .

"This event of Providence is peculiarly suited to touch the tender cords of my heart. She was a kind of darling among us all, and among others beside our family friends. She has left four little sons. Sister Moore, in writing of her, says, 'Another such blow cannot be struck in our family. Among all her numerous relatives, none can fill her place. Heartfelt kindness marked her whole manner. It seemed to reverberate from heart to heart the moment she was announced. The sound of her voice, like some charm, infused a thrill of joy, animating every countenance. Even now, I seem to hear her sweet voice, and see her animated smile, and the welcome of her fine eyes, when lighted with joy on seeing her friends.'

. . . . .

"There is very little prospect that my sister at Hartford will ever be any better. Her bodily health begins to be impaired. She has attacks that are rather epileptic in their character; and these, to some extent, endanger her life.

. . . . .

"I went to school this forenoon as usual. About half past eleven, I was sent for to see Miss Kingsley.* I sat by her dying bed most of the time till four o'clock, when she fell asleep in Jesus. Some of her dying words and her dying prayers we will send you. It has been one of the most precious seasons I have ever enjoyed. M. G. endeavored to write some of her words, to preserve for her friends, and she remarked this evening that it was the happiest day of her life."

TO MISS GRANT.

"IPSWICH, October 6, 1832.

"My dear afflicted sister has finished her work and her sufferings. If you made any inquiries at Hartford, you found that she needed none of your sympathies. It is a great comfort to me, that she was so favorably situated during the last months of her life. The care I have had for her, ever since the death of her husband, has been so great that it now seems as if one of the strong cords, which bound me to earth, was broken asunder. The dispensations of Providence towards her have been very gracious. She was comfortably situated; there was nothing peculiarly trying in her last sickness and death; and now, I trust, she is sitting at the feet of Jesus, clothed and in her right mind. My mother has buried two children in one month, five hundred miles from each other."

TO THE SAME.

"IPSWICH, November 3, 1832.

". . . . . In observing how ignorant the disciples were on some points, after they had been with Jesus three years, I was reminded of our inability to determine the way by which Christ will be most glorified. How easy it would have been for Christ to make them understand that he should

* A pupil from Brighton, Massachusetts.

rise from the dead! But he knew it was not then best that they should understand this clearly. How little do I know what is best! I can pray, without reserve, that the will of God may be done; that the kingdom of Christ may speedily come; that the events which Christ sees to be best may take place, and that we may have hearts to do the whole will of God. But when I pray for particular blessings, I often feel that perhaps I know not what I ask; and it is a delightful privilege to refer the whole to God. I hope that Christians in this school may be fitted to labor in the field of Christ. May the regenerating influence of the Spirit be given, and may many be born of God. How few have been the hopeful conversions the present year! I was forcibly reminded of this to-day, when I inquired who had made a public profession of religion. Almost all, who hope they are Christians. O, may the Lord again return, and may the showers of divine grace descend as in former days."

TO MISS GRANT.

"Ipswich, November 9, 1832.

"A week ago to-day, I mailed a letter for you, which was a little later than I designed, on account of a severe cold. I have now quite recovered. Goodness and mercy follow me continually. I feel so well every morning, when I rise, that I do emphatically *enjoy* health. I never was more sensible of enjoyment from this source. My daily business, connected with school, is peculiarly sweet and delightful. I do not think I ever did love a school so much in so short a time. I do not know how it is, but every thing is so pleasant. From duties in prospect I have none of that shrinking which I often have. There is an unusual evenness and uniformity in my feelings, freedom from excitement, or any rising above the common level. My cup is full and running over, and every future labor, or future scene, seems all that I could desire. I often say to myself, 'How sweet are all my labors! how sweet is life!' In what I have said, I have not referred to religious enjoyment. I find great cause for daily repentance in the sight of God. Though I often walk in darkness, and see no light, I am not left to wander long without any light. In my own experience I have abundant evidence that the Savior is ready, not only to forgive seven times, but until seventy times seven. I have been very much interested, within a few days, in some parts of Scripture which treat of the forgiveness of sin. How boundless is the love of Christ in the way of pardon! How inexpressibly great and glorious is this subject! During a few months past, I have learned a little of the minor prophets. I have just commenced reading these books. I am now reading Hosea. The figurative language in the second chapter is exceedingly forcible. How strikingly are described the treachery, ingratitude, unreasonableness, and wickedness of spiritual departures from God! How exceedingly sinful is sin! How deserving of all the judgments denounced against it! But the boundless love and mercy of God, as exhibited in the promises contained in this chapter, I think most wonderful; and so of all the promises to guilty sinners. How very interesting that Peter should receive an assurance that, though Satan had desired to sift him as wheat, Jesus had prayed for him, that his faith might not fail! Our Mediator will never leave the weakest nor the most unworthy of his followers. He has undertaken in their behalf. He has begun their salvation, and he will complete it. How safe it is to trust in him! Here is all our confidence, all our hope. Here is an unfailing fountain. May we, my dear friend, both of us be permitted to rest under the shadow of his wings. May we walk with the Savior day by day, hear his voice, and listen to his words. May we feel as he would have us feel, think as he would have us think, speak as he would have us speak, and do what he would have us do. It is, indeed, a precious privilege to live, if we can have a single eye to the glory of God. I want you should pray for me daily, that I may have a heart filled with love to Christ, that I may have a zeal according to knowledge in laboring in his service, and that I may have wisdom from above to direct me in the right path. Pray that our teachers may be holy, devoted to God, and faithful in his service; that we may none of us be entangled in the things of this world; that we may all be able so to connect our temporal duties with the great business of eternity that they shall not prove a snare."

During Miss Grant's absence, it was customary for the teachers to send her full accounts of the arrangements of the school, Miss Lyon's instructions, &c. A few disconnected paragraphs, containing some of her remarks, are given here.

"Miss Lyon said to us one day, in school, that if we were unhappy, it was probably because we had so many thoughts about ourselves, and so few about the happiness of others. She asked us to call to mind an unhappy day, and inquire whether we, during that day, had had large desires for the conversion of the world. She also said that, at one period of her life, she used to be dejected and unhappy; but she came to the conclusion that there was too much to be done for her to spend time in that manner. Since that, she had experienced but little unhappiness."

To find the path of duty, "Take all the circumstances, and weigh them candidly, taking the Bible for your guide, and asking God to enlighten your mind. If you sincerely and patiently wait on him, light *will* eventually dawn on your path. It may, at first, be but a faint glimmer; and you may see but one step where you can place your foot; but take that, and another will then be discovered, and if you can see one step at a time, it is all you ought to ask."

"Miss Lyon said last night, she thought she knew the

definite lessons, which the death of her sister and of Miss Kingsley was sent to teach her; one, to pray more; another, to leave nothing undone of all her duty to her personal friends, her relatives, and others."

"I never knew, till last Saturday night, that the command to love God in the decalogue was negative. Do you suppose, as Miss Lyon suggested, that God said to the Israelites, 'Thou shalt have *no other* gods before me,' because they could understand much better how to pluck away the idols, than how exactly to exercise the emotion of love? and does he require us to break away from idols, and, as soon as we have done it, enthrone himself in our hearts?"

Notwithstanding Miss Lyon's engrossing cares, it is gratifying to find that her continued affection and her unwearied kindness to her relatives and friends were wisely directed. This, and other manifestations, show that her superiority of intellect did not overshadow her largeness of heart. It is recollected by many how she watched over the infant child of her youngest sister, which died but a few days before its mother; how she nursed it with her own hands, and ever spoke of it with animation, as in the infant choir above. She also interested herself in the children of her friends, as she visited them from time to time.

The afflicted family of her sister Putnam shared largely in her pecuniary favors, as well as in her affection and care. No pains were spared by her to place the children in families where they would be under a good influence; and until such places could be found, she paid the board of one or more of them, although there was a small property to be divided among them. She also assisted in paying the board of her sister for many months, when it was thought best to separate her from her family without sending her to the hospital. The following extract from letters to her mother, after the death of her sister, will show what she did for her at the hospital:—

"I have received from Hartford an accurate account of sister Putnam's expenses. I shall pay all her regular bills, and the extra charges for nursing and watching. There are some other expenses which I thought it might be best to take from her own funds, so that I can have more for some other purposes. I feel that what I have, should be devoted to the best of objects. After every thing is properly settled, I should think it best that the remaining property of sister P. should be equally divided among the children."

Most of her nieces, of adult age, enjoyed her instructions at South Hadley one year or more. One of them writes that the influence she exerted over them, in early life, in causing them to be educated, and in raising higher their tone of piety, can be known and acknowledged only by their own grateful hearts. A letter to one of them, written at Ipswich, in 1832, will show the motives she held before them.

"MY DEAR A.:

"In advising you what course to take in future, I should be guided very much by your own views and feelings about giving up yourself to do good — to do all you can to render those with whom you may be connected better and happier. I used to think much about leading my friends to endeavor to educate themselves, that they might take a more respectable position in society. This is comparatively of little importance. There is a great work to be performed before that time shall come which is foretold, and many hands are needed to be employed in this work; not only those of ministers and missionaries, but also of females. The labor to be done seems greater and greater every year; perhaps I may say every month and every week. How much is to be done by influence, in a variety of ways! How much prejudice to be removed! What an almost endless catalogue of evils exists among the middle-aged and youth of the present generation! And the children will follow on in their steps, unless some greater and more powerful influence is used. I do most ardently desire that laborers may be raised up, possessing willing hearts and a self-denying spirit. Teachers of the right character can do much.

"Now, my dear niece, will you not, in a measure, forget self, and decide to give yourself wholly to the service of the Lord, to labor in his vineyard, wherever he shall call, and 'whatsoever you do, to do it heartily as unto the Lord, and not unto men'? If this is your decision, and you have evidence that you possess a tolerable aptness for teaching, and can obtain your mother's consent, (do nothing without your mother's consent,) I should think it might be your duty to make even a great pecuniary sacrifice, in order by that means to be prepared to do the greater good. You need that skill in exercising moral power over others which you cannot possess without a thoroughly cultivated mind, and cultivated on the best principles. If your object is to devote yourself wholly to the service of God, and to labor to promote his glory by increasing human excellence and human happiness, I advise you, by all means, to bear the expenses of the journey, and come here to school.

. . . . .

"Your tuition will be twenty-five dollars a year. I will give you enough to pay your tuition bills while here, without any charge, except the charge in Heb. xiii. 16. I should be glad to do more for you in this way, but, consistently with prior obligations, I cannot. I will endeavor to help you plan and economize, and if it should be best that I should *furnish* you with more funds, I should expect that you would pay me interest and principal when able.

"May you be guided in the path of duty, which is the path of peace."

TO MISS GRANT.

"Ipswich, January 15, 1833.

"Is it indeed so, that your dear sister has gone, to dwell forever with the Savior? It is pleasant to think how many, whom we have tenderly loved, have, during the last year, gone home to glory, and are now enjoying that which eye hath not seen, nor ear heard. It brings the heavenly world very near. May we both be preparing for that everlasting rest. But it is a great privilege to live and labor in the cause of Christ."

ON A SCHOOL CIRCULAR. — TO THE SAME.

"I am afraid that their school will be suited only to the higher class, which in every part of our country is a very small class; that their plans will promote distinctions in society; and that, in their view, the improvement of the masses is but a small consideration. But on the whole, I am glad they are about to commence. I trust they will do much more good than harm. They will lead their pupils to gain *knowledge*. They will teach the Bible too, and I hope they will be careful to let the Bible take the lead. Then I care not how closely intellectual philosophy follows after."

TO HER MOTHER.

"Ipswich, January, 1833.

"I should be glad to have you write to me, and tell me all you know respecting the religious state and character of your descendants. I wish to obtain and preserve their names and ages, and keep a record of their deaths, as they may occur. I should be glad to keep some account of the evidence of piety there is among them. May they all be brought into the ark of safety; and whatever may be their temporal condition, may they bear the image of our Lord and Savior Jesus Christ. Will you, my dear mother, pray particularly for your *children*, that they may *all* be *wholly* devoted to the service of God; that they may let their light so shine, that others, and especially those over whom they shall have an influence, may take knowledge of them, that they have been with Jesus? How small a thing is the greatest worldly prosperity, compared with the blessing of true piety in those so near to your heart!

"There are a few cases in school of more than usual religious interest. Our whole number is one hundred. About half are either professors of religion, or indulge a hope that they are Christians. I hope you will pray for us daily, that all who love the Savior may become his *decided, active*, and *devoted* followers; and that all who do not now love God may give their hearts to him, and be prepared for his service. How much is to be done in this dark and wicked world, before all will know and love the Lord! O that a great multitude of laborers might be speedily raised up! The field is white already to the harvest. May your life be spared many years to pray for the prosperity of Zion."

TO MISS GRANT.

"IPSWICH, January 23, 1833.

"It sometimes seems as if I had no place in my letters for small matters, there are so many great things demanding immediate attention. . . . . . I enjoy acknowledging God at our meals very much. I never before realized so constantly his good hand in temporal blessings as since we commenced this exercise. Before the first attempt, the trial became greater and greater every hour. After commencing, it gradually lessened from meal to meal, till now I feel that the privilege far overbalances the trial.

. . . . .

"I have just commenced giving instruction on the Epistles of Peter. We have had two exercises, three verses each. I have looked forward to studying and teaching these Epistles as a kind of feast. But the commencement is more precious than I anticipated. O that I might have a heart to receive into my inmost soul the glorious truths which emanate from many a 'radiant point'! The good Mr. Shepard, of Cambridge, on his dying bed, mentioned to the young ministers around him three things concerning himself—'That the study of every sermon cost him tears; that before he preached any sermon he got good by it himself; that he always went into the pulpit as if he were to give up his account to his Master.'"

TO MRS. H. C. B.

"IPSWICH, May 14, 1833.

"I doubt not you will be glad to receive from my pen a few thoughts, though hastily written. A week ago yesterday I put your name on a list with nearly twenty others, to whom I wished to write forthwith. To tell the truth, I have been so immersed in cares for two or three months, and my brain has been so strained to keep in mind present duties, and not to forget any thing important, that it has often seemed as if things and circumstances which were not needed for present use would be not only forgotten at the time, but even obliterated from my memory. For a week past, in my chamber alone, in a straightforward course of business, in the midst of letters, papers, &c., I have been resting at a great rate. It does seem as if I never gained so much mental rest in a week before in my life. I have had a most curious vacation in respect to calling to mind things and circumstances which I had not thought of for weeks, and which seemed entirely forgotten. To myself I seem almost like one coming to life."

TO MISS H. W.

"IPSWICH, May 23, 1833.

". . . . . Our dear Mr. Emerson has gone home to reap his everlasting reward. He died last week. During most of his sickness, his intellect was clear, and his soul in a heavenly frame. I love to think of him as in heaven. Who was better prepared to enjoy the delights of the heavenly world? May the living walk in his steps.

"My affectionate regards to your parents and all the family."

Miss Lyon having had charge of the school during Miss Grant's sickness and absence, she now, in her turn, consented to spend the summer of 1833 in recreation, and for the preservation of her own health.

In her absence, she kept up a constant correspondence with Miss G., and from these familiar conversations on paper a few extracts are here given. Her first letter is from New York, to which place she went by way of Boston, having gone there to be present at the sailing of a company of missionaries. As her name was afterwards much identified with the cause of missions, it is pleasant to trace the progress of her mind on this subject.

TO MISS GRANT.

"NEW YORK, July 8, 1833.

". . . . . . On my way I was introduced to Mrs. L., who had been to Boston to bid a second daughter farewell, to go and labor in Ceylon. I was exceedingly gratified with her spirit. She appears like a mother who would strengthen the hands and encourage the hearts of her children in the path of duty. Fourteen years ago she went to Boston to bid an older daughter farewell. The daughter now gone was then about six years of age, and remembers but little of her sister. Mrs. L. feels that she is sending this daughter to a mother, and hopes that they will be assigned to the same field of labor. She remarked, that when she viewed the subject of giving up her daughter as a *whole*, she could rejoice and be thankful;

but that when she directed her mind to the particulars, nature sometimes recoiled.

. . . . .

"Sabbath evening, the missionaries received their instructions from the prudential committee, and sailed on Monday. I enjoyed the privilege of being present on both occasions. The scene on board the vessel, on Monday, was calm and lovely. Every countenance seemed softened with tenderness, and yet almost every one reflected, in some degree, the elevated joy, so strikingly manifested by the departing missionaries.

"The monthly concert, on Monday evening, was interesting, as it always is in Boston. Dr. Wisner drew some comparisons between the missions in Ceylon and in certain other places. He remarked that, at some stations under the board, the work had gone on so rapidly that, as might be expected, there is more appearance of religion than reality; and, therefore, there probably will be reaction. Not so in Ceylon. Every inch that is gained seems secure.

"I should like to know more than I do about the Ceylon missions, and, indeed, about all the other missionary operations."

TO MISS GRANT

"PHILADELPHIA, July 10, 1833.

"Yesterday I came to this place. I rose in the morning with the headache, which increased till I reached Amboy. When I took the railroad car, my seat was rather confined; the motion of the carriage increased the pain in my head, and produced an excessive nervous restlessness. It did seem as if I could not go forward; but still I must. I had no protector, no one to take care of my baggage, and engage a hack after I should arrive. I felt, emphatically, that I was a stranger in a strange land.

"After I reached the steamboat, I was, in some measure, relieved; but O, the noise and confusion of men and women

9

of all descriptions; the crying of children from every quarter — on deck, in the cabin, and in every direction. But when I arrived at Philadelphia, I found a carriage without perplexity, which took me to the door of Miss E., where I find a quiet resting-place.

"Little incidents are constantly occurring, which remind me of the goodness and mercy of God. Pray for me, that I may this summer be led in a way which shall bring me nearer to God than I have ever been. Pray that this may be the end of every dispensation of Providence towards me; that every thing may be sanctified by the influence of the Holy Spirit on my heart, without which every means will be lost. O that my whole soul might be conformed to the blessed image of our Lord and Savior Jesus Christ, and that I may bring forth fruit to his honor and glory!

"Dr. Spring gave a most excellent sermon, last Sabbath, from Heb. xii. 1, "Let us lay aside every weight, and the sin which doth so easily beset us." The sermon was to Christians, and drawn directly from the text. I would that I might not lose the impression of the truths contained in this sermon. I hope the Lord will enable me to improve the means of grace this summer, wherever I may be."

Here she was taken sick; and, after describing her situation minutely, she says, with her characteristic frankness, —

"I have written this page just for my own comfort, not for your profit. I am not cast down; I have no painful solicitude.

. . . . .

"I do not think highly enough of ———'s Grammar to use it again. There is a lack of elevation and character about it. It is more like the work of a smart, ingenious *schoolmaster*, than of a man of fine literary taste. ———'s Grammar is too much of the same character. What do you know about ———'s Grammar? I have had it in my heart to examine it as thoroughly as I am capable of doing, but I have not done it. I do not, however, expect to be satisfied. He is too loose a writer to make a good grammar. He may possibly have done more to make this edition what it should be than he did the first; but a man that can write a book for children loosely can scarcely be expected to make a grammar what it ought to be."

TO MISS GRANT.

"PHILADELPHIA, July 22, 1833.

"On Friday morning, I went with Dr. B. to the United States mint, and to the porcelain manufactory. I value these two visits highly. In the afternoon, I went with Miss E. to the House of Refuge. The girls were assembled, and one, who was of age, was that day to leave. They sang a parting hymn, and many of the girls were affected to tears. The neat, whitewashed little rooms and clean beds, the orderly circle of cleanly and decently-clad girls, and the general air of neatness, order, and system came up in my mind, in striking contrast with the many dirty hovels which I have often passed, and the filthy children, the confusion, disorder, and misrule generally attendant on such habitations. That heart must be very hard which cannot rise in gratitude to a kind and good Providence for making such provision for poor, outcast children of wicked, degraded parents. 'O that men would praise the Lord for his goodness, and for his wonderful works to the children of men!' We were late, and our time limited. On that account, we did not visit the boys' department.

"From the House of Refuge we went to the Penitentiary. What abundant evidence have we every where of the wickedness and guilt of man! Man is emphatically the enemy of man. How little, comparatively, have we to fear from the fiercest of the brute creation! As it is only man that we fear, and he only is our enemy, what cause have we for gratitude that the ingenuity and skill of man are combined for our defence!

"Saturday we visited the Old State House, Independence Hall, &c. It was a clear day, and we had a fine view of the city, though, after the business of Friday, we found it rather fatiguing to ascend the many steps. President Jackson was received in Independence Hall, which was richly furnished for the occasion.

"Our course led us next to the navy yard, to see the wonderful ship, (the Pennsylvania,) which truly exceeded all my ideas of its magnitude. I expected to see a great vessel, but not such a mighty fabric. We ascended the many flights of steps to overlook the deck, and felt ourselves richly rewarded for our efforts.

"A visit to the New Marine Hospital completed the business of the forenoon. The architecture of this edifice exceeds that of any other I have visited. If you have seen it, you doubtless observed the plan for ventilation. The walls of the chambers adjoining the passage do not extend entirely up, and yet the beautiful, white, polished arching overhead is such as to give an appearance slightly deceptive, so that, at first view, this aperture for ventilation would not be observed. I would that it abounded in as rich provision for the soul as for the body.

"In the afternoon, we visited the Academy of Natural Science. I closed the week, greatly interested during the last three days, in fine health, except some little suffering in muscles and sinews."

The following extracts from her letters, while visiting some of the fine scenery of our country, are given simply to show her interest in natural objects: —

TO MISS GRANT.

"CATSKILL MOUNTAIN, August 8, 1833.

". . . . . . I remember that, for my own sake, you are more desirous I should dwell on what I see and hear than on the seminary at home, in which my heart is so much interested, but about which I have not indulged one moment's anxiety since I left you. I see enough to make my letters interesting; but these fragments of time, so few and so short, are worth but little in trying to recall and describe what I have seen and heard. And even if I had sufficient time, I have so little tact, that it seems to me my letters, of all things, must be the most insipid.

"I am now twenty-two hundred feet above the Hudson, on one of the peaks of the Catskill Mountains, termed Pine Orchard, snugly settled in a pleasant chamber in the 'Mountain House.'

"The Catskill is indeed a delightful chain of mountains. I have been favored with fine prospects of it at various points. This afternoon, we have taken a drive to see one of the mighty wonders of nature. As from different situations we behold the broad sides, the various summits, and numerous peaks of the mountain, the whole seems like a vast ocean of luxuriant green; at one time, waving gently with the undulating breeze; at another, rolled and tossed by the mighty tempest into lofty billows and deep gulfs.

"The highest peaks of the Catskills are from eight to twelve miles distant from the Hudson. The two highest are Round Top, three thousand eight hundred and four feet above the river; and High Peak, three thousand seven hundred and eighteen feet. Pine Orchard, on which we are situated, furnishes a most extensive prospect. The 'Mountain House' stands near the brink of a precipice, with a bold, commanding front. It is indeed a delightful spot.

"The nearer scenery is composed of the neighboring peaks of the same grand chain. On one hand, they rise with a familiar nearness; on the other, they recede to a more respectful distance. On one side, we behold neighboring summits, rising high above our heads; on another, we cast our eye downwards on the waving tops of the thick trees, with their rolling surface; while in a third direction, rival mountains seem to unite, tipped with the blue summits of more distant and higher peaks.

"The more distant scenery embraces the rich and extensive valley of the Hudson. The view is said to extend about one hundred miles in length and fifty in breadth. But I will not attempt to tell you of the finely-cultivated fields, enclosed by neat, regular fences; nor of the towns, villages, and cottages scattered over the whole prospect; nor of the beautiful groves, whose rich foliage at this season finely contrasts with the sterile appearance of the neighboring fields, just disrobed by the hand of the reaper; nor of the long and winding course of the Hudson, whitened with sails, ornamented with islands, and lined with villages, trees, and wooded embankments.

"I noticed the first impression on my fellow-passengers, as we ascended a very long flight of steps into an elevated piazza, fronting the valley of the Hudson. Scarcely looking after their baggage, almost all, with one consent, stopped to admire and wonder. In the spacious drawing-room within, the numerous visitors seemed full of glee; but without, in the piazza, and on the broad, flat, projecting rocks around the house, the low voice and sweet stillness reminded me of a company in a gallery of paintings."

TO MISS GRANT.

"BUFFALO, August 31, 1833.

"I hastened away from the Falls yesterday, without being half satisfied; with the hope that, by leaving then, I should be able, either by stage or by steamboat, to reach my sister in Fredonia before the Sabbath. The stage, instead of going this morning, as I expected, will not leave until four this afternoon, and, of course, will travel most of the night. As it is rainy, the boat will not touch at Dunkirk at all. My conscience will not allow me to take the stage and travel all Saturday night, if I abide by the rule, 'not to do any thing of which I doubt the propriety, unless I equally doubt the propriety of not doing it.' So here I am, and must stay here, for aught I see, until Monday.

"I have many things on hand, with which I should be glad to fill this sheet. Perhaps you may expect that I should tell you something of the great Niagara, or, rather, that I should tell you how this exhibition of the power of God affected my mind. I cannot tell you any thing about it. I have heard so many things said by one and another who visited the Falls; one saying, 'You will be disappointed;' another, 'You will not be disappointed, if you stay long enough;' a third, 'I do not think it exceeds this object, or that;' and a fourth, 'You never will wish to see any thing more; every grand object will lose its charms after your visit to Niagara.' I have heard many compare it to fleeces of cotton, to banks of falling snow, to the dashing of ocean waves, to the roaring of thunder, &c. I feared that I should be unable to feel the soul-moving power, and I had an ardent desire that I might not acknowledge, even to myself, any second-hand emotions, any influence which did not affect my own heart. But I have been to see for myself, and I am glad I have been. I want to go again; I shall love to dwell on the most distant remembrance. I spent a day and a half, and my time was most fully occupied. I would give you a description of my ramble, but I could not tell you what I saw, what I heard. O, the voice of many waters! I had formed no conception of the scene, or, rather, of the many scenes. Perhaps it is because my powers of conception are so feeble. It does, indeed, mock all attempts at description; it is a stain upon human pride and greatness; it laughs to scorn all the trickeries of art.

"Very much depends, I believe, on the order in which the various parts are viewed. The smaller should be viewed first, and then the greater; and in going from step to step, the soul continually expands to take in the larger views, until we reach the climax. The last step should be to cross over to the Canada side, and there take a view of the whole. This is merely my opinion. I have heard no statement about it; but I am almost confident that it is so."

TO MISS GRANT.

"BUFFALO, September 2, 1833.

"Buffalo is increasing with almost unexampled rapidity, and depends for its growth on its commercial advantages. What a vast influence will be exerted by this single city, during the next half century, on the multitudes of human beings who will spend a few hours or a few days here, either from necessity, or for profit or pleasure! The population is made up of a mixed mass, collected together from different parts of the world.

"O that the Lord would cast the salt of divine grace into this increasing fountain! They do greatly need holy ministers, and faithful, pious teachers in all their schools.

. . . . .

"Saturday afternoon, the rain being over, I made an arrangement for a private conveyance to the Seneca mission, which is about four miles from Buffalo. There I passed a Sabbath delightfully at Mr. Wright's, whose first wife was our beloved pupil, Martha Egerton."

"FREDONIA, September 4.

"My time here will be very much occupied. I did not really think how much visiting I should have to do here. I design to visit all my near relatives twice; once before I go to Detroit, and once on my return. I have in this village only my eldest sister and her family; but I found my sister F. here, from Massachusetts, waiting my arrival. In Stockton, a few miles distant, is my only brother, and his great family; sister Rosina's husband and four children; near by, the only brother of my mother, and his children married and settled around him. Then there are relatives of my relatives, and others from Massachusetts, whom I used to know more than twenty years ago, who will expect me to look in upon them. . . . . .

"The eldest child of my dear departed sister, between six and seven years old, is under the care of sister M., attending school here. I have not seen the other children yet. He seems to enjoy my coming almost as much as an old acquaintance of mature age. He loves to be with me and talk with me, and when he is present, I can think of no one but his mother. His laughing face, every time he looks at me, gives me the most striking conception of that uncommon joy which flowed forth so spontaneously from her on meeting friends, and in which every one seemed involuntarily to share. All say to me, 'None of us *can* be so glad to see you as sister Rosina would be, if she were alive.' O that her children might be trained up for the Lord! I can only commit them to him."

"September 10.

"Since I last wrote to you, my time has been most fully occupied in forming new acquaintances with those I wish to know, and whom I should like to have familiarly acquainted with me. I mean the individuals who compose the three branches of our own immediate family circle. I have been able to accomplish much. I never despatched business faster. I feel considerably acquainted with every one. It has been rather fatiguing, because every thing is adapted so o call forth the powers of the heart. There are so many little circumstances suited to bring before me, in a most vivid manner, the numerous changes which have taken place in our family during the last fourteen years, since my brother came into this country. Till that time, my home was with him. Though he is considerably altered, and appears somewhat bowed down with trials, sickness, and age, yet I find him the same kind-hearted, generous, affectionate brother. O that my visit might be profitable to his children, and to my other family friends! O that the Lord would preserve them from the temptations with which they are surrounded!

"I value the privilege of visiting my friends even more than I expected."

"MADISON, OHIO, September 16.

"I have been a few miles from this place to visit a gentleman, whose first wife was my mother's sister, a very lovely woman indeed. Though I never saw her except on her visits to my mother's widowed home, yet I loved her with a tenderness which is still alive in my heart at this late hour. Her visits were very frequent; and among my earliest recollections is the joy which thrilled through my little heart at the sound of her sweet voice. I had not seen any of the family for many years, and I was anxious to visit uncle for my aunt's sake."

TO MISS GRANT.

"DETROIT, September 18, 1833.

"Every date carries me farther from you. When I left Chatauque county, New York, I hoped to be able to return there this week; but finding it inexpedient, I decided to spend the Sabbath here, and take the earliest boat next week. But one says to me, 'Do not, on any account, take the Ohio, which leaves on Monday. I would not have a friend of mine go in her, for she is always meeting with accidents. On one voyage she caught fire three times; but the New York, which goes on Tuesday, is a good boat.' Another says, 'The

New York is very easy to capsize, but the Superior, leaving the same day, is a large, safe boat.' Another says, 'I should not feel so safe on board the Superior, for she is a very old boat. Besides, it will be just about the time for the equinoctial storm.'

. . . . .

"I agree with you that 'the manner in which recitations are heard has a great effect on the mental discipline of the scholar; and in this point our teachers should excel.' Can we not do much to promote this object the coming winter?

"I am in doubt as to what grammar it is best to use in our lower classes.

"Besides requiring a thorough knowledge of good old Murray, embracing a clear understanding of all his notes and remarks, I have a query whether we ought not to include, as essential to completing our course, an ability to criticize in a philosophical manner his erroneous Latinisms; a knowledge of the particular resemblances and differences between Murray and our preparatory book; and an ability to arrange the differences under two heads, essential and non-essential. Finishing with a book of such an elevated style as that of Murray's Grammar, it would not be so great an evil to have the style of our preparatory book ordinary. What a pity that in our late primary school books there is not more of *elevated* simplicity!"

TO MISS GRANT.

"STOCKTON, September 27, 1833.

"On my arrival at Fredonia, I found that sister F. was sick at my brother's, and I came immediately to this place, where I shall probably remain until I leave this region.

"I feel that I ought to be very thankful for the privilege of being with this sick sister a little while. She was taken ill just after I left for Detroit. It is doubtful what the disease will prove to be, or how it will terminate. She has a broken constitution, which can bear medicine only of the most gentle kind. For two days past she has been more comfortable, and the symptoms are more favorable."

At a later date she writes, —

"My sister, during her sickness, has been in a very desirable state of mind. For the past year, since Rosina's death, she has felt continually that she had not long to live, and has been tried because death seemed to her so much of a terror. She has feared that she should not be reconciled to sickness. But as soon as she was taken sick, her soul was filled with the sweetest resignation. Now, the prospect is, that her life will be spared to labor a while longer in this vale of tears. I have had much this summer to make me think of the last solemn scene of life. It is indeed a great and important thing to be prepared for death. O that I might have my lamp trimmed and burning! that the Lord would save me from sin and everlasting death! What a wonder of grace, if I should be allowed the unspeakable privilege of dwelling forever in the presence of God!"

Her sister recovered from this sickness, and returned to Massachusetts. She was married in June, 1839, and after becoming the mother of an infant, which lived but a few weeks, she died in the triumphs of faith, October, 1840, a short time before their mother.

Miss Lyon cherished a peculiar tenderness for this sister, the "*little one*," when her father was called from his family. In speaking of her to a friend, she said, "Whenever my mind is disposed to dwell on her feebleness and sufferings, I turn from them to the pleasant thought, that God allowed her to live long enough to take with her to glory a little spirit, to sing with her forever the praises of her Redeemer."

TO MISS GRANT.

"ROCHESTER, October 12, 1833

"I am now commencing the last letter but one which I expect to write you before we again meet, and are able to converse face to face. My heart vibrates with tender emotions, as the time draws near when I hope again to sit by your side, enjoying your society as I have in former times. May the Lord prepare me to improve, as well as to enjoy, this precious privilege. Will you unite with me in making it a subject of daily prayer, that the ensuing winter, which we anticipate spending together after so long a separation, may be for our mutual benefit, for the good of our dearly-beloved institution, and for the glory of God? Without God I can do nothing. I am the weakest of the weak."

Her next date was at Ashfield, from which place, after visiting her mother, she proceeded to Ipswich in time to be present at the opening of the winter school.

The following letter to Miss G. was written while the latter was out of town for a few days, soon after the school was organized for the winter.

TO THE SAME.

"IPSWICH, November 16, 1833.

"I have my eye on several members of our school, to whom I think it best to give some individual attention as soon as I can. May I have wisdom from above to give to each such a portion as she needs. How difficult it is to know when to attempt to draw by the silken cord, and when to try a little the firmer cord of authority! It is a comfort that we can do nothing ourselves; but Christ strengthening us, we can do all things which he requires. I would that in all my labors I might keep directly in view the upbuilding of Christ's kingdom.

"In our meeting to-day,* I dwelt on the undoubted fact, that there were living Christians in this school, and it was desirable that every one should find them, and hold with them sweet communion. This I presented among the first steps towards being prepared to commence our mutual labors for the promotion of each other's spiritual growth. I urged the point of every one's finding one or two such spirits before next Saturday night."

TO HER MOTHER.

"IPSWICH, December 3, 1833.

"Perhaps you may have heard that there is at this time in progress a very powerful revival at Andover. It is said to be one of the most glorious displays of divine grace in modern times. Some Christians in this region are hoping that another such visitation is about to return, as the American churches enjoyed two or three years ago. Some gentle dews have descended around us; but there has been in no place, for a long time, so copious a shower as is now witnessed at Andover. In Park Street Church, Boston, there has been, for a few weeks, increasing interest; and in several places around, there are favorable indications. I mention these encouraging things to enlist your prayers, that all this region may again be visited with a refreshing from the presence of the Lord; that his name may be honored in the salvation of souls. This beloved institution you will also remember, as you have delighted to do from year to year. Our present number is one hundred and sixty. Nearly half are hopefully pious. Some appear to be established Christians; some are like many whom we find in all places, who have only a name to live, while we fear they are dead.

"My dear mother, *I* very much need your prayers, that I

* A weekly meeting of the teachers and pupils who hoped they had been renewed by divine grace.

may be revived; that I may have clearer views of salvation by Jesus Christ, and of the wonderful manifestations of God's love in giving his only beloved Son to save a lost world."

TO HER MOTHER.

"BOSTON, December 16, 1833.

"During the past week, I have been attending a very interesting course of meetings in Park Street Church. We hope there is a good work begun in Boston, which will be carried on in this great city, and extend into the country, till the whole region shall be watered. I want you should pray for this city, for this region, and for our school. Pray that sinners, who are out of the ark of safety, may be turned unto the Lord. My dear mother, I want you should pray for me in particular, that I may, from day to day, do my whole duty; that I may know what I should do, and how I should do it; that I may be so faithful to souls, as to free the skirts of my garments from their blood.

"Whether I eat or drink, or whatever I do, may I do all to the glory of God; may all my labors be subservient to the advancement of the cause of our ever-glorious Savior.

"During the past week, I have, as I trust, enjoyed much of the presence of God. The heavenly world has seemed very near, and it has appeared an unspeakable privilege to dwell forever in the presence of the Lord. It is a wonderful mercy that I should be permitted, so guilty and unworthy as I am, to enjoy so much of the presence and glory of my Savior."

TO MISS GRANT.

"BOSTON, December 18, 1833.

"The seasons which I have recently enjoyed have, I hope, through infinite mercy, been profitable. I think I have had a deeper impression than ever before of my inexpressible vileness in the sight of God, and of the infinite and glorious fulness in Christ; a deeper sense of the divine presence and glory; of the real object for which we should live, of the worth of souls, of the duty and privilege of co-operating with Christ in his great work, of the efficacy of prayer, and of the infinite power of the Holy Spirit. When my thoughts go back to Ipswich, my heart rises, crying, 'Lord, what wilt thou have me to do?' I cannot atone for any past neglect, neither would I desire to do it; the blood of Christ is sufficient to atone for all sin. Pray for me, that I may have strong faith in the promises of God, and that I may constantly have the teachings of the Spirit. The same blessings which I seek for myself, I ask for you. May the Lord bless you, and keep you."

The two foregoing letters, as well as the two following paragraphs, were written during a separation of these fellow-laborers for only a few days.

TO MISS GRANT.

"IPSWICH, March 1, 1834.

"You will recollect that yesterday was our communion season. The covenant, when read to Misses G. and A., seemed more solemn and precious to me than ever before. What a privilege it is to make such a consecration of soul to God the Father, the Son, and the Holy Ghost! How precious, indeed, would it be to keep those vows!"

. . . . .

"I should like very much, about the middle of next winter, after I am fairly out of school, to spend five weeks here, and attend to a large class in chemistry."

In a letter to her mother, dated Ipswich, April, 1834, after speaking of the hopeful conversion of a nephew, she says, —

"I consider this a *special* blessing. I have thought of no one in the family circle so much during the winter, as I have of him. He was the eldest that gave no evidence of being born again. I was much interested in his general character when I last saw him; but he seemed far from the kingdom of heaven. Have we not renewed cause to bless the Lord, and praise his holy name? We have surely another pledge of his goodness and everlasting love. And now, my dear mother, I hope you will have an increased spirit of prayer for your children and grandchildren. More than for almost any thing else do I desire to have your life spared, that you may have more time to pray for your large, increasing family. I hope you will stand, at the last day, on the right hand of the Judge, with all your posterity down to the latest generation."

During the summer term of 1834, Miss Grant was journeying in the Western States, while Miss Lyon had charge of their seminary. To the absence of Miss G. at different times, amounting in all to two years, out of the six and a half during which they were connected at Ipswich, and to Miss Lyon's absence from that place, in the mean time, two winters and one summer, we are indebted for many of Miss Lyon's thoughts, which otherwise she might never have committed to paper.

TO MISS GRANT.

"Ipswich, May 6, 1834.

"Yesterday we heard of the death of our former pupil, Miss Farnum. She died last Friday. We have not heard the particulars, except that she had her reason to the last, and was calm in death. It is very pleasant to think of the five individuals who once were members of our family, that we believe are now together with the Lord; Mrs. Wright, Miss Marsh, Miss Kingsley, Mrs. Bishop, and Miss Farnum. How evident is it, that we do not know who it is best should be called home, and who it is best should stay! In times past, life has seemed to me pleasant, and the privilege of laboring very desirable. But my feelings have undergone some change for a few months past. Now, it seems to me that, if God sees it to be best that we should live, it is vastly important that we should labor with all our strength; but that, whenever God may see it best to call us hence, we should cheerfully leave our work at a moment's warning. He who has given us our work to do, can easily commit it to other hands. It is my desire to be in daily readiness to leave all. I believe I do have some foretastes, from time to time, of what I think heaven is, though between these seasons there is much of strange stupidity. These little foretastes, too, as they return again and again, become more and more enriching to my soul, and ravishing to my heart. But the imperfect fruit which I bring forth, and the more imperfect fountain within, form a strange paradox. The grace of Christ is sufficient to cleanse from all sin. This is my only hope, and a precious hope it is."

The reader must have noticed Miss Lyon's confidence in the efficacy of her mother's prayers. She was in the habit of asking them not only for herself and her school, but also for *individuals* under her influence. She was specific in the requests she desired her to bring to the throne of grace. She herself felt that these prayers were an important link in the chain between the Giver of good and the blessing received.

The following extracts not only show this, but also her own exertions in behalf of all around her.

"Ipswich, May 13, 1834.

". . . . . . My dear mother, I want you to pray for the family with which I reside."

After describing the different members, particularly their religious state, she adds, "Another member of the family is a young man, whose mind was injured by sickness when he was a child. He makes himself useful, and is very faithful. As I have seen poor J. go about, I have thought of his soul, and hoped he would at last shine in heaven.*

. . . . .

"Another, for whom I feel great solicitude, is a woman who works in the kitchen. She is about forty years old, and cannot read. She is now absent on a visit. I commenced teaching her to read before she went away, and design to continue it when she returns, or engage some one of the teachers to do it. She has been very much ashamed to let any one know that she could not read. I taught her in my chamber alone. I *do* want you should pray for these individuals. I hope salvation will come to this house.

"The religious state of our school was favorable last term. About twenty indulged some hope of having been born again. In about two weeks, the school reassembles. Pray for us, that the Lord may meet with us."

TO MISS GRANT.

"IPSWICH, May 16, 1834.

"What can any of us do without the blessing of God? I do hope we shall not be forsaken of him. Pray for us all, and especially for the teachers, that we all may be fed with heavenly food, granted day by day, like our daily bread. When there is so much to be done for the blessed and glorious Savior, how important that all our strength, feeble as it is, should be wholly devoted to his service! I am feeling more and more, and with considerable force, that it is much more important that all our powers, greater or less, should

* The reader may be gratified to learn that, after the above letter was written, J., in great simplicity and sincerity, came like a child to Christ, and has since adorned a religious profession by an humble and exemplary life.

be devoted to God, than that our powers should be great; and that it is more important that all our time, whether longer or shorter, should be devoted to him, than that this life should be long. What a privilege to labor, feeling that, while we are spared, God, in his infinite love, can make use of our labors to promote the best of all causes, and whenever he calls us hence, we can lay by our work, as we lay off a garment, and the work can go on just as well without us! How full of wisdom, goodness, and mercy, are all the ways of God! In eternity, we shall forever feast upon his love. Sometimes I have great hope that the Lord will meet with us and bless us this summer; teachers, scholars, and all. To save by few or by many is the same with God. It may be that he will honor his name by remembering us in our weakness, and by taking us all to be his own. It seems to me that this is my heart's desire and prayer to God from day to day.

"Last week, I wanted to tell you how weak I felt. In the first place, a pain seemed to play around my head, just ready to seize upon it, and to unfit me for every thing. It became necessary to watch and guard my efforts as carefully as I would a candle in the gentle breeze. In the next place, my mind was locked as in a cage, and my heart was seized with a painful chill. So much for myself. In looking over the boarding-houses and scholars, I could find so little *salt* on which I could depend that it would not lose its savor, that my heart sank within me. The inquiry, 'How can these boarding-houses be so regulated, and the school so guided, that every thing may be done, which ought to be done, to prepare the way of the Lord, and make his paths straight?' came home to my soul. I felt like sinking; but the thought that the Lord is able was comforting. Yesterday, I seemed to gather some crumbs from my Father's table, which revived my strength of body, mind, and heart."

TO MISS GRANT.

"IPSWICH, June 3, 1834.

"I have a multitude of little things which I should like to say to you. Our school has come together, and the prospect is encouraging. The general aspect is favorable. The cold, wet weather last week made some countenances sad, and seemed to make a few misshapen stones more unfitted to every place. But the sun comes out this week, and other things look rather more comforting. Miss —— is one of these misshapen stones. She has so far been at home most of the days on account of *her health.* I think it doubtful whether she remains.

. . . . .

"I have received a letter from Miss ——, in which she says it is a great trial to hide her talent in a napkin. She is disappointed in getting a situation to teach, as she expected. Now, my dear friend, can you help contrive for this poor child? Can you not find some nook where she can do good, and begin forthwith? If you could find some field of labor, and write to her immediately, how it would rejoice her heart, and mine too, and yours no less."

TO THE SAME.

"IPSWICH, June 5, 1834.

"Last evening, the Life of dear Mr. Emerson came. I seemed to have a visit with the good man as I glanced over the pages one after another. I do hope every one who loved him will enjoy the privilege of reading it. O that I might derive important and permanent profit from this precious book! How large a portion of my life has already gone, and to how little purpose! When I look at such a character as his, whose time was so systematically divided, so filled up with varied usefulness, and who was so persevering on so many different and seemingly opposite points, I feel a kind of stirring influence in my inmost soul, making me feel that

I want to begin anew, like a little child, and live as I should live; though it must be a short life, comparatively. But when and how shall I begin? How shall I live, and how shall I labor?"

The reflections of Miss L., on parting with individuals who caused her unusual trouble, show that the relation she sustained to her pupils affected her spirit deeply. Selfish joy, on being relieved from such burdens, found no place in her benevolent heart. The following letter is an illustration: —

TO MISS GRANT.

"IPSWICH, June 25, 1834.

"I wish very much to give you some more full account of the school than I have done, but have time only to say the same that I have expressed before — that the good hand of our God is upon us in our daily labors and cares. What trials the Lord may see best to bring upon us before the school closes, I know not. The circumstances of Miss ——'s unhappiness have terminated, as I expected, in her leaving the school, and were very trying. She did nothing; was at school only now and then half a day; disliked the school excessively; thought she was sick, and wrote to her uncle, without mentioning it to me, that she could not stay; wrote to her guardian, &c. I told her I thought it best that she should leave. I do not know but I have done my whole duty to her. At any rate, she has gone, and I shall meet her no more till I meet her at the judgment seat. How solemn will then be the account which I must render of my stewardship! May I, from this time forward, feel more and more the solemn truth that I must meet every one that I am allowed the privilege of teaching, and render up a strict account. Pray for me, that I may be faithful to every individual.

"Three or four young ladies were anxious about their

salvation when they entered the school. Others are somewhat interested. Last Sabbath morning, I met twelve at my room, who thought they were decided to make religion their first concern. Two of the number are now indulging some hope."

TO MISS GRANT.

"IPSWICH, July 4, 1834.

". . . . . Returning by way of Beverly, I passed the night in the hospitable home of kind Mrs. B., and spent some time in reading to her and another good lady from Mr. Emerson's Life. It was a luxury, indeed, to read to people possessing such hearts. How justly might he say, 'O, with what eyes, with what smiles, with what hands, with what hearts, with what words, did they meet the feeble remnant of him they once honored as their minister, so much above his deserving!' I love to read his letters. I delight to dwell on his sincerity. Surely, mine eyes have seen one honest-hearted man in this dark, deceitful world. I am distressed with the apparent want of sincerity among Christians on the first and grand principles of duty; and more than all, with my own real deficiencies in this respect. I am distressed that so many momentous subjects of Christian duty should wear so different an aspect in the pulpit, and in the solemn and attentive audience, from what they do in the social circle, and in the business of life. I have often had seasons of being distressed with this subject. In reading Mr. Emerson's Life, all these feelings have been renewed. Is there real cause for this distress? Is it owing to partial views of things? O that my own heart might be sincere, and my hands clean! But I had almost forgotten that I was going to confine myself to business.

. . . . .

"Miss F.'s lucid description of Granville, Ohio, I value very much indeed, and trust I am truly grateful to her for it. Such an aspect of society rouses my soul to almost a flame, when I think what might be done in advancing the interests of the human family, if every good thing might take its proper place.

. . . . .

"Last evening, Mrs. —— showed me an old tract, 'Mary and Martha,' which her daughter had brought from Vermont. I found it was written more than forty years ago, by my grandmother's sister. She was a good woman, in whom the meek and heavenly spirit of Jesus reigned all her life, almost without a spot. She nursed her aged parents till their death, after which she was married, and had one only son, who was content to be brought up by his mother's side, a stranger to the arts of the world. This child has now three little daughters, and for a son has taken the youngest child of my afflicted sister Putnam.

"This little tract brought up a long train of family associations. It seemed an interesting relic of the old, venerated family of my mother's grandfather."

TO HER YOUNGEST SISTER.

"IPSWICH, August 26, 1834.

"Our niece, A. M., has gone to Virginia, to teach. She left us about four weeks ago, and has arrived safely. She has made very good improvement here, and is promising. I think she has some right views about the real object of life, and the real object of education. I do hope she will use her acquirements for the advancement of Christ's kingdom. When you pray for her, I beg you will remember this one thing. What a great mistake has been committed by the followers of Christ, in not believing that every good thing is to be used primarily for the advancement of the Redeemer's kingdom, for the salvation of men! Property, education, time, influence, friends, children, brothers and sisters, all should be devoted to this great object. All can be used, all should be used thus. All who have willing hearts to engage in the great work of coöperating with Christ in saving the world, I do desire should be thoroughly furnished. I would have their power increased, their strength of body and of mind, their knowledge and influence. These things seem to me more and more important and valuable ; not, however, for the worldly-minded, but for the followers of Jesus. When will Christians learn the great lesson of doing every thing for the glory of God? This, I believe, means that every thing should be done, and every blessing be made, to promote the salvation of souls. This is the glory of God, as revealed to us. This is that which we are commanded to promote in all that we do, whether we eat or drink. It is by the church that the manifold wisdom of God is manifest. (Eph. iii. 10.) To the angels, too, it seems that the wisdom of God is made manifest by the church, or by the salvation of man.

. . . . .

"I took this sheet to state a few things about myself; but inadvertently I have turned aside, until it is almost full. You already know that I expect to close my labors here, and my connection with Miss Grant on earth, this fall. I am about to embark in a frail boat on a boisterous sea. I know not whither I shall be driven, nor how I shall be tossed, nor to what port I shall aim. I know not what is before me, nor where will be my next field of labor. I know not when I shall find myself engaged in regular labor in the great work of teaching, for which Providence has fitted me more than for any thing else. But I am not anxious. I have decided to close my labors here, because I felt it to be probable that I could do more good in another field. And now, after breaking asunder a thousand cords, to separate myself from this beloved institution, I feel that I must at present keep myself disengaged from any school, because, by so doing, I have more hope that the way will be open for me yet to engage in the specific field in which my heart is so deeply interested. I never had a prospect of engaging in any labor which seemed so directly the work of the Lord as this. It is very sweet, in the midst of darkness and doubt, to commit the whole to his guidance.

"The next winter I want to spend partly in study, and partly in laying out plans for the future, writing, &c. I wish to be in a family where I shall meet friends, and where I shall have access to a good library, and in a town where I shall not be out of the way of society, for I shall often want counsel. Providence has very kindly given me such a home at Amherst, in the family of Professor Hitchcock.

"The religious state of our school has been in some degree interesting. Many are anxious for the salvation of their souls; some deeply so. A few have recently expressed hope. The interest increases from week to week. I want that you and dear mother should pray for us *much* while the school shall continue, which will be about three weeks longer."

TO MISS GRANT.

"IPSWICH, September 15, 1834.

". . . . . . Messrs. Reed and Matheson, from England, were here last Thursday evening. I regretted exceedingly that you were not present to answer for the school yourself. Mr. M. was in school a short time in the morning, and Mr. R. just before they left town."

Mr. Reed had previously had a personal interview with Miss Grant, at Cincinnati, Ohio, and was very particular in ascertaining the principles and plans of operation in the seminary at Ipswich.

At a later date, Miss Lyon writes to Miss G., —

"What a blessing we have enjoyed in having such a field of labor from year to year! How few are favored as we are! May you, my dear friend, live long, and enjoy the privilege of laboring for a great while to come."

TO HER SISTER MOORE.

"I have not heard from your daughter A. for a long time. I think she will be prepared to do great good, and I hope she will live to do it. I feel satisfied with her present situation, only as a temporary one. I do not think the sphere of usefulness so extensive as she might have in other places. How much greater is the blessing of enjoying a field of usefulness, than a situation favorable to personal advantage! And do you not, my dear sister, regard it as a higher privilege to have your children prepared to do good, than to have them enjoy great worldly prosperity? This happiness I desire and pray that you may enjoy in all your children."

From Miss Lyon's letters to Miss Grant, we now give a few fragments without date; and with these we are brought to the close of their ten years' coöperation in teaching, viz., September 1, 1834.

"They are talking about erecting a building for a female school in this city; but they have had no idea of doing it, except by shares, with the expectation of an income. They look at schools, generally, just as they would at mercantile business. Some persons, who knew I was coming here, hoped that I would render them some assistance about a plan; but they need *something more than a plan.*"

"There is more decided religious influence in this place than in any other village of its size in which I am acquainted. There is more equality among the people, and less aristocracy. But, from what I have learned, I should think the people had not knowledge enough, and fixedness of purpose enough, for their security. They have great zeal and ardor in new things, but in their plans and efforts they are among the most changeable. Their zeal is very apt to be of mushroom character."

After mentioning some young ladies who had refused a field of usefulness, because the salary did not meet their wishes, she says,—

"You see what the views of these ladies are. I could not refrain from saying to myself, If all ladies entertain the same views, what will become of the immense population of our country, whose scale of means and living, in every respect, is so far below these views? How shall the mothers of future generations be so trained, that, with the common blessing of Heaven, they will refuse to give up their children to Catholic influence? What would become of the great multitude of our churches throughout the country, if all our educated ministers were to demand a salary, which should furnish as much better support for their families than the common, enterprising, and industrious farmers and mechanics can procure, as these ladies consider necessary for their personal wants, above what can be obtained by the industry of respectable females in ordinary employments?"

"How soon your school will close! and where will you then be? How I should love to step in some morning and listen to your instructions, and, as in former days, not only enjoy the truth in my own mind, but enjoy it as reflected from many an impressive countenance! Does the Lord bless the truth? Has there been a growth of grace among professing Christians? Do the teachers and pupils have enlarged views of Christian feeling and Christian action? Are their hearts and minds so enlarged, that they can understand and love the principle, that the commands of the Bible are to be obeyed, at all times, in all places, and under all temptations? I do believe that this is a time when efforts in behalf of young Christians are peculiarly needed. In my intercourse with society of late, I have been more and more convinced of this. I have noticed a tendency to giddiness, volatility, and foolish talking and jesting. In some cases, I have been surprised to learn that those in whom I had noticed these things were professors of religion. I am inclined to think that this is more manifest when young ladies and young gentlemen are engaged in conversation with one

another. I recollect meeting a minister and his daughter of fifteen or sixteen. She was introduced to our company. We noticed her apparent thoughtlessness, and spoke of it to each other with a feeling that she was a child, and would need a prudent mother's care. We soon learned, to our surprise, that she professed piety, and would like to go on a mission. This is an extreme case ; but I have seen many others, though less marked, which have led me to tremble for the church. Have we not reason to fear that too many of the young persons in our churches lose sight of the distinction between believers and unbelievers? Is not this a time when there is great need of watchfulness and prayer? O, how important that young Christians should take Christ for their example, and become holy as he was holy, harmless and undefiled as he was! How important that all who are united to Christ, should live in such a manner as to avoid the appearance of evil! May the Lord teach the dearly beloved in our seminary as no man can teach them."

"Several clergymen travelled some distance with our company. Much of their conversation was interesting; but I have some sighs in my heart for a more holy ministry."

"May the Lord guide us in all our plans, and in all our labors. May we feel our dependence, be humble before God, and by his abundant grace be prepared to receive from our heavenly Father great and increasing blessings on the beloved institution which has been our joint care."

PART II.

THE GREAT STRUGGLE

SECTION I.

The Buckland School.

For six successive winters, as has been seen, Miss Lyon was engaged in teaching in Buckland or Ashfield ; assisting Miss Grant at Derry, or at Ipswich, through the summers. That winter school was, in an important sense, the germ of the Mount Holyoke Seminary, and contributed to enlist public opinion in favor of Miss Lyon's later enterprise. In Buckland, where she spent the first two and the last two of the six winters, her school-room was a hall used for social religious meetings ; and, as the pupils increased, the teachers used their own rooms for recitations. The first winter, the school numbered twenty-five ; the last, nearly one hundred. The scholars of one winter were an advertisement for the next. Hiding herself in the shadow of her own loved hills, happy in her work, and seeking only to do it well, she and her assistant were often occupied with it twelve hours out of the twenty-four. Miss Hannah White aided her every winter after the first ; Miss Louisa Billings, now Mrs. Russell, of East Randolph, was the only other teacher regularly employed in the school ; but the more advanced pupils often acted as monitors, when their services were needed.

The school was moderate in its expenses ; the families

near by, sensible of its advantages, made every effort to board the pupils, one family receiving twelve, and another fourteen. The friends of the school opened their houses, not to make a living, but to accommodate the young women, who were expected to wait on themselves as much as they could without hindering the work of the family. They either did their own washing or sent it home. Tuition was three dollars per quarter, and board from one dollar to one dollar twenty-five cents per week. This school becoming the resort of many who had been, or expected to be, teachers, and Miss Lyon aiming to fit them for their work, reading, writing, spelling, mental and written arithmetic, geography, English grammar, and the Scriptures were made leading studies. Herself a pattern teacher in them all, she showed every pupil how to teach. After the first winter, she introduced one or two higher branches, varying the choice so as to meet the wants and wishes of the former pupils. The celebrity of the school in that region was such, that to have attended it one or more winters became a letter of recommendation to a candidate for teaching. If she had the imitativeness, tact, or talent to make her scholars do as well as she had been made to do, she was sure to be employed and to be wanted in the same district the next year. Though the word had not then found its way thither, it was, to all intents and purposes, a *normal* school.

The religious character of the Buckland school, more than any thing else, drew the hearts of the good people toward it. Daughters who went thither thoughtless and bent on pleasure, returned home serious, and bent on doing good. The gentle influences of Heaven falling on the school, its members were turned from the path of sin and death to that of holiness and life, till, to the churches in the vicinity, it became a consecrated spot. In many a working-man's house, at many a family altar, that school was remembered with earnest prayer and with pious gratitude. The absent daughter and her youthful companions were prayed for together, with hope and trust that there they might learn the way of life. Ministers in the sanctuary, when they prayed for colleges, did not forget the school at Buckland. Pastors and people alike felt that, *there*, education was truly a handmaid to religion.

It has already been seen, that, after Miss Grant removed from Derry to Ipswich, she kept her school open through the year, and conferred with Miss Lyon with reference to uniting their labors for winters as well as summers. Miss Lyon was nearly a year considering the questions, Where can I do the greatest good? Where am I called to serve my Lord and Master? At Buckland and Ashfield, she was surrounded by sensible and efficient young women, who looked to her with filial confidence and respect, and who, in most cases, could not command the means to go to the more distant and more expensive school at Ipswich. By them she seemed to be able to take hold of society, as of a sheet knit by its four corners, and raise it towards heaven. For them she had given up all elegant leisure, and hours of literary recreation. Many of them she had pointed to the cross of Christ, and been the instrument of opening to them, in the certain future, the gate of heaven, the entrance to his presence. Her spiritual children, her sisters in Christ, as they were, could she leave them to be guided by other and unknown hands?

She was also in the midst of a community who appreciated her worth. Enough was subscribed by the friends of female education in that region to erect a suitable building for the permanent accommodation of the school. The Franklin Association of Ministers passed resolves, requesting her to continue in that part of the state. Dr. Packard, of Shelburne, and others, personally urged her to continue with them.

In view of these considerations, she was, at first, disinclined to leave her field of labor among her native hills.

Writing to Miss G. on the subject from Buckland, January 22, 1829, she says, "Had you made the proposal contained in your last two years ago, I should have had no doubt about the path of duty. But within this time, I have given encouragement of continuing in this region winter after winter. Within this period, the number of the friends of my school has greatly increased, till now there are many who would not justify my leaving this region, except for obvious and sufficient reasons.

"The present necessities of this region; the experience I have had in attempting, during five winters, to accommodate my plan to the wants of this community; the increased number of schools in the vicinity of Ipswich, compared with the scarcity here; your abundant ability alone to form all your plans; the ease with which you could procure experienced assistants in the winter,—lead me to doubt very much whether we should do right to be together the whole year. In endeavoring to decide, I do not estimate what I should accomplish with you, but compare what you would accomplish with my assistance with what you would do with the assistance of other experienced teachers. This I have considered a just balance, and, weighed in this, you can judge, as well as I, how the subject appears to me. Since I last saw you, the importance of this field has increased in my estimation. May we both be directed from above."

There was one *personal* consideration which weighed much with Miss Lyon in favor of Ipswich. This was her extreme attachment to Miss Grant, whose presence was sunlight to her soul. The peculiar enjoyment she derived from the society of her friend, she felt, should be allowed some weight in the decision of the question. Miss Lyon also saw that her aid was greatly needed the year round in the large and increasing school at Ipswich, especially if the way should be opened for Miss G. to do any thing towards laying the foundation for a permanent seminary.

Miss Lyon's multiplied labors, near the close of the summer term at Ipswich, in 1829, the journey thence to Buckland, and the care and toil connected with commencing her own school there for the winter, together with a severe cold, almost prostrated her. Her friends, as well as herself, saw that she might injure her health, and be lost to the cause of education.

Writing to Miss Grant soon after her school at Buckland commenced, she says of these ills, "Perhaps they were sent in kindness to convince my friends here that my health can fail."

When her friends in the western part of the state saw that she could not with safety labor in two fields so distant from each other, they urged her to locate herself with them. To this request she had but one reply — that she had sacredly pledged her assistance to Miss Grant for summers.

In view of her happiness, her health, and her consequent usefulness, Miss Lyon finally decided to unite with Miss Grant for the two succeeding winters as well as summers, leaving the question as to the place of her labors after that period for future consideration. In a letter of December 9, 1829, communicating this decision to Miss Grant, she says, "It is fully understood, that I leave Buckland because I consider it injudicious to attempt to occupy two fields of labor so distant from each other. Dr. Packard, as well as some others, was disposed to come directly to the conclusion that it was my duty to separate from you altogether, as soon as possible. This question I have carefully avoided, except when I have been pressed upon it. Dr. P. inquired whether I should be ready to leave you, if duty should be plain; to which I could give but one answer. He thought it not best that I should give much encouragement of returning here, at the end of two years, as the matter is so doubtful, but advised me to fix my eye on some one or two confidential friends, and if, in six months or a year, or at any future period I should think it my duty to direct my attention to this vicinity, communicate it to these friends, depending on them to bring the school to the best spot without collision or commotion.

"One year ago, I should not have supposed that I could so quietly and cheerfully have decided to leave this beloved field. The prospect of my future labors is pleasant, but excites no high anticipations. Your society will always be to me a source of the *highest* earthly enjoyment, but I do not mean to make it 'my meat and my drink.'"

This decision was, no doubt, a wise one. She had won confidence and honor in her own country. He whose counsel she devoutly sought, saw that it would forward the work which he had raised her up to accomplish, if she should for a time fully identify herself with the Ipswich school.

When it was found that Miss Lyon was unalterably determined to continue with Miss Grant, an attempt was made to induce the latter to remove to the western part of the state. The Franklin Association of Ministers passed some resolves, and, through the Rev. Thomas Shepard, corresponded with Miss Grant on the subject; but, for reasons not necessary to mention here, the effort did not result in her removal.

Miss Lyon afterwards said that it was at Buckland, surrounded by the young women who have been described in the foregoing pages, that she first conceived the vague notion of "a seminary which should be so moderate in its expenses as to be open to the daughters of farmers and artisans, and to teachers who might be mainly dependent for their support on their own exertions."

Rev. Dr. Packard, of Shelburne, submitted rather than consented to her removing entirely from Buckland. She did not forget the advice he gave her, which is contained in her letter of Dec. 9, 1829. One of her first steps, after deciding to leave Ipswich to embark in her great enterprise, was to communicate her decision to him. He was at Ipswich at the first formal meeting that the friends of the project ever held, was chairman of the general committee, and was the first agent employed to act in reference to the subject. He was a friend when most needed, in the very infancy of the enterprise; and by the time he withdrew, there were others ready to take his place. In one of Miss Lyon's letters to Miss G., written in December, 1834, she says, "In the plan for the proposed seminary, Dr. Packard's whole soul is enlisted. It is his first and great object, occupying his time by day, and many of his thoughts by night. I sometimes think that in interest he will even go beyond myself. In devising ways and means to accomplish it, his mind acts with all its peculiar originality. I have long desired, almost more than any thing, that some gentleman, who has the habit of acting, would take hold of this object as his own, and devote to it his time and his energies. It appears to me his zeal and his action may be *essential* to the accomplishment of this object."

Not only was Dr. Packard a connecting link between the school at Buckland and the Holyoke Seminary, but the ministers who had been so much interested in the former school were among the first to welcome the latter to their vicinity.

SECTION II.

*The Ipswich School.**

THE school conducted by Miss Grant, first at Derry, and afterwards at Ipswich, owed much of its prosperity to the faithful and efficient aid of Miss Lyon, and in turn contributed much to prepare and enlist both herself and the public in the novel work of founding a permanent female seminary. A

* In this account of the Ipswich school, the writer has made free use of an article published in the American Quarterly Register, and also in the last catalogue of Miss Grant.

somewhat full account of that school is therefore demanded, both as a part of her own biography, and of the early history of the institution at South Hadley.

Miss Lyon threw her soul into that school as entirely as if it had been her own. While other teachers, for one reason or another, vacated their places in the school, Miss Lyon stood at her post, coveting the heat and burden of the day. Never had a principal a more faithful and cordial assistant. In after years, did not God remember this faithfulness, in raising up so many fellow-laborers, in whom Miss Lyon's heart could safely trust?

The principal features of the plan on which the Adams Female Academy at Derry * had been conducted by Miss Grant, were as follows: A thorough course of English studies, occupying three years; the arrangement of the pupils, at entrance, in three regular classes, each occupying a year; provision for devoting much time and attention to biblical study and instruction; the exercise of the same care and supervision over the young ladies in and out of school, as if they were her own daughters; while certificates, at the close, were given to those, and only to those, who, on examination, gave evidence of having gained a thorough knowledge of each study in the prescribed course. The academy at Derry was continued on this plan four years, but no sessions were held during the winters.

In the winter of 1828, the Trustees of the Ipswich Academy made arrangements with Miss Grant to occupy their building for a female seminary of a high order, leasing it to her, by permission of the proprietors, free of rent. The responsibility of furnishing instruction and conducting the school was devolved upon her; but they were to afford such aid as they could in carrying the design of the school into effect.

* At the division of Londonderry, the part in which the Adams Female Academy was located took the name of Derry.

The trustees pledged themselves to provide the members of the school with accommodation in families, so that two pupils should have the exclusive occupancy of one room, and that in winter not more than four should study by one fire. From and after the spring of 1830, a house capable of accommodating thirty-three boarders was occupied exclusively for the school. The principal and most of the teachers usually boarded in this family, and its privileges were always in great request. The young ladies there were, of course, directly under the eye of the teachers. They also took the care of engaging boarding-places in town, and of assigning rooms and room-mates, thus securing a great control over the influences operating on the pupils out of school. It was made the business of a particular teacher to acquaint herself with the wants and wishes of the young ladies in regard to their boarding-places, rooms, and room-mates, and to make the best possible arrangements for their personal comfort and accommodation. Those who were in the large boarding-house, and those who were not, bore to the Principal the same degree of responsibility; all had the same regular hours for meals, sleep, relaxation, exercise, and study.

Of the one hundred scholars who gathered around Miss Grant and Miss Lyon at Ipswich in the spring of 1828, more than thirty had been their pupils at Derry. Bringing the spirit of love and obedience, they gave a pleasant type to the school. A part of these thirty felt that they owed a debt, which they could never pay, to teachers who had, in preceding years, held to their lips the waters of life, yea, meekly and patiently taught them to go themselves to the ever-flowing fountain. They evinced their gratitude by a readiness to do all that in them lay, by their influence and example, to assist these teachers in their efforts to make a good school.

The school at Derry and at Ipswich was one in its plans, instruction, and general results. Many older scholars gathered to it, and it numbered among its pupils the daughters of nearly every state in the Union.

In 1831, there were one hundred and ninety pupils; but as there were not suitable and available accommodations for so many, the number was reduced; first, by not receiving any under the age of fourteen; second, by requiring certain qualifications for admission; and finally, by limiting the number of boarders.

From the time that Miss Lyon commenced her labors at Derry till the fall of '34, she was in the school every season, except two winters and one summer. For two years of that time, Miss Grant being absent from the school on account of her health, the care of it devolved mostly on Miss Lyon. For the whole ten years, she was inscribing ineffaceably on the minds and hearts of these pupils her name and character, as she did also on her Buckland and Ashfield scholars. On them she left the impression, that for efficiency, for unpretending goodness, for power to direct and control mind, and for skill in exhibiting divine truth, she had scarce an equal among the daughters of men.

As has been already stated, some account of this school belongs to the history of Miss Lyon, because she did so much to make it what it became, because her service there educated her for her future work, and because that school was really the Holyoke Seminary, dwelling in tents, led by the cloud and the fire, and not yet honored with a name. The active friends of the new seminary, in their drafts upon the benevolent public for its accommodations, every where pleaded that they intended to stereotype the Ipswich Seminary, and afford the same and greater advantages at less expense. It was the known character, and wide and substantial usefulness of the Ipswich school, that gave to those pleas and arguments their power and success.

Two wealthy, active, original, practical minds, whose ruling passion was to benefit immortal souls, had consecrated their thoughts, energies, and affections to the Ipswich school. They taught, not for money, nor for fame, but from the love of God, and to do good. Looking beyond parents and guardians, they received their scholars as from God, and sought to train them, in the morning of their existence, for his everlasting service, and held themselves accountable to him for the manner in which they fulfilled the trust. The great and all-absorbing question with these ladies, by night and by day, in term time and in vacations, was how to prepare the minds intrusted to them for the greatest possible usefulness and happiness, here and hereafter. To this end scholarship, literature, and science were all made subservient. It was to this end alone that efforts were made to provide suitable and permanent buildings for the accommodation of the Female Seminary at Ipswich.

The proportion of teachers employed in the school was about one to fifteen pupils, and the other ladies thus engaged were of one mind with Misses Grant and Lyon. Consecrating their energy, as well as their time, to their work, they did not fall into the way of doing as little as they could and yet escape censure, but they sought to do as much for every pupil as would be of any use to her.

The school, neither at Derry nor at Ipswich, included in its course of instruction needlework, instrumental music, or the foreign languages. It proposed to furnish a thorough English education, to make its pupils intelligent readers, easy writers, and companionable friends, and to give them such a knowledge of liberal studies as would enable them, in an unembarrassed manner, to acquit themselves honorably and usefully in any station of life which they might be called to fill. But before Miss Lyon left Ipswich, the course of study embraced nearly the same branches and text books as that at South Hadley does now. The study of Latin was introduced into Ipswich Seminary in 1835. In a circular which Miss Lyon sent that fall to all the candidates for admission to her new institution, she says, "It is expected that the Mount Holyoke Female Seminary will take the Ipswich Female

Seminary for its literary standard. It is to adopt the same high standard of mental discipline, the same slow, thorough, and patient manner of study, the same systematic and extensive course of solid branches."

Many improvements which are often spoken of as having originated within a few years, were introduced into Miss Grant's school at Derry or at Ipswich.

An hour was assigned to each recitation, and the teacher devoted it to examining the class in the lesson of the day, to explaining, illustrating, or enforcing it, and to pointing out its difficulties, or directing the attention of the class to preliminary questions and questions of instruction. The exercise elicited thought, and accustomed the pupil to express her ideas in a clear, correct, and forcible manner. The standard of recitations was unfailing accuracy, and a majority of the pupils attained it. The teachers, aiming at a thorough and symmetrical cultivation of the mind, selected the studies, and laid their plans for recitations, with reference to that end. The pupils pursued not more than two or three studies at a time, but they were expected to investigate the subjects studied till they had made the ideas their own, if correct, or found out the fallacy, if they were false. Free discussion gave life to the recitation, and stimulated the pupil to make thorough preparation.

Any pupil was allowed to bring a written question on any part of the lesson which she wished to hear more fully explained, and each scholar was liable to be called on for the explanation, except the one who presented the difficulty. The different answers from all sides would increase the interest of the exercise so much that the hour assigned for the lesson would pass rapidly away, and close unexpectedly to all. In the study of mental philosophy, particularly, these discussions were very animated, and completely absorbed the attention of the pupils. Not only was the text subjected to examination and criticism, but questions suggested by the lesson were discussed, sometimes in several successive exercises. The object aimed at was not merely to store away knowledge for a lifetime, but to prepare the pupils to read understandingly on the subject, and to form independent and correct opinions. In all the branches of study, the pupils were led to understand that they were only taking a glance into fields of hidden treasures, which they were to explore in future years.

The government of the school was a kind of theocracy, the teachers standing between the pupils and God, to assist them in learning his will. Yet there was a copious infusion of true republicanism. The regulations were referred to the immutable standard of right and wrong. Is it right? Is it in accordance with the law of love? were questions constantly pressed home, with the hope of leading the scholar habitually to ask them for herself. Conscience was brought to bear on courtesy, neatness, dress, and every thing which affects personal character and usefulness.

A rule, and its reason, were generally given together. Miss Lyon, on requesting the young ladies not to visit each other on the Sabbath, would say, "It is not in our power to make you keep the day holy in your hearts, yet, as standing in the place of parents, we are bound by the fourth commandment to see that you keep it externally." When she told them that they were expected to be at meeting on the Sabbath, she would quote the words of the apostle, "Not forsaking the assembling of yourselves together, as the manner of some is." The likeness of the good man to "a tree which bringeth forth his fruit in his season," was the unfailing sanction of punctuality. In the time of green fruit, Paul's direc tion to the jailer, "Do thyself no harm," was enforced upon the pupils. All violations of physiological laws, such as over-indulgence of the appetite, thin shoes, tight waists. were shown, to the satisfaction of the pupils, to be violations of the sixth commandment. By the eighth, using things without leave, injuring borrowed articles, defacing furniture not their own, and all careless use of common property, was shown to be forbidden. The teachers were glad to have every practical proposition of theirs tested by the Bible. To the remark, that "an eminent teacher was much assisted in governing scholars by studying and applying the laws of nations," they would reply, "How much more, if she had studied and applied the laws of God!" This reply contains the genius of their mode of school government, the controlling of minds by God's methods.

The pupils were led to govern themselves. A new regulation was generally distinctly stated, and its tendency to promote the greatest good, *on the whole*, clearly exhibited. Their consciences and judgments approving, all, or nearly all, the school would formally adopt it, and pledge themselves to its observance. While they were trusted to approve of just and wholesome rules, and to report their success in keeping them, effectual measures were adopted to guard against and to detect insincerity. The teachers seemed to find the golden mean between trusting scholars so much as to make them careless, and watching them so closely as to make them sly and mean.

The system of accounts, that is, of scholars, reporting their success or failure in keeping rules, Miss Grant adopted when an assistant in Mr. Emerson's school. He had requested his pupils not to whisper, unless it was very necessary; but they found it necessary oftener than conduced to their highest improvement. Miss Grant had the care of instructing the whole school, at certain hours, in writing and in English grammar, and, with Mr. Emerson's leave, she took charge of this important item in school discipline. As she met one and another of the more docile and influential pupils, she said to her alone, "If you could avoid whispering altogether, I think it would be an advantage to you and to the school;" and when the pupil said, "I will try," Miss

G. added, "Will you try for a week?" After a large number had pledged themselves to her, she discussed the subject with them all, dwelling on the evils of whispering in school, and clearly showing it to be the floodgate of idleness and disorder. When their minds were in the right state to give the right answer, she put the question, "Would you like to try and avoid whispering, and all communications equivalent to it, till this hour to-morrow?" On the morrow, she bestowed a look and a word of commendation on those who had kept their resolve, and by such means, in a few weeks, banished whispering from the school. She was careful to keep them informed as to what were communications, and to see that the line between truth and falsehood was correctly drawn on their minds and consciences. Though young persons, who are weak in moral principle, may be injured by an indiscreet use of this system, yet, in the hands by which it was at first employed, its fruits were good. One lady, who had a large school of small children, made a rule that every scholar who whispered should lose his recess, and, just before recess, said to her flock, "Those who have whispered this morning may rise," and thought she was pursuing the same plan as Misses Grant and Lyon. Two ladies could not be found in all the United States, who would be more keenly alive to the danger of such a mode of proceeding to a child. Children, at such a school, are trained to falsehood as regularly as to read and spell. The plan is adapted only to minds capable of discriminating between truth and falsehood, and in which reason and conscience have the ascendency over passion and appetite. When this state of mind and moral principle is wanting, Misses G. and L. instructed the candidates for teaching, who were under their care, to delay introducing this system of accounts until, by moral means and appliances, it could safely be done. In their own schools, from week to week, they gave instruction, and bestowed individual labor to implant, or evolve, and to keep in healthful action, principles of truth and integrity; their object being not merely to lead the scholars to faithfulness in the minutiæ referred to, but in all the relations of life.

The following extempore remarks of Miss Lyon will illustrate her method of introducing a new regulation, and leading pupils to self-discipline: —

"Early rising, young ladies, is not rising at any particular hour; for what is early for one, may be late for another. Early rising, for any individual, is rising at the earliest time proper for her under the existing circumstances. The hour of rising should not be decided on in the delicious dreaminess of the half-waking and more than half-dozing state of one's morning slumbers, but the decision should be made when you are up and awake, with all your powers in vigorous exercise. In deciding, you must take into view your age. Young persons, who have not fully attained their growth, need more sleep than those of mature age. You must consider the state of your health. Feeble persons, with constitutions made to run only half the threescore years and ten allotted to man, often need more sleep than the strong and healthy. Some allowance, too, must be made for the temperaments of different individuals. Some require more sleep than others; but those who need a large amount should take their additional sleep in the early part of the night. Who was it that said, 'One hour's sleep before midnight is worth two after?' Yes, Dr. Dwight, a man of large experience and careful observation. Now, young ladies, you are here at great expense. Your board and tuition cost a great deal, and your time ought to be worth more than both; but, in order to get an equivalent for the money and time you are spending, you must be systematic, and that is impossible, unless you have a regular hour for rising. If that hour is five, and you are on your feet before the clock has done striking, then you are punctual; but if you lie five minutes, or even one, after that hour passes, you are tardy, and you must lose a little respect for yourself in consequence. Persons who run round all day, after the half hour they lost in the morning, never accomplish much. You may know them by a rip in the glove, a string pinned to the bonnet, a shawl left on the balustrade, which they had no time to hang up, they were in such a hurry to catch their lost thirty minutes. You will see them opening their books and trying to study at the time of general exercises in school; but it is a fruitless race; they never will overtake their lost half hour. Good men, from Abraham to Washington, have been early risers."

She kept on in this lively strain, till she saw the school prepared to make a proper decision, when she would say, "Now, young ladies, I want every one of you to fix on an hour of rising for a week to come. Be sure not to fix on too early an hour, for it would not injure your character nearly so much to make a mistake, and decide to rise at six, when you might rise at half past five without any injury to your health, as to fail of meeting your own appointment."

In the freshness of the forenoon, their minds unbeclouded by over-eating, over-study, or unhealthy excitement, the pupils would generally fix on an earlier hour for themselves than their teachers would for them.

Miss Lyon would proceed: "All who have decided on their time of rising, for a week, may raise their hands." The irresolute and the sluggish would be unable to come to any decision. She would next say, "You may all rise; *all* means *every one.* Yes, *all* are on their feet now. If you have decided on your time of rising, you may take your seat." The lovers of their own ease and comfort would be left standing, while a large majority of the school were comfortably seated. "As fast as you fix on the hour, you may take your seats," was the curt and effective address to those who were still unable to decide. No one could sit down *undecided*, without acting a falsehood, which was considered in the school dishonorable, as well as wrong. If any were inclined to stand it out, she was patient with them, and willing to stand as long as they did. When all had signified that the decision was made, they were directed to write down their decision, and hand the papers to her, or keep them till she called for them. One of the first remarks on the succeeding day would be, "How did you succeed, young ladies, about rising? You may all stand. Those who were up this morning at the time they set yesterday, may take their seats." A very large majority would be found to have kept their resolutions, and the delinquents could complain of no one but themselves. Having broken their own rules, and fallen short of their own standard, they could not but feel self-condemned.

When there was not time for the teacher to give the reason for a rule, the pupils would still render a cheerful compliance, feeling a childlike confidence that their teachers knew better than themselves what was for their good, and were aiming to promote it. The early hour for retiring, and other specific regulations, were often observed in this manner by pupils, in the early part of the term; but in the sequel all the rules were duly explained. The pupils were led to look at these requirements in the same light as their teachers, and to pronounce them in the hidden recesses of their hearts, as well as by a formal vote, just and good. They appeared to have a hand in the government; but they did what they chose, because they chose what was wise and good. The reins were so hidden in their hearts, and so held in hands of love, as never to be seen or felt by well-disposed pupils; and yet they were turned whithersoever right, reason, and duty led.

No question was ever left to the vote of the school, unless there was a moral certainty that they would decide right. In conversation even with a pupil, Miss Lyon exercised great adroitness in preventing her from committing herself on the wrong side. If there was not time to exhibit a requirement in such a light as to bring the school heartily to concur in it, it was taken for granted that they understood it, and would observe it; and but few disappointed such expectations.

Miss Lyon was firmness itself in case of a refractory pupil. The only outburst of passion that was ever manifested in the school at Ipswich was at a time when she was presiding. A pupil, of woman's height, refused to go into the assembly-room at nine in the morning. Miss Lyon said to her, "*You must go* into the large room." The young woman was in the library. As she refused to move, Miss Lyon requested two other pupils to assist her. The young lady not helping herself at all, they drew her from the library through the entry and a recitation-room into the assembly-room. The scholars, all in their seats, looked on with amazement. When she was fairly in the room, so that the door could be shut, Miss Lyon, who was in the desk, said to her aids, "That will do;" and turning to the school, she said, "You may study," and the young lady, on the floor, was left to her own reflections. She continued a member of the school several terms, and though she was always a source of anxiety and care to her teachers, she never after attempted openly to contend with the authority of the school. Notwithstanding the school was nearly petrified with astonishment, yet, at the word, the scholars turned their eyes to their books, and saved their exclamations for another time and place.

The pupils felt a lively interest in the reputation, character, and usefulness of the school. Near the commencement of the term, Miss Grant or Miss Lyon would speak of the magnitude of the work with which the teachers were intrusted, in a very solemn and impressive manner, and say they should be crushed under it, were it not for the hope that their scholars would help them in sustaining it. After showing them that the responsibility lay on the scholars as well as on the teachers, the speaker would say, in tones of love, "And now, my dear pupils, may we depend on you to help us bear this burden? Will you unite your efforts with ours in promoting the welfare of this beloved seminary? Your predecessors have made the school what it is; will you see to it that it does not suffer in your hands? Will you leave it as good as you found it?" Every heart and every eye would answer, "Yes." "I thought we might, I feel that we may, lean on you," the speaker would say; "and if you will each take good care of one, we can take care of the rest." Those teachers could send electric thrills from heart to heart, and their appeals were not lost upon their pupils. They were made to feel that the reputation and character of the school were part and parcel of themselves, and must be secured, rather than their individual gratification. In such connections, the maxim, "What will not do for all to do, will not do for one," was repeated and applied; until, if a scholar wished to ask for an improper indulgence, the motto would be brought to her remembrance, and her request would die in the asking. The leading scholars were sure to be on the right side, and to strengthen the hands and comfort the hearts of their teachers. The only way in which the teachers showed partiality was by employing their favorites in doing sundry little services for them, or for the school. The desire to be thus selected and distinguished was sometimes almost inordinate.

The government was maternal, not merely in name, but in truth. The teachers manifesting a tender regard to the natural and right feelings of their pupils, a jealousy of their reputations, and a lively interest in their concerns, many of the scholars made them their confidential friends. When a scholar was seen going wrong, she was not arraigned before the "faculty," but a teacher, taking pains to meet her privately, without mentioning her specific fault, would ask her if she was doing as well as she was capable in that particular

The pupil would generally answer truthfully. "And would you like to improve on this point," uttered in a tone of kindness, was the next question. The next time the same two met alone, a like truthful answer would generally be given to the inquiry, "How did you succeed on the point of which we were speaking?" None but the untoward pupils themselves know how this motherly way of proceeding binds the heart in love to a kind and faithful reprover. It is seldom that, in a school so governed, the amputating knife is necessary, but the case does sometimes happen; and it has been said, that Miss Lyon would expel a scholar in just as good humor as she received her. "I am sorry for you," she would say, "but the good of the institution requires it." Every unnecessary exposure of the faults and weaknesses of scholars was avoided, and it was an established rule with the teachers not to speak of such defects among themselves, unless the good of the school, or of the individual, made it necessary. "Speak of them, as if they were your younger sisters," was the direction to the newly-initiated teachers. In a teachers' meeting, if any one spoke jestingly of a scholar's capacity, Miss Lyon would hush the speaker immediately, saying, "Yes, I know she has a small mind, but we must do the best we can for her."

They labored, and that with great success, to start their pupils on a voluntary course of self-denying action. Scarce a term passed but the command, "Thou shalt love thy neighbor as thyself," was held up, day after day, in new and interesting relations. They would exhort their pupils to forego many little indulgences, that they might have wherewith to meet the calls of charity, and then would be sure to see that the call was forthcoming. When the pupils, under the exhibition of the truth, were led to feel it a privilege to deny themselves for others' good, their teachers sought to stereotype the benevolent emotion by hallowed benevolent action. In this, they had their eye on an end far beyond the adding of a few dollars to the resources of a philanthropic society. Looking forward, they saw that, to make their scholars open-handed and charitable women in coming years, they must see that they made a liberal use of small means, while under their eye and influence.

The teachers always set a good example to their pupils in this respect. They generally headed a subscription paper with handsome sums. The "tithe" which Miss Lyon contributed to objects of benevolence was gradually increased, till it became nearer one half than one tenth of her income.

The study of the Bible held a very prominent place in the Ipswich school, as a means of intellectual as well as of moral discipline. It has already been seen, that when Miss Grant first went to Derry, she gained the consent of her employers to occupy one seventh of the pupils' time and energy in the study of the Scriptures. Miss Lyon fully concurred in an arrangement, which secured the Bible's being studied more in a year than any other book. The Bible lesson, conducted much as in a well-ordered Bible class, occupied the school an hour on Monday morning; and every pupil was expected to spend at least two hours in preparation for this exercise. Not only were the two hours' study and investigation recommended, but the teachers secured its being given. It was very well understood in the school, that the more improvement any one had, the longer she could profitably employ herself on a given passage. In the social exercise of Monday, while much attention was paid to the biographical and historical incidents, the points of moral interest and practical application were especially presented, and the discussion of abstract and useless questions was avoided. This lesson was reviewed on some other day of the week.

Lessons of common sense and propriety, and principles of every-day action, were enforced by words of holy writ. The writer recollects seeing one of their pupils, a woman of fine understanding, refuse to draw lots for a berth in a steamboat, saying to the servant, "I would rather not draw. If any berth is left after the other passengers are provided for, I will take it; if not, very well." She had been impressed with the explanation of Prov. xvi. 33. Many a one in middle life, when she hears the common proverb, "Better that ten guilty escape than one innocent suffer," is reminded of Prov. xvii. 15, which her teacher had placed in juxtaposition with the former. Another cannot join in the thoughtless merriment occasioned by a person's assuming the garb of the other sex, because she remembers Deut. xxii. 5, once so impressively pronounced in her hearing. Some scholars, who gave little heed at the time to such lessons, may have forgotten them; but many are acting upon them from day to day, and transmitting them from generation to generation. "O, Ipswich! my wife is always quoting Ipswich," said a husband, who was not sorry that his wife could never forget the wisdom she had learned there.

At Ipswich, an arrangement was made to give each young lady half an hour for retirement. This greatly promoted serious reflection. The arrangement was a matter of necessity. As the result of biblical instruction, an extensive interest in personal religion would be awakened. Many scholars would anxiously ask the way of life. Night and morning, one and another of the pupils would be found in the entries, on the stairs, or in a family room, apparently out of their proper places. To the question, "Why are you here?" they would reply, "My room-mate wished to be alone a little while." So many pupils were thus thrown out of their rooms, as to give an air of disorder to the house, and occasion some waste of time. To meet the difficulty, the teachers made an arrangement in the families, that for one hour in the morning, and one in the evening, the scholars might have the use of a family room, half of them being in the family room, and half alone in their own rooms, at the same time, thus securing to each the privilege of a season of retirement twice a day. The command, "Enter into thy closet, and when thou hast shut thy door, pray to thy Father which is in secret," was faithfully applied and enforced. The teachers explained to the school, that, standing in the place of parents, they had provided means and opportunity for obeying this command. The scholars were informed, that the manner of spending this season of retirement was left to their own choice; but they were exhorted to spend it in the manner and spirit for which it was given, and carefully instructed, that if they wasted it, on their own souls rested the responsibility. Their attention was directed to parts of the Bible most helpful to devotion. They were advised to pray in a whisper, or in a voice which should not prevent the season being strictly in secret, and they were instructed how to spread out their sins and recount their mercies before God.

This plan, like the system of accounts, was suited only to a school where the moral sentiment was high. It was adapted only to a school of serious and reflecting persons, who, in a majority of cases, would make good use of their time. On such scholars, even though some of them had lived a prayerless life, it often made an abiding impression for good. One hour a day alone, an hour which the person may, to be sure, spend as she pleases, but which she distinctly understands is given her to commune with her own heart and with God, and which is thus improved by her companions, is not only an opportunity, but a strong inducement, to her to think of her moral relations, to open and study her Bible, and to bow before God. Said a Holyoke pupil, "My conscience would not let me study any thing in my half hour less serious than Wayland or Butler."

Much effort was made for the religious improvement of professing Christians. Miss Grant and Miss Lyon, or one of them at least, would see them together before the first Sabbath of a term, and, in a fervent and effective manner, urge them, for the sake of their own growth in grace and their influence on their impenitent companions, to honor that holy day. Instruction particularly adapted to their case was given from the desk. At a weekly meeting, in which they all assembled, practical subjects were presented with earnestness and close application. What Christian was ever with those teachers a term without hearing the passage, "Whether ye eat, or drink, or whatsoever ye do, do all to the glory of God," expounded? and who did not carry away with her a livelier sense of its meaning and power than she had carried there? Any one who has read Miss Lyon's work on missions, must have seen that her conceptions of eternity, of an eternity of sorrow, spent under the frown of God, were awfully distinct, vivid, and controlling. How her hearers would almost hold their breath, as she dwelt on this subject! "Take," she would say, "any slight trouble, or trivial suffering, bodily or mental, a throbbing tooth, a tedious, complaining, disagreeable room-mate, and think, 'I am to bear this pain a year, night and day;' or, 'I am to have this companion always in my presence for twelve months.' That seems long. Yet hope lends strength to bear the evil. A year, you say, and it will be gone. When one day is past, you subtract it from three hundred and sixty-five, and rejoice that you are one day nearer the end of your trial. Let the load accumulate to the utmost that can be endured by mortal frame, or conceived by mortal mind; let the year before you be one of suffering, of anguish, of remorse, of grief like that which separates the soul from the body, and yet you cannot die. You are doomed to a living death, always dying, yet never to die; for this is the import of those solemn words, the second death; — a year spent in such agony, how long, how slow its moments roll! Yet hope lends her pencil, and the happy future appears beyond, in dim, but certain light. Let years be added and multiplied, till the sum reach a number equal to all the years of all the lives of all the sons and daughters of Adam, and let the soul be strung to endure suffering to the utmost stretch of its capacity in all these years, yet in the infinite ages of eternity, there would come a period for these sufferings to cease. Relief, however distant, would lighten the woe. But 'the smoke of their torment ascendeth up *forever* and *ever*.' It is an everlasting punishment; the worm dieth not, the fire is not quenched. No sun shall rise on that darkness, no time shall measure out those groans. It will be one blank scene of woe, with nothing to mark its duration; and when the soul shall ask, 'How long?' nothing but that awful '*How long*' shall echo from its prison walls. O, forever, *forever!* Think of this word and its import. Add life to life, and age to age, and you have not approximated it." Many a pupil could say, in a manner recognized at once by her companions as Miss Lyon's, "You won't do so again, will you, dear;" but no one could ever imitate her manner in such remarks as these. They were the embodiment of her own experience. "Souls bought and redeemed from all this woe," she would say, "how should they show forth the glory of God! How should they feel toward the multitudes in danger of perishing for lack of the bread of life! Who that has been redeemed, and permitted to linger on the shores of earth a while to represent her ascended Savior, would not wish to eat and drink and live to the glory of God? Who but would rejoice to give all her money, her time, her talents, her influence, to this great cause, the salvation of the perishing? When you are about spending a single shilling, remember, that shilling might carry leaves of healing to those who are sick unto death, unto the second death, and ask whether you are investing it to God's glory. The question for the Christian is not, 'Is it right for me to buy this little elegance for myself?' but, 'Would it be wrong for me to do without it?' You waste ninepence worth of paper. That single ninepence might have sent the bread of life to the famishing." Her sympathy for the heathen was ever alive and active, and she communicated her own feelings of indebtedness to them for Christ's sake to many of her pupils. She led them to feel that all they were, and all they had, were indeed the Lord's, to be actively and constantly employed in his service.

Professors of religion met weekly in circles of ten or twelve, for conversation and prayer. One person was chosen to act as a leader, and each gave in turn a report as to her fidelity and enjoyment in closet duties, her trials, her conflicts, and her labors with the impenitent. The members of the same circle became intimate as Christians and attached as friends, and went forth from school sympathizing fellow-laborers in the kingdom of Christ. The professors of religion, residing in the same family, met for prayer in one of their rooms on the Sabbath. The tone of piety among the professors of religion had a very important agency in making religion honorable and desirable in the eyes of the impenitent. A good Christian character was felt to be the most valuable of possessions.

To the teachers, the Bible was the source of light divine, and they sought to cast its radiance on every mind. They felt under no obligation to be instructed in this particular, and asked no parent's creed. They never spoke of sects, but industriously inculcated the doctrines of the Bible, as they understood them, asking leave only of God and their consciences. They looked on secular studies as the scaffolding by which they might reach their main object, to make known the will of God. Miss Lyon used to say of teaching such studies, that it was but "hewing the wood, and drawing the water," humbly and patiently to be done, indeed, in the hope that it would lead to an opportunity to do something infinitely higher and better.

Two or three mornings in a week, the Principal occupied from fifteen to thirty minutes at the hour of nine, A. M., when the newly-waked spirit was all unworn, in illustrating and enforcing some particular scriptural truth. The Ten Commandments, for example, the Sermon on the Mount, the first chapter of 1 Peter, and many other parts of the Bible, were presented in a practical manner, text by text, and clause by clause, to attentive listeners. Miss Lyon always took her full share of the biblical instruction, but it was not till the morning lectures devolved upon her in consequence of the absence of Miss Grant, that she developed her full power of interesting scholars in the discussion of religious truth. At Derry, and for the first two or three years at Ipswich, she seemed to study and teach the Bible much as she would any thing else. Her intellect, rather than her heart, was interested. She admired it, examined it closely, sought out its application with care, and awakened in her scholars the same intellectual interest in its contents. This careful study, no doubt, contributed to the power with which, in after years, she came before the school. For years before she left Ipswich, it was a rich entertainment to hear her unfold the hidden wealth of some apparently obvious text. She came to her hearers in the fulness of the gospel of Christ. Unseen things, in her mind, were living realities, and seemed to become such to those to whom she described them. Her faith was substance; and her imagination, fertile and sacred as the garden of the Lord, was put under its tuition. She had a great deal of moral intuition, and she never exhausted that fund of great first truths to which the human heart echoes a response, and which find their way directly, when properly presented, to the consciences of intelligent moral beings. Her manner was simple. There was not the slightest appearance of speaking for effect, or trying to speak eloquently. The speaker was in the shade, where she evidently wished to be, completely hidden by the truth she was holding forth. She did not crowd ideas before the mind, but would dwell on one important thought, present it in different lights, illustrate it in several ways, and detain her hearers on it till they were as fully possessed with it as she was. How many have heard her thus dwell on the passage, "Whatsoever a man soweth, that shall he also reap," until their minds were all pervaded with the great truth, that they were to meet the deeds of every day hereafter! A part of her power lay in securing continued attention to one single, but great and solemn conception. Active as was her own mind, and easy as it was for her to grasp large ideas, and to survey many almost in a single breath, she could parcel out truth in those small proportions in which common minds are obliged to receive it. The superior scholars, who loved to give themselves up to a kind of moral exhilaration, and those of spiritual discernment, who watched the effect of truth on other minds, were never weary of her religious instruction. Those who were worldly in their views, who delighted most in the pleasures of sense, or in mere intellectual acquisitions, sometimes complained of the length of her lectures; but such complaints were not often heard.

The vividness with which she evidently saw and felt the very truth she was uttering, was one secret of her power. If she had ever a flitting doubt of the certainty of future retributions, that doubt was never known or suspected by her most intimate friends. The foundations of her faith never wavered. It seemed as though the principles of our holy religion were interwoven with the fibres of her soul. The world to come was as present to her thoughts as this world to her eyes. Her confidence in God was as simple and true as a child's in its mother. She felt the Savior to be present with her, her friend, her counsellor, her adviser, sustaining and directing her as really as though she had seen him at her side, had leaned bodily on his arm, had heard his lips respond to her petitions, and seen his wounded, but almighty hands reach down deliverance.

The commands of God were as practical to her as the commands of a father to the docile child at his knee. She ran the way of his commandments. They were welcome to her soul. It was hardly a self-denial to her to keep them. It was to her a delightful fact, that the eye of God never wandered from her, and one of which she seemed ever joyfully conscious; somewhat as we are conscious of light and the presence of the sun, even though our minds are intensely occupied with a different class of subjects. She delighted to discover the great principles of God's government in his word and works, in providence and grace. In this science she was an apt scholar, ever learning and ever coming nearer those great and magnificent truths, which doubtless she still studies and comprehends more fully than when she tabernacled in clay, and yet still sees a boundless ocean beyond. When she undertook to bring these truths before the minds of her pupils, the effort conduced to make them clearer to her own spirit's eye. While feasting others, she was herself feasted. It was because God was so glorious to her, that she made him glorious to her pupils. What she spoke of was reality to her, and hence her words had an indescribable power. Her energetic way of saying the most common thing absolutely constrained you to attend; but there was something more than that in the calm, subdued, unearthly tone in which she dealt out heavenly wisdom. When she opened the terrors of the law before her hearers, it was a dying sinner spreading the most awful truth before dying sinners. It was the warning voice of one who saw the yawning gulf. She would point to the dark, shelving, fatal precipice without a gesture, without a motion, save of her moving lips, her hand laid devoutly on that well-worn octavo Bible. She would uncover the fiery billows rolling below, in the natural, but low, deep tones with which men talk of their wills, their coffins, and their graves. If she had been to Westminster Abbey, and had been describing its treasured monuments, she would have awakened no more sense of reality. This *faith* was the mainspring of her power. She said little by way of entreaty. She never begged and besought her pupils to serve God, as though the Infinite could not do without them. Religion was not degraded by representing it as begging for votaries. Sometimes she would lift the curtain, and give her auditors a glance into the holy of holies. When the soul was ravished with glories that no tongue can fully describe, she would turn, and say so effectively, "But there will be no vacant seat there. If any one chooses to break away from the vows her parents have taken for her, if she chooses to separate from her Christian friends, her absence will not be felt in that happy throng. Heaven will be full without *her*." She set life and death before her pupils. In the name of her Savior, she offered them salvation. She held forth the hope that they might find, if they sought. She offered pearls only to the discerning. That waiting soul, how she would describe its capabilities, its ever-growing susceptibility to joy or woe, its continued existence, its identity through all this infinity of experience, as if she had herself been through it all. It was not the words, nor the manner, nor the thoughts, but it was the whole effect, which was wonderful. It was the conception her hearers formed of the truth she exhibited. With what a sense of present reality would they feel, that a thousand years hence they would remember as though it were but yesterday, sitting on those seats, accepting or refusing offers of mercy. She would carry the soul forward into the midst of the glowing realities of eternity. Such conceptions will outlive death and the grave. They are still the aliment of the souls that then began to feed on them. They fill the mind in its most solemn moments, but they cannot be described. Like the things shown to Paul, they are unutterable. They were none the less impressive because they cannot be detailed. Miss Lyon worked her way down to the depths of the soul, and planted seeds there to germinate, and grow, and yield fruit in the after life. It is no proof that bread has not been eaten, that the substance of it can no longer be discerned.

The truth seldom failed to produce its legitimate fruits. It was almost sure to lodge in some minds. In the course of a few weeks, the solemn look, the suppressed sigh, and absorbed attention, would be manifest to the observing teacher. The school would be more and more serious. It would be increasingly evident that great thoughts were occupying their attention, but the pupils themselves would not be aware of any general change. Often, when a meeting for conversation was appointed for such as desired more particular and individual instruction as to the way of life, every one who went to the appointed room would expect to find herself nearly or quite alone, but to her surprise would see her most intimate friends among the inquirers. The teachers never appointed such a meeting, until they were certain of a good attendance. If they knew of only two or three who desired such instruction, they met them informally, or by a private appointment. These meetings for special religious instruction and conversation were, however, attended frequently by a large part of the pupils who were not professors of religion. For several years in succession, more than half of those who entered the school impenitent, and remained for any length of time, went away with a warm and permanent interest in the Redeemer's kingdom.

SECTION III.

Unsuccessful Attempt to endow the Ipswich School.

When the trustees of the Adams Female Academy invited Miss Grant to take charge of it, they stated to her their design of making it a permanent school of a high order.

Entering into this design, and forwarding it all in her power, she had become, when she left Londonderry, exceedingly interested in the idea of a seminary which should be to young women what the college is to young men, and was full of the earnest purpose of doing what in her lay for embodying this conception.

For some time after her removal to Ipswich, Miss Grant was so entirely occupied in instructing and providing for her increasing school, and in exercising a mother's oversight of more than a hundred pupils, scattered in companies of two, four, six, and eight, all over the village, that she had but little time or strength left to labor for the object of her thoughts and hopes.

Miss Grant naturally conversed much with Miss Lyon on the subject of the establishing of a seminary, with buildings, library, and apparatus, owned as colleges are, where successive generations of young ladies might be trained for respectability and usefulness; but Miss Lyon entered into the project very slowly. "Never mind," she many a time said, between 1824 and 1829, — "never mind the brick and mortar; only let us have living minds to work upon." How different were her feelings in 1836, when, on the occasion of laying the corner-stone at South Hadley, she writes, "The stones, and brick, and mortar speak a language which vibrates through my very soul."

Not far from 1830, Miss Lyon became convinced of the utility of such a seminary, and entered into the project, not merely, as before, from sympathy with Miss Grant, but also from her own firm and deep conviction that the thing was both desirable and necessary.

The following extracts from a joint letter of Misses Grant and Lyon give an outline of what they considered necessary for establishing the school at Ipswich on a permanent basis: —

. . . .

TO THE TRUSTEES OF IPSWICH FEMALE ACADEMY.

"IPSWICH, February 17, 1831.

"GENTLEMEN:

"You doubtless recollect that, in September, 1829, a committee from your board was appointed to inquire what was necessary to secure the continuance of our school in this place. Since that time, it has been repeatedly asked, by persons in different and distant towns, what would be an inducement to the present teachers to remove from Ipswich, and locate themselves in a situation favorable to the prosecution of their object. Before giving such encouragement to the friends of science, literature, and religion abroad, as shall seem at all like a pledge for our removal, we deem it proper, and it is in accordance with our feelings, to state to you what provision we consider essential for establishing a female seminary on a good foundation, with the prospect of making it permanent.

"The first requisite is a seminary building, free of rent, containing a hall of sufficient size to accommodate one hundred and seventy-five scholars, several recitation-rooms, a laboratory, a room for a library, and a reading-room. Some way should be devised to have this building furnished with books of reference, and the apparatus necessary for illustrating the several branches taught.

"The second requisite is a boarding-house, completely furnished for one hundred and fifty boarders, to be situated contiguous to the seminary building, and surrounded by a few acres of play-ground. The rooms in the boarding-house should be pleasant and airy, so finished and furnished as to give ladies as favorable a situation, while pursuing their studies, as is afforded to young men at our colleges, or other seminaries. The care of the conduct of the scholars, and the general internal arrangements of the house, must devolve on the teachers.

. . . . .

"It would be necessary that the pecuniary affairs of the

establishment should be committed to an agent appointed by the trustees, to whom he should be responsible.

"Yours, very respectfully,

"Z. P. Grant,

"Mary Lyon."

As the result of this movement, prospective trustees were appointed, and a pamphlet of eight pages, entitled "Proposals and Conditions," was printed and circulated. The pamphlet contained the substance of the preceding letter, a statement of the difficulties arising from the teachers and pupils being so separated and scattered, and various specifications as to the contemplated buildings and conditions of subscription.

The prospective trustees of the proposed school held several meetings, passed sundry resolutions, and made many inquiries; but finding the public unprepared for the project, the zeal of several of them entirely failed. The apathy every where met with may have been occasioned by Miss Grant's absence from Ipswich, and her personal inability for active service in teaching.

In a letter of Miss Lyon's to Miss Grant, in February, 1832, she says, "Things are preparing for the next meeting of trustees. I did think of advising to have it delayed till your return; but on the whole, I consider it best to adhere to my uniform principle, to retard nothing, but rather forward every step as much as possible, and trust Providence for the result."

The following letter of Miss Lyon to Professor Hitchcock, dated at Ipswich, February 4, 1832, will show her feelings at that time on the subject of the proposed school: —

"Rev. and dear Sir:

"Knowing that you are interested to learn any thing about the proposed plan for a permanent female seminary, which has been agitated by some of its friends for more than a year, I make no apology for this communication. The friends of this object, I think, are beginning to look upon it in a more extended view, and are beginning to consider it an important object, as connected with the prosperity and advancement of female education in general, and not simply as a *very good* thing to promote Miss Grant's and Miss Lyon's school, and facilitate their usefulness. These local, private, and personal views, I think, should be far removed from this object. Could I but be permitted to labor in the portico, and spend my days in clearing the ground for that which is destined to continue, and to exert an extensive and salutary influence on female education, and on religion, from generation to generation, it would be the height of my ambition. What permanent female seminaries are now in existence? What one in New England, of a high character, is necessarily, from its plan, destined to outlive its present teachers? Ought this so to be? Are not a few permanent female seminaries needed? — say one or two in a state? Could there be a few of this character, designed exclusively for older young ladies preparing to teach, and soon to go forth and exert an influence in a variety of ways on the cause of education and religion, — a place of resort, where those from different parts of the country, designing to spend their lives in doing good, might come together, together receive instruction, form and mature their plans, and exert over each other's views and feelings an extensive and powerful influence, — would not great good result? Might not such seminaries have an extensive influence in removing that false mantle of charity, which has been thrown over a great many *little* schools, and great ones, too, which have, to a great extent, had the moulding of the female character, but which have not been what they should be?

"The prospect now is, that this subject will be presented to the public in some form or other. The attempt may be fruitless. The institution is to be entirely new, not having any connection with that which is the present field of our labors. To give the public confidence, it has been considered very important to obtain an able board of trustees. This business has been on hand several months. It is now settled. Seven have been appointed as trustees elect, and have accepted, and, if the plan should go forward, will obtain an act of incorporation, and will become the trustees. They are the following: Hon. William Reed, Marblehead; Rev. Dr. Fay, Charlestown; Professor Emerson, Andover; Hon. Rufus Choate, Salem; George W. Heard, Esq., and William Heard, of this town. They have had one meeting, and have appointed a committee of inquiry.

"It is generally understood that the location should be in Ipswich, but it is not absolutely necessary. Some of the trustees, I believe, consider it somewhat doubtful whether this is the best location, and, if it is not, will be disposed to make inquiry about other places. Not much has been said about it, however. Feeling that a genial soil would be of vast importance in this first attempt, I have been exceedingly desirous that the locations on Connecticut River should receive at least a little attention, before it is finally settled in Essex county. It is not best that I should say much about it; but these trustees are capable of looking at facts as they are, if their attention should be directed to the subject. The location is to be decided before the object is presented to the public, probably at the next meeting of the trustees. My only desire is, that the state of feeling in your vicinity should be tested, and the facts laid before the trustees. I do not know that there is any way by which it could be done, but I thought it barely possible that some benevolent individuals might devise some plan. I write these things to you merely because I can do nothing more than to mention it to some of my friends in that vicinity. It would not be well that the subject of this communication should be known generally. There is no objection to your mentioning it to individuals, if you should think it desirable. One reason why I feel desirous that your part of the state should be the proposed location is, that I think it might affect the public in general more favorably, and there would be a greater prospect of success. If you think it a vain thought, a foolish and impracticable scheme, my only request is, that you would commit this sheet to the flames, and bury the whole in oblivion.

"It is true that this plan was started in view of Ipswich, and, of course, the trustees were chosen from this vicinity, and there is no hope that it could be transferred, unless it should be obvious that it will meet with more success and more encouragement from the public by being located in that part of the state. It is rather probable that an attempt will be made in Ipswich, and perhaps in the vicinity, to ascertain what amount can be raised for the object. If an attempt could be made at the same time in the valley of the Connecticut, the object being fully understood, it seems to me somewhat probable that the west would so far exceed the east, that it would be very manifest that that was the most suitable location. In such a case, it would be very important that a part of the trustees should be from that vicinity. This board can make changes in their own body, such as they shall deem expedient; and if they shall decide that the public will not accept of Essex county as a location, such a course will probably be taken. Besides, twenty-five gentlemen, in different parts of New England, are appointed as a board of visitors, if the plan should go into operation.

"If any thing should be attempted on this subject in your part of the state, would it not be inexpedient to name any definite location, nearer than to say, a location in Massachusetts, on or near the Connecticut River? Doubtless Amherst or Northampton would be the place. Each would have its peculiar advantages, and I am by no means sure which would be the most favorable.

"Nothing can be done on a subject like this, without the attention of a few benevolent individuals, whose time and talents are exceedingly precious, and whose hands are already full of other great and important concerns. None but such men could do the work. None but such could excite an interest on this hitherto neglected subject. None but such could carry it forward. None but such could give any hope of success.

"If any thing should hereafter be done on this subject, would it not be well that the *leading friends* should not all be from Amherst or Northampton? If it should be thought best to make any inquiries on the subject, perhaps you would think it well that some benevolent gentleman, yourself or some other one, should correspond with some gentleman of this board. Some members have devoted considerable attention to the subject, others have but just glanced at it yet. I could mention with what individuals it would be most favorable to correspond.

"I must now, my dear sir, beg that you will not look on this subject in the view of personal friendship, and feel under a kind of obligation to treat it with some little respect. Unless it commends itself to your judgment as one which has a high claim on our benevolence, I could not ask you to devote to it a single moment of your very precious time. But if it has such claims, I would most gladly raise my feeble voice, entreating all who would befriend such an object to lend a helping hand."

In the summer of 1832, at the suggestion of Mr. George W. Heard, one of the proposed trustees, Miss Lyon prepared the following sheet, which was printed, and, under the sanction of the prospective board, was sent to many of the friends of the Ipswich school: —

NEW ENGLAND FEMALE SEMINARY FOR TEACHERS.

Several friends of education and of evangelical religion are considering the expediency of attempting to raise funds to found a permanent female seminary in New England.

General Object.

The main object of the proposed institution will be to prepare young ladies of mature minds for active usefulness, especially to become teachers.

Character.

1. Its religious character is to be strictly evangelical.
2. Its literary character is to be of a high order.

Location.

This has not yet been selected. An attempt will be made to embrace as many of the following requisites as possible in the location:

1. That it be central for New England.
2. That it be surrounded by a community marked for intelligence and public spirit.
3. That a liberal proportion of the funds be raised by the town and its immediate vicinity.
4. That the particular spot be healthy and pleasant, a little removed from public business, and so situated as to be free from all other encumbrances.

Funds.

The amount of funds should be sufficient to furnish the following accommodations: —

1. Several acres of land.
2. Buildings sufficiently capacious to furnish from one hundred to two hundred pupils with accommodations for school and boarding.
3. Furniture.
4. An ample library and apparatus.

Domestic Arrangements.

It is proposed that the domestic department should be under the direct superintendence of such persons as are qualified for the trust. In order to give as much independence and facility to the trustees as possible, in organizing the establishment, and in order to avoid difficulties in filling offices from time to time, it is proposed that all the furniture should be owned by the corporation.

Boarding-House.

The plan which has been proposed for the buildings is suited,

1. To give to the young ladies superior privileges, both for retirement and for social intercourse, and in an eminent degree to promote health, comfort, and domestic happiness, and intellectual, moral, and religious improvement.

2. To furnish each member with a small chamber, exclusively her own.* The great advantages of such a privilege can scarcely be realized, except by those who have often felt that they would give up almost any of their common comforts, for the sake of such retirement as can be enjoyed only in a separate apartment. To persons of reflection, the advantages will doubtless appear much greater than the extra expense, especially when it is considered that this institution is not designed for younger misses, but especially for the benefit of ladies of maturer age.

Family Discipline.

The family discipline is to be entirely distinct from the domestic concerns. This, together with the general improvement of the pupils out of school, is to be committed directly to the teachers. The family discipline should be very systematic, but of a kind adapted to the age of its members. The whole should resemble a well-regulated voluntary association, where the officers and members are all faithful to their trust.

The plan which has been proposed for buildings is particularly suited to promote family discipline, and to render it at once easy, systematic, and pleasant to all.

1. It is such that the whole family will naturally and necessarily be arranged in a convenient number of sections, each of which can be easily directed by an appropriate head.

2. It is such as to bring all the young ladies under a direct and natural supervision. This will tend at once to secure order and propriety, and at the same time to exclude all necessity of any thing like apparent watchfulness or nice inspection, even if the age and character of the members of the institution should not render every thing of the kind needless.

Specific Objects to be accomplished.

1. To increase the number of well-qualified female teachers. The present want of such teachers is well known to all particularly engaged in the cause of education. This deficiency is the occasion of placing many of our schools under the care of those who are not competent to the undertaking.

2. To induce many who have already become teachers, to make further improvement in their education. This institution will furnish such ladies with a full course of instruction, and with society

* This feature of the plan was not Miss Grant's, and Miss Lyon afterwards gave it up.

adapted to their age and character, and will give them a more suitable and pleasant home than can now be found connected with any of our female seminaries.

3. To exert an influence in bringing as much of the labor of instruction into the hands of ladies as propriety will admit. This seems important, on account of the many public demands on the time of benevolent, educated gentlemen, and the comparatively few demands on the time of benevolent, educated ladies.

4. To lead the way toward the establishment of permanent female seminaries in our land. That there are no female seminaries of this character is, we believe, a fact. Those which appear to have the strongest claim to such a standing are so dependent on their present teachers, and their funds and accommodations are to such an extent the property of private individuals, that it would not be safe to predict even their existence the next century.

This circular bears strongly the impress of Miss Lyon's mind and hand.

In November of this year, the attention of Miss Lyon was turned to Amherst as a location for the school. Dr. Humphrey, President of Amherst College, wrote to Miss Lyon, saying, "Mount Pleasant school is at an end. The teachers and pupils are dispersed, and the buildings are soon to be closed. Providence has, so to speak, thrown Mount Pleasant into the market, and we should be glad to see such a seminary as yours there, if it should be thought an advantageous location."

"The situation of Mount Pleasant," writes Miss Lyon, "is delightful. There are about fifteen acres of land connected with it." The owner was willing to sell it at its market value, or rent it at six hundred dollars per annum. There was no hope of raising a sum sufficient for the purchase. The utmost that could be hoped was, that the rent might be met for three or five years by the friends of female education. It would accommodate only about half the number of boarders that were at Ipswich. Objections were made by some to locating a female seminary by the side of an institution for young men; but Miss Lyon thought that the advantage to the pupils of attending college lectures might, in a good degree, counterbalance that disadvantage. She was very desirous at first that the school should be removed to Amherst. November 29, 1832, she wrote to Miss Grant: "I am in favor of endeavoring to secure Mount Pleasant, because I have next to no faith that the public are now prepared to raise a sum sufficient to meet the necessities of the institution, unless it is done by stepping stones, and those must be laid by the actual progress of the institution. You know this is the way every thing is done in New England. Amherst College, and all the other institutions of the kind, have been founded by commencing operations, by forming a nucleus, and then calling for assistance.

"Might it not be a good plan, rather than to do worse, to make an attempt at Amherst, but not with the certain expectation of permanence? Would not the fact that the school was in operation there, be of assistance in obtaining the funds? and might not the accommodations there be a stepping stone towards better?"

Miss Lyon's interest in the removal of the school to Amherst was such, at this time, that she even advocated Miss Grant's removal, on her own personal responsibility, in case the trustees, above mentioned, did not see sufficient encouragement to warrant them in hiring the place for a course of years. She even offered, in Miss Grant's absence, to go forward herself in the removal. But she afterwards became convinced that such a removal was inexpedient.

As Miss Lyon saw more and more plainly that the attempt to endow the Ipswich school was likely to fail, she began to revolve the idea of engaging in teaching in a distinct field from Miss Grant. A letter to Miss G., of December 9, 1832, contains the first mention of this subject. It follows, nearly entire: —

"I take my pen to introduce a subject, which has agitated

my mind for several months. Is it not your solemn duty and mine to review the question, whether my services are needed as much in our beloved seminary as in some other portion of the Lord's vineyard? This is a question of deep solicitude with me. For a long time, *previous* to the present year, I felt that the question was settled. I had made a kind of decision, that I should not mention the subject to you again. For some time after the above query arose in my mind, the trial of mentioning it to you seemed greater than I could bear. Often, when alone, I have found relief in tears. The burden of my prayer has been, that if it were most for the glory of God that I should continue to labor with you, the path of duty might be made plain, and if it were his will that I should labor elsewhere, the way might be laid open, that you might see it, and both of us be prepared for the separation.

"In taking the superintendence the past year, I have seen that very many of the things which you and I do, when we are together, can be as well done by our experienced teachers. In the present improved state of the institution, there is really no more business that would come under the head of superintending than can be done by one of us. Of the labor which needs our experience, and even *mind*, some could be done nearly as well by one as by two; some just as well, and some could be done better. I have been led to make a little calculation how much might be done by the assistant teachers, and what is the least amount of labor which it is indispensable that the principal should accomplish, in order that the institution may flourish. After a while, the query involuntarily arose in my mind, whether my services were really needed here, whether the experience I had gained was not more needed somewhere else, in this needy, impoverished state of the world. I did not intend to mention the subject till you returned; and in the event of my leaving, I supposed it would probably be best for us to take a year to plan for it.

"But since your proposal that I should journey next summer, a new query has arisen, whether my leaving *then*, and not returning, might not be a less injury to the school than my leaving at any more distant period; whether it might not cause less excitement, and be less the means of increasing your labor. I should very much need more time to collect and arrange the fragments of improvement which we have been enabled to make, which are now more in my possession than in yours, in order that I might transmit them to you in the best order. But it would undoubtedly be my duty to take some time to become refreshed, and during that time I could collect these items from memory, notes, &c., and arrange them for your use about as well as if I were on the spot. I could have no object so important, and surely I could have none *so very dear* to my heart, as that of leaving this dearly beloved seminary, this darling of my heart, under the most favorable circumstances. Now, my dearest sister, the subject is before you. Will you commend it to our heavenly Father every morning with me? My faltering pen has obeyed my will; I have succeeded in telling what I would. And now I beg, that while this question is under consideration, you will never allude to personal considerations on either side, for they are not the data by which this interesting question must be decided. It would be to us both a needless trial of our feelings. You will ask about our great plan. I do not think there is one chance in twenty for it to succeed. If it should, a different course might be taken."

TO MISS GRANT.

"January 10, 1833.

"When I consider the apparent expectations of those who are ready to say, 'It is a good plan,' it does not appear to me probable that you or I shall live to see a female seminary in New England, such as we desire, so endowed as to become permanent. Yet I do hope, that the interest excited and the information communicated by this attempt will terminate in more favorable accommodations for this school. If even this could be effected, I should consider myself amply repaid for all my exertions."

Alluding to difficulties which had arisen about Amherst, she says, "It seems rather discouraging, when I look over the last two years. How much time and strength I have spent in thinking, feeling, conversing, and planning on this subject, and to how little purpose! How many plans I have drawn and altered, and how many sheets written and burnt! I am not, however, disheartened. I am ready to attempt any thing which seems pointed out by Providence, even without any surety of success."

Two days after she writes, "I have never known such an overwhelming interest in the great plan as I have for a few weeks past. It does appear to me that it is a good plan, and one which God in his own time will own and bless. I know of nothing which I should not be ready to do, nor any sacrifice which I should not be ready to make, to promote the object."

Again, in the same letter, "Every thing connected with the great plan, in which we have been interested, takes hold of my inmost soul, and at once seems to prostrate all my powers."

TO MISS GRANT.

"BOSTON, February 4, 1833.

"I have seen Rev. Daniel Crosby, of Conway, this forenoon. He is an energetic man, and his talents are much respected abroad. He is a young man, and not worn out. Perhaps Providence will make use of him to accomplish this object. He says, it needs to be taken hold of by those who have not every thing else in their hands, and by those who will not be crushed by difficulties. He seems to grasp the whole subject at once, and to see its importance. He says, 'If all the attempts shall fail now, the effort will prepare the way to raise the forty or fifty thousand dollars some twenty years hence.'

"I feel more and more that the whole business must, in name, devolve on benevolent gentlemen, and not on yourself or on myself. I do not feel so much afraid as I did that they will not take the right steps, but I feel much more afraid that they will not act at all. If the institution is ever founded, it will be safe only in the hands of God, and under God, in the arms of the whole benevolent community, including not only the rich, but the poor. If any thing at all *should* be done, the less you and I have to do with the business part of the affair the better. Fewer needless, unkind remarks will be thrown out, less jealousy will be excited, and our private influence will be more extensive and useful in directing matters for the good of the institution. It is desirable that the plans relating to the subject should not seem to originate with *us*, but with benevolent *gentlemen*. If the object should excite attention, there is danger that many good men will fear the effect on society of so much female influence, and what they will call female greatness. They will think and say, 'Miss Grant and Miss Lyon want to do some great thing, to have a large sum of money raised, and a great institution established, and to see themselves at the head of the whole, and then they will be satisfied.' I imagine I have seen a little of this already, and if more interest were to be felt in the cause, more jealousy might be excited."

TO MISS GRANT.

"February 13, 1833.

"I have written to you about Amherst, and the views of Mr. —— and his friends. Their plan, at best, would make the institution all a personal affair. I thought it best, on my own private responsibility, to pull down some of their castles, if possible. Their zeal did not seem to be very great, when they had learned that the plan was one which would allow little or no prospect of income to the steward, to merchants, and to others engaged in the concern."

On the 20th of February, 1833, Rev. Mr. Crosby wrote to Miss Lyon, communicating the following preamble and resolution of the Franklin Association: —

"Inasmuch as this association has heretofore taken some measures in regard to a female seminary, founded upon the principles of the seminary at Ipswich, and inasmuch as the subject is again, in the providence of God, open to investigation, therefore, —

"*Resolved*, That a committee of two be appointed from this body to meet individual friends of the Ipswich Seminary for the purpose of inquiry and consultation; and that this committee be requested to call upon other gentlemen for advice and counsel, as they may see fit."

To Mr. Crosby's letter, containing the above resolve, Miss Lyon replied: —

"I received yours of yesterday. I have most ardently desired that this meeting might take place, hoping that it might be the first link in a chain of means to draw the interest of the Christian community to this object. If such an interest can be secured, the time will ere long come, when friends will be raised up to sustain the labor, and even bear the reproach of being chimerical, if need be, as all who lead in any great and good cause must expect to be called.

"The gentlemen of this region, that I think it most important should go to Amherst, are, Mr. G. W. Heard and Rev. Mr. Felt. I expect to be there as you suggest. The most important thing now is, to lay the subject before those who are capable of becoming enlisted in its favor. He that can now awaken an interest, will do more than he, who, at some future time, shall be willing to bestow largely of his abundance.

"I hope, dear sir, that all who are ready to devote some of their precious time to looking at this cause, in its feeble and forlorn state, and to inviting their brethren in the Lord to look at it, will hereafter receive an abundant reward.

"If the proposed institution should ever be founded, I hope and pray, that from generation to generation it may assist the church in fulfilling her covenant obligations to her own children, and in grafting many a wild olive branch upon the true vine. Unless the building can be the Lord's, let it never be built; unless the Lord go with us, let us not go up."

TO MISS GRANT.

"IPSWICH, February 24, 1833.

"I begin to doubt whether you will consider it expedient to go to Amherst on the best terms on which there is any hope that we can go. The highest of my hopes is only that by some means, the rent can be collected by dollars and cents from the farmers and mechanics all over Franklin and Hampshire counties, in order to make an experiment of three years. The greater prospect is, that, at the close of that period, the school will be thrown on the public without a home. But I am inclined to hazard, for nothing will ever be done without it on this subject. I cannot see one important step toward the 'New England Female Seminary,' which can safely be taken at present, and perhaps not for many years to come, unless this experiment at Amherst can be tried. If an agent for raising funds should now be sent out, in towns where he would need to raise one or two thousand dollars, he might not raise more than twenty or fifty. As the subject has gone forward for three years past, the public will not be prepared to be called on for money for twenty years to come.

"The plan of finding a location where they will do something handsome seems equally fruitless. It is known at Northampton how the matter stands; but the people there manifest no wish to do any thing about it. At Worcester, nothing can be done. There is no inducement to go to Brookfield. If Mr. Felt were now to visit every town suitable for a location in the state, to ascertain what amount could be pledged, if the school should go there, I believe that Ipswich would bear the palm.

"Interest and zeal, I think, are what we now need. This is not the time to inquire how the money can be raised; but it is needful now to put forth every nerve and sinew to awaken an interest among ministers and other good men, till they shall feel that the object is good, and that it is feasible. But this interest cannot be awakened so much by writing, preaching, and the like, as by putting certain secret springs into action. Now, if any thing is done at Amherst, I think it should aim only at an experiment for three years, with the express design of preparing the way for a permanent seminary. If this experiment can be made, borne on the broad shoulders of an associate body of gentlemen from different parts of the state, as their plan, I have a hope that these gentlemen would so bring the subject before the public, that it would be safe, before the close of the three years, to solicit of the community the sum of forty thousand dollars."

In the conclusion of this letter, which follows, we have the first *distinct hints* of those modifications of her plans which enabled Miss Lyon to triumph over all difficulties.

"One point more. The funds for Amherst College have been collected, not from the rich, but from liberal Christians in common life. At the commencement of that enterprise, the prospect was held out that it would be a college of high standing, where the expenses would be low, and that it would be accessible to all. This was like a mainspring, without which it is doubtful whether it would have been possible to raise the funds. I am inclined to think that something of this kind may be indispensable to our success. The great and honorable among the good will not listen to our cause; but perhaps the more humble in life, led forward by their own ministers, may befriend this important but forsaken object. If so, if there is any class of Christians that we should seek to gratify, it must surely be the benefactors, whether high or low. If the same class of Christians who support our missionaries should contribute principally to the raising of the funds, is it not important that the style of the whole establishment should professedly be plain, though very neat? If it were *really* plain, would it not be more respectable to have it professedly so?"

The following interesting letter alludes again to the matter of a separation: —

TO MISS GRANT.

"IPSWICH, March 1, 1833.

"Yesterday was my birthday. Thirty-six years of my life are gone, and now I am one year more than middle aged. To look back step by step, it seems a long life, and the remaining years in prospect seem few and short. But my life and strength may be prolonged for many years to come. I would that it might be so, if it is the will of the Lord. But in one thing I can rejoice, — that, as long as the Lord of the vineyard hath any need of my feeble service, he will allow me the unspeakable privilege of living and laboring; and when he sees it to be best that I should labor no longer in this dark, wicked world, which has been promised to the Savior as his inheritance, then may I be prepared to lay down this tabernacle with joy and rejoicing, and go to dwell with Christ, which is far better. Daily, my dear sister, do I endeavor to ask for you the same blessings which I ask for myself. O, this vast field, which is white already to the harvest! May laborers be raised up in great numbers, to gather in the harvest, which is continually wasting away. May those who are in the field labor while the day lasts. May you and I be so directed, that we shall spend the remainder of our days in that manner which shall be the means of the greatest possible results.

"One thing I have, for several weeks, wanted to propose to you. It is this: If Providence should ever make it plainly our duty to occupy different fields of labor, and to dissolve our legal connection, I should deem it one of the greatest earthly blessings which I could possibly enjoy, to keep as many of the cords which now bind us together unbroken as could be done under existing circumstances; that we should assist each other in forming plans; that we should visit each other often, write to each other often; that we should each feel that, next to our own field of labor, that of the other is the most endearing — the field to which we have pledged our services, our influence, our hearts. A union somewhat like this would be to me an unspeakable satisfaction; it would seem to save my bleeding heart from sinking under the stroke of a separation; and my judgment says, that such a union would be suited to advance the great cause to which we have consecrated our lives.

"Two days ago, I received yours, written January 10, replying to mine of December 10. After sending mine, I felt that I could leave it all with God. After that, however, there was a solemn weight resting on my soul; a feeling that one step had been taken toward accomplishing the greatest change that has ever taken place in my situation and labors, and probably the greatest that ever will take place in my life. But after receiving a few lines in Miss C.'s, acknowledging the receipt of mine of December 10, I felt that all, for the present, was done, — that God, in his own time and manner, would by his providence point out the path of duty, and

I could most cheerfully and quietly wait. The peace and freedom from solicitude which I have been permitted to enjoy, with regard to the final issue, have been uncommon. When I have opened your letters, I have had no painful solicitude to find a line indicating your opinion on the question. But since the reception of yours two days ago, my mind has been most intensely occupied, and I can now give you only a few of my general, scattered thoughts.

"A few words about my feelings. If it should be plain, or equally probable, that you and I could both of us accomplish as great an amount of good to spend our remaining days together as we could to occupy different fields, it would be a blessing which would be most grateful to my heart; or, if it should be equally probable that we could accomplish as much good during our lives, to continue together three years more, and then separate, I should be grateful for the privilege of being with you so much longer.

"Now I will endeavor to write according to my judgment, though my opinion is not made up on any point. The reasons why it seemed to me, that were we ever to occupy different fields of labor it might be better that we should commence soon, were two, — one relating to my own usefulness, the other to yours.

"If I should separate from you, I have no definite plan. But my thoughts, feelings, and judgment are turned toward the middle classes of society. For this class I want to labor, and for this class I consider myself rather peculiarly fitted to labor. To this class in society would I devote, directly, all the remainder of my strength, (God permitting,) — not to the higher classes, not to the poorer classes. This middle class contains the main springs, and main wheels, which are to move the world. Whatever field I may occupy, it must be an humble, laborious work. How I can get a footing sufficiently firm for my feet to rest upon for the remainder of my days, and where my hands can work, I know not. But by wandering around, and by resting from my labors a year or two, perhaps Providence might open the door. I should seek for nothing permanent, to continue after my death, as to the location of my labors; but I should consider it very desirable that I should occupy but one more field, that I should make but one more remove, till I remove into my grave. I shall soon be literally forty years old; and if I am ever to leave my present field of labor, and begin entirely anew, it seems desirable, for my future usefulness, that I should begin soon, before many more of my remaining days are gone, or much more of my remaining strength exhausted.

"If I should journey next summer, it might be better, for you and for the school, that I should not return at all, than that I should return to spend merely a year or two. It might be less hazardous to your strength to go right forward alone, than to have these changes. You want I should write how I judge, and feel inclined to decide. I wish I could tell you more definitely than I can now. My mind seems exceedingly reluctant even to incline to one side or the other. One thing, however, is clear. Considering your views and feelings, I do not think it best that we should separate so soon as this spring, at any rate. How long it is best that we should continue together, I do not know. As your letter has been so long delayed, perhaps it will not be best to attempt to settle these questions till we meet face to face.

"Your arguments against a separation *now* are weighty. I have considered most of them in some form, though, perhaps, not with the distinctness with which you have expressed them. My query of December 10 I designed not specifically to be, whether we ought to separate this spring, or in one, two, or three years from this time; but generally, whether it was best that we should continue together permanently, or that we should separate as soon as it could be effected to good advantage; say, at the most suitable time in the course of two or three years. I do not think I expressed this clearly. Looking at the subject in the form of this last query, I will dwell a moment on the main arguments. 1. The hope of founding a permanent seminary. This is so great an object, that it would be right to sacrifice considerable good for the sake of a small probability of success. But we must guide our steps by probabilities. My feelings are most deeply interested in this cause, and so strong is my belief in its utility, that I do believe that such a work will be effected at some future day, perhaps some twenty or fifty years from this time. But if it must be delayed entirely for several years, I have thought that there was nothing that we could do together which we could not do separately. And as the probability in my own mind, founded, I think, on evidence, was altogether on this side, it seemed my duty to decide according to this probability, knowing, that if any indication of Providence should appear in favor of the great object, either before it should be time to act, or before I should take fast hold of any other, (which time must be considerable,) we could again unite our labors as before. My candid judgment has been, that the probability that such a seminary would be founded during our day has been constantly diminishing; but I have felt it my duty not to say much about it, but to put forth every possible effort, till we should professedly give up the subject for the present. If, in my own mind, the chance two years ago was equal to one in five, it is now reduced to not more than one in fifty; I would say to one in one hundred, or five hundred, if we except the ray of hope which beams from the possibility that an experiment may be made at Amherst, and the possibility that something favorable may grow out of such an experiment, if it should be made. My belief has been, that unless something unexpected should be brought forward by the wheels of Providence, the time has nearly come, when it will be your duty and mine professedly to relinquish the object, — not our interest in the plan, but our attempts for its execution. This I have not expressed before, and now it pains me to acknowledge my conviction. My conviction arose from the manner in which the scheme is regarded by various individuals, who, I think, are a fair index of the public. The public, as such, know nothing of any consequence about the object, and care less than they know. The public, as such, know not, and care not, how Miss Grant and Miss Lyon are united, or when they separate, or how, if the school at Ipswich can go on well.

"A few words about the importance of the prosperity of Miss Grant's school. I consider it more important that it should continue to flourish during her life, or during her ability to labor, than any other school in the land, which is the property of a private individual. But, after all, it is short-lived. I view it as just like Mr. Emerson's school. It was very important that Mr. Emerson should prosper during his days of labor, and that he should have a place where he might put forth his strength to peculiar advantage. But where is his school now? If we ask, 'Where are his labors?' I would say, 'All over the earth, and their record is on high.'

"If the plan for the permanent seminary does not succeed, I have long felt that you and I must continue to labor, and make no more attempts for any thing permanent to result, except what is planted permanently in the hearts and in the lives of those over whom God may give us a direct or indirect influence. I consider it so important that your school should continue to flourish during your remaining days of labor, that I ought to take a course which would diminish my present usefulness, and hazard my future usefulness, rather than greatly to hazard the prosperity of Miss Grant's school, and her usefulness thereby. A small hazard may be justifiable.

"This letter has cost me more hours than any letter I have written you this winter, and I fear it will cost you more to read it; and how little it contains!

"If the experiment is made at Amherst, the hand of Providence would, undoubtedly, make it plain duty for us to continue together."

May 2, 1833, on the same subject, she writes, "I am very glad, my dearest friend, that you propose to endeavor to learn that you *can* do without me. I should rejoice to have you learn this lesson fully, even if we should hereafter decide that it is our duty to continue through life to labor together."

In reference to the anticipated meeting at Amherst, Miss Lyon wrote, on March 14, 1833, —

"I consider the friends of the original plan as having all failed, except Messrs. Felt and Heard. The subject is now about to assume a new aspect, and to have a new beginning. Will it not be best to endeavor to operate on a new circle of friends, who have hitherto known but little on the subject, rather than on those who have known *something*, and cared *less*? Is it not also very desirable to exert an influence through *gentlemen*, rather than directly by ourselves? Without a strict adherence to this purpose, in the preparatory steps, I think the plan will utterly fail. This purpose, adhered to, will increase our labor, but it may turn to much more account in the end."

The aspect of things had so changed, that the gentlemen who acted as nominal trustees of the proposed New England seminary judged it expedient to dissolve the board. A meeting for this purpose was called in the early part of April, 1833. In a subsequent letter, Miss Lyon writes, "I do not know that I have told you of the dissolution of the board of prospective trustees. On the 18th of March, a circular letter was sent to each, requesting his attendance at the meeting, or a written answer, authorizing some one present to vote in his stead, on the question of a dissolution. The meeting was held on the day before the annual fast. Messrs.

Felt, G. W. Heard, and William Heard were present. One of the absentees sent a letter to Mr. G. W. Heard, authorizing Mr. H. to give his vote in favor of dissolving. The others did not reply, but there was a quorum present, and the business was completed. In the letter just referred to, it is very justly said, 'The board of the proposed female seminary has not been organized in vain. It has done something to bring the subject of female education more fully before the public mind, and the consequences may be important and salutary. I do not perceive that this board can attempt any thing more; and I must confess that the best men in the community do not favor our plan of a female seminary so much as I anticipated. I wish Miss Lyon and her coadjutors to know that I am as favorable to female education as ever.'"

April 6, 1833, Miss Lyon writes to Miss Grant, "I think there are more than nine chances out of ten that the door of Providence will be closed against all future operations towards founding a permanent institution."

The proposed meeting at Amherst was appointed to be held on the 25th of that month. Referring to it, she says, "If this effort should fail, it seems to me evident that it will be the duty of Messrs. Heard and Felt, and of ourselves, to take a different attitude; to give up all thought and expectation of doing any thing directly for the object, but only to disseminate knowledge which may operate on the next generation. If the effort now commencing should fail, I think that we should select a favorable location for usefulness, and settle down for life, disclaiming all expectation that any plan for a permanent seminary will ever succeed in our day. We may describe the advantages of such an institution, what the public ought to do, and what they probably will do in the next generation. We might always speak as if the public were not now prepared for such an undertaking, and would not be prepared for many years. When it is evident that all has been done that can be on our part, would there not be essential advantages in our taking this attitude? It would be more according to the common leadings of Providence that we should in this way collect the materials, and that the temple should be built by our successors."

These apparently fruitless efforts were not without their uses. A certain class of the community had become familiar with the subject of founding a permanent female seminary, and some few were sorry that the scheme had failed. Miss Lyon's own soul had become completely permeated with the subject. She knew not her own heart when she spoke, in her letter of April 6, 1833, of giving up all thought and expectation of doing any thing more towards the object, in case the effort in which she was then engaged should fail. She had learned to lay plans for buildings for a school and family in an economical and convenient manner. Most thoroughly was she taught that, for efficient aid, she must look not to the honored and wealthy, who were already laden with responsibilities, and drained by constant calls for charity, but to men comparatively retired and unknown. She saw that it might be necessary to commence operations on a small scale, and work with such means as she could command, and by the experiment win public confidence and public aid to assist more largely in the enterprise. She moderated her expectations as to friends, till, at one time, she felt that she could work, if only two or three gentlemen and ladies would cordially sustain her by their influence and coöperation. She was convinced, to a degree to which no abstract reasoning could have conducted her, that the argument from the superior literary and scientific advantages of a permanent school could not be relied on for gaining the attention of the community, and securing their interest; but that some peculiar and tangible feature, addressing itself to the feelings and perceptions of the middling classes of society, must be used as a lever for moving public opinion and obtaining the needed funds. These lessons were of great use to her in her future and successful labors.

SECTION IV.

Miss Lyon's Plans modified and matured.

MISS LYON's inventive mind continued earnestly to revolve the question, "How can a permanent seminary for ladies be secured?" Imperceptibly to herself, her plans were more and more modified, until she found a way to the hearts and purses of the friends of education. We give extracts from her letters, showing the progress of her mind in the solution of the problem.

In the following letter, we see the first germ of a peculiar feature in the Holyoke school as to the domestic arrangements. It is written to Miss Grant.

"IPSWICH, April 16, 1833.

"I believe I once said something to you about having an institution at the west, with the style plain, the food simple, almost all the labor done by the teachers and scholars, and the expenses very low. Involuntarily my spirit has been stirred within me to try such a plan on a small scale, but I have heretofore subdued these emotions."

After speaking of the inexpediency of her attempting any thing of the kind, she says, "But I have thought very much about it, with a view of having some other person execute the plan, if any one could be found who would do it well. I should not wish to undertake it, unless two or three judicious gentlemen

16*

and ladies should fall into it most cordially and most ardently. One idea more has passed across my mind, which, however, I do not think there is one chance in twenty that it would be wise to adopt. It is this: Might it not be of advantage, as a preparatory step for testing the practicability of the object, to make an experiment for a year or two on a small scale, say of thirty, forty, or fifty scholars, in New England? A failure here would be less unfavorable than a failure at the west." Her reasons for ultimately establishing her school at the east, rather than the west, will be found in a subsequent letter, dated July 5, 1834. On the 25th of April, Miss Lyon was at Amherst, at the meeting already mentioned. She writes, "A committee of seven was appointed to call another meeting, in reference to the proposed seminary. It will probably be held in Boston, about the time of the religious anniversaries; but whether it will be of sufficient interest to advance the business a single step, I think doubtful." Again, some six weeks later, she writes, "There was a meeting appointed in Boston, in reference to the plan of a seminary. Very few were present. The meeting was adjourned; and the adjourned meeting utterly failed. There were not enough present to organize, and there the business, in my view, has come to an end. I do not think it best to make any attempt to revive the subject again. The *indications of Providence* appear to *me* plain."

Miss Grant returned to Ipswich in the spring of 1833, and resumed her place in the school. Miss Lyon, according to previous arrangements, spent the summer in journeying and visiting. Her mind, during her travels, was constantly laboring at the problem which she had, as yet, been unsuccessful in solving. On her return in the fall, she continued her connection with the Ipswich school; but she devoted much time and strength to maturing and modifying her plans. February 26, 1834, she wrote to Miss W., "During the past year, my heart has so yearned over the adult female youth, in the common walks of life, that it has sometimes seemed as though a fire were shut up in my bones. I should esteem it a greater favor to labor in this field than in any other on which I have ever fastened my attention." With Miss Grant's concurrence and approbation, she prepared the following circular during that winter. It was obviously intended for any and all friends of an enlarged Christian education, as well as for those to whom it was particularly addressed.

To the Friends and Patrons of
Ipswich Female Seminary:

It has long been a subject of deep regret to individuals, familiarly acquainted with the character and influence of this institution, that many promising young ladies, for the want of pecuniary means, should be denied its privileges. These friends of universal education and of religion have fixed their eyes on one and another of their acquaintances, who would be greatly benefited by the advantages of this seminary, and who have ardently desired to enjoy them for at least one year, but whose desires have hitherto been in vain. In behalf of such individuals, the inquiry has often been made, whether board in some families in Ipswich could not be furnished at a lower rate than usual; and whether they could not render some assistance by labor, so as partly to defray the expense, and thus bring these privileges within their reach. Efforts which should meet, in any degree, the wants of this interesting portion of the community, would, without doubt, find a response in many a benevolent heart. Could the expenses be reduced one third, or one half, a great number, who now almost despair of ever being able to realize the object of their ardent desires, would be made to rejoice in the possession of opportunities for instruction and improvement, which they would value more than silver or gold. Many others, whose resources will not now permit them to enjoy these privileges more than one term, or one year, would derive scarcely less benefit from such a provision. To effect such an object, could not a separate and independent institution, similar in character to the Ipswich Seminary, be founded and sustained by the Christian public? Could not this be effected by some plan like the following?

1. Buildings for the accommodation of the school and of boarders, together with furniture and all other things necessary for the outfit, to be furnished by voluntary contributions, and placed, free from encum-

brance, in the hands of trustees, who should be men of enlarged views and of Christian benevolence.

2. Teachers to be secured possessing so much of a missionary spirit that they would labor faithfully and cheerfully, receiving only a moderate salary, compared with what they could command in other situations.

3. Style of living *neat*, but very plain and simple.

4. Domestic work of the family to be performed by the members of the school.

5. Board and tuition to be placed at cost, or as low as may be, and still cover the common expenses of the family, instruction, &c.

6. The whole plan to be conducted on the principles of our missionary operations; no surplus income to go to the teachers, to the domestic superintendent, or to any other person, but all to be cast into the treasury, for the still further reduction of the expenses the ensuing year.

From a careful review of the above principles, would it not be safe to calculate on a reduction of one third, and perhaps one half, from the expense of board and tuition at Ipswich? Such a reduction could not, indeed, be expected to meet the wants of the more needy and dependent. The design would be to benefit more directly a very large and interesting portion of the industrious and enterprising, who are able to do something for their daughters, and who would be induced to make far greater efforts in behalf of their education than they now do, could they secure to them equal advantages to those of one of our best and most respectable female seminaries at so moderate an expense. If the standard of female education among this class could by any means be raised, and its influence more extensively diffused, every department of society must sooner or later experience the beneficial results.

The difficulty of raising funds would doubtless be the greatest obstacle to such an undertaking. But there are many individuals in different parts of our country, who confidently believe that something of the kind could be effected, if the proper course were taken to interest the public. The object should be brought forward with very broad and liberal views, without any semblance of local interest. It should be presented as a public enterprise, for the public benefit, claiming equally the patronage of every part of New England. To effect this, and to secure public confidence, no special favors should be granted to the town where the institution is established. For example, none should be received into the school, unless they enter the establishment as boarders, subject to all its regulations, in the same manner as those from abroad.

The location would be a matter of special importance. It should be one which would be viewed with a favorable eye, not only by the immediate vicinity, but by the community in general; and one for which funds could as easily be raised as for any other location. The spot selected should be adapted to the growth and prosperity of such an institution. It should be alike suited to nourish the tender plant, and to support the lofty oak.

To Thomas White, Esq., of Ashfield, who had been deeply interested in her Buckland and Ashfield schools, she forwarded a number of these circulars, for distribution among the gentlemen of his acquaintance, accompanying them with a letter, from which some extracts are given.

"IPSWICH, March 5, 1834.

"I have long felt a great desire that the advantages of a seminary like this should be brought within the reach of the common people generally, and that by some means the expenses should be reduced to a level with their ability. I do wish our farmers would look at this, and see what can be done. If they would take hold of it vigorously, I do think something could be done, perhaps something which would secure the interests of thousands of their posterity. While it is desirable that every benevolent man should be able to grasp all the benevolent objects of the day, and do something for all, I doubt not but the best interests of the whole are promoted by having one mind directed to one object, and another to another. I have been thinking that if this object should be brought up, and viewed in its true light, some of our fathers in the cause of benevolence might select it as the child of their prayers and of their charities. Who would be more likely to begin upon it than our wealthy farmers?

"And now, my dear sir, in your old age, would you not be glad, with a few other kindred souls, to be the means of commencing a great work, which, in importance to the welfare of our country, of the church, and of the world, shall not fall behind the home missionary, or any other of our leading benevolent societies? Would you not gladly see such a work begun, and advancing? And how would your heart rejoice, if, before you sleep in the dust, you could see it rise and spread as our foreign missionary operations have done? This, I believe, may be accomplished, and he who, first putting his hand to the work, shall say to others, 'Come, and do likewise,' will deserve a place with Mills, with Robert Raikes, and others of like eminence. I do long to have some one or more gentlemen look at this object, till they are ready to do something for it. I would gladly do as much of the work as I can, and I find other ladies ready to join in it.

"I have long had a secret hope that the time would arrive, when I could consistently give up my present sphere of labor, and in some way devote my life, my strength, and all my powers to this object. That time has now arrived; and, after laboring half a year longer for this seminary, I expect to close my connection with it."

The following letter of Miss Lyon to her mother seems like a peep into her very soul: —

"Ipswich, May 12, 1834.

"My very dear Mother:

"I do not expect to continue my connection with Miss G. after this summer. I have for a great while been thinking about those young ladies who find it necessary to make such an effort for their education as I made, when I was obtaining mine. In one respect, from year to year, I have not felt quite satisfied with my present field of labor. I have desired to be in a school, the expenses of which would be so small, that many who are now discouraged from endeavoring to enjoy the privileges of this, might be favored with those which are similar at less expense.

"The course of instruction adopted in this institution, and the course which I have endeavored to adopt when I have instructed among my native hills, I believe is eminently suited to make good mothers as well as teachers. I have had the pleasure of seeing many, who have enjoyed these privileges, occupying the place of mothers. I have noticed with peculiar interest the cultivated and good common sense, the correct reasoning, the industry and perseverance, the patience, meekness, and gentleness of many of them. I have felt, that if all our common farmers, men of plain, good common sense, could go through the country and witness these mothers in their own families, and compare them with others in similar circumstances, they would no longer consider the money expended on these mothers as thrown away.

"Since I have lived to see so many of these ladies in their own families, I have felt more than ever before, that my field of labor was among the most desirable. I have felt that I could thank Him who has given me my work to do. O how immensely important is this work of preparing the daughters of the land to be good mothers! If they are prepared for this situation, they will have the most important preparation which they can have for any other; they can soon and easily become good teachers, and they will become, at all events, good members of society. The false delicacy, which some young ladies indulge, will vanish away as they see most of the companions of their childhood and youth occupying the solemn and responsible situation of mothers. It will no longer appear like a subject for which no care should be taken in the training of daughters.

"While, in the good providence of God, I have been permitted to occupy a field of labor where I could aid in preparing some who must mould the character of future generations for their great work, and while I have enjoyed much in my labor, I have not been quite satisfied. I have looked out from my quiet scene of labor on the wide world, and my heart has longed to see many enjoying these privileges, who cannot for the want of means. I have longed to be permitted to labor where the expenses would be less than they are here, so that more of our daughters could reap the fruits. Sometimes my heart has burned within me; and again I have bid it be quiet. I have sometimes speculated, and built airy castles, and again I have bid my mind dwell on sober realities. I have thought that there might be a plan devised by which something could be done. I have further thought, that if I could be entirely released from all engagements and all encumbrances, perhaps I might in time find some way opened before me for promoting this good object. With this view, I decided some time since, if Miss Grant's health should be sufficiently restored, to propose a separation. That time has now come, and we have agreed to close our joint labors next fall. Miss Grant is to be absent through the summer term, to improve her strength, and we shall spend most of the vacation here together, in getting ready for the winter, and then I expect to leave this scene of labor forever.

"I do not expect immediately to commence in any other field. I very much want six months or a year to read, write, plan, and do a thousand other things. I do not expect to be idle. This may seem like a wild scheme; but I cannot plead that it is a hasty one. I have had it under careful consideration two years or more, and for one whole year the question has been weighed by Miss Grant and myself.

"I hope and trust that this is of the Lord, and that he will prosper it. In this movement, I have thought much more constantly, and have felt much more deeply, about doing that which shall be for the honor of Christ, and for the good of souls, than I ever did in any step in my life. I want that you should pray for me, my dear mother, that I may in this thing be guided by wisdom from above, and that the Lord would bless me, and make me a blessing. My daily prayer to God is, Lord, what wilt thou have me to do? If the Lord go not with me, let me not go up hence.

"Perhaps you may inquire, what course I expect to take,

and where is to be my future scene of labor. This I do not know. The present path of duty is plain. The future I can leave with Him who doeth all things well."

Miss Grant journeyed to Ohio during the summer of 1834. The following letter of Miss Lyon to her, soon after she left Ipswich, is in answer to objections brought against the plan of having the teachers in the proposed school receive a comparatively low compensation. She never received more than two hundred dollars per annum for her services. She had always a home in the seminary beside.

"IPSWICH, May 6, 1834.

"Is it not true, that, on extraordinary occasions, it may be the duty of benevolent individuals to labor without expecting to receive that which is their just due? Does not any good object, which has not yet gained the public confidence, often furnish such an occasion? In such emergencies, has not the church always been able to furnish some who are ready to turn a deaf ear to louder calls, and continue to do so, while the necessity lasts! Was not the apostle Paul one who acted preëminently on this principle? How plainly does he teach, that the laborer is worthy of his reward, and that the Lord hath so ordained, that those who preach the gospel should live of the gospel. Yet he used not this power, lest he should hinder the gospel, and lest his good should be evil spoken of. That necessity has passed away, and it is no longer desirable that in Christian lands the gospel should be without charge. But do not some of our missionaries adopt a similar principle? How great are their sacrifices, compared with those of ministers at home! What minister in a Christian land would not sooner relinquish one half of his salary, and even one half of the remainder, than subject his children to the evils to which the children of missionaries are exposed? What reward is given to missionaries for all this sacrifice? Does it not appear, that even justice, to say nothing of mercy, would compel those who send them forth to pledge at least the education of their children? This would be but a small return for the debt of gratitude due to some of our missionaries from the churches. But this return, the most precious of a pecuniary kind that can be made, the Christian public are not sufficiently enlightened to render. But the missionary cause has not been forsaken on this account. Louder calls do not turn the devoted missionary from his purpose. Is not this the condition of the object under consideration? Is it not very important that mothers should be so trained, that they will be proper educators for the children of the church? To effect this, is there not great need of female seminaries, cheap but good schools? And is there any hope of establishing such schools without the aid of the benevolent Christian public? And while the public are so little prepared to contribute liberally to an object like this, may it not be expedient that those who first enter the field as laborers should receive as a reward so little of 'filthy lucre,' that they may be able to commend themselves to every man's conscience, even to those whose minds are narrow, and whose hearts are not much enlarged by Christian philanthropy? If such a course should be desirable at the commencement, how many years, or how many scores of years, must elapse before it would be no longer needful, time and experience alone can decide."

In the latter part of May, about the time of the religious anniversaries, she writes to Miss Grant, "I saw Dr. Packard last week in Boston. He has gained the sanction of the Franklin and Hampshire Associations of Ministers to any attempt that may be made to establish a female seminary within their bounds. He intends to ask for a vote of approbation from the Pastoral Association; and again from the General Association of Massachusetts, which meets in Berkshire county the last of June. Dr. P. says, that he is sixty-five years old, and can only do a little of the work at the outset, and somebody else must carry it on. Who that some one else is to be, no one knows."

Alluding in the same letter to her separation from Miss Grant, she says, "I do believe that an overruling Providence will remember your faithfulness in Mr. Emerson's school, and that you will always have given to you kindred hearts, able teachers, as your health and other circumstances may require. He tempereth the wind to the shorn lamb, but on the hardy sons of the forest he causeth the winds and the tempest to beat. It is good, my dear friend, to commend you to our heavenly Father."

To a gentleman at Andover, who had expressed an interest in her plans, and had suggested Andover as a good location for her contemplated school, she writes, under date of July 5, 1834,—

"Rev. Mr. K. called on me yesterday, making some inquiries in your name, relative to my plans for future labors. I have been desirous of an interview with you, that I might learn your views on several particulars.

"I have decided to close my connection with this institution, with a hope of using my limited influence towards advancing the belief that female schools of an elevated character may be furnished at a very moderate expense. I have much stronger desires to do something towards establishing some general principles on female education than to accomplish much myself. But I do hope that Providence will open a door, where I may labor directly in a school in behalf of this great and important cause, as I believe I can do more in this way than in any other.

"I have no definite spot in view where I may spend the remnant of my strength in behalf of an object which for a long time has seemed to drink up my spirits. I have not been so affected, because this object is more important than many others, but on the same principle that I should be more moved by the cries of a drowning child, where no deliverer was near, than by those of one actually in the arms of relief. I have no doubt there will be many objections raised. To avoid these, as far as possible, as well as to rouse a candid attention to any features which may be somewhat new and peculiar, I have supposed that, in many particulars, it would be of great importance to meet the views of the judicious part of the community. On this account, I have been desirous that a location might be selected by a committee, so appointed that they would be regarded as a kind of representative of the public. Whether it is practicable to create such a committee, I do not know. I have conversed with two or three gentlemen on this point, who think that some plan can be devised by which the thing may be brought about. It was suggested that something towards the object might be done at the General Association, that met at Lee last week. But on such occasions, the multiplicity of objects, each of which has several warm advocates, generally presses out an object of this sort, which has so few warm-hearted friends.

"You will, of course, perceive that I cannot now give any definite opinion with regard to Andover as a location. If it should be judged by gentlemen from different parts of New England to be a favorable, or the most favorable, for which there is any probability of raising funds, I should not shrink from undertaking even there, though it would be a location attended with difficulties.

"The question of the expediency of my devoting myself to this object in some place farther west has been several times mentioned to me. That influence needs to be put forth in the more western states, as in New England, cannot be doubted. The opinion, which has so universally prevailed here, that female seminaries of the first respectability must necessarily be expensive, has overspread the whole

State of New York, and marched on farther still, keeping pace with every effort in behalf of female education. As I believe, with many others, that this opinion is an error, and a highly injurious one, this is the point on which my mind centres more than on any other, and on which I wish to use an influence as far as I can. Considering the vast importance of the more western portion of our country, and the more abundant zeal, and the greater rapidity with which they carry any thing forward, when they are once convinced of its importance, I have been half inclined, at times, to look upon some spot beyond the limits of New England as more desirable for experiments on this subject. But, considering that improvements in education seldom make any progress eastward, my purpose to live and labor in New England has, during the last six months, become fixed and unchanging."

TO MISS W.

"Ipswich, August 1, 1834.

"My dear Miss W.:

"How long, very long, it is since you have written to me, or I to you! I can hardly realize that I have so little intercourse with those whom I so tenderly love, those whom I once met daily face to face, and with whom I held delightful intercourse sometimes from hour to hour. But it is even so. I have not written to dear A. for a great, very great while. How was my soul knit to her soul! Seldom have I loved any one so much, dear Miss Grant excepted. But we have long been separated, perhaps to meet no more on earth. Long separation breaks up the vividness of affection, but the strength still remains. How delightful will it be to have this affection renewed in heaven! I have to bid dear Miss Grant farewell, no more to live with her on earth. This separation has not severed my heart, but it has so shaken it as to render it most tenderly alive to all emotions of affection, which have sometimes seemed to lie dormant in my heart. I love more

17*

than ever to dwell on those friends who shared the warmth of my heart in my younger years.

"I suppose you have heard that I am endeavoring to establish a *manual labor school* for ladies. I have heard so. But as it is not true, I wish the mistake could be corrected. I will tell you what I should be glad to have done. You know it has become very popular for our highest and best seminaries for young men to be moderate in their expenses. It is not a sufficient recommendation for a college to be expensive. But how different is it with regard to female seminaries! Even at the present time, almost in the middle of the nineteenth century, do not many value them according to their expensiveness? Is it not rather gratifying to young ladies to attend expensive schools, when perhaps their brothers would rather glory in pursuing their studies at a moderate expense? Is there not a general feeling that female education *must* be costly, and that those who cannot pay the price must do without it? Is not this the reason why ladies are more aristocratic than gentlemen, and why their aristocracy is founded on so much more despicable principles? Would it not be a less evil for the farmers and mechanics through the land, who must spend all their time in laboring to support their families, to have scanty stores of knowledge, than for their wives, who must train up their children, to be thus scantily furnished? I will now tell you what I wish could be done. I wish the same public interest could be excited to extend female education to the common walks of life that exists with regard to the education of young men. If the church would do the same for young ladies that she has done, and is continually doing, for young men, the work would be accomplished. O that the church would take our highest female seminaries under her direct control, protection, and support! And do you not believe that this will be done at some future time? But this cannot be done, unless means are used to secure the confidence of common Christians.

And if any institution should ask for public support, would it not be desirable that, in some particulars, it should present certain marked features which would be approved by common Christians? On this account, I have thought that, in the proposed seminary, it would be well to have the domestic work done by the members, not as an essential feature of the institution, but as a mere appendage. But this mere appendage ought, by no means, to give the name of *manual labor* to the scheme. I have not the least faith in any of the proposed kinds of manual labor, by which it is supposed that females can support themselves at school, such as raising silk, attending to grape-vines, spinning, sewing, &c. I should expect that any attempt of the kind would become a bill of expense, rather than an income, to any female seminary. After the acquaintance I have had with many cultivated and interesting families, where the daughters, in a systematic manner, performed all the labor, I have the greatest confidence that a system might be formed, by which all the domestic work of a family of one hundred could be performed by the young ladies themselves, and in the most perfect order, without any sacrifice of improvement in knowledge or of refinement. Might not this simple feature do away much of the prejudice against female education among common people? If this prejudice could by any means be removed, how much would it do for the cause! Some of the specific features of the great object in which I am engaged will seem to some of our friends like new views, different from my former ones. Not so new as might seem; they are of no very recent date. The only difference is, that I did not consider it expedient, while I was connected with Miss Grant and this institution, to say much about these views. I should be very glad to see you a day or two, and talk over this whole subject."

Miss Lyon remained in the school at Ipswich till the term

was finished, but, for several weeks before its close, her thoughts and energies were absorbed in her scheme, and it was evident to the other teachers that she had a great work before her, and was straitened until it should be accomplished. Her plans during the summer had assumed a definite form, and she was fully ready to commence her prospective labors.*

SECTION V.

The true Principles of Success discovered and applied.

On September 6, 1834, a few gentlemen met in Miss Lyon's private parlor, in Ipswich, to devise ways and means for founding a permanent female seminary, upon a plan embracing Miss Lyon's favorite views and principles. It had been suggested that the first movement towards the object should be made in the Essex County Teachers' Association; but Dr. Packard, who was in Ipswich as the informal representative of his part of the state, objected that in such bodies there was apt to be much talk and little progress, and suggested, instead, the calling of a meeting of a few friends of education for the purpose. The point being yielded to

* "Miss Grant, after Miss Lyon left the school at Ipswich, continued to cherish the hope of obtaining a permanent foundation there; but the speedy failure of her health disabled her from assuming any extra labors or responsibilities, and after a few years compelled her to relinquish the idea of ever again imparting instruction to those she could call her pupils. As the lady of the Hon. William B. Banister, of Newburyport, she is now enjoying and adorning that circle of intelligence and worth with which she is surrounded, with the grateful respect of nearly two thousand pupils, who owe, as it were, their own selves to her instruction and care." — *Independent*, May 3, 1849.

his judgment, some dozen gentlemen, of known benevolence and candor, were invited to attend the proposed meeting. Miss Lyon writes, on September 8th, "Dr. Packard came here last Wednesday evening, and left this morning. We talked much of the time, for three days, respecting the proposed seminary. A meeting of a few gentlemen was held on Saturday, and Rev. Drs. Dana and Packard, Professor Hitchcock, Rev. Mr. Felt, Mr. George W. Heard, Mr. David Choate, and General Howland were appointed a committee to make a commencement, and go on (provided they are successful) to appoint trustees, &c. A circular is soon to be printed, with the doings of the meeting."

The committee appointed at this quiet meeting, which was scarcely known to twenty persons out of the room where it was held, supplied their own vacancies, and increased their number from time to time, as the progress of affairs required, and stood before the public as the responsible agents for establishing the proposed seminary, until, a charter having been obtained, and trustees appointed, their services were no longer needed. Some of them became trustees, and others resigned their places on the committee.

The first contribution towards the funds of the projected seminary was also made in Ipswich, soon after the meeting just mentioned. Miss Lyon proposed to raise one thousand dollars from ladies, as a fund for the contingent expenses of the undertaking. The school over which she was presiding had been accustomed, once or twice a year, to unite in a contribution to some one of the leading benevolent societies. She proposed to them, on that occasion, to make her projected seminary the object of their charities. A free-will offering of two hundred and sixty-nine dollars was the result. She next applied to the ladies in Ipswich, who contributed four hundred and seventy-five dollars more towards the proposed thousand. Miss Lyon herself went from house to house, to solicit subscriptions. The Ipswich ladies have a vivid recollection of her farewell visits that autumn. She represented her object as calling the most loudly for aid, because, though very deserving, it was the most unknown, unnoticed, and unappreciated by the benevolent community. She talked, now with the lady of the house, now with the husband. She told the husbands, in a very good-natured but earnest way, that she had come to get them to cut off one little corner of their estates, and give it to their wives to invest in the form of a seminary for young ladies. She held before them the object dear to her heart — the bringing of a liberal education within the means of the daughters of the common people, till it loomed up to them, for the time, as it did ever before her eyes. She put it to the lady whether, if she wanted a new shawl, a card-table, a new carpet, or some other article of elegance in her furniture or wardrobe, she could not contrive means to procure it. She spread out the whole subject, talking so fast that her hearers could hardly put in a word, anticipating every objection before it was uttered, and finally appealing to their individual humanity and benevolence. She uttered no falsehood; she poured out truth; she offered arguments to make out her case; and, last and best of all, she carried the will of nearly every person with whom she labored. Ladies that, in ordinary subscriptions to benevolent objects, did well to put down their fifty cents, gave her five or ten dollars of hard-earned money, collected by the slow gains of patient industry, and gave it of their own free will, yea, gave it as a privilege from which they would not have been willing to be debarred. They paid it on the spot, grateful that it had come to their hands at such a time as that. Every dollar of that money was well invested. All of it brought her a hundred per cent. It was, as Miss Lyon always called it, the corner stone of that noble edifice. She carried the story of the liberality of those ladies from town to town. Wherever she collected the ladies to awaken their zeal in behalf of her undertaking, there, with her impassioned eloquence, she stirred up the spirit of emulation by holding up the example of the Ipswich ladies; and in the next two years those five talents gained many more.

She wrote letters to former pupils of the Ipswich school, soliciting their aid in making up this contingent fund. She went herself to ladies with whom she was acquainted, in the towns about Ipswich, and invited them to contribute to it. Such was her perseverance, that, in less than two months, the sum was very nearly raised. It was a pledge of her future success. She used to say that it was a thorough commitment of all concerned to the object. The special effort to raise this fund, together with her labors in school, made her almost sick. She writes to Miss Grant, October 7, "I do not recollect being so fatigued, even to prostration, as I have been for a few weeks past, since I have been connected with the institution, except during your sickness in 1828, and a year ago last spring. The school business, as usual, accumulated; the business relating to my future enterprise hung in suspense all summer, and then required nearly a week of my time near the close of school, besides absorbing much strength of intellect and of the inner soul."

When, from long and close application, Miss Lyon became brain-weary, it was her practice, at this period of her life, to sink voluntarily into a state of partial stupor for one, two, or three days, as the case might require, keeping her bed most of the time, and taking very little food. From such seasons of rest she would come forth rejuvenated, and ready for a campaign that would exhaust any body else. She *could* arrive at that state in which she seemed to lose the power of stopping the wheels of thought. This seems to have been the case just before her final sickness.

Always preferring that the proposed school should be located in the central or western part of the state, after leaving Ipswich, she took up her abode for the winter at Amherst.

She attended some of the college lectures, and reviewed the natural sciences, that she might be the better fitted to superintend the education of her future scholars. She improved every opportunity that offered for conversing on her project with the intelligent gentlemen whom she met. Whenever there was a prospect of forwarding her plans by her presence in any other part of the state, she was sure to be promptly there. Some very important questions were settled that fall and winter. One was, whether the funds should consist of free donations or of proprietary subscriptions. Dr. Packard devised an ingenious plan, with many guards against abuses, for raising funds by scholarships, their owners to have the right of sending scholars at less expense than others. While Miss Lyon saw that the plan would, as its author contended, open purses far more readily than a call for free donations, she also feared that it would be attended, in future years, with many perplexities. Soliciting Miss Grant's advice on the subject, she says, "Dr. Packard has said to me several times that he was forming a screw, composed partly of benevolence and partly of selfishness, which he was designing to put upon the purses, and which he was confident would draw out the money; and when he had time, he would explain it to me. This week he has laid it before me. We have talked about it, most of the time, for three days. I saw objections which appeared to me so great, that I doubted whether it would be right for me to go forward." The plan was to have scholarships of two hundred and fifty dollars each, to be owned in whole, half, or quarter shares, the owner or owners being at liberty to send a pupil for fifteen dollars a year less than others. After much free and friendly conference, the committee, at a meeting at Ipswich in December, at which Dr. Packard was present, decided to depend on the free-will offerings of an enlightened public.

The question of location was settled that winter. The towns of South Deerfield, Sunderland, and South Hadley each offered handsome subscriptions, if the seminary might be located within its limits. The members of the committee in the vicinity of the places were of different opinions on this question. The gentlemen in Essex county — Dr. Dana, Mr. Felt, Mr. Choate, and Mr. Heard — held the balance in the meetings, and, from their residence, as well as their characteristic candor, they were not likely to be influenced by local considerations. Miss Lyon was intensely interested in these questions, but she left them to the committee with satisfaction, rejoicing that they did not depend on her voice. With Mr. Heard she had held more conference than with any other man. Evening after evening, while she was connected with the Ipswich school, she had spent at his house, conversing with him on her favorite object. He and Mr. Felt both went to the Connecticut River region, visited the towns in question, and surveyed the ground for themselves, in order to be able to give an intelligent vote. Mr. Choate, but for imperative illness, would have done the same. Dr. Dana took pains to inform himself through Messrs. Heard and Felt of the arguments, and generally was present at the meetings of the committee that winter.

A meeting of the committee, at which South Hadley was fixed upon as the location provided the subscription there could be raised to eight thousand dollars, was held at Worcester, January 8, 1835. It was the wish of the gentlemen that Miss Lyon should be there, that they might be able to consult her in the course of the meeting. The thermometer was below zero on the night when she, with Mr. Hitchcock, left Amherst in the stage for Worcester. Having taken some warm food and commended themselves to God, they took their seats in the stage some three or four hours before sunrise, each wrapped in a buffalo robe. Miss Lyon said she never suffered less from a journey in her life. From Worcester she wrote to Miss Grant, —

"Last evening, about midnight, Mr. Felt came and told

me that the question of the location at South Deerfield was decided in the negative. My heart was filled with gratitude to Him who directs all events according to his own infinite wisdom. The other two places are to be considered to-day. Between them I had no choice, and it did appear to me that I could commit the whole to God more entirely than ever before. The decision, as Mr. Heard will tell you, is in favor of South Hadley."

The location being fixed, the time had come for giving a name to the proposed institution. Some articles appeared, not far from this time, from the pen of one of the general committee, in which the suggestion was made that it should be called the Pangynaskean Seminary. Though the term Pangynaskean was pure Greek, and was fully explained to designate that seminary in which all the powers of woman — physical, intellectual, and moral — should be cultivated, those who were hostile to the enterprise laid hold of the name, and made it the occasion of sarcastic remark. Some of Miss Lyon's friends were afraid that the excitement about it would endanger the success of the enterprise. The author intended by the use of the term to designate the leading features of the proposed school, and by its novelty to awaken the public attention. Finding he had done this, he was not alarmed because a few editors, unfriendly to the project, attempted to make it ridiculous. Those very articles did far more good, in one single case, than all the harm that could possibly have flowed from them. They fell under the eye of a benevolent lady in Connecticut, and enlisted her sympathy and efforts. In the providence of God, she soon after became united to a gentleman in Boston, of liberal heart and means. Miss Lyon had heard his name, and had been told that he might regard her undertaking with favor. A gentleman who had married one of her Buckland scholars, and who is now a professor in one of our theological seminaries, commended her to his friendly notice. She found an open ear. His wife opened her doors and her heart to Miss Lyon and her coadjutors. When, after their first interview with her, this gentleman said to his wife, "How much do you think I had better give to Miss Lyon," she replied, "I thought, perhaps, you would give five hundred dollars." The husband was surprised; but he slept upon the subject, and rejoiced the hearts of the friends of the cause by affixing that sum to his well-known name. It was the first, but by no means was it the last five hundred dollars which he gave to that cause. The time, influence, and sympathy which he and his partner have to this day given to it, have been worth more than thousands of silver and gold.

Alluding to the name mentioned above, Miss Lyon, in a letter to Miss Grant, says, "I wish a little could be said to lead that part of the community who *would* attend to things and not to words only, to direct their attention to the magnitude of the object, rather than to *one undesirable, temporary* word, and to lead those who *would* expend their zeal in promoting that which is good and important, and not in opposing trifles, to spend the time and interest they have to spare in aiding the great cause with which the new institution is connected, rather than in opposing and ridiculing the mere suggestion of a peculiar name."

The next letter is to her mother.

"AMHERST, April 2, 1835.

"MY VERY DEAR MOTHER:

"I would be glad to visit you this spring before I go east, but you know the travelling is bad; and besides, Professor Hitchcock is now giving a course of lectures on geology, which I have long desired to attend, and I have thought I ought to make special efforts to hear them. They are given three times a week, and I have been able, so far, to attend every lecture." After speaking further of her regret at not being able to visit her, she says, "I have been to Ipswich twice this winter. The last time I staid two weeks. There, I have enjoyed much that relates to this world, and much, I hope, that relates to a better. There, more than any where else, I have looked out upon this broad and wicked world, till my heart has longed that laborers might go forth to reap the harvest, which is already ripe for gathering. When I have there looked around on those committed to my care, how has my heart gone forth in their behalf, that they might be ready to do with their might what their hands find to do!

"I often feel that my life is far advanced, and that I can do but little more myself. But this great work is all to be done through human instrumentality. How small a portion of it has yet been done! O that I might do a little more, before I depart hence! But my greatest hope is, that I may have the privilege of encouraging, stimulating, and strengthening some, who may continue to labor when I am laid in the grave. It is so pleasant for me to go to Ipswich, I am rather glad that I occasionally have business which calls me there. But it awakens many tender and sad emotions. Sometimes I fear that I never shall have another field of labor, where I can do so much good. But if the Lord has more work for me to do in the world, he will provide it for me, and point out the way.

"For special reasons, I think it best to keep myself disengaged from any school, till the new school goes into operation in South Hadley. But the work goes forward very slowly. It will be a great while before I can expect the privilege of laboring there. Will you, my dear mother, pray for this new institution, that God will open the hearts of his children in its behalf, and that the Spirit of God may rest on its future teachers and pupils, that it may be a spot where souls may be born of God, and saints quickened in their Lord's service? It is my heart's desire, that holiness to the Lord may be inscribed upon all connected with it, and that a succession of teachers may be raised up, who shall there continue to labor for Christ long after we are laid in our graves."

TO MISS GRANT.

"AMHERST, April 8, 1835.

"I have been thinking whether the buildings might not be commenced this summer, laying out ten or twelve thousand dollars, on such a plan that the buildings can be extended when more funds are obtained. Considering the field yet to be gone over, would it not do to presume on a few thousand dollars? Would it not do, by some sacrifice, to turn what is subscribed to be paid in future years into ready money? I fear to let the present season pass away without having any thing done on the buildings, lest friends may be discouraged, and enemies take occasion to injure the cause. I wish Messrs. Heard and Choate would look at this subject, and come and attend the meeting next Wednesday.

"It seems to me also desirable, that every important branch of the business should be committed to a small executive, to men who are qualified to do the definite things needed, and are known to be willing to work for this cause. The business to which I refer is *finding* and appointing agents, devising ways and means of raising funds, making arrangements towards building, making contracts, obtaining plans, &c."

At the meeting of which Miss Lyon speaks in the preceding letter, the contemplated institution received the name of the "Mount Holyoke Female Seminary."

In the fall of 1834, while Dr. Packard still felt a father's zeal and interest in the enterprise, he succeeded in enlisting in its behalf Rev. Mr. Hawks, of Cummington. One evening in November, they came to Amherst, to confer with Miss Lyon, and she then and there held her first interview with her future friend and co-worker. He helped her com bat the doctor on his proprietary plan. He was then a young man, and happily settled ; but he obtained leave of absence from his people, providing them a supply for the pulpit, and engaged for a few months in an agency for the seminary. Under about the same date as the last extract, she says, "I am very well satisfied with Mr. Hawks. The query begins to arise in my mind, whether early efforts should not be made to secure his services for the summer. This matter ought to receive the immediate attention of the committee." He was continued in his agency. At that crisis, when it required a clear eye and a strong heart to embark in the cause, Mr. H. gave himself sincerely to its advancement. Miss Lyon often went with him in his pilgrimages, aiding his arguments with her presence and conversation. From the evening in which they met at Amherst to that of her death, no person was a more patient listener to her many and varied plans, nor a more efficient co-worker with her in giving these plans life and form.

"NORTON, May 19, 1835.

"MY DEAR MISS GRANT:

"I am not fully decided about my manner of spending the summer. I design to make one excursion, which will occupy a few weeks, to visit my relatives, to visit South Hadley, Amherst, Northampton, and some other towns in the vicinity of South Hadley, and perhaps some in Franklin county, to exert an influence in favor of our cause. I think I shall take this excursion about the time of commencement at Amherst. Considering that it must be at least two years before I can commence teaching at South Hadley, I think it is best to spend some time in study, though I should not think it wise at my age to give up active labor for study. The time being providentially thrown on my hands, the case is different. I should prefer not to say much about it, because I do not expect to make much progress, or to retain much of what I gain ; but much more, because it seems ridiculous for a lady of forty to be trying to make over her education.

What time I do devote to study, I can probably take much better this year than next, and I can find no better place than this. Here, no one inquires what I am doing, or how I spend my time."

Miss Lyon attended the "General Association" of Massachusetts, which met at Framingham in June of that year, as she was on her way from Norton to the western part of the state. She was detained a few days at Framingham. From that place she writes to Miss C., —

"Give a large share of love to Miss A. from me. I want to see her, to talk with her about the good which she can do, by being a member of the school the *first* year. Ought we not to ascertain what young ladies of our acquaintance, who are advanced in their education, intend at some time to become members of the institution, and lay before them the good that they would do by joining the school, the very first year?

"I have been sleeping and resting since I have been here. I wish you could sleep and rest as much. Do tell me all about your frail, mortal tenement; and may your soul be in health and prosper."

By Miss Lyon's private efforts, three ladies of distinguished abilities were led to complete their school education at the new seminary the first year. Every class since has been several times as large, but perhaps no one, according to its numbers, has embraced more talent, intelligence, and genuine self-denying benevolence. They all live to mourn the departure of their revered instructress. All of them are the wives of active clergymen. One continues in the Bay State, one dwells in the Great Western Valley, and the third sojourns on India's sunny plains.

The original committee of seven, who had been appointed

at the first meeting in Ipswich, September 6, 1834, added to their number, from time to time, the following gentlemen: Rev. Roswell Hawks, Rev. William Tyler, Rev. John Todd, Rev. Dr. Joseph Penney, Rev. Joseph D. Condit, Mr. William Bowdoin, and Mr. Samuel Williston. The committee held a meeting at the house of Mr. Williston, in Easthampton, on June 10, 1835. They voted to invite the ladies in the vicinity of the Connecticut River, in Massachusetts, to raise a thousand dollars towards the object, and to address a circular to the friends of Christian education. The following extracts are from that circular: —

After much deliberation, prayer, and correspondence, the friends of the Redeemer have determined to erect a school for the daughters of the church, the object of which shall be to fit them for the highest degree of usefulness. The justly celebrated school at Ipswich embraces the principal features which we wish this to possess. We will state the outlines of our plan.

1. The seminary is designed to be permanent; to be under the guardianship of those who are awake to all the interests of the church. It will not, under God, depend upon the health or the life of a particular teacher, but, like our colleges, be a permanent blessing to our children, and to our children's children.

2. It is to be based entirely on Christian principles; and while it is to be furnished with teachers of the highest character and experience, and to have every advantage which the state of female education in this country will allow, its brightest feature will be, that it is a school for Christ.

3. It is located at South Hadley, Massachusetts, on the banks of the Connecticut, at the foot of Mount Holyoke, in the centre of New England, easy of access from all quarters, and amid the most lovely scenery. In selecting the location, the committee had in view centrality, retirement, and economy, morality, and natural scenery.

4. The buildings are to be adequate to receive and board two hundred young ladies.

5. It is designed to cultivate the missionary spirit among its pupils; the feeling that they should live for God, and do something as teachers, or in such other ways as Providence may direct.

6. The seminary is to have a library and apparatus equal to its wants; to have its internal arrangements such that its pupils may

continue to practise such habits of domestic economy as are appropriate to the sex, and without which all other parts of education are purchased at too dear a rate.

7. The seminary is to be placed on such a foundation by the Christian public, if they sustain our views, that all the advantages of the institution may be afforded so low, as to be within the reach of those who are in the middle walks of life. Indeed, it is for this class principally, who are the bone and sinew and the glory of our nation, that we have engaged in this undertaking. The wealthy can provide for themselves; and though we expect to offer advantages which even they cannot now command, yet it is not for their sakes that we erect this Christian seminary, and thus ask the funds of the church. In regard to this, we hope and expect that it will be like our colleges, so valuable that the rich will be glad to avail themselves of its benefits, and so economical that people in very moderate circumstances may be equally and as fully accommodated. We expect that distinctions founded on such incidental circumstances as wealth will not find a place within its walls, any more than they do at the table of Jesus Christ.

8. In order to establish such a seminary, the committee believe that the Christian public must be invited to contribute a sum not less than thirty thousand dollars. While every thing is to be done on a scale as economical as possible, yet the committee feel that the materials and work should all be the first of their kind. Of this sum, the village of South Hadley has contributed eight thousand dollars, which, with the subscriptions of the few who, in addition, have been invited to contribute, makes the sum already raised about one third of the amount specified.

TO MISS GRANT.

"June 29, 1835.

"Rev. Mr. Todd requested Rev. Morris White to endeavor to bring the seminary before the Massachusetts Association of Ministers, and to obtain some resolves in its favor. He succeeded in presenting it, and it was voted to appoint a committee of five to report on the subject. Mr. White was not included in this committee, and probably not an individual, who was known to have any interest in the object, or to understand any thing about it. The design was to have some resolves passed, and perhaps have something said on the subject. At the meeting of the committee, one objected because he was president of the board of trustees of an academy; a second was much more opposed, and Mr. W. was about where you would expect. Mr. M., a quiet, good man, would do nothing any way; Mr. C., a candid man, the youngest of the five, was favorable to the enterprise. Mr. White told me how the business stood. He and Mr. C. took it into their hands with the design of bringing it to a close in some way not injurious to the object. Mr. White saw the committee together again, and told them that he only wished to have some general resolves passed, recommending the object, but as they were opposed to it, he was ready to withdraw the proposition. This had the effect of bringing them to terms, and they finally reported three resolutions, which were carried so quick as to allow no opportunity for a word to be said, if any one had been disposed. The first was in favor of Christian education among females, the second granted that sufficient efforts had not been made, the third recommended Mount Holyoke Female Seminary, and any other institution which designs to effect a similar object."

TO HER MOTHER AND SISTER.

"Northampton, July 23, 1835

"I cannot undertake to tell you where I have been, and what I have been doing, since I last saw you. I seem to be ever busy, and yet I accomplish nothing. I wander about without a home, scarcely knowing one week where I shall be the next. In this way, I expect to live, *at least* until one year from next spring, the earliest possible time that our new institution can open. And then, I may only make a change for a situation of overwhelming cares. But I have no doubt that I am following the leadings of Providence. His dealings towards this new enterprise have been such as should lead me to trust wholly in the Lord. Every token of success has been rather strongly marked by his hand; and every trial and discouragement have been such, that when good comes, we feel constrained to say, 'This is the work of the Lord.'

"In looking back, I feel that, whatever may be the result, I can never regret that these things were not directed differently. It seems to me more and more that this institution, and other similar ones, are a necessary part of the great system of means now in operation for the conversion of the world. When I look abroad and see how much abounds that is contrary to the spirit of the gospel, I sometimes feel it to be a precious privilege to pray, 'Thy kingdom come; thy will be done on earth, as it is done in heaven.' Whatever we are permitted to do, in accordance with these desires, is a precious privilege. The feeble efforts which I am allowed to put forth in coöperating with others, in laying the foundation of this new seminary, I feel will probably do more for the cause of Christ after I am laid in my grave, than all I may have done in my life before. Do not cease to pray for this seminary, that in every succeeding age it may be most sacredly the Lord's; and that no wicked hand may ever be allowed to turn it aside from its consecration to the Redeemer."

TO MISS GRANT.

"NORTHAMPTON, July 24, 1835.

"How vain would it be for us to hope by our present efforts to make our situation more comfortable or quiet! We have every reason to believe, that the more we seek to draw the public to aid us in doing good, the more perplexing will be our cares and labors. But then we shall not shrink from this, if we can thus lay a foundation for our successors to labor abundantly for the cause of Christ."

In August, Miss Lyon went to Ipswich, to take Miss Grant's place in school, while the latter went on a journey. She writes to Miss G., —

"IPSWICH, August 23, 1835.

"MY DEAR MISS GRANT:

"I now feel so well, that I am trying to renew my feeble attempts in behalf of the religious interests of this school, and to ascertain the character and wants of individuals, both among the professedly pious and those not so. The prospect, I hope, is in some respects a little more favorable than I dared express in my last. Yesterday evening, there were not quite so many at meeting as sometimes, but they seemed to keep along with the subject with unusual attention, and there was more solemnity than at any other time. I had before endeavored to dwell upon the unreasonableness and criminality of ever 'doing wrong,' or, in other words, of *sin*. Last evening, I dwelt upon the suitableness and justice of punishing those who sin, and upon the nature and degree of that punishment which God, who knows, has decided to be just what sin deserves. I purpose at another time to take up the way of escaping punishment. O that their hearts might be opened to accept of pardon in this wonderful and glorious way! I invited those to come to my room, this morning, who could decide, in *external* things, to do all that they considered their duty. So many came, (twenty-eight,) that I almost feared they did not understand me. The meeting was solemn, more so than last Sabbath morning. There were so many, that I only talked to them all together, and I had some thoughts which I was glad to communicate to them."

"SOUTH HADLEY CANAL, October 1, 1835.

"MY DEAR MISS GRANT:

"I expressed in my last a very earnest request that you would visit us next week. I now repeat the invitation and urge the request. I wish Mr. Choate could be here one day, or a part of a day, before the time of the meeting. Come yourself directly to Rev. Mr. Condit's. Dr. Penney had simply been put on the committee, but all we could say was, that he was a general friend. He has on his hands a larger weight of gratuitous business than most other ministers, besides having the care of the largest church in the United States. And he has been abroad a part of the summer on account of his health. My heart almost failed me as to attempting to invite his attention to this object, but as I supposed that with him much wisdom existed on some important particulars, I thought it best to try. On Monday, Mr. Tyler proposed to take me to Northampton. He called with me at Dr. Penney's. Mr. Tyler expressed the difficulties he felt on account of Mr. Todd's absence. Dr. Penney said the business ought to go forward, and that he regarded the object as very important; but that he knew nothing about the state of the business. He was ready to enter into the subject thoroughly, and devoted his whole time to us till about the middle of the afternoon of the next day. He inquired definitely what had been done, and endeavored to point out the course of procedure now. He convinced Mr. Tyler that it was his duty to go forward and make an arrangement for the meeting of the committee. He aided him in deciding on the time of the meeting, in laying out the business, and in settling what was to be done beforehand. I have decided to stay here till next Monday morning, and try to rest. I have had much solicitude, because I could see no way in which any thing was to be done, when so much needed to be done. But I am greatly relieved for the present, and Mr. Tyler about as much as I am. It is very easy to converse with Dr. Penney. A child would feel no embarrassment in consulting him in the most familiar manner. Thus a kind Providence has caused light to shine on our path just for the present. Mr. Todd's absence, which we have so much regretted, has rendered it more evident to Dr. Penney that his aid is now needed, and this has been the occasion of his becoming more acquainted with the particular business of the institution."

TO HER SISTER.

"NORTON, October 24, 1835.

"MY DEAR SISTER:

"You will doubtless be glad to know something about the Mount Holyoke Seminary. The work goes on slowly. I hope they will be able to commence building next spring. We have much to try our faith, and much to excite our hopes. I love to look at the hand of Providence as connected with this enterprise. With how much wisdom and goodness are trials and blessings mingled together in our cup! The work of endeavoring to found and build up this seminary is one which I trust the Lord will own and bless. But I do not expect that it will be carried forward as on flowery beds of ease. This I have never asked. I only ask that it may receive the smile of Providence in that way which shall best promote the interests of the great cause to which it is consecrated. I hope that in your prayers you will commend this enterprise to God."

The general committee, at their meeting, October 7, invited Miss Grant to unite with Miss Lyon in taking charge of the contemplated seminary. Miss Lyon cordially seconded this invitation. While Miss Grant had the matter under consideration, Miss Lyon addressed to her the following letter: —

"October 27, 1835.

"I have thought of you very much since we separated. I greatly fear that the trying questions which are now taxing your mental energies, besides the care of the school, just now at the commencement, will be more than you can sustain. May the Lord give you strength equal to your wants, and may he give you wisdom from on high to guide your thoughts, and your views, and your present important decisions. When all human help and human wisdom fail, and all knowledge of future events, as connected with present causes, seems entirely cut off, how sweet it is to go to One who knows all from beginning to end, to One who can direct our very thoughts, and who can take us individually by the hand and lead us in a plain path! Every thing appears to me dark with Egyptian darkness, except as I turn my thoughts to Him who is the fountain of light. I dare not pray for any thing in particular, but only that the will of the Lord may be done, that all interested in this institution may be humble and submissive, that his will towards this enterprise may be done, as it is done toward those on whom he smiles, and not as it is done toward those whom he chastens and afflicts. My daily language is, 'Lord, thou knowest; not my will, but thine, be done.'

"How often have I endeavored to consecrate all the part, all the interest which God has given me in this contemplated institution, most sacredly and solemnly to his service! and how often have I endeavored to pray that no one who has any thing to do in building it up may ever call aught his own! O that every one who puts a finger to the work, by giving the smallest contribution of time, of money, or of influence, might feel that this is a work of solemn consecration, a work to be reviewed in the light of eternity! For a few weeks past, I have thought a little too much about gaining the approbation of the wise and good, as compared with my desires that every thing connected with it may receive the approbation of God."

TO MISS GRANT.

"AMHERST, December 23, 1835.

"MY VERY DEAR SISTER:

"It is sweet to review our past years, the time of our first acquaintance, the commencement of our connection, and the many years we spent so delightfully together, and in some degree, as I hope, profitably to the best of causes.

When I look back and compare my own views and feelings, fifteen years ago, with what they are now, I am constrained to believe there has been a very great change. Comparatively, it does seem to me now a great privilege to live and labor for the cause of Christ in any place, and under any circumstances, where He may direct; and, if possible, a still greater privilege to lead others to attempt and to do more than I can ever myself accomplish. It seems to me, uniformly, as if my strength was mostly spent, and my years, a great proportion of them, gone. But if I may be permitted to do something more, it will be indeed a great privilege. In this respect, life seems to me a greater and greater blessing.

"I anticipate trials in future, such as I have never yet known. I expect them, from indications of Providence already manifested toward the enterprise in which I am engaged. Sometimes my heart and spirits seem to sink under the prospect, and I am almost ready to exclaim, 'When will the work of my feeble hands be done, that I may go home?' But through the mercy of God, these seasons do not often occur, and do not continue long. Generally, I feel that the dark, portentous cloud which hangs over the future is under the direction of Him who led his chosen people by a pillar of cloud and of fire. I do hope that in some way the remainder of my life may be instrumental of more good than my past life has been, though it may be in a manner very different from what I anticipate. The years which I have had the privilege of spending with you have done more to fit me to enjoy so great a blessing than almost all other circumstances. Such a view gives a peculiar sweetness to the remembrance.

"Have you seen Dr. Channing on Slavery? Really, I did not know that he had such a great soul, so much of the noble spirit of former days, composed of mildness and decision.

He deals in great principles, instead of that personality which is the order of the day. In seeking after truth, it is delightful now and then to come to a stream which we can recognize as flowing from the great fountain, and which has not been subdivided into endless ramifications, till we forget that there is any fountain-head ; or, to speak without a figure, till we forget that there are any great principles, on which we can rest unshaken amid all the clashing of opinions and sentiments. Dr. Channing has a suitable word of reproof, alike in season for the south, in their present excited and threatening attitude, for the abolitionists, in their furious and misguided zeal, and for the anti-ultras, who, in their *prudence* and caution, are in danger of making concessions, tacitly at least, which are suited to endanger our first principles of duty, rather than hazard the odium of being called by some one *ultra*, and of being claimed by some of the ultra parties. This last class need reproof, perhaps, as much as either of the others, though in different degrees. And from this class we have more fear that truth will suffer than from any other. I lament most deeply the havoc which misguided zeal is now making with the dearest interests of our country and the church ; but should this fire sweep over the whole country, consuming all that is combustible, the soil will be left, the foundation will be unshaken. But I dread to have the foundations broken up. I dread to have those who are the stability of the times driven, by the scarecrow of ultraism, from their high post in defence of truth, the rights of man, and the duties of the church. Dr. Channing's reproofs must come down with great weight on every conscience that puts on the coat so finely fitted. How much more heavily will reproofs bear upon the conscience, which come from great principles, than those captious fault-findings which fill many of our newspapers! I am delighted with the spirit in which this book is written."

TO MISS CALDWELL.

"January 11, 1836.

"In C. I visited the family of Mr. A., who, probably, during the past twenty years, has given more to benevolent objects, in proportion to his property and family, than any other man in New England. I was delighted with their godly simplicity, their systematic mode of benevolent action, and their well-balanced views of things."

In C. Miss Lyon visited two maiden sisters, (the Misses M.,) who were living comfortably on some property left them by an honored brother. Out of their moderate means, they subscribed one hundred dollars each to the object. Owing to circumstances which they could neither foresee nor control, they soon after lost their property; but, rather than be denied the luxury of helping the good work, they labored with their own hands, and earned the money to meet their subscription as it became due. With such money was the institution built. With the prayers of these and kindred spirits was every stone and every brick consecrated to the Lord.

The act of incorporation passed both houses of the state legislature February 10, 1836, and was signed by the governor the next day. The instrument named as trustees Messrs. William Bowdoin, John Todd, Joseph D. Condit, David Choate, and Samuel Williston, and empowered them to hold real and personal estate, not exceeding in value one hundred thousand dollars, to be devoted exclusively to purposes of education.

On March 2, the trustees met at South Hadley. They accepted the act of incorporation, added Rev. William Tyler and Rev. Roswell Hawks to the board, elected officers of the board, appointed an executive committee from their number, and took measures for obtaining plans and estimates for carrying forward the contemplated operations.

On the 13th of the following month, the trustees met again in South Hadley. In reference to the meeting of the 13th April, Miss Lyon writes from Boston, April 25th, —

"The late meeting of the trustees at South Hadley was as favorable as could be expected. A committee was appointed to attend to the preparations towards building, and more general responsibility was committed to Mr. Hawks than heretofore. Mr. Joseph Avery, of Conway, was added to the trustees. At an adjourned meeting at Northampton, on the 19th, Deacon Andrew W. Porter, of Monson, was appointed a trustee. We have had our eye on him for some time. He has had more experience in superintending workmen and in putting up buildings than any one on our board. Benevolent, disinterested, and of sound judgment, he is also one of the first of accountants. He is an acquaintance of Mr. Tyler, and at South Hadley Mr. T., with Mr. Hawks and myself, agreed to meet at Monson the next day. When we reached Monson, the gentleman we went to see was absent, not to return till Saturday night, and on this account I did not leave Monson till the following Tuesday. I was much interested in my visit there. Both Mr. P. and his wife can look at our cause.

"I have been endeavoring to ascertain whether we can depend on Mr. and Mrs. Safford's firm support, whenever it is desirable to bring our cause up here. The Lord is, I believe, inclining their hearts in our favor."

The three gentlemen alluded to in the preceding letter entered fully into Miss Lyon's plans, became trustees of the seminary, and were as active in promoting its interests as though it had been their own private business. The first named gave for several years much of the surplus revenue of his rock-bound but productive farm to the good work in which she was employed. Like Miss Lyon, he could not endure to see a mill of the sacred funds of the institution spent for a fruitless purpose. When, on one occasion, a plan had been purchased of an artist, at an artist's price, which, as Miss Lyon thought, was not available for her purpose, the bill was voluntarily met from his own purse, in addition to his large subscription. It was a kind deed, which gave Miss Lyon great satisfaction. Her private funds had suffered many drafts, and were ill able at that time to bear another.

Mr. Porter, for several months, left his own extensive and lucrative business to the oversight of others, and went every Monday morning in his own carriage to South Hadley, and there, till the sunset of Saturday, gave his financial skill and rare business abilities to overseeing the erection of the seminary building. It was in his hospitable mansion that she spent her very last season of rest, and refreshed her soul for the heavenly employments on which she was so soon to enter.

To no one is the institution more indebted for pecuniary aid than to the friends of whom she said, in the last letter, "The Lord is, I believe, inclining their hearts in our favor." But for the coöperation of these men, we cannot see how the enterprise could have gone forward. Who can doubt that the Lord helped her to find them, and to set her object before them, and inclined their hearts and minds to receive and understand the complicated plans of a woman so unlike all other women they had ever met? It was to herself a providential interposition that, at a crisis when many wise men, even in the church, could not comprehend her plans, and assist in their execution, such men as these lent her their efficient aid.

TO MISS CALDWELL.

"BOSTON, May 24, 1836.

"When I was last in Boston, I thought it best that Mr. Hawks should come here this week, hoping that something might be done for our cause. But the times grow worse and worse, and doing any thing now is entirely out of the question. I know not where I am going to be, nor what I am going to do. 'Take no thought for the morrow' comes to me often with force. I seem continually to know less and less about the future."

TO MISS C. E. BEECHER.

"July 1, 1836.

"I thank you for your interest in my plans, expressed in the sincere way of criticism on one point. I think, however, you do not fully understand them.

"The terms high, low, and moderate tuition mean very different things in different parts of the country. In the aristocratic south, where all the wealth is concentrated on large plantations, and in some of the speculating portions of the north, where wealth flows in as in a day, and in some of the most prosperous mercantile and manufacturing places, these terms are understood differently from what they are among the general community of New England. The latter, tilling a sterile soil, and uniting economy with prudence, are enabled, by the slow gains of patient industry, to provide comfortably for their children, and send them to school in their own neighborhoods, to sustain the ordinances of the gospel, and to reserve something to be cast into the treasury of the Lord, in order to send the gospel to the heathen, to raise up ministers, to build up colleges and seminaries at the west, and to supply the destitute of our own land, who are less able or less willing than themselves, with the sacred ministry.

"Our plan is to place tuition at what will be regarded by the New England community, including the wealthy and the educated, with farmers and mechanics, as moderate tuition.

Here I would have you distinctly understand that we do not adopt this standard because we consider ourselves under any obligation to *man* so to do. Neither do we consider it necessary that other institutions should adopt the same standard, or that this institution should certainly abide by it evermore, though at present it is essential to our success.

"I have not been alone in considering it of great importance to establish a permanent seminary in New England for educating female teachers, with accommodations, apparatus, &c., somewhat like those for the other sex. Honorably to do this, from twenty to forty thousand dollars must be raised; and such a sum, raised for such an object, would form almost an era in female education. For years, Miss Grant and myself made continual efforts to accomplish the object; but all our efforts failed.

"I am convinced that there are but two ways to accomplish such an object. First, to interest one, two, or a few wealthy men to do the whole; second, to interest the whole New England community, beginning with the country population, and in time receiving the aid and coöperation of the more wealthy in our cities. Each of these modes, if practicable, would have its advantages. The first, if done at all, could be done sooner and with very little comparative labor. The second would require vastly more time and labor; but if it were accomplished, an important and salutary impression would be made on the whole of New England. Having adopted this second course, we have been for some time going forward with as much success as we could expect. We have enlisted for the work. I have regarded it as a work for life. In laying our plans, we examined carefully every step. In the commencement of any great enterprise, the community often are not prepared to act upon the most important considerations, when they can be moved by less important, but more tangible, circumstances. During my long but fruitless efforts in connection with Miss Grant, I became convinced that the community were not disposed to appreciate the most important advantages of an institution thus endowed, such as its superior character and its permanency. I was also convinced that, to give the first impulse to this work, something must be presented which is more tangible, and of real, though of less, value, and be made to stand out in bold relief. For this purpose, we have chosen the reduction of expenses, as compared with other large seminaries, not aided by the public. Every step we take proves it a good selection. We carefully avoid all extravagant statements ; indeed, we usually state only general facts, leaving each to make his own estimate and draw his own conclusions. There is an expectation that economy will be practised in the establishment, and that the funds, gathered by little and little, will be reserved for the good of the institution, and not for private emolument, and that there will be such a reduction of expense as the nature of the case will allow. Here is our pledge, and we must redeem it. In doing this, the first object to be gained is good management in the boarding department. Let that be secured, and all else will be sure to follow. I do not expect to have the direct care of the boarding department, but I hope to secure the coöperation of persons skilled in domestic economy, and disposed to use their skill faithfully for the great cause. The department of instruction, including tuition, I expect to superintend myself ; and it is essential to success in the boarding department that I should set an example of economy in my own. Unless I do, I cannot lift up my head in efforts to exert an influence on this point in every other department. I do not mean to ask any other one connected with the institution to make such sacrifices as I can cheerfully make. This may not be necessary for my successor, but it is necessary in my case, at least for a few years.

" Again, we have held up to New England people the advantages of a teachers' seminary, with ample facilities for boarding and instruction, free of rent, of so superior a character that a supply of scholars could be secured without receiving those who were immature and ill prepared, and who are always a heavy tax on the time of teachers. We have shown that the same money will, in this way, do more to provide instruction for young women qualifying themselves to teach, than it would do in our country academies. After these professions, shall we ask for higher tuition, at the same time that we are asking for benevolent aid to carry forward our enterprise?

"Thus I do feel confident that we must retain our plan for tuition, or abandon the enterprise. But we must not give up the work. To indulge even a fear as to our final success, would be a cruel distrust of the kindest Providence. While I do not consider ourselves under any obligation to *man*, we are under solemn obligations to *God*, to adopt this course. We are compelled by the principles of expediency, so beautifully exhibited in the precepts and practice of the apostle Paul. If any injury should result to the cause of education from our adopting this moderate standard of tuition, it will be as nothing compared with the great good to be accomplished; less far than the injurious results of Paul's example, on the support of the gospel ministry, which results he so carefully guards against in the ninth chapter of 1 Corinthians.

"I express myself with more confidence on this subject, because it has been with me, for two or three years, a matter of careful consideration; but further, because our laborious and indefatigable agent is of the same opinion, and all his intercourse with New England people has tended to confirm it. Having been wholly devoted to the enterprise for a year and a half, he probably knows more of the views of the New England community on this point than any hundred others. Careful in all his movements, he never has occasion to retrace a single step. Whatever may be thought of my sanguine temperament, he cannot be charged with being over-zealous. But his deficiency in zeal is more than made up by his unwearied labors, his never-ending patience and perseverance, his sound common sense, his careful observation of human nature, and his intimate acquaintance with New England people.

"You speak of the importance of raising the compensation of teachers. In a list of motives for teaching, I should place first the great motive, which cannot be understood by the natural heart, Love thy neighbor as thyself. On this list, though not second in rank, I have been accustomed to place pecuniary considerations. I am inclined to the opinion that this should fall lower on a list of motives to be presented to ladies than to gentlemen, and that this is more in accordance with the system of the divine government. Let us cheerfully make all due concessions, where God has designed a difference in the situation of the sexes, such as woman's retiring from public stations, being generally dependent on the other sex for pecuniary support, &c. O that we may plead constantly for her religious privileges, for equal facilities for the improvement of her talents, and for the privilege of using all her talents in doing good!"

September 6th, she writes to Miss Grant, "I have very much wanted to know whether Mr. H. would exert any influence in our behalf in Boston. When I came from Norton last week, I thought it best to come through Boston and test the question. I cannot tell you how much I dreaded it. I sent a line to him, asking his advice in such a manner that I knew he would not give it, unless he would also give his aid. I mentioned that I should call directly after dinner, and that I was to leave the city at four. I called. His look, and his manner of shaking hands, left no doubt what would be the issue. I spent a little while conversing on the subject, when he told me that he could not give me advice, as he could not go forward in this object. He said he felt himself pledged to aid the Ipswich school, and that he did not consider it his duty to engage in our enterprise. I do not know whether he designed to be understood that he would not contribute to it, or only that he would not take any responsibility about it. I asked him whether there was any objection to my saying, that the reason he could not engage in this was, that he was pledged to Ipswich. He replied that it was the truth, and that he felt no objection to its being stated. I came away with mingled emotions. I felt as if I had undergone a severe operation. On the whole, gratitude seemed to be the preponderating emotion — gratitude that I had gone through this trying effort, and that the question was finally settled; and especially that so good a reason could be assigned for its being settled in the negative."

The site for the seminary had been selected at a meeting of the trustees, held on May 19, 1836.

July 7, she writes, "Mr. Tyler has never been satisfied with the site selected. Mr. Bowdoin, who was not at the meeting when the question was decided, also dislikes the selection. Mr. Hawks and myself like it more than we dislike it. To-day we have been to the spot, measured the ground, taken the relative elevation, and discussed the subject abundantly. I am not very partial to the spot, but I dread to have the subject again agitated."

On the 18th of the same month, she writes, "Mr. Tyler and Mr. Bowdoin were so much dissatisfied with the selection of site, that it was thought best to call a meeting of the trustees to reconsider the subject. See how one source of solicitude follows quickly on the steps of another!"

Again, on the 31st of July, she writes, "The trustees held a meeting on Thursday;" and adds, "They confirmed the doings of their last meeting respecting the site."

In a letter of September 6, she details other discouragements. She writes, "After the excavations for the cellar and basement story were nearly completed, an apparent defect was discovered in the foundation, and we had great fears that the question of site would be again agitated. The foundation was examined by a gentleman well acquainted with such things, and it was decided to be safe, but better to go back a little. It was removed back twenty-five feet farther from the road. I wish it could have gone much farther back, but this was something I could not control. It is sixty feet from the road, which is very wide, and makes the distance more tolerable. But the same man who decided on the foundation raised a doubt about the bricks which had been purchased, and there was great fear that all must be rejected, and no more could be obtained till they were made next summer. Several days more of suspense succeeded, when the bricks were examined by a superior judge, and pronounced not bad, pretty good."

It might have been as hazardous as Miss Lyon supposed to have the question of site again reconsidered. She feared that the trustees would be divided on the question more and more strongly, and that, unable to see alike, some of them, whom the cause could ill afford to spare, would desert it. But some, who are familiar with the ground, cannot but regret that a more eligible situation had not been chosen from among the beautiful building spots in South Hadley. After the erection of the edifice, Miss Lyon was accustomed to preclude all criticisms on the selection, by taking her visitors to the upper story, and directing their attention to the magnificent views from the southern and western windows.

The corner stone was laid October 3, 1836. On the 7th, Miss Lyon writes from South Hadley to Miss C., "We had a fine day for the laying of the corner stone. I should have enjoyed your being present. It was a day of deep interest. The associations were very tender. That is an affecting spot to me. The stones, and brick, and mortar speak a language which vibrates through my very soul. How much thought and how much feeling have I had on this general subject in years that are past! And I have indeed lived to see the time, when a body of gentlemen have ventured to lay the corner stone of an edifice, which will cost about fifteen thousand dollars, and will be an institution for the education of females. Surely the Lord hath remembered our low estate. This will be an era in female education. The work will not stop with this ins itution. The enterprise may have to struggle through embarrassments for years, but its influence will be felt."

At their meeting in South Hadley, October 3, the trustees added Rev. Dr. Heman Humphrey, and Professor Edward Hitchcock, of Amherst College, to their number.

Miss Lyon writes to Miss Grant from Boston, October 25, 1836, "Some interesting incidents have occurred during the last two weeks. Our enterprise is one of incidents. The good people in Conway have made a handsome subscription for our seminary. Besides, Rev. Melancthon G. Wheeler, their minister, is going to labor for a few weeks, to help us in raising funds. The officers in Amherst College supply his pulpit gratuitously during his absence."

Mr. Wheeler, in those few weeks, did good service for the cause, obtaining in one place, where he had previously been settled, five hundred dollars, and in other places in that vicinity handsome donations.

About this time, Miss Lyon addressed a circular to ladies of her acquaintance, the drift of which will be seen from the following extracts: —

The enterprise of founding this institution was commenced about two years ago. The work has since been going forward slowly. The first edifice is now erecting. It is ninety-four feet by fifty, and of four stories, besides the basement. It will furnish good public accommodations for the school and the family, private chambers for the teachers, and for eighty young ladies. Additions are to be made hereafter, as the liberality of the Christian public shall furnish the means. If there is no delay on account of funds, this first building can be finished, and a school of eighty scholars commenced, the latter part of next summer.

The time has now come when we must make our arrangements

for furniture. For this we must depend principally on ladies. We have no doubt but the call will be promptly met. In all our progress, ladies have been prompt to do all that we have asked. It is true that we have been careful to avoid extending our requests beyond their ability. The first contribution in behalf of this object was made by ladies. The institution had then assumed no name, nor place, nor legal standing. The whole enterprise was less in appearance than a man's hand, when a few ladies came forward, and generously raised one thousand dollars to meet incidental expenses. This was a noble beginning.

Though I have no doubt that all the furniture can be easily made out by ladies, and merely by a written invitation, without the interposition of an agent, yet, to effect it promptly, some regular plan will be necessary. We shall propose to distinct towns, or parishes, the plan of furnishing one chamber each by a united contribution from the ladies. The other parts of the furniture will, we hope, be promptly supplied by other means, perhaps principally by donations from individuals. This plan has been examined and approved by several judicious ladies. Some towns are now ready to commence the work of furnishing a chamber, and the teachers and pupils of one school,* under the care of a lady from the Ipswich Female Seminary, have already given a donation of one hundred and thirty dollars, to be expended in other articles of furniture. Will not other schools, with their teachers, follow this example? and especially those instructed by ladies from the Ipswich Seminary, on whose influence over the community this enterprise has been able to rely with so much confidence? Will not many ladies feel it to be a privilege to make a large donation, to furnish some specific articles of furniture?

But the business of furnishing chambers needs immediate attention. The sum necessary for one chamber will be from fifty to sixty dollars; fifty dollars will furnish the essential articles, though some other conveniences would be very desirable, and might be procured for a few dollars more. This will be left optional with the donors. Let one efficient lady, in almost any place, either alone or with one or two to aid her, commence the work with decision, and perseverance to carry it through, and it will be done; while, in the most flourishing town, it would not be accomplished unless some one lady should undertake the work as her own business. I should advise that the contribution should be very general, embracing a great number of ladies. It may be best to request, that the largest contri-

* Wheaton Female Seminary, at Norton, Massachusetts.

bution should not exceed five dollars. Individuals who are able to do more might give a separate donation in addition, to be appropriated in some other way. Perhaps, in some cases, the bedding and some money might be advanced by some young ladies' sewing society, and the remainder raised by a general contribution from ladies of all ages. The plan of operation must, however, vary according to the circumstances of different towns.

And now, dear madam, would not the ladies in your place consider it a privilege to furnish one of these chambers? Would you not consider it a privilege to bring the subject before them so fairly, that they will do it with promptness?

Among the means essential to the safety of the nation, many are convinced of the necessity of urging into the field a multitude of benevolent, self-denying female teachers. Many of the most candid and discriminating, who have the advantage of observation on this subject, are convinced that all other means without this will be insufficient. Fill the country with ministers, and they could no more conquer the whole land and *secure* their victories, without the aid of many times their number of self-denying female teachers, than the latter could complete the work without the former. But what can be done? Most of the calls which come to New England, and are multiplying every year, must be returned unanswered. The seminary at Ipswich, whose teachers are found in every part of our country, and whose influence has done so much to prepare the way for this enterprise, is compelled even now to return a negative reply to a multitude of calls every year. And the necessities of the country are yet scarcely beginning to be known.

This work of supplying teachers is a great work, and it must be done, or our country is lost, and the world will remain unconverted. If we begin, we must go on; the more we do, the more we must do. The more we attempt to supply, in this particular, the wants of our country, the more its wants will be made manifest. What instrumentality shall ever meet this demand? Why is it, that so much should have been seen, and acknowledged, and felt on this subject, without an attempt to apply the sovereign remedy, which has been so successfully applied to every other want? It has seemed that the church had been fully convinced, that there was but one grand means of meeting any great public demand of the Redeemer's kingdom — a union of disinterested labors and contributions is this grand means. When the church early felt her need of the services of young men, she began to found colleges; and as the demand for their services increased, and became more manifest, she went on founding colleges, till more than eighty have been reared in our country, and more than thirty theological seminaries. But this was found to be not sufficient, and the American Education Society came into existence, and has been going forward with an increasing magnificence and glory, scarcely equalled, except by the importance of its object. All these are so many public voices from the church, calling upon young men, and entreating them to enlist in her service. But what has been the voice of the church to female teachers? Has it not been, "*We need not your services: go on to serve yourselves — to serve the children of this world — to serve the mammon of unrighteousness. We can save our country, and convert the world without your aid.*"

After these remarks, you would expect that I should feel deeply interested in the success of Mount Holyoke Female Seminary. Had I a thousand lives, I could sacrifice them all in suffering and hardship for its sake. Did I possess the greatest fortune, I could readily relinquish it all, and become poor, and more than poor, if its prosperity should demand it. Its grand object is to furnish the greatest possible number of female teachers, of high literary qualifications, and of benevolent, self-denying zeal; and every other good must, if need be, be sacrificed to this great object.

1. The institution is to be only for an older class of young ladies.

2. Every scholar is to board in the establishment. This will give great unity to the plans of the institution, and will greatly facilitate the improvement of those for whom it is designed.

3. In laying out the minutiæ of the plan, great care is taken to furnish points of attraction to those who would gladly become benevolent, self-denying teachers, should the cause of Christ demand it, and points of repulsion to the more inefficient and self-indulgent, and to those whose views and desires are bounded by themselves and their own family circle.

4. This is to be an institution of the highest opportunities for improvement, and of very moderate expense. This is a union not yet found in so high a degree in any large female seminary in the land, and not to be found, except it be the production of disinterested benevolence.

5. The general course of study, and the general character of the instruction, are to be like those at Ipswich.

6. The institution is placed on a firm legal basis. An act of incorporation has been obtained, and the board of trustees consists of the

following gentlemen: Dr. Humphrey, and Professor Hitchcock, of Amherst College; Rev. Mr. Condit, of South Hadley; Rev. Mr. Tyler, and William Bowdoin, Esq., of South Hadley Canal; Rev. Mr. Hawks, (permanent agent;) David Choate, Esq., of Essex; Deacon Andrew W. Porter, of Monson; and Mr. Joseph Avery, of Conway.

7. The institution is to be permanent, continuing onward in its operations from generation to generation. A considerable sum has already been subscribed to this object, and by some hundreds of individuals in more than sixty different towns. How unlike the principle so long acted upon, that Christians are not required to contribute for the building up of any female seminary, unless it be established in their own town! As the number of self-denying friends is continually increasing, the sacred cords of obligation are becoming stronger and stronger.

These are some of the general principles, and this the grand object of the institution. And is it too much for Christians to indulge high hopes of usefulness to the cause of Christ from this institution, founded on such principles, and contemplating such an object, and going forward in improvement, and in increasing usefulness, from generation to generation? May the Lord grant that the high but reasonable hopes of the friends of the Redeemer may be more than realized in coming years. In the many hundreds, if not thousands, of teachers which it will send forth, it will doubtless be an instrument of good, far beyond the present grasp of my feeble comprehension.

But this is not all. This, in my view, is not the most important result of this grand experiment on the benevolence of the Christian community. It has an important bearing on the great subject of adopting suitable means for supplying our country with well-qualified female teachers, and it is testing the great question of duty on this subject. This constitutes its chief importance. It is like the signing of the Declaration of Independence; the battles were still to be fought, but the question of independence was then settled. It is like fitting out our first little band of missionaries. The great work of evangelizing a world was still before the American churches; but the grand question of duty, and the mode of meeting duty, were then settled, never again to be seriously doubted. Let this enterprise be carried through by the prompt liberality of the Christian community, and it will no longer be doubted whether the work of supplying our country with well-qualified female teachers shall be allowed a standing among the benevolent operations of the day. The work will still be before us, but the principle on which it is to be accomplished will be settled. Another stone in the foundation of our great system of benevolent operations, which are destined, in the hand of God, to convert a world, will then be laid. When the last stone in this foundation shall have been laid, we shall only need to go forward and build, to modify and mature, to carry out our principles to their results, till the work is finished. But the foundation stones must all be laid. Every fundamental principle must be settled. They are mutually to sustain and support each other. Take away any one, and all the others will suffer by the loss. And who can tell how much every great effort of the church, during the last thirty years, has been kept back, because it has never been acknowledged, in practice, that the work of supplying our country with a sufficient number of well-qualified female teachers must be accomplished by a voluntary sacrifice of time and money, proportioned to the greatness and importance of the object?

The work of bringing this institution into operation has been longer than was anticipated. But the progress of the enterprise in taking an acknowledged standing among the benevolent operations of the day has exceeded the expectations of its warmest friends. I doubt whether any benevolent object, not excepting even the missionary cause, has ever, within two years from its commencement, made a greater advance in gaining access to the understanding and hearts of the people. How true it is, that Christians have but little faith in any object, till they have made sacrifices for its sake! The eyes of many are now turning towards this new enterprise. Many have rejoiced that so noble a design has been formed in the heart of New England. They have hoped that it may be only the beginning of a great and glorious work of benevolence, which shall in this department meet the demands of the church. Many hearts have been filled with hope, as they have beheld this enterprise commenced and carried forward in obedience to the great command, "Love thy neighbor as thyself."

And now, dear madam, will you allow me to appeal to your benevolence in behalf of this cause? There may be some gentlemen, in the circle of your friends, whose heart the Lord will incline to favor this object, and whose hand the Lord will open in its behalf. If so, you will bear it in remembrance that several circumstances combine to place the institution just now in circumstances of great necessity. I do most earnestly desire that all, who have it in their hearts to do something for this object, may speedily do that which has been put into their hearts. There may be some ladies in your circle of acquaintance, who will feel it to be a privilege to make an uncommon sacrifice for the benefit of this cause, and make out in its behalf a generous donation, either to the principal fund, or to supply some of the more expensive articles of furniture. But the question of furnishing a chamber is one to which a direct reply is particularly requested. It is important that the reply should be DECISIVE, and as early as convenient, so that, in case the answer should be negative, (which, however, I do not expect,) a substitute may be found.

An effort, which had long been contemplated, was made in Boston in March, 1837. Its results are chronicled by Miss Lyon, in a letter to Miss Grant, under date of March 13: "Thursday evening, though it was so rainy, we had a very interesting little meeting in Deacon Safford's parlor. The gentlemen thought there would be no impropriety in admitting three ladies to hear what was said on the subject — Mrs. S., Miss C., and myself. Deacon Safford wished to have us present, and asked the opinion of several gentlemen, who approved of it. Rev. Messrs. Cogswell, Anderson, Blagden, Winslow, Rogers, and Boies, with some fifteen or twenty laymen, were present. Mr. Anderson made some very pertinent and effective remarks, and read a part of your letter in connection with them. At the close of the meeting, a subscription was taken up of a little more than three thousand dollars, which has since been increased to four thousand. The largest subscriptions were, one of one thousand dollars from Deacon Safford, two of five hundred dollars each, and four of two hundred and fifty dollars each, from other individuals.

On the 17th of March, she writes again to Miss Grant, "Dr. Anderson has lent me your letter, and I have read it to several, and all are very much interested in it. It makes a fine impression, and is much suited to benefit the great object. I want leave of you to use it at my discretion, and I will engage to make a good use of it."

We give a part of the letter which Miss Lyon valued so highly, below : —

"IPSWICH, February 23, 1837.

"REVEREND AND DEAR SIR :

"I have just learned that it is still undecided whether any united effort shall be made in Boston in behalf of the Mount Holyoke Female Seminary. I do hope the benevolent men in our metropolis will not dismiss this subject without a careful examination. The question is not, whether the plan of that seminary, in all its minutiæ, is adapted to their taste, or whether it is as good as their united wisdom could devise; but it is whether they will lend a helping hand in building up an institution founded on Christian principles, and designed for the education of female teachers.

"Woman, elevated by the Christian religion, was designed by Providence as the principal educator of our race. From her entrance on womanhood to the end of her life, this is to be her great business. By her influence, not only her female friends, her scholars, and her daughters are to be affected, but also her sons, her brothers, the young men around her, and even the elder men, not excepting her father and his peers. Considering the qualifications which the mothers in our land now possess, is there not a call for special effort from some quarter to render them aid in fitting their daughters to exert such an influence as is needed from this source on our infant republic, on our Christian country? Never before was the call for pious, well-qualified female teachers so urgent and so reiterated from every part of our land. Never before were there so many energetic, talented, benevolent females disposed to qualify themselves to do something towards educating the rising race for the service of the church. How shall the many destitute children in our country be rightly guided without a teacher? How can females teach without being prepared? And how can a sufficient number be prepared without public aid?

"We ask, therefore, for aid, not for the sake of an individual, not for the sake of the female sex, but we ask it for our country, nay, more, for the *world.* We ask it, that our Redeemer may be glorified, in having a more holy seed to worship him on the earth, and a larger and more glorious train to manifest his image, and show forth the wonders of redeeming love to all eternity.

"My soul kindles while I write; but I forbear, for I am exceeding the limits of my strength. For the last twelve days, I have been unable to attend to my school, have been mostly confined to my room, and much of the time to my bed. My failure is caused partly by the late great demands on me to supply female teachers to the destitute, but principally by a series of efforts to sustain an institution, without such means as it would be economy for the Christian public to furnish, and such as I think they would long since have gladly afforded, if the subject, in its bearings, could have been presented to their view. From my present prostration I have a prevailing hope that I may again rise; but I have scarcely the shadow of a doubt that my labors will be curtailed many years in consequence of my increased burden, for the want of what comparatively small funds would have furnished.

"When I shall reluctantly leave that course of toil which, for its results, I have ardently loved, with my dying breath would I plead that the public would immediately do something to rear and uphold Protestant institutions for the education of females."

The trustees, at their first annual meeting, April 12, 1837, elected Deacon Daniel Safford, of Boston, a member of their board.

On the 29th of May, Miss Lyon writes to Miss C., a lady in the seminary at Ipswich, on the subject of raising funds for furniture: "I very much want to see you and others whom I place among the particular friends of Mount Holyoke Female Seminary. We are now in a very great strait about obtaining furniture, &c. If I should visit you, could the whole school devote from one to two hours to the subject? I do not expect that they will contribute any thing to this object while they are members of the school, but only use their influence in its behalf when they go to their various homes.

"I would by all means have the teachers choose their object of benevolence, present its claims to the scholars, and lead them to give abundantly and cheerfully; but I do more and more feel it to be important that young ladies engaged in study, and spending freely on themselves for board and tuition, should give liberally to the treasury of the Lord. This is essential to their cultivating right principles, to their forming right habits. Are not young ladies, as well as young men, while engaged in study, in danger of excusing themselves from contributing liberally, because they are spending their money to prepare themselves for usefulness? By fortifying themselves with this excuse, through their whole course of education, may they not almost form the habit of feeling that every thing of large amount, that is to be cast into the treasury of the Lord by their own hands, must first pass through the channel of self, to fit it for the Master's service? Ought not young ladies, in a course of education, carefully to economize in the least expenditures, lest something which ought to be put into the treasury of the Lord should flow into some other channel? I hope the teachers in Ipswich will be faithful on this subject."

The funds of the seminary needing help, and the treasurer not being able to borrow all that was wanted, Miss Lyon writes to Miss Grant, September 6, 1837, —

"I take my pen to ask of you a very great favor. I want to use five hundred dollars this fall, which is not due me till February; and if I could get it of some personal friend, like yourself, who would not talk about it, it would be a very great relief, besides being a very great accommodation. I do not suppose that you can let me have this as well as not. I suppose it will cost you effort and care, and I regret to add to your labors in your present state of health. But I thought if you knew just how much I needed it, you would prefer that I should ask you."

EXTRACTS FROM A LETTER TO HER MOTHER.

"South Hadley, September 6, 1837.

"My dear Mother:

"I want you should let me hear from you often. Letters sent to this place will find me very soon; indeed, I must be here now most of the time. I have so much letter writing to do, that I seem not to have time for much else. And yet I have five times as much as I can do which I wish to do. But I must do what I can, and let the rest go undone. There is scarcely a mail which does not bring me a letter; yesterday's brought five. Most of them require an answer, and many of them will require two or three before I get through with them. Among all these letters, I should now and then like to receive one from my own dear mother. As for myself, my head is filled with such a variety, that I can write nothing except it is on business. Our building is going on finely. The seal to every thing about it must soon be fixed. My head is full of closets, shelves, cupboards, doors, sinks, tables, &c. You will think this is new work for me, and, indeed, it is.

"Give my love to father. I hope he will have the presence of God, and be prepared for a long and happy eternity, where he will feel no more of his infirmities, and where all can *hear* [Mr. Taylor was deaf] distinctly the song of Moses and the Lamb."

These last two letters, one to Miss Grant and one to her mother, were written precisely three years after the meeting in Miss Lyon's parlor at Ipswich, of which Dr. Packard was chairman, and David Choate, Esq., Secretary, where the first resolves were passed to attempt to found a permanent female seminary of a high order.

These years, as Miss Lyon's letters abundantly show, had been with her years of much and increasing toil. For the cause to which she had given her life she dared do any thing that became a woman, and any thing which she deemed not wrong in the sight of God, that appeared to have any tendency to further her object. She went hither and thither by public conveyances, with Mr. Hawks, or any other friend of the enterprise. Travelling the road from Boston to the Connecticut often, she could scarce ride any ten miles of the route without being recognized by some fellow-traveller, whose cordial salutation would introduce her to the company. All felt very well acquainted with her, as soon as they heard her name, and she would soon be invited to detail the progress of the enterprise. Being infallibly certain that the object would commend itself to the good common sense and best impulses of true New Englanders, she improved every opportunity of unfolding its merits to any who seemed capable of comprehending them, whether acquaintances or strangers. She could make herself heard easily, although the road might be a little uneven, and would expatiate on the subject as freely as in her own parlor. She did not talk louder than many fashionably-dressed boarding-school girls do in public conveyances, the difference being that the latter inform the company of their own personal affairs, while she discussed principles as enduring as the human race, and as vital to human welfare as they are enduring. Many a man can say, "I saw Miss Lyon once; I met her in the stage coach; an original character, quite." One young lady certainly enjoyed her instruction the first year of the school in consequence of such a casual interview of her father with Miss Lyon. The father had penetration enough to discover that she understood female education, and could so train young women in the way they should go, that when they were old they would not depart from it.

Miss Lyon's friends used to be tried at the wandering kind of life she led during these years. It was far more trying to her to lead it than to them to witness it. How contentedly did she stay at home, ever after home was her field of labor! The difficulty with which she was drawn from it, even in a vacation, shows that it was repugnant to her feelings to lead a public life. When her familiar friends undertook to remonstrate with her on the subject, they always found her fully aware that it would be in better taste to sit down in some secluded nook, and from its loopholes watch the movements and success of the agents; but she insisted that it was better to violate taste than not to have the work done. She claimed that the exigency of the case required of her the sacrifice of her personal feelings, because her presence in every part of the field was essential to the prosperity of the enterprise.

Feeling that the cause for which she toiled was the Lord's, she was willing to make herself of no reputation for its advancement. Certain that her feet were on a rock, she stood firm and fearless of sinking. Along with unbounded trust in God, she had a reasonable and intelligent trust in herself; and both combined to help her cling tenaciously to her darling object. So long as what she did was not sinful, she left the consequences entirely to that Providence whose agent she felt herself to be. "What do I that is wrong?" she would say to the friends who expostulated with her on the subject. "I ride in the stage coach or cars without an escort. Other ladies do the same. I visit a family where I have been previously invited, and the minister's wife, or some leading woman, calls the ladies together to see me, and I lay our object before them. Is that wrong? I go with Mr. Hawks, and call on a gentleman of known liberality at his own house, and converse with him about our enterprise. What harm is there in that? If there is no harm in doing these things once, what harm is there in doing them twice, thrice, or a dozen times? My heart is sick, my soul is pained with this empty gentility, this genteel nothingness. I am doing a great work. I cannot come down." Thus she justified her multiplied toils, travels, and sacrifices. Though naturally desirous of human approbation, yet, if she was sure she was right, she could go forward, though her dearest friends thought she was wrong. There were many persons, first and last, who came into her plans for a time, but, unable to see things just as she did, silently withdrew. She saw the hand of the Lord as clearly in their withdrawal as in their enlistment. She often remarked that the right persons were always raised up in every strait, and that it was wonderful how they would fall away when there was nothing more for them to do; doubtless, she added, to teach her not to trust in an arm of flesh; and then, in the next extremity, the Lord would raise up others to fill their places. The truth is, that, happy in expedients, and fertile in combinations, when one door was shut, she could always find another, and though God was truly the mover, she was as truly his instrument.

Those who did not entirely agree with her had too much confidence in her earnest and benevolent intentions to try to thwart her plans. She was, as they thought, and as she very well knew, set in her opinions; but she was set only when sure she was right. She understood the subject better than any gentleman, because she had studied it a hundred times as much. When she differed from any of her coadjutors, the result generally proved that she was in the right. The trustees came, as one of them said, to be afraid to oppose her plans, because they had so much proof that the Lord was with her, and that what she proposed to do he had purposed to prosper.

Her courage never forsook her. "It is," she used to say, "one of the nicest of mental operations to distinguish between what is very difficult and what is utterly impossible." She was gifted with the necessary discrimination. After the question of site for the building had been reconsidered again and again, after the foundations had been reëxamined and removed back twenty-five feet, after the quality of the brick had been questioned and tested anew, and the walls were moving slowly upward, the structure fell to the ground. The workmen were at their breakfast when the disaster occurred. "Then," said the agent, "I did dread to meet Miss Lyon. 'Now,' thought I, 'she will be discouraged.' But as I went towards the scene of confusion, I met her coming towards me, as smiling and cheerful as ever; and when she arrived within speaking distance, she exclaimed, 'How wonderful! no one killed, no one hurt; the men all at their breakfast, not a hair of their heads touched!'"

As has been seen, Miss Lyon herself took charge of obtaining funds and articles for furnishing the house. In addition to crockery and cutlery for about one hundred persons, in addition to parlor furniture and kitchen utensils, forty scholars' rooms were to be provided with bedsteads, beds, bedding, tables, washstands, chairs, and mirrors. Extracts from the letter which she sent to many ladies have already been given. Finding her bodily presence more powerful than her letters, she went to many towns and met the ladies, to inspire them with zeal for the work. When questioned as to the motives from which some gave under her persevering eloquence and prolonged urgency, she would reply, "Get the money," closing her hand, to suit the action to the word, — "get the money; the money will do good."

The summer and fall of 1837 she spent mostly at South Hadley. Rev. Mr. and Mrs. Condit, who lived in the house next north of the seminary, took her into their family as they would a sister. How grateful was she ever to them, and to the Providence that thus inclined them! She fully appreciated and highly valued the uncommon refinement and taste of Mr. Condit, which did not, on his part, prevent him from perceiving her worth through a rather uncourtly exterior. To any playful remark on her energetic movements, he would pleasantly say, pointing to the seminary, "If she were more of a woman, she could not have done all this." In case of any difficult question of duty, as when he was offered a professorship at Amherst, he would say, "I think I shall see the way of duty; Miss Lyon is praying for me." One of her last deeds of grateful love was devising a plan for his widow's comfort, which she did not live to execute.

She slept and ate at Mr. Condit's for several months before she removed into the seminary. Her days were spent in the unfinished edifice, overseeing workmen, and doing many things which needed to be done, much as an efficient lady of moderate means would superintend a house she was building, in the absence of her husband. She looked after the drawers, cupboards, closets, shelves, latches, and hinges, and saw that the church's funds were applied to promote the convenience and welfare of the church's daughters. When the joiner work was done, she made ready for the mason; when the masonry was done, she made ready for the painter; and when the painter had done, she saw to the drying. The workmen might complain of her interference and dictation, but it was little she minded the complaining, if the work was only done to her mind. Deacon Porter could not always be on the ground, and when he was, numberless questions came to her for a solution. She could make up her mind quickly. It did not take her all day to decide whether the floors should be yellow or marble-color, or any other question of like consequence. But it must be confessed that, in these small matters, she often revoked her decisions, for reasons not at first seen, to the annoyance of workmen, who cared only to get to the end of their job.

Though a small thing, it shows the self-control she had attained, that, though in youth, with nothing to do but study, she carried her book to the table, hardly allowing herself time to eat; yet at this period, in the whirl of cares and duties, she never failed to be at table ere Mr. Condit asked the divine benediction, always staid till the table was formally dismissed, and was as punctual at prayers and in retiring as she ever required any of her South Hadley pupils to be.

It was the finishing and furnishing work, above described, which was before her, September 14, 1837, when she addressed the following lines to Miss Grant. The school was to open November 8, about seven weeks after the date of the letter from which the extract is taken.

"I should like to tell you many things. When I look through to November 8, it seems like looking down a precipice of many hundred feet, which I must descend. I can only avoid looking at the bottom, and fix my eye on the nearest stone, till I have safely reached it. I try to take the best possible care of my health. I have had more real sick days with headache and the like, during the last few weeks, than usual; but, on the whole, I am very much sustained by a kind Providence."

SECTION VI.

Striking Adaptation of the Scenes through which Miss Lyon passed, to fit her for the great Work before her.

[ALTHOUGH some of the delineations of character in this section belong more properly to the last part of the work, the compiler is very glad that one who uses so graphic a pen, and who was so familiar, from intimate personal intercourse, with every shade of Miss Lyon's character, has given us these interesting sketches, even at some expense of logical order.]

Events reveal God's decrees, and time unrolls his purposes. Tracing one thing back to another, Miss Lyon's training, from her very birth, seems to have a connection with her great work. The first thirty-five years of her life were a preparation for the rest. That work consisted in discovering and realizing the need of a permanent female seminary, in awakening the Christian community to see and feel that need, in raising the funds necessary to supply it, in planning and erecting the buildings, and in commencing and sustaining operations there, until what was at first matter of experiment became matter of history. To the mind that sees God in every thing, it is interesting to observe the way in which he prepared her by his providence and grace for this work.

The work to be done needed a strong, inventive, earnest, enthusiastic mind. It needed a spirit that could not be looked down by opposition from the honored and the wealthy, nor discouraged by any common obstacles, together with a body able to fulfil the purposes and plans of such a spirit. Miss Lyon had both.

She was descended, as we have seen, from a healthy, long-lived ancestry, and expected herself, with good reason, to live to old age. The physician who attended her in her last illness, and was well acquainted with her, said that she had six times the strength of constitution, both physical and mental, of a common woman. Who that witnessed her watchings, her toils, her endurance, in the prime of her days, will not assent to his opinion? We hear, upon good authority, that when a member of the Sanderson Academy, she was engaged in study twenty hours out of the twenty-four, save the few and hurried intervals in which she took her meals and went to and from her boarding-house to the academy. Yet we hear of no faltering in health, no breaking down from hard study. Her large, strong frame teemed with as strong a life. At twenty-five years of age, her mind ran seemingly without weariness, and appeared as active at night as in the morning. One of her signal victories over herself in after years was breaking up her late study hours, and retiring habitually early. It cost her much resolution, but she always felt that she had her reward.

A sound mind in a sound body was her birthright. But he who breathed into her clay so much more vital fire than he commonly sees fit to bestow upon an individual, next adapted her outward circumstances to its safe keeping. She was not born to ease and affluence. She was not cradled on down. She did not tread on soft carpets, loll on cushioned sofas, ride at first in her basket cradle, and afterwards in a coach. So doing and faring, she might, by middle age, have become so enervated in body and mind as scarce to adventure to set the sole of her foot upon the ground for delicateness and tenderness. Nor was she given to literary parents, who, proud of the prodigy, might have suffered her to rock and read from early morn to dewy eve, and, by the most successful hot-house nurture, might have made her a paragon indeed, but might as likely have opened for her an early grave. She was thrown into a neighborhood where talent and genius were little talked of and slightly valued. The honored parents to whom she was committed, like those of the babe in Bethlehem, were pious, common-sense, self-dependent, hard-working people. They sought first the kingdom of heaven, and all things needful to them and theirs were added with it. In their little and quiet nest, seven mouths opened wide for bread; and the loving parents, day by day, filled them, not with stones nor dainties, but with what they craved — sweet, light bread. What though they wandered around their secluded homestead shoeless in summer, the warm stockings and the strong, thick shoes awaited them in winter. Mary, like the rest, and like the generality of children, was left to her own resources, to look after her own comfort, and provide for her own amusement. Her own genius made her playthings. Summer's sun browned and crimsoned her beautiful skin, the rain and the wind played with her fair hair, the ice, the snow, and the hail were her wonder and her pastime. Her young hands and feet were soon employed in healthful work or errands of love. She went to bed sleepy and rose refreshed.

Multitudes of entertaining books did not cloy her appetite for knowledge. Even the district school was so far from their corner of the world, that she could enjoy its privileges only when her mother was able to make some shift to get her boarded nearer the school-house. The Bible was the first and best book in their family library. From her earliest infancy, her parents had read it, with becoming seriousness, as often as the sun roused them to the duties of a new day. Her mother told her its stories before she could read them for herself. Mary, for want of other books, had read it much, and treasured up its words of wisdom in a singularly tenacious memory. She turned leaf after leaf in another book, that never tires by repetition. Their little brown house, snugly nestled under the hill, (see Sketch, at the end of Part I.,) was surrounded by the wildest scenery. Her young and eager curiosity turned to nature for its refreshment and supplies. The roses, the pinks, and the peonies, the buds, the blossoms, and the fruit, the rocks, the cliffs, the hillocks, and the dells, as she herself tells us, employed her opening mind.

No feeling of degradation ever once rose in young Mary's heart. She was never an object of charity. After her father's death, her mother husbanded their little income so thriftily, that it met their simple wants, and left them their mite for charity. Miss Lyon used to enumerate it among her early mercies that she never knew a servile, cringing fear of those born to better things than herself. Her mother, the sun of their little circle, the admired of all admirers in that retired neighborhood for her goodness and skill, walked a queen among them. Her children knew it. So, while Mary, unfettered by custom and fashion, in her short and scanty robe, ranging from one end of the farm to the other, was manufacturing bone, flesh, and sinew, that could stand the drafts of future days, she yet felt herself as good as the best.

As Mary grew in strength, she was busily and laboriously employed. She knew what it was to labor, working with her own hands. Her far-sighted mother had no drones in that little hive. She worked in the most agreeable of all circumstances, in the society and under the eye of that cheerful, capable, sensible mother. Up with the lark, from sunrise to sunset she went from one sort of work to another, never tired, never unhappy, never discontented. How beautifully she always spoke of woman's sphere of labor! "So much variety, such pleasant work!" she used to say, "so unlike the monotonous task of drawing out the waxed end, or driving the peg all day long."

When, at her second marriage, her mother removed to a new home, Mary remained under the paternal roof, sole mistress and servant in front room and kitchen, doing a hired girl's work for a hired girl's wages, but lending head and heart, as well as hands, to her beloved employer. She was not merely keeping house for a brother; she was educating herself for her future and more important labors. Though not naturally very *handy*, she brought to her work strength, energy, prudence, and perseverance. She always gave her mind to the thing she was doing, whether it were preparing a meal, calculating an eclipse, teaching a child to cipher, listening to a sermon, or writing an essay on female education.

Miss Lyon's perseverance carried her through every thing she undertook. With all her acknowledged inaptitude for mechanical pursuits, she could spin and weave as well as any of her kinswomen of those days. The blue fulled cloth habit, which she wore at Derry and Ipswich in 1827 and 1828, she spun and wove herself. She could make a batch of bread or a tin of biscuit without wasting a dust of flour. She could *clear-starch* as well as any laundress in the land. Gloves and window curtains she could net evenly and cleverly. Whatever her later correspondents may think, she once wrote a very fair and legible hand. There is in the writer's possession a remnant of a muslin neckerchief which she embroidered with her own hands, and it does credit to her needle. She took all the greater pleasure in doing these and the like things because they came hard to her.

Not only in her lowly home did Miss Lyon work willingly, "laying her hand to the spindle," and "taking hold of the distaff," but when she went to school she sometimes paid for her board, in the family where she was received, by assisting about the house. Notwithstanding these hinderances, she learned more than any one else, and her mates loved and respected her just as well as though she had paid her board with money. This circumstance, and the strait which made it necessary, she never forgot. It fitted her the better to understand the limited means and inward longings of her fellow-women. It recurred to her in after life as an argument that her plans were feasible. It contributed to set the current of her great soul towards the middle classes, the respectable, independent yeomanry of the land, too poor to be idle, too rich to accept charity.

It was necessary that a hand should be provided, in due time, to lift her from the vale where she had hitherto been so safely reared. Thomas White, Esq., of Ashfield, kindly and thoughtfully afforded his aid. He was like a father to her, not merely when, at length, her praise filled the churches, but in her early and obscure youth, when it required a discerning eye to see the masterpiece as yet hid in the shapeless marble. The many essential helps, which, as she delighted to acknowledge, he lent her, when she was "creeping her way along" to usefulness, belong rather to his life than to hers, and but few of them can be mentioned here. They were not so very costly to him, but they were above price to her; and, left undone, we cannot see how she could have found her true place in the world's history. He did not dream that he was placing a new star in the firmament, whose rays would gladden thousands along the path to usefulness, or that her name would carry his, like sweet incense, to every quarter of the globe. But he did know that she was a poor girl, with a good mind, the wonder of all her teachers, and that she needed help. He loved to see woman educated, and he freely gave her counsel, sympathy, influence, and often a charming home and more substantial aid. Miss Lyon always chose to bear her own pecuniary burdens, and Mr. White would not probably have thought it the best way of helping her to assume them fully himself. Hundreds of dollars would not have gone so far, in helping her upward ascent, as the steady, cordial, efficient friendship and counsel of such a man. With it came also the gentle and delicious influence of a highly-cultivated, sensible, intelligent lady, the wife of Mr. White, the mother of his favored children. That circle of brothers and sisters will, for Miss Lyon's sake, pardon the giving to the world what she more privately communicated to the writer. Her history would be incomplete without this notice.

It was by the earnest recommendation of Mr. White, that the privileges of Sanderson Academy were offered her gratuitously. It was by his persevering arguments and persuasion, that the person who had charge of the remainder of her patrimony was led to submit the mode of spending it to her own discretion, when she wished to undertake what was regarded as the romantic expedition of going to Byfield to school.

To this sum she added what she had been able to save from the small wages of seventy-five cents or a dollar a week, for teaching in any district where she could find an opportunity, and a few more dollars which she had earned by weaving heavy blue and white coverlets, a kind of work requiring strength equal to that of a man, and therefore commanding more pay than common labor. When, with these added sums, she was able to defray her expenses for a summer at Byfield, there were not, as now, railroads; and the three days' journey was made in Mr. White's carriage, beside a daughter whom he was conveying to school, and his own hands held the reins. As all they knew of the place was its distance from Boston, and what they had learned from advertisements, they missed their road, went miles out of their way, and could find no one who had ever heard of Byfield; and Miss Lyon, with all her courage, took turns with the friend by her side in crying like a child.

It was also by the earnest arguments of Mr. White that she was afterwards employed as an assistant in Sanderson Academy. The principal thought that he, like his predecessors, needed a man to aid him. "Try her," said Mr. White, "and see if she is not sufficient." He tried her, and found her a host.

When she decided to leave Ashfield and go to Derry, he became surety for her, at the stores in Northampton, for over forty dollars' worth of clothing. That green velvet bag, which seemed to the Derry and Ipswich scholars to have a perpetual life, was one of her purchases at Northampton.

As, with her growing success, she not only earned the money to pay her debts, but was able to lay by something for a sick or a rainy day, Mr. White was the father to whom she carried her savings, who husbanded them with care, and turned them over for her with his own, and, without any commission, made her five dollars ten. It is to his careful oversight, as well as to her strict economy, that at her decease the American Board received so considerable a bequest from her savings. His house was a home to her at any and at all times after she went to Byfield. She entered without knocking, and ever met with a hearty welcome. In the midst of her labors, in 1836, she writes to a daughter of the family, "When I am wandering about, it is pleasant and consoling to think that under the roof of your dear home I can have a resting-place when I need." We can almost see her now shaking hands with Mr. White at the door, but intent on the end of her journey, saying, in the same breath with, "How do you all do?" "Could you take me over to Hawley to-night, Mr. White?" "Well, come in, Miss Lyon, and we will see," he would answer. "Your horses in the barn?" she would ask, hardly seeming to heed his remark. "I want to see about some furniture for the new seminary, and I must take the stage back to-morrow morning." The ride to Hawley would be accomplished, the warm supper and best bed awaited her return, and she would depart the next morning with the blessing of her old friends. They reached the end of life's journey but a little before her. The following letter was written to one of the family soon after their death: —

"South Hadley, Dec. 14, 1848.

"My very dear Friend:

"I have received your letter, and should have replied immediately, but I wanted to write a little besides, on mere business. I wanted at least to express a little of that full heart of sympathy which I have had in your behalf. But now a severe headache on the one hand, and a conviction that I must not let another mail pass on the other, will give me but little opportunity. Allow me to say, that in the bereavements through which you have passed, I, too, have felt that I had lost a father and a mother. Who else living has any such claim, comparatively, to a place in my heart? These events have brought fresh to my mind my first acquaintance with your dear family, and the many acts of unfeigned friendship, which I received, as I was creeping my way along toward an humble place in my Master's service. In a very special manner do I remember your father's great parental kindness to me. With what a cheering face would he ask me to come directly to his house from the stage, and depend on him to carry me to see dear mother, just as if he expected it, and in a way to make me feel perfectly at home! Your house has indeed been to me a sweet home! I must go and see that dear home before it is broken up.

"I have many things which I want to say, but cannot with pen and ink. Shortly, I hope, I may see you face to face. If there is any time that I should not find you at home, please write and let me know. I wish I could meet your brother, and his wife also, it would seem so much like meeting a remnant of the family."

Miss Lyon never forgot her old friends. Their names, faces, and kind deeds were treasured in the depths of her capacious soul, and if she did not turn the leaf to read them every day, it was not for lack of love, but of leisure. There was always some one in the circle of her friends in whom her heart rested, with whom she loved to talk over her own affairs, opinions, and feelings, and to whom she confided a thousand little interests, which concerned nobody but herself. Open and frank to all, she was completely transparent to this chosen friend.

Miss Lyon never had a secret that required the veil of night to screen it. In commenting on the passage, "Blessed are the pure in heart," she used to tell her pupils that this characteristic designated such blamelessness of word and deed, that its possessor need not blush to see any thought of hers written, in capital letters, on the white wall back of her, and fronting the whole school. Her own words were conformed to this standard. Her soul was refined and pure. Whatever faults she had lay on the outside. Nothing but pearls and diamonds fell from her lips. In seasons of the most intimate communion, her words were often apples of gold, which one could have wished to preserve in pictures of silver. Among the multitude of friends she left, none can be found who entertain a higher estimate of her worth than the four who successively held the highest place in her affections.

Amanda W. was the first of these favored ones. Miss Lyon used to designate her as "my earliest friend." Their intimacy was both rational and romantic. Miss Lyon often likened it to the love between David and Jonathan. Its commencement, while they were in their teens, and members of the Sanderson Academy, has been described in a letter of the survivor. They studied the same books, and under the guidance of their teacher, Mr. Burritt, they calculated eclipses and made an almanac together. Miss Lyon could learn all the faster by the side of her beloved Amanda. On religious subjects they had full fellowship with one another. They walked to the house of God in company, and while there Miss Lyon loved to steal a glance at her friend, as they listened to the same discourse, and the consciousness that they were both enjoying the same thoughts would double her high pleasure. She had a woman's heart along with a masculine understanding.

There came a time when this love was tested. She was impatient of a rival. But as they pursued their onward course, a home missionary found out where Amanda W. lived. The result can easily be guessed. One was taken, the other left. For a time there was a struggle in Miss Lyon's loving heart; but she soon resigned the first place with a good grace. None but an unmarried lady, similarly situated, can understand the conflict which such an engagement may occasion. Once passed, Miss Lyon rejoiced that her friend was mated to her mind, and was to walk the ways of life with one who truly appreciated her, and who would not fail to give her the place in his family and circle of acquaintance that of right belongs to the wife of an educated man. She was happy in seeing them all in all to one another. When a letter arrived in his well-known hand, she would be as glad for Amanda as Amanda for herself. She often spoke of the eloquent look with which the husband would gaze on her friend after she was legally his. To the few who were privileged with Miss Lyon's most entire confidence, nothing is more wonderful, than that she, who never had husband or children, could so fully and easily sympathize in all the mysteries of wedded and parental love. Though she never added match-making to her multitudinous cares and labors, she always congratulated her friends on making such as suited them. However she may, now and then, have regretted parting with a prominent and efficient fellow-laborer, however she might try, — while the question was under consideration, to prove that the opportunity was a temptation to be shunned, rather than an opening to be entered, — yet, when the matter was once settled, no word of regret ever escaped her lips. She would aid in the necessary preparations, and the lady's own mother would not have felt more pained at a disappointment.

In due time, Miss W. was married. The last farewell was spoken, and the friends separated, each going to her own appointed work. For a time the correspondence was brisk and regular. They whispered one another's names, evening and morning, at the mercy seat, before their common Redeemer. But time kept pressing new duties into the domain of each. Miss Lyon felt the need of a present intimate friend, and made choice of another. She went on adding store to store, and friend to friend, the favor of man to the favor of God. Her life became identified with the history of female education in New England. Her successful labors were an era in its annals. Her early friend had been busy in a different way, and her oldest daughter, grown to woman's size, had found a welcome home in Mount Holyoke Female Seminary. Urged by her aged parents, the mother, once the youthful Amanda, came from the west to visit her native hills. She went first to South Hadley, but as it was anniversary week, there was no room for her in the inn. She asked the landlord to provide her a room in the neighborhood, but he told her he knew of none that was not already engaged. "Do you not know Miss Lyon," said he. "I did know her a good many years ago," she replied. "Well, go right to her," he said; "she will find you a place." The lady hesitated. Her own name was strange in that region of the country. Miss Lyon's was known every where. The young woman whom she had left, twenty years before, unknown and unnoticed, it was the fashion to call the wonder of the age. She hardly expected to be remembered, much less to be known.

She found her way to the seminary, was waited on into the parlor, and word was sent to Miss Lyon that a lady would like to see her. The messenger soon returned, instructed to conduct her to Miss Lyon's private parlor. The climate, the fever and chills peculiar to it, hard work, and spiritual expenditures had altered Mrs. F. She looked service-worn, and really needed labelling. Her old friend, on the contrary, dressed in her best style, and flushed with the excitement of the occasion, was so unchanged in form, feature, complexion, and manner, that Mrs. F. would have known her in the centre of Europe. She held back the rush of her heart, and, after the first civilities had passed, said, in a common tone of voice, and with a calm aspect, "I called to see if I could have a room at the seminary." Miss Lyon was standing. She began to rub one hand over the other, and to balance herself first on one foot and then on the other, in just the style we have all seen her when she was placed in embarrassing circumstances, and to say she was very sorry, but at this time they were full, and asked her if she could not get a room at the public house ; it was a very good house, she believed. "I have been there," replied her friend, "and they sent me to you." Well, Miss Lyon said, really she did not know what could be done, but at the examinations their rooms were all engaged ; she was sorry, very sorry, but they could not receive her. "I don't think you know me, Miss Lyon," was the short and familiar reply. The tone and words were electric. "O, yes, I do know you, Amanda, I do know you! There is room, there is room!" she exclaimed, clasping her to her heart, just as she used to do when they were young together, while the tears streamed down her cheeks, and her struggles of affectionate joy forbade her speaking in sentences of any great length. By crowding scholars together more than before, a good room was provided for the stranger's use ; and while she tarried at the seminary, no attention was omitted that would contribute to her comfort or gratification.

Miss Lyon ever regarded her connection with Mr. Emerson's school as an important era in her life. In conversation with Mr. Hawks, only a short time before her death, she remarked that she owed more to Mr. Emerson than to any other teacher. In teaching, no less than in learning, it is of the greatest consequence to get a right start, and she always felt she first received that from Mr. Emerson. Previous to her enjoying his instruction, the intellect rather than the heart had occupied her attention ; from him she learned to give to each its due proportion. I asked her once about the story of her learning the Latin grammar through in three days. "O," she replied, "It was at one of those schools where they do nothing but *study* and *recite;* not at all so good for the character as Mr. Emerson's. You just learned what was in the book. I traced out the likenesses and differences among the declensions and conjugations, and could commit any thing to memory quick, when I was young; and as to the rules of syntax, they are so much like those in English grammar that it did not take long to learn them. So you see," she said, "it was no great feat after all." She went on to praise Mr. Emerson's school as the one where she treasured up great principles of action, and met with a complete change as to her views on education.

Any one who is curious enough to leave the cars at Lynn, and ride out to Saugus, or at Newburyport, and ride out to Byfield, will find that it was neither peculiar beauties of scenery, elegant edifices, nor superior accommodations, that drew the hundreds of young ladies around that venerated man. Difficult is it to realize that these are the spots where so many young ladies once assembled to garner up thoughts and principles, making a circle blessed with as much sense, vivacity, and intelligence as is gathered in any of our female seminaries of the present day, though that be saying a great deal.

The Memoir of Mr. Emerson, published by Crocker & Brewster, Boston, in 1834, contains a valuable letter of Miss Lyon, in which she takes up his views of female education, and his treatment of ladies. That letter gives a clew to the great success he attained in his efforts to extend and improve female education. While he admitted that, in some respects, woman is the weaker half, he contended that she was made for something better than ornament, show, or household drudgery, and honored her with conversation as sensible and elevated as he bestowed on his fellow-man. In nature and providence his ears were open to the voice of God, calling on woman to be the principal educator of her own sex and of children of both sexes, and his own heart and voice echoed back the heavenly call. He took the high Christian ground, so grateful to the mind of every thinking woman, that she is intended to be neither the slave nor the pet, but the companion, of man, the partner of his thoughts, as well as the assistant in his devotions. All his plans and efforts for female education were founded on this assumption. The wife of his youth, his first and early love, a bright intelligence, was the mate of his understanding as well as of his heart. His second wife, who was also early snatched from his side, possessed splendid talents, a keen relish for literature, and brilliant powers of conversation. If Miss Lyon's remark, that "men judge of the whole sex by their own wives," be just, Mr. Emerson's sentiments on that subject pay an invaluable compliment to all the ladies who were called to sustain to him that endearing relation. Whatever may have been the occasion, Mr. Emerson could perceive and value mental acumen and moral worth in one sex as easily as in the other. In the letter referred to above, Miss Lyon says that he regarded learning without discretion just as Solomon did beauty in the like case. Every female seminary in New England, whose aim it is to train young women to discriminate nicely in ethics, to see the wrong, and yet the right pursue, to discipline their mental faculties, to enrich their minds with varied and practical knowledge, and to render them fit companions in hours of thought and effort, and able help-meets in the emergencies of life, owes much to Mr. Emerson's humble, unpretending, and happy efforts. He turned the attention of ladies at school from the fancy work of the fingers to the great subjects of thought in science and religion. He discussed with them questions in metaphysics, such as had been before mostly shut up for the divine and his theological student. He knew how to draw out the latent thoughts which the possessor was scarce conscious of entertaining. His active mind was constantly throwing out its rich and varied meditations in the form of apt and ingenious questions.

Mr. Emerson had two classes of pupils. The one, sent

by their parents, and too young or immature to appreciate his lectures, yawned, and wondered when he would get through; yet most of them carried away so much of his counsels and instructions as to make them better educators, when they came to be teachers and mothers, than they otherwise would have been.

The other class had lived long enough to know the value of a good education, and deeply to feel their own need of it. When they cheerfully denied themselves luxuries, and made other efforts to aid their brothers in acquiring a liberal education, they could not always refrain from sighing, and saying to themselves, "O, there is no college for girls to go to!" Mr. Emerson's seminary, better than any thing else, met the deep inward wants of this class; and they left their homes, the schools they were teaching, and their other engagements, to enjoy for a term or two his instructions. Some, too deeply involved in business to go themselves, used all their influence, and made every exertion, to give to a younger sister the privileges they felt obliged to forego for themselves.

All the pupils caught more or less of the sentiments of Mr. Emerson, but on the class just described not a word was lost. They profited by every exercise — scientific, moral, and religious. All the scholars felt that their teacher was a good man, living in such nearness to God and to eternity that unseen things were to him substance; while this class emphatically responded to his sentiments, and adopted the great principle on which his daily conduct was based — that of doing the greatest good to the largest number for the longest possible time.

The school at Byfield was superior to any that Miss Lyon had ever attended, in the society of mature and cultivated minds which it afforded; in giving the first place to efforts for enlisting its pupils in the work of blessing the world, and in leading them to adopt principles of faith and action; in making the Bible prominent among its text books, and referring all questions of ethics to its decisions; and in aiming immediately at the conversion of sinners and the edification of Christians. Many there learned the way of salvation, some entering its strait gate under the eye of their heavenly-minded instructor; others treasured up his instructions, and, months or years after they left the seminary, turned their feet into the path pointed out by their beloved teacher.

Mr. Emerson's was the first of a series of schools open and inviting to young ladies who had taught, who expected to teach, or whose age and circumstances indicated that they were soon to enter into active life in situations of responsibility and influence.

Miss Lyon's prodigious powers of mind, her docility, her good will to all about her, and her unclouded temper, made her from the first an object of special interest to her teachers and companions. No pupil of her own was ever more industrious, more yielding, or more respectful. At twenty-four years of age, and after having taught for several seasons, her obedience and submission were as implicit as she ever desired to see in her own scholars. When, at any subsequent period, a self-sufficient pupil endeavored to thwart her plans, she was not compelled to reflect, "This is the way I used to treat my teachers." It is worthy of remark that very generally, and some years with scarce an exception, her scholars were all like herself in this respect, one with her in plans and efforts. Truly, as she meted out love and trust to her teachers, in that summer of 1821, so were love and trust measured out to her for years afterwards. While her instructors took delight in their pupil, and sought to mould her wonderful powers aright, she in gratitude, spoken and unspoken, treasured up every hint, and endeavored to put it in immediate practice. With fear and trembling, uncertain whether she were saint or sinner, she ventured to class herself with those who loved the Lord; and in no knowledge did she grow faster than in that of God and his will. How often have her pupils heard her quote the precepts and sayings of "my beloved teacher, now in heaven," the style in which she always spoke of him after his removal thither!

At Byfield, Miss Lyon became acquainted with Miss Z. P. Grant, a teacher in Mr. Emerson's school. No one person probably had such unlimited sway over her, for any ten years of her adult life, as had Miss Grant for the ten in which they were associated together. Miss Lyon justly attributed very much of the shaping of her aims, plans, and efforts to this companion of her toils and friend of her soul.

It was a part of her providential training that she should be thrown for years under the strong and permanent influence of one who could appreciate her talents, perceive her power, and foresee, to some extent, her future eminence, and who, at the same time, felt solemnly responsible to God to do all that in her lay to render this younger friend more meet for the employment of their common Savior. Justice to the dead will allow no less to be said of the living. Her love and esteem for Miss Grant were undiminished with passing years. Who, of all her Holyoke pupils that heard her, can ever forget the unaffected glow with which she would announce to them, that her particular friend, Miss Grant, of whom they had often heard her speak, had come to make her a little visit! and how her face would shine, as, smiling through her tears of joy, she would tell them that she wanted they should all avail themselves of the opportunity to go to the parlor and be introduced to her!

May the writer, as the friend and pupil of both, be allowed to ask, who, with more unmixed delight than Miss Grant, witnessed the increase of Miss Lyon's power, her growing influence and fame? It gave her only joy to see her younger and healthier friend, whom God had called to build the temple which it had been in her own heart to build, increase, while she felt that she herself must decrease. With admiration, she saw her grow in favor with God and man. It was with reverence, as she met her from year to year, in South Hadley or Newburyport, that she saw her becoming more and more assimilated in moral loveliness to the blessed God. She could not entirely forget that, in those years in which they had daily intercourse with one another, she had assisted Miss Lyon to walk more firmly in the ways of piety, and to grasp closer the Savior's hand. Yet she loved, in her turn, to open her own heart to her friend, to stimulate herself by learning, that she, who once doubted whether she loved Jesus at all, now felt herself as truly and as surely accepted of him as she had ever felt herself accepted of an earthly friend. How precious to Mrs. B., in their late interviews, to hear her dwell almost with ecstasy on the name and perfections of the blessed Immanuel, and to see how entirely the fibres of her soul seemed interwoven with the interests of his kingdom and the glories of his character!

Who mourns more truly her own loss? Who sympathizes more deeply in the joy of the happy saint than this beloved associate of her early years? Late, but sure, may she have a seat by her side, and renew those sensible communings which are now for a season interrupted.

Miss Lyon's school at Buckland, which was truly the germ of the Mount Holyoke Female Seminary, was composed mainly, as has been seen, of young women who had been trained to wait on themselves, to consider the mind more than raiment, and education better than the most palatable dainties. Equally removed from luxurious effeminacy and abject dependence, neither fearing the rich nor despising the poor, they sought to turn their time and means to the best account, to make the most they could of themselves for the high purposes of usefulness and duty. Their minds and hearts were open to receive the great truths and principles which Miss Lyon revelled in presenting, and, as it were, infusing into the minds of others. Becoming acceptable teachers in that part of the state, they made Miss Lyon known as a capable, efficient, and benevolent woman, untiring in her efforts to benefit the young. "O," said Miss Lyon, in after years, "how I used to enjoy my labors in the western part of the state! and how hard it was to me to break away from that beloved spot! I used to wish I could find some retreat in the woods where I could gather all the young women, and explain to them the great principles of benevolence, and set them to doing good." What she was able to do, only revealed the more fully what remained to be done. She often quoted a remark of Dr. Lyman Beecher's, "The wear and tear of what I cannot do is a great deal more than the wear and tear of what I do." Of the few, comparatively, for whom she labored there, she lived to see some eminently useful. Their history would exhibit the fruit of Miss Lyon's labors, fruit "whose seed is in itself," thus yielding its hundred fold.

One of those pupils may be referred to as a specimen. For six successive winters she was under Miss Lyon's care. With her she studied arithmetic and grammar, geography and history, astronomy and chemistry. With Miss Lyon, too, she studied the Bible, and, under its light and guidance, sought first the kingdom of heaven and its righteousness; and from this early choice she has never wavered. Her mother had trained her to habits of courtesy, self-denial, and patient labor. There was but little in her external life to alter, when she subscribed herself the Lord's. Her habits are all unobtrusive. Her spirit preferred, and prefers, retirement. But she learned from her teacher that the business of her ransomed spirit, while it is permitted to tabernacle in clay, should be to make this world the better for her presence in it. Who, save the pupils themselves, can ever know the impressive manner in which Miss Lyon could say, "O young ladies, as they bear your body to its resting-place, may all who have known vou be able to say, 'She hath done what she could!'" Thus educated, and thus impressed, this beloved pupil of Miss Lyon, some sixteen years ago, left her father's rural home, closed behind her that pleasant chamber, so comfortably and neatly furnished, bade farewell to the superior privileges of New England society, and took up her abode in a western territory. Miss Lyon's blessing went with her, and the blessing of many has fallen upon her since. She became an inmate in the house of a married sister, who, as to the good things of this life, was far differently situated from their parents in the old country. In a small room of their small house, she opened a school for any who wanted instruction. Fifteen timidly came in. She took them, such as they were, French, Dutch, and Yankees, taught them what they most needed to know, spent time, energy and pains upon them, as though they had been princes, and she were to be richly remunerated for her labors. Plain in her person, and simple in her manners, almost as much out of sight as moles or miners, she labored to do good to those fifteen youthful minds. Others soon came in. The private dwelling becoming too strait for the school, the next year a house was built for its accommodation. The number of pupils often exceeds one hundred. Very many of the younger people of that region have been under her instruction. Her youngest scholars are children unable to speak plain; her oldest, in the winter, are often masters and sailors of the vessels that ply on the lakes in summer, and these are among her most docile, studious, and agreeable pupils. On the Sabbath, when there is preaching in the school-house, it is her business to keep her little scholars in due order. When they are not favored with preaching, as well as when they are, the Sabbath school is held in this same school-house, in which, besides being the superintendent, she has charge of a class of twenty of the younger scholars. Every one in that part of the state — for it is no longer a territory — knows her, loves her, and reverences her.

The man who represents the town in which she lives, in the state legislature, at this very writing, was for ten years her pupil. Perhaps Miss Lyon herself, in the same situation, could hardly have been more useful than this lady. A number of her schoolmates at Buckland and Ashfield have been called to labor among the heathen in lands beyond the seas; and though they may be more conspicuous, they are not more self-denying, more patient, or more Christ-like. Her vacations are short. The one room of her narrow schoolhouse is her dwelling for the most of her waking hours. When she can stand the additional labor, she opens it for an evening school in grammar, spelling, and the like, and among her pupils come parents as well as children. Some from the old countries have learned at this evening school to read, write, and cipher. She has always on hand stockings to knit, or garments to make for the orphans and the destitute among her varied flock. While she is doing much service for her Master, chills and fever, toil and time, are bringing her nearer every week to his glorious face. A few more years, and her humble soul, laying aside its weary, aching, and way-worn tenement, shall pass the portals of heaven, and enter on its promised rest. What a happiness to Miss Lyon, as she looks from her Father's presence, from the heights of heaven, on this distant ball, the scene of her earthly labors, to behold not one, but many such streams of influence, destined to deepen and widen as long as earth and time shall endure! She has had many equals in disciplining minds and imparting information; she has had few in training characters for usefulness and happiness. The durable impression for good that has been made on the multitude of living minds brought under her control; the intellect unrolled in her presence, on which, by God's grace, Holiness to the Lord has been inscribed in deathless letters; the hearts of immortals, starting on an unending existence, which have been swayed aright; the souls which, under the influence of her fervid eloquence, have been kindled with zeal to go and do likewise; — the greatest of her privileges is to have been a co-worker with God in bringing about such results; this, and nothing less, is the imperishable work of her life. Its fruits must meet her, not only when she glances from heaven to earth, but at every turn of her walks in paradise. The brick walls, the library, the apparatus at South Hadley, nay, even the cheapening of education to the daughters of our country, were but the external conditions to this work, and valuable only as they conduced to its accomplishment.

It was the good spirit and happy efforts of her pupils at Buckland and Ashfield that recommended Miss Lyon's enterprise to the sensible, industrious, independent citizens of that part of the state. It was at a comparatively early period in its history, that such men as Mr. David Mack, of Middlefield, and Mr. Roger Leavitt, of Heath, put their shoulders to the wheel. They were both, at that time, old men. Miss Lyon went to see them, and laid her plans before them. Recollecting how much they had seen her accomplish in her winter school, they had faith in her ability as well as in her benevolence. Mr. Mack subscribed five hundred dollars. Colonel Leavitt, a well-known friend to emancipation, inquired whether she would receive colored young women into the school, and seemed at first unwilling to contribute, unless she would pledge herself to do so. They discussed the subject some time. She said that it was a matter for the trustees rather than herself to act upon, but for her own part she would have no objection, provided the young women should be qualified according to the requirements for other pupils, and she presumed the trustees would have none. He subscribed according to his ability without any more definite pledge.

For the first year, the school was a very difficult one. The building was hardly finished when it commenced; the furniture was not all procured; one plan was continually interfering with another. Many of the students, who, under her guidance, carried the institution safely through that most trying season, were from the hills westward of the seminary. Those beloved names, from whatever quarter they came, how many of them are now, as then and ever since, working women, serving their day and generation, wishing no reward but that best one of all, a peaceful conscience and an approving God!

What her Buckland school did for Miss Lyon in the western, the Ipswich Female Seminary did for her cause in the eastern and central parts of Massachusetts.

The numbers of gifted and mature minds which went forth from the bosom of that seminary, year by year, scattering blessings in their track, bore its influence far and wide, and made the school known as a place of rare intellectual training, but more especially as a place where character was formed on practical, common-sense principles. It sent forth good scholars; but its crowning excellence was, that it sent forth good characters.

Many young ladies, from families in easy circumstances, went there for one, two, or three years, as they could gain the consent of their parents, to improve and extend their education. Their fathers denied themselves the pleasure of their presence and society, and furnished them the opportunity of enriching their minds, that they might the more satisfactorily and honorably meet the duties of life. The daughters left home, perhaps, with no further view than to increase their own mental resources, to acquire riches that moth cannot corrupt, nor thieves take away, nor ennui approach, and to increase their power to bless the circles in which, as members of families, they were or might be cast. The training of minds to honor, glory, and immortality, the only profession open to woman, was set before them till their souls glowed with zeal to enter on the work. "Do not think of filthy lucre and immortal minds together," Miss Lyon would say. "Teach, as Christ taught, to do good. Dollars and cents can never pay the faithful minister, nor the faithful teacher. The field is all white, and whoever has a willing heart may sharpen her sickle and help gather in the harvest." The young women, touched by pictures delineating the want of cultivated and able teachers, and by appeals to their natural desire to be doing something of some account, and to their benevolence, would return to the lovely firesides they had left, better fitted to adorn and cheer the groups around them. But some of them would ask to go forth to educate others. Fathers, with trembling lips, would ask, "Why do you want to go away? Is not your father's house a pleasant home to you? Is there any thing you want that you do not have? Why do you wish to leave us?" The daughter pleaded that a younger sister would be company, eyes and feet for her parents; that *she* could be spared, and not much missed; that, in some other spot, she might minister to the wants of young minds; and by such considerations would win the father's consent to her departure. Filial and affectionate though she were, she would seek and find a circle of immortal minds to whom she could transfer the impressions she had herself received at Ipswich, and at the same time deepen them on her own mind.

Miss Lyon considered her pupils intrusted to her by God, on purpose that she might excite this very spirit in them. The love of employment, of bringing something to pass, as natural to young women as to young men, she would awake and draw forth in behalf of the poor, the benighted, and the ignorant. "Do not say you would like to take a few music scholars," she would say, "or to assist in an academy; but remember Christ was the Friend of sinners. Labor for the degraded. Take hold where no one else will." She used to tell her scholars at South Hadley, that she hardly considered a lady educated until she had some experience in teaching children. She once said to an assistant, who had only taught in schools of young ladies, that "it was a defect in her education as a teacher, that she lacked experience in teaching children." "Begin at the lowest round of the ladder," she would say to candidates for teaching, "and if you hear a voice, saying, 'Come up higher,' then ascend cheerfully, but not exultingly."

There was another large class in the school at Ipswich, the bone and sinew of the institution, whose means were limited, and who were more or less dependent on their own resources. By various expedients they had raised the means to defray their expenses. The money they brought was sometimes the bequest of a mother, or their portion of a deceased father's estate, eked out by industry and economy; or it was the loan of a brother, an uncle, or a friend, who was willing to trust the young woman, and run the risk of her refunding it by her subsequent earnings. In some cases, the daughter took the dowry intended for her at her marriage, or anticipated the division of the homestead, with the understanding that what she received was to be accounted for in the future and final settlement. Not what were their circumstances, and who were their fathers, but what they were themselves, and what they could be made, were the questions asked in reference to all these pupils, by the teachers. With them, goodness was the first thing, industry and application the second, and talent the third.

Misses Grant and Lyon did not always know the straitened circumstances of their pupils. A few days since, the wife of a prosperous manufacturer spoke of them with filial regard. She said, "I went to school to them at Derry one quarter. I earned the money with my needle to pay my tuition, and fit up my clothing. This man," pointing to her husband, "paid my board, and it was quite a bill for him to pay then. My mother was a widow, and unable to help me. I never missed answering a question in any lesson while I was there. It was there, too, that, as I hope, I met with that great change in my affections which altered my whole destiny. I have often told my husband, that for worlds I would not have those few months blotted out of my history. I could go but one term. I could not, then, bring myself to tell them the reason, and I have never met either of them since."

Though this lady did not feel like opening her heart on this subject to her teachers, many others felt no such restraint. Both Miss Grant and Miss Lyon have frequently loaned to irresponsible young women the money to defray their expenses at Ipswich, and in almost all cases payment has been honorably and faithfully made. How few could they aid, compared with the number who needed help! Miss Lyon had known many, in the ten years of her connection with Miss Grant, who, by the slow gains of patient industry, had earned in a district school, in a millinery shop, in making dresses, or even in tending looms and jennies, the means to place themselves under her instruction. She had found such often apt to learn, and capable of large thoughts and high aims. She had seen how much they needed more time at school to make them useful to the extent of their abilities. When poverty of means and wealth of soul were united, her sympathy was strongly moved. To her was given wisdom to devise and strength to execute a plan for meeting the wants, not of here and there one, but of a multitude who come, who are coming, and still will come to the seminary of her founding. Her acquaintance with such young women was a most material circumstance in stirring up her fertile mind to the plans and efforts which resulted in the Mount Holyoke Female Seminary. This class of scholars contributed largely to making the Ipswich school a glory to Massachusetts, and others like them in character have done a like service to Miss Lyon's institution. Their unobtrusive influence has been worth uncounted gold. Let that class be taken away, and all the teachers in New England cannot keep the school in its past and present position.

If the Holyoke Seminary were merely a place where intellect was to be sharpened, and information gained, we might not care much for its existence. Whenever it becomes merely, or chiefly, the arena for mere mental struggles; when the mind comes to be disciplined there at the expense of the heart; when ambition supplants the love of doing good, and the moral powers are thrown into the back ground,—should that time ever come, the Mount Holyoke Female Seminary can be spared from the world. We need disciplined mind, if we can have it on the side of Christ. We want our susceptibilities enlarged and increased, if it may be for usefulness and happiness here and in heaven; but we care not to render them the more acute and sensitive for uselessness and woe here and hereafter. We want our leading women to be Christian women, strong in principles, efficient in duty, and then the more of solid acquisition and elegant accomplishment the better. So long as that school shall be true to the principles of her who was for more than eleven years its life, so long will it bless the church and the world.

Those pupils of the Ipswich Female Seminary who have now been described, wherever they were, met the plans of Miss Lyon with faith, hope, and corresponding effort. One from the far south, whither she had gone to teach, and where she had married, contributed one hundred of the first thousand dollars. As the standing representatives of the institution Miss Lyon declared it her aim to stereotype, they disposed the community to favor her projects and lend her pecuniary aid. This they did in common with every woman who had been made wiser and better by her connection with the school in question.

There was another large class, in the seminary at Ipswich, who had been allowed to have their own way, to be waited on by mothers and grandmothers, till, even in their youth, the grasshopper had become a burden, and the questions, "What shall we eat? what shall we drink? and wherewithal shall we be clothed?" were the all-absorbing topics of their daily lives. Some such were waked from the lethargy into which they had been rocked, to see where they stood, to lay hold on the work of self-reform, and to endeavor to regain, as well as they could, the ground they had lost. Many such are now adorning the spheres in which they move far better than they would have done, had they never breathed the genial influences which surrounded them, while they were at Derry or at Ipswich. Yet habits are often stronger than principles, and some, who saw the right and adopted it in theory, whose sentiments were all in favor of self-denial and efficient labor, have unconsciously lost ground, and feel condemned when they lay their past purposes and their actual and present lives side by side. The love of dress and show, which they once fancied slain, has shown its head too often since. They have catered to appetite, and given themselves up to pleasures that perish in the using, till one who hears their conversation from day to day is tempted to ask how they can expect to be happy in a kingdom which consists not in meats and drinks, and where they neither marry nor are given in marriage. Little by little, under one pretext or another, they have given up the self-denials which, in the zeal of youth, were resolutely undertaken. Though they are less vain, frivolous, and sensual than they would have been without their early impulses, resolves, attempts, and conquests, they are still far from where they hoped, fifteen or twenty years ago, to find themselves at this stage of life. They cannot spend their lives in embroidering fire-screens and slippers, making bedquilts out of a thousand pieces, ruffling and trimming their children's dresses, without feeling a little uneasy, and recollecting that the work in hand is not the chief end for which life was given to a thinking woman. One of this class may sometimes be found floating along with the gay and butterfly multitude, apparently unconscious that she has not a whole eternity before her for decking and feeding her frail and failing tabernacle, discoursing of nothing beyond the changing fashions and the passing events of the day. Yet now and then, all unwelcome, must come a reminiscence, even to such, of school days, as if but yesterday, and plant a thorn in her bed of flowers. None of them can entirely forget the patterns shown them in those favored hours, nor the lofty views they once entertained. An inward dissatisfaction mars half their apparent pleasures.

There are many to whom that school was the school of Christ, who intelligently gave themselves away to do his will, and have never looked back; who, with energy and grace equal to the conflict, have gone on conquering and to conquer, and have fewer struggles now than formerly, because they are approaching the heavenly rest. They are overcoming; the white stone, destined for those who run well to the end, begins to be in sight. Unfailing virtue, a perfect love to God, that cannot be drawn aside, is in full view as their prize and reward. Some have already reached the goal and received their crowns. I see a shining band around their dear departed earthly leader on yonder heavenly plains. They are a group of her own disciples, whom she led in the way to heaven. They met her freed spirit at the pearly gate. They hail her welcome to their celestial home. They lead her to the great white throne, and stand around her with affectionate gaze, as she mutely wonders at Him who sits thereon. Anon, I see her raise her hands, and hear her exclaim, in the pleasant voice of olden days, "O! O! such glory! This is indeed more than I ever conceived!" and in fuller, richer strains than any of the group, cry, "Glory to Him that sitteth on the throne, and to the Lamb forever and forevermore!"

Whatever may have been the means, it seems to have been a part of God's plan that Miss Lyon should remain unmarried, on purpose that she might give herself wholly to her work. She looked well, often very well, always bright and intellectual, and often conversed handsomely. There was a freshness and an originality in her thoughts, sure to interest persons of sense. That dependence, so aptly likened to the clinging ivy, was perhaps incompatible with her force of character and physical strength. It was not often that a hiding of her power beneath a soft and subdued womanliness made her so much the more engaging. She was careful to rise up before the hoary head, and honor the face of the old man, to pay to every one the respect due his age, character, or station. At the same time, she made the impression on every one with whom she had any thing to do, from the common day laborer to the president of a college, that if she had set herself to do any thing, it was of no use to oppose her. It is not strange that, with this wonderful energy, the graces peculiarly feminine were with her the result of careful recollection. Though many a gentleman would go to such a woman for counsel or aid, would confide in her judgment, or forward her plans, it is no reflection upon her to remark that few comparatively would be drawn within love's silken meshes.

On the other hand, Miss Lyon was not so ignorant of herself as not to know her own comparative superiority. This idea occupied no more room in her capacious mind, engrossed no more of her attention, than the other just alluded to, that she had no great power of fascination. Both ideas were equally familiar to her, and while the one gave her no particular pain, the other gave her no peculiar pleasure. But she would never have sold herself for nought. She could not have looked confidingly up to an ordinary man, and she had too true a sense of propriety to look condescendingly down upon a husband. In her early youth, before she went to Byfield, it was only now and then that a mind to match her own crossed her path; but after that period, she certainly met with many sensible and educated men. When she made up her mind not to be married, she was more than thirty years old. She made it up deliberately, in view of her comparative usefulness in wedded life and in teaching. The occasion of her decision was a tempting offer of matrimony, which she thought held out as good a prospect of a life of love and happiness as any she could expect. When she had once fully decided on giving her undivided labors to the advancement of female education, it was fixed beyond reconsideration. The answer to any letter of a particular character thereafter was quickly despatched. If the bishop of all the churches had thrown an apple of gold in her path, she would not have stopped in her race to pick it up. But between the day in which she sold the *et ceteras* towards beginning housekeeping which she had collected, like her sisters before her, and the day in which she made up her mind to give herself wholly to the work of female education, there was time enough for her to have been sought and won by any person who could have commanded her respect and love. A warm heart beat in that broad chest, which, once appropriated, she would never have wished to recall. She was without ambition to be known; and, settled for life, she would have moved along in an even, lovely course, like her noble mother before her. Her life might have been many years longer here below, but the Holyoke Seminary would be among the things yet to come. Whatever were the means or the occasion, we cannot but see a providence in the fact that she did not become encumbered with domestic cares, but remained heart-whole for the work of her life.

Miss Lyon was a living witness to the great truth she often uttered in the ears of her pupils, that "mind, wherever it is found, will secure respect." She won the esteem, respect, and love of the high and the low, the rich and the poor.

She never felt any pride on account of her elevation; she never lost her sympathy with persons in humble life. Her sympathy with the middle ranks of society was the main-spring of her last great efforts. She desired, as has been seen, to see females of limited means furnished with facilities for mental and moral improvement. She sought to build up a school where the pupils should be of sufficient maturity to take in great and ennobling views of God and human life, but not so old that she might not hope to see them impelled by new and higher motives, take new aims, and set their faces resolutely towards the true and the good. The leading characters in all our religious and benevolent enterprises, the controlling minds which preside in all the distinguished posts of usefulness, are, she was accustomed to say, neither from the wealthy classes nor from the wretchedly poor, but from the substantial yeomanry of the land. "Influence exerted on that class," said she, "tells every where. Educate the women, and the men will be educated. New England influence is vastly greater than its comparative size and population would indicate. It is the cradle of thought. New England mind carries the day every where, and the great business is to get the New England conscience enlightened and accurate." She would not meddle with politics. But she said, "Let the ladies all understand the great doctrine of seeking the greatest good, of loving their neighbor as themselves, let them indoctrinate the children, their sons, in this fundamental truth, and we shall have wise legislators."

She used to say that it takes as much mind and character to descend as to rise with dignity. The weak, uneducated woman, who happens, as the wheel of fortune turns round, to be on the upper side, is so elated as to be spoiled, and the same character, when the wheel descends, is unreasonably depressed; while the woman of mind, of fixed principles, of good education, appears the same under all reverses;

never foolishly elated, nor miserably depressed. One great reason why she would have the ladies of our republican country educated was, that they might have ballast amidst the fluctuations of life. She said all this as if she herself stood apart, a spectator of society; and such, to some extent, she was. She never sought the patronage, society, favor, or notice of the gentry. "We are on the top wave of popularity, just now," she would sometimes say of her school, just as she would say, "They live in a great house, and have plenty of money, but they are little bits of folks. You understand what I mean; they think they must have their say in every thing." Such people's neglect could not hurt her. The rich were to her no more than the poor, save as she could unclasp their purses and obtain their money for benevolent ends. She extracted money from the rich, and influence from the clergy. She never sought patronage, but laughed at the word, and said it was the teacher who did the pupils and their parents a favor, and not they the teacher. Intelligence, capacity, and goodness were the articles she put in her inventory of valuables. The parade of wealth, the glitter of pageantry, could create no illusion for her eyes. They were to her but the rattles and the trinkets of babyhood. She looked at the things which were enduring. The boast of family was but a waste of breath in her ears. She knew no satisfaction in ancestry beyond the remembrance of their piety. Her own ancestors, as far as she could trace them, had, she said, been pious, and she used to say that she thought they might have been so back to the time of Christ. She made no war on the factitious distinctions of society. A school and a church, she said, knew no such distinctions. Women, it is often said, rise with more difficulty than men. She never felt any such difficulty. She never sought to rise, but only sought to do good. She had no jealousy of her sex. She valued herself at her true worth, and took it for granted that every body else did. Her life was a beautiful illustration of the great truth that persons rise to eminence not by seeking distinction, but by seeking a worthy end.

Another item in Miss Lyon's adaptedness to her work was her constitutional indifference to such things, in her personal appearance, as dress, and what, in common parlance, is called gentility. She was not schooled to observe " nice customs." Her mother took all pains, by example and precept, to give her that adorning which is incorruptible, and which is of great price in the sight of God; which money cannot buy, nor artificial rules confer; and she succeeded. Her beloved daughter wore ever, where all who approached her could see it, the ornament of a guileless, pure, humble, enlightened, and intensely benevolent spirit. The mother taught her to be honest, to be kind, to shun every thing mean and wicked; but she did not take so much pains to drill her in the most approved mode of standing, sitting, walking, eating, and dressing. These she left to Nature, who does not always teach according to conventional rules and forms. Her friends can afford to admit that she did not excel in the graces of the drawing-room. In her early and susceptible years, her attention was not turned to her appearance. The getting a thing done so engrossed her thoughts, that none were left for the manner in which it should be done. Perhaps no training could have educated her to live to be dressed and fed. Clothing and food were means, not ends, in her nomenclature, and it does not seem as though all the powers and principalities beneath the skies could have wrought her into a worshipper of the toilet. She was born to a different destiny. There seemed wanting, what teachers cannot give, a natural bias to that branch of study. Dress could not get between her and the sun. She did not feel above attending to it. On the contrary, she considered it a duty to dress conformably to her station. She had not so much instinctive perception of what is tasteful in outward adorning as many ladies possess and exercise. If she was sometimes seen in the drawing-room when every hair did not know its place, and some article of her apparel would not bear the closest scrutiny, she was never guilty of that far greater offence against a classical taste, of being over-dressed. She had a correct theory. With Hannah More, she held that the perfection of the art is so to dress that no one will recollect, two minutes afterwards, any thing that you had on. She sought simplicity, neatness, correspondence. She often told her scholars that dress should answer to the age, employment, health, and position of the wearer, and to the season, the weather, and the occasion. It cannot be denied but that she sometimes fell short of her theory. Nature would get the better of rules. She had to study a question in dress as closely as most ladies would one in political economy, which she, in her turn, would grasp almost intuitively; and if she sometimes made mistakes in her lessons, it was no more than they do in theirs. It was the greatest drudgery of her life to attend to it. It was that which gave her most frequent occasion to exercise self-denial, and to improve in the grace of patience. Perhaps she needed a mistress of the robes as much as Victoria, because weightier affairs pressed such things out of her notice. No gift from a friend or pupil was more acceptable to her than a pretty cap or collar. In any thing pertaining to school, she seldom asked counsel till she had made up her own mind, and then what she wanted was approbation; but in matters of the toilet she was grateful for advice. When she stood before the glass, her thoughts were at the world's end, or above it. Her room-mate in 1834 says she well remembers her standing before the mirror in their room, adjusting her bonnet strings, and saying at the same time, in an impressive manner, "Well, I *may* fail of heaven, but I shall be very much disappointed if I do;" and then slowly and emphatically repeating, "very much disappointed." We have as little reason to complain of inattention in our dull scholars, as the dress-makers sometimes had who worked for her. "You must find mind as well as fingers," she would say; "I expect you to do the contriving as well as bring the patterns."

It is matter of gratitude that the shade of a color, the form of a hat, the texture of a shawl, the fit of a glove, or the adjustment of a lock of hair, did not assume an aspect of such supreme importance in her eyes, as they seem to do in those of many a Christian lady. Else how could she have found time and mind for the magnificent structures she has bequeathed to her sex and her country? When I think of her early indifference to this subject, her deep-seated aversion to wasting one minute on gratifications that perish in the using; of her great soul, seemingly unconscious of a body, save as it was crowded for want of room; of the multiplicity of her cares, the magnitude of her conceptions, the work she brought to pass, and all the good in which she had a hand,—I wonder, not that, now and then, her outward robes fell short of conventional elegance, but that she did, so much of the time, reach her own true ideal. Had she been fastidiously nice in matters of dress and etiquette, had she stopped to measure every step, and to estimate the force of voice she should give to every word, and to consider what people might think or say about the particular way in which she moved her feet or her arms, she could never have borne the heat and burden of the day through those memorable years from September 6, 1834, to November 8, 1837. Blessed saint! that body, so long thy patient care, wrapped in its snowy shroud, lies peacefully in its quiet resting-place. The shining vestments which thy free spirit wears infinitely more than meet thine own ideal, and they shall never be soiled, never wear out, nor ever tire on the vision of thy sister spirits.

PART III.

THE VICTORY GAINED AND SECURED.

SECTION I.

The first Year of the new Seminary.

WE have now followed Miss Lyon through the first forty years of her life, during the first twenty-four of which, at home, or near home, she was the diligent scholar and the obedient daughter; trying her hand, also, sometimes as teacher. Next we have seen her abroad most of the time as a teacher for thirteen years. Afterwards, we have watched her with deep interest, as she went through the arduous struggle of founding the Mount Holyoke Female Seminary. In the autumn of 1837, its walls had been erected, and its rooms were ready to receive eighty pupils. The means were now in her hands of making the grand experiment towards which she had so long looked forward with intense interest. Though she had gone forth alone, with a simple sling and stone, to meet not one, but many giants, their headless trunks all now lay at her feet; and well might she have raised the shout of victory. But, though thankful to God that he had at last given her a place where she could firmly plant her feet, little thought she of exultation while so much remained to be done, while the great experiment remained untried, and especially while so many of the most judicious and benevolent Christians had little or no confidence in its success. Such was the fact, and she knew it. The evidence had met her so often in her efforts to obtain influence and subscriptions, that it would have paralyzed the exertions of one whose faith had not been almost equal to vision. But now the matter was to be put to the trial, to decide who was right. And she took hold of the work with all her powers of body and mind.

Although our readers have probably a tolerably good idea of the plan of the new seminary, from the descriptions already given of the schools at Buckland, Derry, and Ipswich, as well as from several circulars, yet it is desirable to give a brief account of the character and condition of the whole enterprise when the school was first opened, in the autumn of 1837.

The Buildings.

The annexed drawing gives a clear idea of the edifice, as seen from the south-west, Mount Holyoke being seen at a distance on the left. The main building is ninety-four feet by fifty, five stories high, though the lower one is partially below the ground in front, but not in the rear, as the surface here slopes easterly. The basement story is devoted to a large domestic hall and a large dining hall, with six smaller rooms. The second story has a large hall for school exercises, forty-eight by sixty feet, a library and reading-room, a natural history cabinet, three parlors, and several private rooms. The third story has a chemical laboratory, a philosophical cabinet, two recitation and lecture-rooms, and several private rooms for pupils or teachers. The two upper stories are exclusively devoted to private rooms, sixty-two in number. All the private rooms for teachers and pupils amount to eighty-five.

This main building will accommodate one hundred and seventy pupils well. Subsequently, a wing has been extended back, containing twenty-five additional rooms for teachers and pupils; so that two hundred and twenty young ladies can now be accommodated in the private rooms in the whole building. It was Miss Lyon's intention to erect a corresponding wing at the north end of the main building, where now only some outhouses stand. But the trustees have not yet carried this design into execution, as they intend to do ere long. In the rear of the main building is a large court, surrounded by buildings, and devoted to the purposes of the laundry.

To the east of the buildings the ground slopes towards a stream of considerable size, which forms the boundary of the promenades in that direction, and which the trustees intend shall be used for the purposes of bathing, when suitable buildings are erected on its margin. The grounds are capable of forming agreeable and beautiful walks, which, when laid out tastefully, and well shaded, will undoubtedly be more attractive than the streets, now so much used for exercise.

The upper stories of the seminary command extensive and delightful views of Holyoke and Tom, with the intervening valleys and gorges. But as the ground opposite the buildings is higher than their base, the lower stories do not present views so attractive. This was the grand reason why some of the locating committee felt dissatisfied with the present site. But it is useless now to agitate that question. We can only say that there is much about the site that is beautiful, although in a town so rich in fine prospects, locations might have been found more commanding and delightful. With a few hundred dollars expended upon the grounds, they might be made exceedingly pleasant. But hitherto the more important wants of the institution have prevented the trustees from devoting much money to objects of taste. And yet they are aware that such objects have an important bearing upon the intellectual and moral training of young ladies. Of this Miss Lyon was fully conscious, as the style in which the seminary is built evinces; for though

the outlines and finishing are plain, they are in accordance with good taste.

The buildings were all planned by Miss Lyon, not indeed without consultation with others. This was a great labor, and severely taxed her powers. Yet so well was it done that but few subsequent changes have been found desirable.

The domestic Arrangements.

These were peculiar to this seminary in two respects. First, all the pupils were required to room and board within its walls. The nearest inhabitant of South Hadley cannot send a daughter thither who does not conform to these rules; and without doubt they are important to the complete success of the institution.

The second peculiarity consisted in the domestic work being all performed by the members of the school, so that no hired female help is admitted. This feature of the plan was entirely original with Miss Lyon; and it was the one that was most objected against by her judicious friends, many of whom were so fearful of it that they dared not recommend her plans while this scheme formed a part of them. On the other hand, it was this feature that gave the plan most interest with a large and highly respectable class of the community, who are very anxious to have their children taught how to perform the ordinary processes of housewifery. So that, in fact, while this part of the plan alienated many judicious friends, it conciliated a still larger number, and was, no doubt, the most important means employed in obtaining funds. But we shall shortly let Miss Lyon give her own views on this point.

The Course of Study and the Instructors.

This course has always embraced three years, and three classes — the junior, the middle, and the senior. The requisites for admission and the studies of the whole course, as they were at first arranged, are given below, as they were stated in the second annual catalogue. When the first was published, the course was not fully arranged.

Terms of Admission.

The studies requisite for admission are an acquaintance with the general principles of English grammar, a good knowledge of modern geography, Goodrich's History of the United States, Watts on the Mind, Colburn's First Lessons, and the whole of Adams's New Arithmetic.

None are received under sixteen years of age. Except in extraordinary cases, no candidate will be accepted expecting to enter after the year commences, or to leave till its close.

Studies of the Junior Class.

Ancient geography; ancient and modern history; text books: Worcester's Elements, Goldsmith's Greece, Rome, and England, and Grimshaw's France; Day's Algebra begun; Sullivan's Political Class Book; Lee's Physiology; Outline of Botany; Outline of Natural Philosophy; Smellie's Philosophy of Natural History; English Grammar — Murray's Grammar and Exercises, Pope's Essay on Man.

Studies of the Middle Class.

Day's Algebra finished; Playfair's Euclid begun; Abercrombie on the Intellectual Powers; Marsh's Ecclesiastical History; Beck's Botany begun; Beck's Chemistry; Wilkins's Astronomy; Newman's Rhetoric; Geology; Alexander's Evidences of Christianity; English Grammar continued — Young's Night Thoughts.

Studies of the Senior Class.

Playfair's Euclid finished; Olmsted's Natural Philosophy; Beck's Botany continued; Paley's Natural Theology; Whately's Logic; Whately's Rhetoric; Intellectual Philosophy; Wayland's Moral Philosophy; Wayland's Political Economy; Butler's Analogy; Milton's Paradise Lost.

Particular attention is given to composition, reading, and calisthenics through the whole course. The Bible lesson is recited on the Sabbath and reviewed during the week. Regular instruction is given in vocal music, and in linear and perspective drawing. Those who have attended to instrumental music can have the use of a piano a few hours in a week.

Subsequently, some changes were made in the studies, as the following list of them, from the twelfth annual catalogue, will show : —

Studies of the Junior Class.

Review of English Grammar; Latin, (Cornelius Nepos;) History, (Worcester's Elements, Goldsmith's Greece, Rome, and England, and Grimshaw's France;) Day's Algebra; Playfair's Euclid and Wood's Botany commenced; also Smellie's Philosophy of Natural History and Marsh's Ecclesiastical History.

Studies of the Middle Class.

Latin; Cutter's Physiology; Silliman's Chemistry; Olmsted's Natural Philosophy; Olmsted's Astronomy; Wood's Botany continued; Newman's Rhetoric; also Alexander's Evidences of Christianity.

Studies of the Senior Class.

Playfair's Euclid finished; Wood's Botany continued; Hitchcock's Geology; Paley's Natural Theology; Upham's Mental Philosophy, in two volumes; Whately's Logic; Wayland's Moral Philosophy; Butler's Analogy, and Milton's Paradise Lost.

All the members of the school attend regularly to composition, reading, and calisthenics. Instruction is given in vocal music, in linear and perspective drawing, and in French. Those who have attended to instrumental music can have the use of a piano a few hours in each week.

None of the studies in these lists were put down for popular effect, but the pupil might be sure that they must all be thoroughly studied. It will be seen, therefore, that the course was of an elevated character in all the substantial branches of study important to females.

The teachers with whom the school opened were as follows: Miss Mary Lyon, Principal; Miss Eunice Caldwell,

Associate Principal; Miss Mary W. Smith, Miss Amanda A. Hodgman, Teachers; Miss Abigail Moore, Miss Persis C. Woods, Miss Susan Reed, Assistant Pupils.

Miss Caldwell was Miss Lyon's pupil at Ipswich, and also a teacher there; and knowing her superior skill, Miss Lyon was anxious to secure her services for the opening of the new school. She was, moreover, Miss Lyon's confidential friend, the third one upon whom she lavished the affections of a generous and devoted heart. Miss Caldwell, (now Mrs. Cowles,) in Part II. of this memoir, has spoken of the first two, viz., Amanda White and Z. P. Grant; but delicacy forbade her to name the third. Yet the fact should not be omitted, since it will show the reader how intimately acquainted Mrs. Cowles must have been with Miss Lyon's character. The fourth special friend was Miss M. C. Whitman.

It will show how well known and esteemed were these associate principals, and also what a preparation there was in the public mind for such a school, to state that the very first year of its existence it contained one hundred and sixteen pupils. How so many were stowed away in a building adapted, according to Miss Lyon's previous statement, to accommodate only about eighty, it needs more knowledge of economics than I possess to explain. Solomon represents it a very difficult matter to dwell even with one *brawling woman in a wide house.* But where humility and affection reign, we find that a great many quiet and modest women can dwell peaceably together in a single habitation. This has been the experience at South Hadley almost every year since the school was opened. For the fact is, that many more have applied for admission every year than could be well accommodated, and the teachers have always been induced to receive more than would be desirable till more rooms were built.

Expenses of the School and Salaries of Instructors.

The amount of term time in the seminary, embraced in three sessions, is forty weeks. For board and tuition during that time, not including fuel and lights, the charge was fixed at first at sixty dollars, and has ever since continued the same. This sum is scarcely more than a third of what is charged at most female seminaries in the land where the same elevated system of instruction is given; and it seems difficult to most persons to conceive how so low a rate has enabled the school to sustain itself, and even to get relieved of a debt of some thousands of dollars. It shows the great sagacity of Miss Lyon's views, however, that she judged so accurately of the proper sum, when probably her most judicious friends would have told her, if consulted, that it was far too low to meet the expenses of the school.

But when we inquire as to the salaries of the teachers, we see one of the secrets on which this lady founded her opinion. She meant that missionary self-denial and economy should be exercised by all who had any thing to do with the seminary; and she meant to set the example herself. She fixed her own salary at two hundred dollars, with board, fuel, and lights; and when subsequently the trustees urged her to take more, she always refused. Her successor, Miss Whitman, on account of feeble health, was induced to take three hundred dollars. The salaries of the other teachers have varied from one hundred and twenty to two hundred and twenty-five dollars, with board.

Religious Instruction.

This was considered the most important object for which the institution was founded; and, therefore, every thing else was held as subordinate to this. But such views did not make it necessary, save in peculiar exigencies, to interfere with the regular literary exercises. Nor was it necessary to make religious exercises and instruction take the precedence of the literary as to time. But the former were made to assume such a position as to show to all the school that the teachers really regarded religion, and especially personal piety, as of more consequence, a thousand times, than every thing else. A religious influence was made, as it were, to permeate every thing else, and to advance religion was the grand ultimate object of all literary efforts, and, indeed, of every action.

The number of religious meetings during the week was not large. On Sabbath evening was one for those without hope, and several prayer meetings of professors at the same time. During the week, one meeting was held by professing Christians alone; another monthly or semi-monthly, and sometimes oftener, for missionary purposes. At these meetings it was usually customary for Miss Lyon to take up some passage of Scripture, and deduce instruction from it in the way of an extemporaneous sermon. This she did, also, several times in a week at morning prayers; in all, about five times a week. For these exercises she usually prepared a skeleton of the subject. To all these religious labors we must not forget to add a Bible class by the other teachers on the Sabbath, whose lesson was reviewed during the week.

I have given only a brief outline of the state of the seminary when first opened, and of the plan of its organization, because I prefer to let Miss Lyon speak for herself. A year before the school was commenced, she sent a circular to ladies in different places, soliciting their aid in furnishing furniture for the rooms. But this has been already given on page 232, Part II. Some months later, but before the opening of the school, she prepared a "General View of the Principles and Design of the Mount Holyoke Female Seminary," which was printed by the trustees; and in 1839 she got out another pamphlet, entitled "Tendencies of the

Principles embraced and the System adopted in the Mount Holyoke Female Seminary." From these last two productions we shall make somewhat copious extracts, both because they give definitely Miss Lyon's views and plans as to the seminary, and contain many important suggestions concerning female education.

Principles and Design of the Mount Holyoke Female Seminary.

This institution is established at South Hadley, Massachusetts. It is to be principally devoted to the preparing of female teachers. At the same time, it will qualify ladies for other spheres of usefulness. The design is to give a solid, extensive, and well-balanced English education, connected with that general improvement, that moral culture, and those enlarged views of duty, which will prepare ladies to be *educators* of children and youth, rather than to fit them to be mere teachers, as the term has been technically applied. Such an education is needed by every female who takes the charge of a school, and sustains the responsibility of guiding the whole course and of forming the entire character of those committed to her care. And when she has done with the business of teaching in a regular school, she will not give up her profession; she will still need the same well-balanced education at the head of her own family and in guiding her own household.

1. This institution professes to be founded on the high principle of enlarged Christian benevolence. In its plans and in its appeals it seeks no support from local or private interest. It is designed entirely for the public good, and the trustees would adopt no measures not in accordance with this design. It is sacredly consecrated to the great Head of the church, and they would not seek for human approbation by any means which will not be well pleasing in his sight.

2. The institution is designed to be permanent. The permanency of an institution may be considered as consisting of two particulars — first, its perpetual vitality, and second, its continual prosperity and usefulness. The first is to be secured in the same manner that the principle of perpetual life in our higher institutions for young men has been so effectually preserved. A fund is to be committed to an independent, self-perpetuating board of trustees, known to the churches as faithful, responsible men; not as a proprietary invest-

ment, but as a free offering, leaving them no way for an honorable retreat from their trust, and binding them with solemn responsibilities to hundreds and thousands of donors, who have committed their sacred charities to their conscientious fidelity. Give to a literary institution, on this principle, an amount of property sufficient to be viewed as an object of great importance, and it is almost impossible to extinguish its vital life by means of adversity. How firmly have our colleges stood amidst the clashing elements around us, and the continual overturnings which are taking place in the midst of us!

The usefulness of this institution, like all others, must depend on its character. This may be very good for a time, where there is no principle of perpetual life, as is the case with some of our most distinguished female seminaries. Amidst all their prosperity, they have no solid foundation, and in themselves no sure principle of continued existence. Could we secure to our public institutions the continued labors of the same teachers through an antediluvial life, the preservation of the vital principle would be a subject of much less consequence. But in view of the present shortened life of man, rendered shorter still by disease and premature decay, and in view of the many changes which are ever breaking in upon the continued services of those to whose care these institutions are committed, every reflecting mind must regard it as of the very first importance to secure to them this principle, especially to a public seminary for the raising up of female teachers.

3. The institution is to be entirely for an older class of young ladies. The general system for family arrangements, for social improvement, for the division of time, for organizing and regulating the school, and the requirements for entrance, will be adapted throughout to young ladies of adult age and of mature character. Any provision in an institution like this for younger misses must be a public loss far greater than the individual good. Their exclusion from the institution will produce a state of society among the members exceedingly pleasant and profitable to those whose great desire is to be prepared to use all their talents in behalf of the cause of education, and of the Redeemer's kingdom; and it will secure for their improvement the entire labors of the teachers, without an interruption from the care and government of pupils too immature to take care of themselves.

4. The young ladies are to take a part in the domestic work of the family. This also is to be on the principle of equality. All are to take a part, not as a servile labor, for which they are to receive a

small weekly remuneration, but as a gratuitous service to the institution of which they are members, designed for its improvement and elevation. The first object of this arrangement is, to give to the institution a greater degree of independence. The arrangements for boarding all the pupils in the establishment will give to it an independence with regard to private families in the neighborhood, without which it would be difficult, if not impossible, to secure its perpetual prosperity. The arrangements for the domestic work will, in a great measure, relieve it from another source of depressing dependence — a dependence on the will of hired domestics, to which many a family in New England is subject.

The other object of this arrangement is to promote the health, the improvement, and the happiness of the pupils; their health, by its furnishing them with a little daily exercise of the best kind; their improvement, by its tending to preserve their interest in domestic pursuits; and their happiness, by its relieving them from that servile dependence on common domestics, to which young ladies, as mere boarders in a large establishment, are often subject, to their great inconvenience. The adoption of a feature like this, in an institution which aims to be better endowed than any other existing female seminary in the country, must give it an attitude of noble independence, which can scarcely fail to exert an elevating influence on its members.

This cause is the humble, but firm and efficient patron of all other branches of benevolence. What the present generation is beginning to accomplish for the salvation of the world it seeks to preserve and carry forward with increasing rapidity. Whatever of conquest is now gained it seeks to secure forever from the encroachments of the enemy. It seeks to lay the foundation strong, on which, under God, the temple, with all its increasing weight, is to rise, and be sustained, and to secure it from injury and decay. It looks abroad on a world lying in wickedness. It beholds with painful interest the slow progress of these United States in carrying the blessings of salvation to the two hundred millions, who are the estimated proportion of the inhabitants of this benighted world to be converted to God through our instrumentality. And as it attempts in vain to calculate the time when the work shall be accomplished, it would fain increase its progress a hundred fold, by training up the children in the way they should go. It has endeavored to fix an eye on the distant point of futurity, when, according to a fair and reasonable computation, this nation, with all its increasing millions, and the inhabitants of the whole earth, shall be supplied with faithful, educated ministers of the gospel. And as it inquires, in vain, "When shall these things be?" and as it attempts, in vain, to count up the millions on millions who shall go down to everlasting death before that time *can* arrive, it would fain strive, with unparalleled efforts, through the children of our country, greatly to multiply the number of ministers during the next generation, and to carry forward the work in an unexampled and increasing ratio through the generations which shall follow.

The object of this institution penetrates too far into futurity, and takes in too broad a view, to discover its claims to the passing multitude. We appeal in its behalf to wise men, who can judge what we say. We appeal to those who can venture as pioneers in the great work of renovating a world. Others may stand waiting for the great multitude to go forward, but then is the time when these men feel themselves called upon to make their greatest efforts, and to do their noblest deeds of benevolence. Thus we hope it will be in behalf of this institution.

We commend this enterprise to the continued prayers and efforts of its particular friends, of all those who have enlisted in its behalf, and have given of their time, their influence, and their substance. We would invite them to come with us around the same sacred altar, and there consecrate this beloved institution, as first fruits, to the Lord, to be devoted forever to his service.

This enterprise, thus far, has been under the care of a kind Providence. It has not been carried forward by might, nor by power; but in every step of its progress the good hand of God has been upon it. Let all its friends bring in the tithes and the offerings, and let them commit the disposing of the whole to Him who can accomplish the work which his own hands have commenced, and he will pour out upon this institution, and the cause with which it is connected, and upon the children and youth of our country, and of the world, a blessing, that there shall not be room enough to receive it.

Tendencies of the Principles embraced and the System adopted in the Mount Holyoke Female Seminary.

The enterprise of founding this seminary was commenced nearly five years ago. More than three years were occupied in preparing the way, in raising the funds, and in erecting the building now occupied. It was ready for the reception of scholars November 8, 1837.

The original plan was to provide for two hundred. Only the first building has yet been erected. This can accommodate only ninety. Though it is a noble edifice, and well adapted to its end, it is but a beginning. Full one half of the funds must yet be raised. In order to finish the plan, at least twenty thousand dollars more will be needed for the buildings, besides perhaps five thousand dollars or more for furniture, library, and apparatus.

This seminary is specific in its character, and, of course, does not provide for the entire education of a young lady. Such a provision may be found expedient in foreign countries, where all systems can be brought under the rigid rules of monarchy, without being subject to the continual encroachments and changes necessarily resulting from a free government. But in our country it is doubted whether female seminaries generally can attain a high standard of excellence till they become more specific and less mixed in their character.

1. *Religious Culture.* — This lies at the foundation of that female character which the founders of this seminary have contemplated. Without this, their efforts would entirely fail of their design. This institution has been built for the Lord, that it might be peculiarly his own. It has been solemnly and publicly dedicated to his service. It has been embalmed by prayer in many hearts, and consecrated around many a family altar. The donors and benefactors of this institution, with its trustees and teachers, have felt a united obligation to seek, in behalf of this beloved seminary, "first the kingdom of God and his righteousness." Endeavors have been made to raise the funds, and to lay the whole foundation on Christian principles, to organize a school and form a family that from day to day might illustrate the precepts and spirit of the gospel. Public worship, the Bible lesson, and other appropriate duties of the Sabbath, a regular observance of secret devotion, suitable attention to religious instruction and social prayer meetings, and the maintaining of a consistent Christian deportment, are considered the most important objects of regard, for both teachers and scholars. The friends of this seminary have sought that this might be a spot where souls shall be born of God, and where much shall be done for maturing and elevating Christian character. The smiles of Providence and the influences of the Holy Spirit have encouraged them to hope that their desires will not be in vain.

2. *Cultivation of Benevolence.* — This is implied in the last particular, but it needs special care in a lady's education. While many of the present active generation are fixed in their habits, and will

never rise above the standard of benevolence already adopted, the eye of hope rests with anxious solicitude on the next generation. But who shall take all the little ones, and by precept, and still more by example, enforce on them the sentiments of benevolence, and, aided by the Holy Spirit, train them up from their infancy for the service of the Redeemer? Is there not here an appropriate sphere for the efforts of woman, through whose moulding hands all our children and youth must inevitably pass?

How important, then, is it that the education of a female should be conducted on strictly benevolent principles! and how important that this spirit should be the presiding genius in every female school! Should it not be so incorporated with its nature, and so wrought into its very existence, that it cannot prosper without it? Such a school the friends of this seminary have sought to furnish. They would have the spirit of benevolence manifest in all its principles, and in the manner of conferring its privileges, in the mutual duties it requires of its members, and in the claims it makes on them to devote their future lives to doing good.

3. *Intellectual Culture.* — This trait of character is of inestimable value to a lady who desires to be useful. A thorough and well-balanced intellectual education will be to her a valuable auxiliary in every department of duty.

This seminary has peculiar advantages for gaining a high intellectual standard. The age required for admission will secure to the pupils, as a whole, greater mental power, and the attainments required for admission will secure to the institution a higher standard of scholarship.

4. *Physical Culture.* — The value of health to a lady is inestimable. Her appropriate duties are so numerous and varied, and so constant in their demands, and so imperious in the moment of their calls, as will render this treasure to her above price. How difficult is it for her to perform all her duties faithfully and successfully, unless she possesses at all times a calm mind, an even temper, a cheerful heart, and a happy face! But a feeble system and a nervous frame are often the direct antagonists of these indispensable traits in a lady's character. A gentleman may possibly live and do some good without much health; but what can a lady do, unless she takes the attitude of an invalid, and seeks to do good principally by patience and submission? If a gentleman cannot do his work in one hour, he may perhaps do it in another; but a lady's duties often allow of no compromise in hours. If a gentleman is annoyed and vexed with

the nervousness of his feeble frame, he may perhaps use it to some advantage, as he attempts to move the world by his pen, or by his voice. But a lady cannot make such a use of this infirmity in her influence over her children and family — an influence which must be at all times under the control of gentleness and equanimity. Much has been said on this subject, but enough has not been *done*, in our systems of education, to promote the health of young ladies. This is an object of special regard in this seminary.

The time is all regularly and systematically divided. The hours for rising and retiring are early. The food is plain and simple, but well prepared, and from the best materials. No article of second quality of the *kind* is ever purchased for the family, and no standard of cooking is allowed but that of doing every thing as well as it can be done. The day is so divided that the lessons can be well learned, and ample time allowed for sleep; the hour for exercise in the domestic department can be secured without interruption, and a half hour in the morning and evening for secret devotion, also half an hour for vocal music, and twenty minutes for calisthenics. Besides, there are the leisure hours, in which much is done of sewing, knitting, and ornamental needlework; and much is enjoyed in social intercourse, in walking, and in botanical excursions. This institution presupposes a good degree of health and correct habits. But little can be done in this seminary, or any other, for those whose constitution is already impaired, or whose physical habits, up to the age of sixteen, are particularly defective. This institution professes to make no remarkable physical renovations. But it is believed that a young lady who is fitted for the system, and who can voluntarily and cheerfully adopt it as her own, will find this place favorable for preserving unimpaired the health she brings with her, and for promoting and establishing the good physical habits already acquired.

5. *Social and domestic Character.* — The excellence of the female character in this respect consists principally in a preparation to be happy herself in her social and domestic relations, and to make all others happy around her. All her duties, of whatever kind, are in an important sense social and domestic. They are retired and private, and not public, like those of the other sex. Whatever she does beyond her own family should be but another application and illustration of social and domestic excellence. She may occupy the place of an important teacher, but her most vigorous labors should be modest and unobtrusive. She may go on a foreign mission, but she will there find a retired spot, where, away from the public gaze, she

may wear out or lay down a valuable life. She may promote the interests of the Sabbath school, or be an angel of mercy to the poor and afflicted; she may seek in various ways to increase the spirit of benevolence and the zeal for the cause of missions; and she may labor for the salvation of souls; but her work is to be done by the whisper of her still and gentle voice, by the silent step of her unwearied feet, and by the power of her uniform and consistent example.

The following elements should be embraced in the social and domestic character of a lady: —

(a.) *Economy.* — Economy consists in providing well at little comparative expense. It necessarily implies good judgment and good taste. It can be equally manifested in the tasteful decorations of a palace and in the simple comforts of a cottage. Suppose all ladies possessed this in a high degree, how much more would be found in families of comfort and convenience, of taste and refinement, of education and improvement, of charity and good works!

This institution, it is well known, is distinguished for its economical features. Economy, however, is not adopted principally for its own sake, but as a means of education, as a mode of producing favorable effects on character, and of preparing young ladies for the duties of life. The great object is to make the school really better. An economical character is to be formed by precept, by practice, and by example. Example has great effect, not only in furnishing a model for imitation, but also in proving that economy is practicable, which is one of the most essential requisites for success. Let a young lady spend two or three years, on intimate terms, in a family distinguished for a judicious and consistent illustration of this principle, and the effects cannot be lost.

(b.) *A suitable Feeling of Independence.* — There are two kinds of dependence, very unlike in their nature, but both inconsistent with the highest degree of domestic bliss. To one of these ladies in cities and large towns are more particularly subject; but it is an evil from which ladies in the country are not wholly exempt. It is a feeling of dependence on the will of servants. Every lady should be so educated, as far as it can be done, that she will feel able to take care of herself, and, if need be, of a family, whatever may be her situation in life, and whatever her station in society. Otherwise, if she remains in these United States, she may be rendered unhappy by constantly feeling that her daily comforts are at the control of her servants, who in such cases are often unfaithful, unreasonable, and dissatisfied. The withering effects of family perplexities on the social character is well known to every observer of domestic life. On the other hand, how much happiness often results from a suitable feeling of independence. A lady in one of our large cities, who is distinguished for having faithful servants, considers the secret as lying in her feeling of independence. If one, in a fit of caprice, proposes leaving her, she has only to say, "You may go to-day. If need be, I can take care of my own family until your place is supplied."

Against this kind of dependence this institution seeks to exert its decided influence. The whole aspect of the family, and all the plans of the school, are suited to cultivate habits entirely the reverse. In the domestic independence of the household all have an interest. The daily hour for these duties returns to each at the appointed time, and no one inquires whether it can be omitted or transferred to another. No one receives any pecuniary reward for her services, and no one seeks with her money to deprive herself of the privilege of sharing in the freedom, simplicity, and independence of her *home*.

There is another kind of independence entirely different in its nature, but equally essential to a high degree of domestic happiness. This is the result of economy already considered. It is the power of bringing personal and family expenses fairly and easily within the means enjoyed. The whole system adopted in this seminary is designed to give a living illustration of the principle by which this power is to be gained. This ability will be of immense value in active life. It will prepare one to sustain the reverses of fortune with submission, or to meet the claims of hospitality and charity with promptness. This kind of independence might be to the great cause of benevolence like an overflowing fountain, whose streams will never fail.

(c.) *Skill and Expedition in household Duties.* — Let a young lady despise this branch of the duties of woman, and she despises the appointments of the Author of her existence. The laws of God, made known by nature and by providence, and also by the Bible, enjoin these duties on the sex, and she cannot violate them with impunity. Let her have occasion to preside at the head of her own family and table, and she may despair of enjoying herself, or of giving to others the highest degree of domestic happiness. Does she seek to do good by teaching? The time, we hope, is not far distant, when no mother will commit her daughters to the influence of such a teacher. Does she seek to do good in the Sabbath school?

How can she enforce all the duties to God and man in their due proportion while she contemns one of the most obvious laws of her nature? Would she endeavor to show the poor and the ignorant how to find the comforts of life? How can she teach what she has never learned? Does she become the wife of a missionary? How does her heart sink within her, as her desponding husband strives in vain to avoid the evils resulting from her inefficiency!

This institution is not designed to conduct this branch of a young lady's education. It would not take this privilege from the mother. But it does seek to preserve the good habits already acquired, and to make a favorable impression with regard to the value of system, promptness, and fidelity in this branch of the duties of woman.

(d.) *An obliging Disposition.* — This is of special importance in forming a lovely, social, and domestic character. Young ladies at school, with all the conveniences and comforts which they should have, and with all the benefits of system which they should enjoy, can have but little opportunity for self-denial. This little should be used to the best advantage. To bring every such opportunity to bear on the character has been a leading object in all the plans of this institution, in the organization of the school, and especially in the arrangements of the family. As the domestic work is done entirely by the young ladies, the varied and mutual duties of the day furnish many little opportunities for the manifestation of a generous, obliging, and self-denying spirit, the influence of which, we trust, will be felt through life. "He that is faithful in the least is faithful also in much," is a motto for the daily guidance of this household.

(e.) *A Spirit of Gratitude and a Sense of Obligation.* — Domestic life is little else but a continued scene of conferring and receiving favors. How much of happiness depends on their being conferred with the manifest evidence of a willing heart, and on their being received with suitable tokens of gratitude! These two lovely traits go hand in hand, not often to be separated. The formation of a character that *can* be grateful is an object of special importance in a lady's education. Parents should seek to give to their daughters privileges, and especially the means of education, in a manner suited to lead them to realize that they are favors for which gratitude is due.

To a spirit of ingratitude the genius of this institution is specially opposed. On entering this seminary, young ladies can scarcely avoid feeling that they are sharing the fruits of benevolent efforts, that they are enjoying privileges which they cannot purchase, that they owe a debt of gratitude to the founders which gold and silver can never cancel, and which can be met only by a useful Christian life.

These are some of the influences which this institution has a tendency to exert on its members.

The principles of the system carried out and extended would also have a favorable influence on the cause of education.

1. *In furnishing a Supply of female Teachers.* — Teaching is really the business of almost every useful woman. If there are any to whom this does not apply, they may be considered as exceptions to a general rule. Of course, no female is well educated who has not all the acquisitions necessary for a good teacher. The most essential qualifications are thorough mental culture, a well-balanced character, a benevolent heart, an ability to communicate knowledge and apply it to practice, an acquaintance with human nature, and the power of controlling the minds of others.

But it is not enough that a great number of ladies are well educated. They must also have benevolence enough to engage in teaching, when other duties will allow and when their labors are needed. Female teachers should not expect to be fully compensated for their services, unless it be by kindness and gratitude.

There are many other chords in female hearts which will vibrate much more tenderly and powerfully than this. There is a large and increasing number of educated ladies, who will make the best of teachers, but who can be allured much more by respectful attention, by kindness and gratitude, by suitable school-rooms and apparatus, and other facilities for rendering their labors pleasant and successful, than they can by the prospect of a pecuniary reward.

The spirit of this seminary is suited not only to increase the number of educated ladies, but to enforce on them the obligation to use their talents for the good of others, especially in teaching. It is hoped it may also lead them to be more willing to take *any school* and *in any place* where their services are most needed.

2. *In promoting the Prosperity of Common Schools.* — Whoever will devise means by which reading, spelling, arithmetic, geography, and grammar shall receive as thorough attention in common schools as they deserve, and whoever will throw inducements before the older female scholars to remain in them longer and attend thoroughly to these branches, as an example to others, will do much to elevate their standard. Such an influence this seminary seeks to exert.

3. *In counteracting certain errors which have prevailed to some extent in female education.*

First Error. Tasking the Mind too early with severe mental Discipline. — The evils of this course are beginning to be felt by careful observers of the human mind and of human character. When the effort is attended with the greatest success, there is generally the greatest injury. The most discouraging field which any teacher was ever called to cultivate is the mind of a young lady who has been studying all her days, and has gone over most of the natural and moral sciences without any valuable improvement, until she is tired of school, tired of books, and tired almost of life. As this institution proposes to conduct young ladies through a regular intellectual course, after the age of sixteen, its influence will be against this error.

Second Error. Deferring some Parts of Education till too late a Period. — Among the things neglected till *too late a period* are the manners, the cultivation of the voice, including singing, pronunciation, and all the characteristics of good reading, gaining skill and expedition in the common necessary mechanical operations, such as sewing, knitting, writing, and drawing, and acquiring, by daily practice, a knowledge and a love of domestic pursuits. To these might be added some things which depend almost entirely on the memory, such as spelling, and others which are suited to lay the foundation of a literary taste, such as a judicious course of reading, practice in composition, &c. Those who are to attend to instrumental music, the ornamental branches, and the pronunciation of foreign languages, must commence early.

Third Error. Placing Daughters too young in a Boarding-school or large Seminary. — A common boarding-school is not a suitable place for a little girl. She needs the home of her childhood, or one like it. Direct individual attention, such as can be given by no one who has the care of many, is the necessary means of forming her character, of cultivating her manners, of developing her affections, and of nurturing all that is lovely and of good report. She wants the uninterrupted sympathies of a mother's heart. She needs a constant and gentle hand, leading her singly along in the path of safety and improvement. Perhaps the evils of a boarding-house are most unfavorable on her character just as she is entering her teens. Who can guide this self-sufficient age but the mother, who has gained a permanent place in her affections and a decided influence over her life? Who but the mother, who first taught her to obey, can lay on her the necessary restrictions without exposing her to form the unlovely trait of character gained by complaining of those whom she should love and respect, and who deserve her gratitude?

4. *In giving just Views of the Advantages of large female Seminaries.* — Such institutions furnish peculiar privileges, which cannot be secured by smaller schools; but in most cases they have not been able to produce their legitimate results. They have often suffered for the want of accommodations and other facilities for successful operation, from their temporary and unsettled existence, from their want of system, and sometimes from too public a location, and too public an aspect in their features. Their efforts also to accommodate all ages and all classes often prevent their having any fixed or determinate character. This institution seeks to avoid all these evils, and to develop the real advantages of a large seminary.

In order that a lady may have the most thorough education, she should spend a number of years in close intellectual application, after her mental powers have acquired sufficient strength, and her physical system sufficient maturity, and after she has all the necessary preparation. This must be during the best part of her life, when every year is worth more than can be estimated in gold and silver. Facilities for success should be given her, which will be an ample reward for the sacrifice of so much time. Whoever has undertaken to organize a school has had abundant evidence that all these points cannot be gained where the number is not large. This seminary is able now to secure all these advantages in some degree, but not so perfectly as it will when the two hundred can be received.

The influence of a large seminary on the social character is also important. The very discipline necessary to preserve little girls from exposure to injury, and to cultivate the principles of virtue and loveliness, is attended with some necessary evils which will need a pruning hand at a maturer age. Not the least prominent of these is a narrowness of soul, giving her limited views of others.

The spirit of monopolizing privileges is to some extent the effect of giving to a little girl all that individual care and affectionate attention which her cultivation demands. A large seminary, and more especially a large family, have a tendency to remove this. The young lady needs to feel herself a member of a large community, where the interests of others are to be sought equally with her own. She needs to learn by practice, as well as by principle, that individual accommodations and private interests are to be sacrificed for the public good; and she needs to know from experience that those who make such a sacrifice will receive an ample reward in the improvement of the community among whom they are to dwell.

5. *In giving the Claims of large female Seminaries an acknowledged Place among the other Objects of public Beneficence.* — The claims of those for the other sex were admitted two hundred years ago; and the colleges, academies, and theological seminaries, all over the land, show that the wise and the good have not been weary in well doing. How ridiculous would be the attempt to found colleges in the manner that some female seminaries have been founded! Suppose a gentleman, having a large family depending on him for support, finds his health not sufficient for the duties of his profession. Casting his eye around, he looks on the office of a president of a college as affording more ample means, and a more pleasant and respectable situation for his family, than any other he can command. But a new college must be founded to furnish him the place. He selects a large village in New England, or at the west, or at the south, as may best favor the accomplishment of his object, and where he can find buildings which he can buy or rent on some conditions, though they may be far from being adapted to such an end. He purchases his apparatus, or has none, and procures professors on his own responsibility. Thus prepared, he commences, making his charge to the students such as will meet the rent of buildings, furniture, and apparatus, and the salaries of his professors, besides furnishing a handsome support to his own family. What could such a college do to encourage thorough and systematic education in our country? But this is scarcely a caricature of the manner in which some female seminaries have been founded.

We cannot hope for a state of things essentially better till the principle is admitted that female seminaries, designed for the public benefit, must be founded by the hand of public benevolence, and be subject to the rules enjoined by such benevolence. Let this principle be fully admitted, and let it have sufficient time to produce its natural effects, and it will be productive of more important results than can be easily estimated. Then our large seminaries may be permanent, with all the mutual responsibility and coöperation which the principle of permanency produces.

Such was the beginning of what we call a victory in this enterprise. In reality, so great were the obstacles in Miss

Lyon's way that she could not for a moment lay aside her armor. Less than half the money requisite to complete the work had been obtained, and several new features, heretofore untried in educational projects, were to be put to the test. It was, therefore, still a struggle so severe as hardly to permit the leader in it to draw her breath freely. But the first year was now coming to a close, and success had smiled on the enterprise, inspiring still stronger hope for the future.

The anniversary at this seminary is always a season of much interest, and attracts many visitors. The first one has been a model for all the rest up to this time. It happens in August, and on Thursday. For at least two days previous, public examinations are conducted in the seminary hall, which is very spacious. On the forenoon of Thursday, it is crowded by listeners. Several selected young ladies read compositions, written, however, by other members of the school. About noon, the pupils, teachers, and trustees go in procession to the church at a little distance, where an address is delivered by some gentleman, previously selected. The diplomas are then delivered, with a brief address, by the secretary of the trustees, to the senior class. Afterwards, the school, with invited friends, return to the seminary to dinner. It may be interesting to read a brief account of the first occasion of this sort in a letter from Miss Lyon to Miss Grant.

"SOUTH HADLEY, August 27, 1838.

"MY DEAR MISS GRANT:

"We have finished our first year. I did want to see you here very much. I send one of our compositions, which perhaps you may enjoy hearing read some time for your amusement. I will also send the impression of our seal. You will observe that the device is designed as an illustration of the quotation of Scripture. Our examinations were Monday afternoon, Tuesday forenoon, and Thursday forenoon. On Wednesday, more than half our young ladies went to Amherst to commencement. The remainder prepared for the next day. The trustees and clergymen were invited to dine with us on Thursday, and some other individuals. We extended our tables to accommodate about forty more than our own family. We had them just filled. This added considerably to my cares. But the agitation of the question about going to the meeting-house on Thursday afternoon seemed almost to add more, when I had just all I could do. It came up once or twice, and was settled in the negative, as I felt a great reluctance to it. After Dr. Hawes came, on Wednesday evening, the subject was again discussed. I found that the trustees, Dr. H., and the other gentlemen were all becoming decided that it was best to go to the meeting-house; I thought it the most modest to acquiesce. The certificates were given at the close of the services, but no other exercise differed from a common public meeting. It did not appear unsuitable, as I thought it would, and I was very glad that I consented. The meeting-house was full, and I think some of our donors would have been dissatisfied if we had met in the seminary hall. Our certificates were signed by Miss Caldwell and myself, and simply countersigned by the secretary of the board, Mr. Condit. Of course the giving of the certificates devolved on Mr. Condit. He did it in his neat, elegant manner. Dr. Hawes's address was good common sense. Mr. Boies, of Boston, made the first prayer, and Dr. Carr the last. I think of you often, very often; I love to think of you when I am alone, and no one present but God, our covenant-keeping God. I should love just to look on you from day to day, and give you a little of heartfelt sympathy; but you have a Friend that sticketh closer than a brother. My heart's desire and prayer to God is, that this Friend may be ever with you, with his consoling presence."

The certificate or diploma delivered on these occasions is upon parchment, in the style of the college diploma; but the form is in English, as follows: —

"A. B. has completed the prescribed course of study at the Mount Holyoke Female Seminary, and by her attainments and correct deportment is entitled to this testimonial.

"Given at South Hadley, &c.

"MARY LYON, *Principal.*

"———, *Secretary.*"

At the top of the parchment is an elegant vignette, representing a palace, in front of which, on the right, a quarry is represented, with blocks of stone in various stages of preparation for architectural purposes. On the left are several ladies, intended to represent teachers and pupils; and beneath the whole is written, "That our daughters may be as corner stones, polished after the similitude of a palace." — *Ps.* cxliv. 14. The seal of the institution, bearing a somewhat similar representation, is attached by a ribbon to the parchment.

This instrument is a very neat one, and the whole appropriate, save that the engraver took the liberty to alter the palace so as to make it quite Oriental, by adding domes and minarets to the towers, quite in the Turkish style. The only palace that I know of in Western Europe which is thus surmounted is the anomalous pavilion erected at Brighton, in England, by George the Fourth.

SECTION II.

The History of the Seminary and of Miss Lyon from the Anniversary, in 1838, to the Time of her Death, in 1849.

Perhaps a part of the title of this section might properly have been omitted, for the history of the seminary is essentially that of Miss Lyon. Not, indeed, that she neglected her duty to others and to other objects. Abundant proof has been furnished, in the previous pages of this memoir, that she was always alive to every call of duty, from whatever quarter it came. But in fact, nearly all her duties lay within the sphere of the seminary. Constituting but one great family, its relations, literary, religious, and benevolent, really reached the whole family of man. It was those relations that made her intense devotion to its interests pure and expansive benevolence, instead of selfishness. When we find a person urging with great exclusiveness the claims of a literary institution started to promote the interest of a sect, or party, or town, or of individuals, we rightly call it selfishness, and know that his zeal may nourish some of the worst feelings of the human heart, viz., pride, party spirit, sectarian exclusiveness, avarice, and ambition. But when, as in this case, the very constitution of the seminary excludes all pecuniary benefit to individuals, or to place, and makes its grand object to be the good of the world, intense devotedness to its interests becomes only a school for the cultivation of benevolence, and almost every other virtue.

So carefully and judiciously were all the arrangements made in starting the new seminary, that although several of its characteristics had never before been put to the test of experiment, very little change became necessary after the trial of the first year. Hence, although minor improvements were subsequently introduced, with slight modifications of some rules, yet the history of its operation for the first year tells its story for the subsequent years. Hence the materials for this section of the memoir are not very abundant.

Let it not be thought, however, that during any part of these eleven years Miss Lyon was resting upon her oars. Such were her habits, that this would have been next to impossible, so long as she had strength to ply them. Her letters, indeed, speak not unfrequently of her going abroad to the residences of certain friends, in order to rest. But even at such times, she usually accomplished about twice as much as ordinary women, in the way of writing or consulting about plans for the seminary. True, the affairs of the school moved on noiselessly and harmoniously. But she was careful to watch the movements of every wheel, and to learn the force of every spring and weight. Especially did she stand by the *new* machinery, and not unfrequently was she obliged to draw largely upon her resources to supply the requisite propelling force. These eleven years, therefore, were among the most busy periods of her life. For a considerable part of that time, the pecuniary means of the institution were not equal to the demands upon its treasury; and she felt herself called on to watch this part of the enterprise with as careful an eye as any other. To the domestic department, also, she gave special attention, and probably expended more mental labor and anxiety upon it, in order to arrange and simplify the system, than upon any other branch of the seminary.

Teachers and Pupils.

THE following figures exhibit the number of teachers and pupils in the seminary from its commencement to the present time. The summation at the bottom, however, does not exhibit the number of different teachers and pupils, because many of them continued through several years.

	Teachers.	Pupils.
1837–38,	4	116
1838–39,	5	103
1839–40,	6	119
1840–41,	5	113
1841–42,	9	172
1842–43,	14	183
1843–44,	13	205
1844–45,	19	255
1845–46,	17	182
1846–47,	15	188
1847–48,	14	235
1848–49,	14	229
1849–50,	16	224
1850–51,	13	244
Total,	164	2568

We have seen that, at first, Miss Caldwell was associate principal with Miss Lyon. But the former continued only one year, having been previously invited to take charge of the Wheaton Seminary at Norton. Till 1842, Miss Lyon was sole principal. But that year, Miss Mary C. Whitman and Miss Abigail Moore were connected with her as associate principals. This arrangement continued till 1846, when Miss Moore married Rev. Ebenezer Burgess, missionary at Ahmednugger, in India, and accompanied him thither, leaving Miss Whitman as associate principal. She continued in that place till 1848, when her health became so poor that she was obliged to leave for several months. During her absence, Miss Lyon died, and she returned and stood at the head of the seminary until, in 1849, she was chosen to succeed Miss Lyon as permanent principal. But her health gave way in a few months, and she has been compelled to leave the institution, probably not to return. As senior instructor when Miss Whitman left, the charge of the seminary devolved upon Miss Mary W. Chapin, who has ever since acted as its principal. Two of her associate teachers, who had been long connected with the institution, have also been removed since Miss Lyon's decease, namely, Miss Curtis by death, and Miss Hazen as a missionary to Persia.

It was regarded as a kind Providence that brought to Miss Lyon's help two associates so well qualified to have charge of the seminary even alone, as were Miss Moore and Miss Whitman. They undoubtedly contributed very much to the prosperity and success of the school; and so long as they remained, the trustees did not fear that the school would suffer essentially, even though Miss Lyon should be called away. It had often been said, that it must fail so soon as she should die; when Misses Moore and Whitman also were called away, its most steadfast friends began to share this apprehension. But the care of the seminary has passed into other hands, and yet never was it in a more prosperous state than now. These facts show, first, that the principles of permanency lie in the system itself, and do not depend upon the lives of individuals. Secondly, they show how admirably every thing in the operation of the plan had been arranged by Miss Lyon. She had had ample time to overcome the friction of the new machinery, to add new wheels and springs where they were wanted, and to strengthen and arrange every part for exigencies. Thirdly, we hence learn how well Miss Lyon knew how to train up young ladies to enter at once upon the most difficult trusts as teachers; for all those who have successively been called to take the high responsibility of directing the affairs of the seminary have been connected with it almost from the beginning; and should Providence see fit to make even further inroads upon those who stand first on the list of teachers, the trustees have learned that they have little to fear. Indeed, in the last instruction which Miss Lyon gave on earth, she taught them never to fear any thing which God does.

The whole number of teachers that have been connected with this institution to the present year, or during its first fourteen years, has been fifty-five. Their names are as follows, in the order of seniority: Mary Lyon, Eunice Caldwell, Mary W. Smith, Amanda A. Hodgman, Abigail Moore, Sarah Brigham, Persis C. Woods, Mary C. Whitman, Sarah H. Torrey, Susan Reed, Helen Humphrey, Lucy T. Lyon, Roxana R. Parsons, Sophia D. Hazen, Fidelia Fiske, Mary M. Stevens, Ann R. Mowry, Catharine A. Wright, Martha R. Chapin, Susan F. Hawks, Mary W. Chapin, Ann R. Webster, Hannah O. Bailey, Margaret Mann, Lucy M. Curtis, Mary H. Humphrey, Marie F. Browne, Catharine A. Porter, Nancy A. Foote, Mary E. Graves, Persis G. Thurston, Ann Maria Hollister, Susan L. Holman, Martha C. Scott, Rebecca W. Fiske, Mary E. Barker, Mary B. Metcalf, Emily Jessup, Harriet Johnson, Aurelia P. Wellman, Helen Peabody, Hannah C. Scott, Mary A. Munson, Mary E. Yale, Lucy M. Ainsworth, Caroline H. Merrick, Maria E. Mason, Hannah G. Gilman, Emily W. S. Bowdoin, Mary L. Brown, Lydia G. B. Rogers, Martha L. Newcomb, Elizabeth Titcomb, Mary Titcomb, and Mary J. Murdock.

The whole number of pupils on the catalogues, as given above, amounts to two thousand five hundred and sixty-eight; of course, the same names are here sometimes repeated. The actual number of different ladies, who have received instruction here, is between seventeen and eighteen hundred; of these, four hundred and fifteen (including the class of 1851) have finished the course of study, and received diplomas. The pupils have come from the following states and countries: —

Massachusetts,	Connecticut,
New York,	New Hampshire

Vermont,	Iowa,
Rhode Island,	Kentucky,
Maine,	Alabama,
New Jersey,	Georgia,
Pennsylvania,	Virginia,
Ohio,	District of Columbia,
Illinois,	Cherokee Nation,
Michigan,	Canada,
Missouri,	Turkey,
Mississippi,	Sandwich Islands.
Wisconsin,	

Trustees.

The names of the trustees at the commencement of the seminary, in 1837, have been already given. In 1838, Hon. Samuel Williston was added. In 1843, Hon. David Choate resigned, as did Dr. Humphrey in 1845. In 1847, Mr. Condit died, and Rev. E. Y. Swift was chosen a trustee, as was Rev. Samuel Harris in 1848.

The Domestic Department.

We have seen how the peculiar feature of the school, which leaves the domestic labor in the hands of the pupils, operated during the first year. But success for so short a time scarcely lessened the scepticism of those opposed to it. "How long must it be tried," said I, to a judicious friend, who thought it must fail, "how long must it be tried to satisfy you?" "Five years," he replied; and although, when the five years had ended, the success was still complete, he was no more satisfied than at first; nor even when almost twice that period had elapsed; for in such a case we may apply the sentiment of the satirist, —

"A man convinced against his will
Is of the same opinion still."

Very few besides Miss Lyon had strong confidence that this plan would be successful or desirable. And, therefore, the trustees took care not to make the fate of the school depend upon it. Even now it might be given up without essentially interfering with the prosperity of the school. Yet it has certainly had extraordinary and uninterrupted success for nearly fourteen years, and is doubtless regarded with great interest by a large part of the religious community. Those who have had the oversight of the plan, and have seen most of its operation, would consider it a great calamity to be obliged to give it up, and resort to hired help in the family. They are confident that this great family have got along much more pleasantly than by the only other plan which could have been adopted; to say nothing of the reduction of expense which has been thereby effected, and which is a feature of great importance in its bearing upon the missionary, as well as eleemosynary character of the institution.

The entire success of this experiment, for so many years, is a striking testimony to the sagacity and remarkable executive power of Miss Lyon. No one was ever more ready to distrust her own judgment than she, when judicious advisers opposed it. Yet here she had to go forward in opposition to the decided opinion of those whose judgment in almost every thing else was law. Nay, the scheme was met with ridicule by wise and good men. She went with one of the agents to solicit aid from a wealthy and benevolent individual, from whom she had hoped much. She remained at the public house while the agent broached the subject, expecting at least to be invited to call upon the family. But when the subject was fairly before the gentleman, he turned to his daughters, and asked them how they should like to attend a school where they must work in the kitchen; and then merely inquired where Miss Lyon was, and sent his respects to her; but she was not invited to call. When the agent gave her an account of the interview, she buried her face in her hands, and bowed down her head upon the table for a few moments, and then appeared as cheerful as ever, and felt confident that all was for the best.

I give this example as an index of the general state of feeling regarding this subject, among the most respectable class of citizens, when the effort was made to obtain funds. But Miss Lyon knew that with four fifths of the yeomanry of New England, a very different state of feeling existed. She turned, therefore, to them, and found that sympathy which had been denied her in higher circles. Indeed, without this feature of the school, it is the opinion of the principal agent in obtaining funds, that he could not have succeeded.

When this plan was first put into operation, and seemed to answer well, those opposed to it predicted, that when the novelty of the scheme had passed by, it would become unpopular, and must be abandoned. But when they found that five, and even ten, years' experience seemed only to give greater perfection to its operation, — when, on visiting the seminary from time to time, they saw how admirably the domestic affairs were managed, and how well cooked and palatable was the food, — then they predicted that, as soon as Miss Lyon should be removed, this peculiarity must be given up. Yet more than two years have now elapsed since that event, and never were the domestic arrangements managed more satisfactorily than now. I know not what other period of time will be fixed on as the fatal moment when this system must fall, unless it be the close of the present century. In that case, unbelievers will, at least, be saved the mortification of acknowledging that Miss Lyon's judgment in this matter was better than theirs.

Anniversary Addresses.

The following list shows what gentlemen have given the Anniversary Addresses, and on what subjects, when they were published : —

1838. Rev. Joel Hawes, D. D.
1839. Rev. Rufus Anderson, D. D. Education of the Female Sex.
1840. Rev. Mark Hopkins, D. D. Female Education.
1841. Rev. B. B. Edwards, D. D. do.
1842. Rev. E. Hitchcock. Waste of Mind.
1843. Rev. Lyman Beecher, D. D.
1844. Rev. E. N. Kirk. The Greatness of the Human Soul.
1845. Rev Joel Hawes, D. D. Looking-glass for Ladies.
1846. Rev. J. B. Condit, D. D. Christian Love the Essential Element of Moral Power.
1847. Rev. Heman Humphrey, D. D.
1848. Rev. Edward Beecher, D. D.
1849. Rev. E. Hitchcock. A Chapter in the Book of Providence.
1850. Rev. William C. Fowler. Taste.

Religious History of the Seminary.

We have seen that the religious character of the schools with which Miss Lyon had been connected, before coming to South Hadley, was the trait that had endeared them most to religious men. They looked, therefore, with deep interest to the Holyoke Seminary, to learn whether a high tone of piety would be there also associated with a high literary standard. So commonly had they been disjoined, that it had come to be a question whether their union were practicable. During the first year, amid the distractions and exciting novelties incident to starting a new and complex system of education, there was scarcely room for that calm reflection, and that deep and thorough self-examination which are essential to genuine revivals of religion. Moreover, the number of pupils destitute of the Christian's hope the first year was very small, not more than one in ten or twelve. But in every subsequent year to the present, (1851,) there has been witnessed in the school long-continued seasons of special interest in personal religion. Most of these works of divine grace had a thoroughness and extent almost unheard of in the modern history of the church. But I am fortunate in being able to present here a brief summary of these revivals for the first nine years of the institution, from the pen of Miss Mary C. Whitman, who was connected with it almost from its commencement; first as a pupil, then as a teacher, an associate principal, and finally as principal; and whose whole soul was as intensely devoted to the school as that of its founder; so much devoted, indeed, that nature gave way under labors too severe and unremitted. Miss Whitman's letter on this subject, written at my request, was dated in 1846.

"The school has been in operation nine years, and each year, since its commencement, there has been some decided religious interest, unless we except the first; several times amounting to a deep and extensive work of grace. Among the pupils of the first year, there were but ten or twelve who were not hopefully pious; and although there was a general consistency of character and deportment, and great zeal in building up the new institution, there was no marked religious interest, and Christians seemed to be in a state of spiritual stupidity and worldliness. During the second year, God seemed to manifest his acceptance of the consecration to himself, which had been made of the institution, not by a visible cloud, but by a baptism of the Holy Ghost. Every member of the school appeared to be deeply affected, and all but one or two indulged the Christian hope. This revival seemed to give that religious character to the school which its founders desired. The work was very rapid and with great power, and occurred in connection with the fast for literary institutions. Its effects were felt for several successive years. This was especially the case the third, which was the following year. This year *all indulged the Christian hope.* The work was gradual, and there was a progressive continued interest from the first week of the school till the close of the year. The presence of the Spirit was manifested from the first, by attention to instruction, the tearful eye, and exhibition of tenderness of feeling whenever the subject of personal religion was introduced. The number of cases of hopeful conversion this year was nearly the same as the preceding, or about thirty. The fourth year the religious interest still continued, somewhat diminished in its power, yet manifest through the year. Christians were not so generally and deeply affected as at some former times, yet there was an interesting growth and maturing of Christian character; six or eight only remained, at the close of the year, without hope. The fifth year our building was enlarged, and our numbers greatly increased. There were in many cases a decided and interesting development, and settling of religious principle, and also several cases of hopeful conversion of an unusually marked character. The number expressing hope was perhaps about seventeen, being nearly half who entered without hope.

"The following year, the sixth, was one rich in blessing. A more careful division of responsibility and labor among the teachers was made, and from the commencement of the year there was an increased personal effort in relation to every member of the family. God crowned these efforts with abundant success. From the first there was an attentive listening to instruction, and truth seemed to be taking a deep hold of the understanding and conscience. But it was not till March that the Spirit of the Lord came upon us with great power, and at once a large number stood up on the Lord's side, having received the breath of life. The work was sudden, rapid, and powerful. We could only stand still and see the salvation of God in our midst. Some cases of conversion were of a very marked character, and of great interest. Of the sixty-six who entered the school without hope, only six remained destitute of it. The missionary interest this year received a new impulse by the departure of Miss Fisk, one of our teachers, on a foreign mission, and there was an increase in the missionary contributions. During the seventh year, there were about thirty cases of hopeful conversion, but no powerful and general work.

"The last year, the eighth, there were very few cases of hopeful conversion, and very many passed through the whole year apparently without receiving any religious impression. The present year has thus far been one of greater blessing. Very soon after its commencement, there appeared cases of marked interest, and generally an unusual tenderness on the subject of religion. Through the whole of the first term, there was a gathering of interest, which, towards its close, appeared to promise a return of the scenes of former years. The vacation dispersed our family, and since the commencement of the present term, the state of feeling has not reached the point which seemed to be gained before vacation. During the last term, there were about twenty cases of hopeful conversion, and a number have occurred the present term. In all cases where there was any depth of interest the last term, it has continued till the present time, and some have resulted in hope. The indications of a gradual and protracted work of grace are perhaps now more encouraging than at any previous time this term."

Nearly five years have now elapsed since the above account was written, and yet all of them have left a similar testimony to the special converting influences of the Spirit of God in the institution. I cannot state the number apparently converted, save that in 1850 between forty and fifty were thus blessed. This work occurred, it will be perceived, since the death of Miss Lyon. Even the few months of 1851, which have passed before this sentence was written, tell the same story, so joyful to the Christian's heart. It shows us that Miss Lyon's presence and prayers are not necessary to secure the agency of the Holy Spirit, as some have imagined. Yet so far as means are concerned, doubtless the system which she adopted, and the example of fidelity which she has left, have still a most important influence. May we not hope that that influence will be identified with the institution as long as it stands?

Some would imagine, from this account, that, to secure such an almost uninterrupted series of spiritual blessings, extraordinary and peculiar means must have been employed. But nothing of this kind has ever been done. A person might live for weeks in the seminary, during one of these revivals, and yet see nothing unusual, save a deep solemnity and tenderness during religious exercises. Those exercises would not be much multiplied, nor would the literary exercises be suspended or diminished, unless in individual cases of deep seriousness. Both teachers and pupils would seem to be deeply engrossed in their studies, and would be, in fact, during the hours appropriated to study. Nor would the subject of religion be obtruded upon the visitor, or introduced, unless he manifested an unusual interest in the state of the school; and then would he find, what he hardly suspected before, that in the hearts of those teachers and pious pupils there was a deep fountain of religious feeling, that was ready to gush forth and overflow if the channel was once opened. He would learn that in their closets and private fidelity to their pupils and companions lay the secret of such an almost constant divine influence.

It is well known to the Christian familiar with revivals in our churches, that such a work is not to be expected without a previous season of deep humiliation, anxiety, and prayer, on the part of ministers and private Christians. But so often had I witnessed the absence of all outward signs of any special religious interest, when I knew that there were many anxious inquirers in this seminary; so calm and cheerful did the principal and her band of teachers appear; and so much interested in literary and secular objects, — that I began to doubt whether here might not be an exception to this almost universal experience of the church. But in looking over Miss Lyon's correspondence since her decease, I find that the suggestion is entirely unfounded. Not a revival has ever occurred in this seminary, nay, I doubt whether a single conversion has taken place there, which was not preceded by deep humiliation and agonizing prayer on the part of teachers or pious pupils. I think that the letters already given in Parts I. and II. of the memoir will show this in respect to the other schools in which Miss Lyon was engaged. And I am glad to be able to present several others in this place, which disclose the state of her feelings previous to and during some of the revivals in her seminary.

The readers of this memoir ought to understand that probably Miss Lyon never had the thought pass through her mind that one of the letters given in this work would ever be published. They are obviously the honest, unsophisticated outpourings of her heart, for the most part into the hearts of personal friends, and give us the true and exact state of her own feelings and views. They are not all conformed exactly to the strict rules of rhetoric, but I have not dared to alter them much, lest I should weaken their force.

One of the most frequent modes in which Miss Lyon manifested a deeper interest than usual — such an interest as Christians very well know usually precedes a revival — in the religious state of the school, is a confession of spiritual stupidity, and a request to Christian friends that they would offer special prayers in behalf of the school or of individuals. She was no believer in the frigid doctrine which self-styled philosophy would impose upon us, that prayer is of no use to move God, but only to move ourselves. She believed that God would be influenced as really by the prayer of faith as any earthly friend. Hence she felt that by multiplying petitions for great blessings, an answer might be more surely expected. She probably had but few friends to

28

whom she appealed for such aid. But they were individuals in whose ardent piety she felt the fullest confidence. One of them was her mother, as we have seen at an earlier date.

The following are extracts from two letters to Mrs. Bedortha, niece of Miss Lyon and sister of Mrs. Burgess in India. One of the letters is a reply to an invitation to her house, intimating that if her health should require her to leave the seminary, she would feel it a privilege to furnish her with a home.

"South Hadley, December 9, 1846.

"My dear Niece:

"I write so seldom, except on business, that I need some inducement to do it. Still, I should be gratified to write to my friends often, and far more gratified to hear from them more frequently. I received your kind note in L.'s letter, for which I am very much obliged. Nowhere except at my own dear home should I expect to find a more quiet resting-place than by accepting your hospitality. I should love to be with you a while, and should love to become acquainted with your dear little one, even at this age. Precious treasure! may it be a treasure for heaven.

"My health is much better. The thought of visiting you, which flitted across my imagination, I think I shall not indulge this cold, cold winter. I shall no doubt find it best to be a keeper at home.

"I want to ask you to remember our school in your prayers, particularly at this time. It is the season of the year when there are more external circumstances favorable for giving a special attention to religion than at any other time. I have not been able for several weeks to attend meetings or give religious instruction. Miss W. has had some aid from Mr. C. and Mr. H. There are some favorable indications, but no decided interest. We feel it to be an important time. We have a larger number impenitent this year than ever before, and a much larger number among the senior class.

As Providence has seemed to confine your field of labor to a smaller circle this winter than sometimes before, perhaps you would like to unite in spirit with us, and adopt our work as your work, and labor with us, and pray with us in heart. May it not be that God will bless you in this work, and give you, even among us, some souls as your crown of rejoicing in another world? What an unspeakable privilege is it that we may go in the name of Christ and ask for whatever we need, with such a full and sure promise as we have!"

This letter is without date, but postmarked February 20.

"MY DEAR NIECE:

"We have just commenced our second term. The last month of last term we experienced a precious reviving season. Not far from fifty expressed the Christian hope. I wanted to write to you, and ask you to pray for us. Not more than half have been brought into the kingdom. The remainder, who are without hope, have no special interest generally. There are some exceptions. Will you not beseech God in our behalf that he will not leave us? To-morrow is the day observed by many Christians as a day of fasting and prayer for literary institutions. This day is observed by us. I should love to ask you and other friends to pray for us. But it is pleasant to think that God can teach them to pray for us and others, though I ask them not.

"Our dear Mr. Condit is gone. A great breach his death has left in many hearts, especially in mine. We know not how his place will be filled, but our waiting eyes are unto God.

"My last letter from your sister in India enclosed one for your mother. I hope it may be followed with God's blessing, and comfort the heart of your mother. I think your sister has been in a very desirable state of mind ever since she left the country."

TO HON. DANIEL SAFFORD.

"SOUTH HADLEY, October 27, 1848.

"I know you are always interested in our welfare, and especially in our spiritual progress. In many respects we are blessed and prospered. In our religious prospects I scarcely know what to say, my heart is so divided between hope and fear, and has been for many weeks. For a long time, I have hoped that there was a silent influence, which would finally result in the glory of God. There is but little which can be seen by human eyes, or talked about by human tongues. I scarcely dare inquire, lest I may put forth a finger to disturb the gentle onward influence. What, how much, or how little God is now doing we can all say we know not now, but we shall know hereafter. I hope we may then know that it is more than we now can speak about. One thing is sure — it is a time for prayer. I know you will not forget us at the throne of grace. The name of one and another is brought to me by some teacher, from time to time, as one who was venturing to indulge some hope in a Savior's love. But I have made no attempt to designate. Where they will finally be found I know not. Our vacation is very near. Its disturbing influence I very much fear. But we must look to God. In him alone is our hope. How peculiarly true it is that the Holy Spirit is the gift of God! The manner in which inquiries are made sometimes about God's visits of mercy to this institution distresses me, lest we should look for this spiritual blessing in the ordinary course of events. Whenever God comes, it is in his own way, disappointing all human expectations, and taking glory to himself alone. I love to ponder many things of hope and fear in my heart alone, beholding anew our own weakness, our own exceeding unworthiness, and trusting with new confidence in the mighty power and amazing goodness of God."

How does the following letter open to our view the inmost heart of Miss Lyon! and what a heart it is! Need we wonder that prayers from so pure and holy a spirit should secure an almost constant divine influence to the institution?

TO MRS. PORTER.

"SOUTH HADLEY, October 27, 1848.

"MY DEAR MRS. PORTER:

"I do greatly desire to commune in heart with you. I want especially to beg an interest in your prayers. May God give you a spirit of prayer in our behalf. My heart is trembling with hope and fear. The still small voice of the Spirit, which has been whispering in our ears, still hovers over us. I dare not say much, for I know not what to say. I may know hereafter what God is now doing, though I know not now. I fear that I may know hereafter, as I do not now, how the Spirit is grieved. But I hope that I may know that God is even now doing a greater work in the secret recesses of the heart than is visible to our eyes. We transferred our Thursday evening meeting this week to Tuesday evening, (last evening,) and brought all together. Mr. Laurie came in and conducted it. He has not met us before. I trembled, as I fear every change at this time. I had felt it desirable that he should come in once at least this term. If the path of duty was plain, I did endeavor to pray that God would give him some crums of bread to scatter to the hungry. My prayer was answered. He spoke extemporaneously from short notes, but with much freedom, and quite to the point. I felt this as a special favor from the hand of God. I think he spoke to our school only once last year, and then he did not seem to enjoy it much. This will explain my solicitude and my gratitude to God for his goodness. I felt before and after the same as I do in my own case. None but God knows how the responsibility of giving religious instruction to those candidates for eternity weighs on my heart. Sometimes, beforehand, my soul is weighed down with fear and trembling and anxious solicitude, which finds no relief but in God. When I have finished, and God has given me some enlargement of heart, I am overwhelmed with gratitude, and with a view of my own unworthiness for such a blessing. Then I can only pour out my heart in prayer that the Spirit may carry truth to the heart, though given in great weakness. Sometimes the spirit within weighs down the body, and sometimes the body treads the spirit in the dust. O this body of death! Thanks to God for the victory through Jesus Christ our Lord! You will see where, and when, and for what to pray in my behalf."

TO MRS. SAFFORD.

"South Hadley, March 9, 1843

"My dear Mrs. Safford:

"As I have a little business on which I must write this morning, I will take this opportunity to say a few things on the subject so near my heart. On my return, I found things in some respects a little more favorable than when I left. The general seriousness has increased somewhat, and considerably in one small section under the care of one teacher. The teachers have had some increase of interest, and are making some new efforts in their sections. Among those who have most of a heart for such a work there is a growing conviction of the great need of a thorough, powerful revival, to break up the fallow ground, to give a new current to thought and feeling among the younger and least experienced Christians, among the coldest, most lukewarm, and most backward professors, and among some who stand on middle ground. Thursday morning is one of the three mornings in the week when I reserve a half hour for religious instruction and devotional exercises. I have just met the pupils in the hall. I took occasion to spread out before them our present position, with our necessity, our danger, our fear, and our hope, mingling all along my own feelings, my own solemn convictions of the urgency of the case. I stated my own views, that something must be done, though entire darkness was spread over the path of duty. I told them that a little while ago I came to them to ask of them a missionary. I would not go from one to another, lest I should not find the best. And the Lord so stirred up the willing hearts that we all believed that we had sent the one whom he had called and qualified for the work. And now I came to ask for a willing heart to unite with me in prayer for this great thing, as this seemed our last refuge. The scene was very interesting to my feelings. How I should love to have had you with us, to mingle in our sympathies and prayers! There was a very tender spirit this morning, an atmosphere in which it was very easy to breathe and to speak too. Probably little circumstances might have some effect. It is so seldom that I leave this beloved household for a single day, that my meeting them after an absence of only a week and a half is suited to awaken some tender emotions on both sides. Such things are the veriest trifles in themselves; but my sentiment is, that the most trifling circumstances should be used for the same great end. With regard to efforts in behalf of the impenitent, all is dark. But amidst the darkness, and with a burden on my heart which I cannot describe, there is something in my soul which seems like trust in God, that is like a peaceful river, overflowing all its banks. Light can shine out of darkness, and I have great hope that we shall receive a blessing, whether or not the providence of God shall permit Mr. Kirk to come and share with us in our labors, our joys, and our sorrows.

"I have increasing views of the importance of a whole work of the Spirit, a universal work, one which shall reach our whole church of more than one hundred, all young. You recollect Mr. Kirk's vivid description of the difference between passing through the deep valley and rising up into a revival, and leaping immediately into the sympathies of a revival. We need experience of his first to fit us for the varied and important remaining duties of the year. On this account, I have some query whether it may not be better that Mr. Kirk's visit should be deferred a little longer. If he could stay two or three full weeks, I would as soon that he would come to-day as ever. But if he cannot stay but one week, and possibly even less, it is very important that he come at the right time, and expend his power in the best way. His fear that he could not stay long enough is my great fear. It seems to me like a very desirable thing that certain minds, certain difficult cases, should come under the influence of a powerful mind and warm heart, like Mr. Kirk's, and we all need some stirring means; but my own will has ever been graciously kept in an even balance concerning this thing. I am prepared to rejoice or to acquiesce as soon as the will of the Lord shall be made known.

"Now, whatever may be in relation to these things, let me ask and beseech you three, [Mr. and Mrs. Safford and Mr. Kirk,] my dear sympathizing friends, to grant me one petition. Will you every day offer a short prayer in our behalf, which shall arise from your inmost heart, till you hear from me again, which shall be soon? Only ask God, our heavenly Father, in the name of Jesus, our blessed Redeemer, and you shall have your request."

FROM MISS WHITMAN TO MRS. SAFFORD.

"South Hadley, March 16, 1843.

"My dear Mrs. Safford:

"Miss Lyon requests me to write a few lines, just to tell you the reason why she has not written, and to ask a continuance of your prayers for us. She is now quite unwell with a cold, and thinks it duty to reserve her strength for the religious exercises of the school. To-day she is perhaps rather better than yesterday, yet I have some fears that she may have a fever. The physician was yesterday somewhat apprehensive of a lung fever. Should she remain entirely quiet, it would undoubtedly do much towards a restoration; but as the present religious state of the school is, this seems very difficult. You will perhaps recollect that Miss Lyon was absent three Sabbaths previous to her return from Boston. She found, on her return, that there had been considerable increase of feeling, and a state of apparent preparation for the reception of truth, which was not so manifest when she left. By all the indications, it appears that we are approaching a very important crisis. There seems to be an increase of the spirit of prayer and of desire for spiritual blessings on the part of Christians, and among those who are yet impenitent there is not perhaps one who is not more or less affected, and some are deeply impressed. The solemn countenance and tearful eye, whenever the subject is personally introduced, show that the Spirit is operating. We feel very much the need of fervent, importunate prayer to bring us the rich blessing which seems so near to us, and which appears to be delayed only for us to seek it. Our meetings this week have been increased. The regular recess meetings are very promptly attended. These have been occasionally lengthened, and a daily sectional meeting of half an hour has been added from the recreation hours, the time usually devoted to reading. Among some members of our sections there seems to be quite a revival spirit. As teachers, we feel that we very much need the prayers of our friends, that we may be prepared, by the reception of a large measure of the Spirit, to be leaders of the flock. As teachers, may I not ask a special remembrance in your prayers? Our need is great and very pressing. Since her return, Miss Lyon has been giving some connected instruction upon the subject of prayer. It will indeed be a mysterious providence should she now be unable to speak to us."

MISS LYON TO MR. SAFFORD.

"FRIDAY MORNING, March 17, 1843.

"DEAR SIR:

"The present state of our school is exceedingly critical. May you have a mind and a heart to pray for us. The testimony from every source — from the teachers, from the prayer meetings, from meetings for the impenitent, from individual conversation among Christians and among the impenitent — is all the same, proving beyond doubt that the Spirit of God is moving with a gentle influence on the face of the waters. Still, there is not that point and decision which must be attained, or we shall fail of the blessing. The great and distressing doubt which rested on my mind about using any extra means myself has, in the providence of God, been somewhat removed. That interesting state on many things, such as missions, the general path of duty, &c., seems now changing to an increasing desire for the direct and special influences of the Holy Spirit. Our regular business goes forward just as usual, but many have been looking up their leisure time for religion. The teachers are most of them very much engaged in gathering up the fragments of time, that nothing be lost. I have had a short extra meeting for the impenitent every day. I have been able to meet all my appointments, though sometimes I have concentrated all the strength of three or four hours into half an hour. Every thing I do is such a privilege. It is such a privilege, too, to depend daily and hourly for light, for strength, and for hope on our heavenly Father, through Jesus Christ, our Redeemer!

"It is so difficult for me to stop writing! My heart is so full! But I fear you cannot read this. If not, let it go as of no great importance."

"SOUTH HADLEY, March 21, 1843.

"MY DEAR MRS. SAFFORD:

"I must write you a few lines this morning, though I can say but little. I want to ask your prayers especially in two or three respects. Respecting our state generally I have little to say, only that the Lord is doing his own work in his own blessed way. The work is going forward apparently with great rapidity, stillness, universality, gentleness, and power. I believe I mentioned about sixty who entered the school without hope. I should have excepted some eight or ten as the fruits of the drops of mercy which have been falling upon us from month to month during the year. I suppose now not less than one half of the sixty are indulging a hope of pardoning mercy through the blood of Christ. A large number of hopeful conversions have occurred in three days, including the Sabbath. The Sabbath is of indescribable value to us. There can be no community to which it is more important. In times of revival, it seems always to be the day that God delights peculiarly to honor. At other times, it seems to be worth more than all other days in bringing the thoughts into captivity to the will of Christ.

"You will ask what means we are using. They are so small that I can hardly tell what they are, and yet they are numerous, simple, and, through the infinite condescension of God, they seem to be adapted to our state. In the use of means, we simply walk, day by day, by the light which is so graciously shed on our path. We cannot, we would not look forward. Our studies go forward, as usual, with all their regularity, our family duties with all their accustomed order. But we feel that we can and ought to turn aside from other sources of social improvement and enjoyment, that all the fragments of time may be gathered up and devoted to the great and grand business of seeking a divine blessing to descend on all this family. The teachers are all of one mind and one heart in this thing. We use our fragments of time just when they happen to come, and just for the object for which they seem at the time to be most needed. The prayer meetings are sometimes fifteen minutes, sometimes half an hour, and sometimes longer, according to circumstances. Some of the teachers have quite a prayer meeting in fifteen minutes at recess in the evening with their sections. They have adopted the practice in these little daily meetings, long ago, of having the prayers unsolicited. This turns to a favorable account just now. Sometimes they find time for three or four prayers in fifteen minutes. They can return to their duties with renewed energy and submission, if not of pleasure in their studies. The teachers really seem to be emphatically the leaders of the flock. In the meetings for the impenitent I have no very definite plan. My waiting eyes are unto God. From day to day, thus far, the path of duty has been plain. The almost Egyptian darkness which rested on my mind about the path of duty was but a contrast to that light which shines from day to day. I have no knowledge of future duty, and I ask for none. It is so sweet to carry every burden and every care to the throne of everlasting love, and of perfect confidence through the Lord Jesus Christ. My lungs have not allowed me the privilege of individual conversation, but the teachers and others are instant in season and out of season.

"But my sheet is full, and I fear the mail will be gone, and I have not told my errand. First, I want you should pray daily and unitedly with great fervency for ———. She has some rather peculiar associations, as I suppose. She retains her hope, but something in her character revolts from every thing social in feeling or action. I cannot find that an individual in the house has been able to approach her successfully in the least degree on the religion of her heart or life. I have met minds in a similar state, and, as a matter of judgment in her case, have avoided meeting her on the subject, hoping that some door might be opened in her behalf before the year closes. Many things may be done and said in time of a revival that cannot be done and said at any other time. This may be the favored time for her. I have approached the subject gently, and hope I may have the privilege of doing something more. I think it not best that she should know that the subject passes between us. But I hope you will really pray in her behalf.

"We have some individuals that seem among the most hopeless. They are among the righteous towards men. They have passed seasons of conviction, and perhaps indulged hope once or twice. Here they are clothed now in the self-righteousness of not being deceived this time. Do pray for them.

"My continued desire and prayer is, that this whole family as a family, and every individual as an individual, may be baptized by the Holy Spirit. We are experiencing some interesting reconversions among those who have long indulged a hope."

"SOUTH HADLEY, Saturday Eve, March 25, 1843.

"MY DEAR MRS. SAFFORD:

"I cannot tell you how rejoiced I was to receive your letter. I had so long been looking and longing for it. I knew you were praying for us, but I wanted to have you tell me so. We are in greater need than ever of the power of prayer. As you hear from us, from time to time, I trust that you will not cease to give thanks to God, and to pray without ceasing, making all our requests known to God. It is sweet to think of you as praying in our behalf, if you cannot come and see us. We are on the verge of another holy Sabbath. It is a great event for us to pass a holy Sabbath. O that a great, a very great blessing may descend upon us! The past week has been a wonderful time. Of that sixty over whom I mourned so much, and wept so much, and prayed so much, the week I was with you, only a remnant are now without hope. But some very trying cases are left. O for that all-prevailing prayer in their behalf which shall be heard! Several professors of religion have given up their hope, and a few have disclosed the fact that they have had no hope for a long time. Some of them are now walking in light, and others are shrouded in thick darkness. But the Lord has wrought for us such great things that we can but trust him in every time of need.

"*Monday Morning.* — We have decided to devote this day as a day of fasting and prayer. This is the first day this year that we set apart to such a blessing on ourselves as individuals and on our family as a family. It is a great and a solemn thing to set apart such a day. It is a great thing voluntarily to give up all our business for a whole day, that we may meet God in the inner sanctuary of his holy, spiritual temple. I trust this day is brought by many hearts as a willing offering, and that it will be accepted through the blood of the everlasting covenant.

"I have many things which I want to write, but I cannot now. I should be glad to tell you how the Lord has led us along by his own right hand. I should love to give you one simple page from my own soul. Do write very soon."

More letters of Miss Lyon respecting the revival of 1843 have come into my hands than of any other special work of grace. That she had similar feelings and made similar efforts at other times cannot be doubted. But it is fortunate that we have her views so fully in respect to that powerful work.

TO MRS. BANISTER.

"SOUTH HADLEY, March 8, 1843.

"MY DEAR MRS. B.:

"I have been absent a short time, and on my return yesterday found your two letters. You ask about the spiritual interests of our school. I was just thinking of writing to you on this very subject, that I might beseech your prayers at this time, for it is one of great darkness, of anxiety, of hope, of fear. In temporal things we have been greatly blessed. We have a much greater supply of teachers than usual. Misses M. and W. have applied their minds closely to reducing every thing under their control to the most beautiful order and symmetry, and with great success. Our young ladies are very youthful, more and more so every year; but there is so much docility, such a sweet atmosphere all around, that I feel, from day to day, that our home is a sweet home. There is more missionary interest than usual, and more desire among some Christians to be prepared for the service of God. But, alas! one thing is lacking — the direct and powerful influences of the Holy Spirit. A few gentle drops have descended, but we have enjoyed no plentiful shower, and this we greatly need. According to all former experience, the harvest time for this year will be past in four or five weeks. Then will come the finishing up of the term and the spring examinations. After that will follow the short summer term, a most favorable time for fixing last impressions, for attempting to lead Christians into green and living pastures, but not a favorable time for the work of the Holy Spirit in breaking up the fallow ground by conviction and conversion. Nearly sixty of our number are without hope. As teachers, as Christians, as an institution, we greatly need the effects of a powerful revival. I fear to make any extra effort; I fear to omit it. I know not what to do. The way seems greatly hedged up. I fear to go forward; I dare not stand still; I cannot go back.

"I went to Boston to help fit off one of our teachers as a missionary to the Nestorians. I made arrangements to be absent a few days longer, that I might have time to look over our sad, very sad state, and that I might inquire of the Lord a right path in which to walk. I wanted exceedingly to go to N., and also to M., on my way home; but I thought it my duty to stay in one place, to make no calls, to do but a little business, and only attend meetings as I could. I have seldom had so profitable a week, when I have had so much physical and mental rest, and so much, as I humbly hope, of spiritual refreshing. I have been greatly interested in examining the subject of prayer. Since I returned, a few more drops have fallen. But how so great a work can be done in so short a time I know not. All is yet darkness, but I hope and trust that light will shine out of darkness. Now, I have one urgent request to make of you. It is, that you would set apart a little time every day to pray in sincerity and in truth for us. Pray that God would, in his own way, do a great work here, and give us a great blessing. Pray that we may be taught what the Lord would have us do. Will you thus pray every day till you hear from us again, which shall be soon? For a few days, I design to study daily two passages of Scripture, praying that I may be led by the Spirit to receive into the understanding and heart just what the Holy Ghost has revealed in these wonderful passages — Luke xi. 5–13, James i. 5–8. Would you like to study these daily with me, as you pray for us?"

What a different meaning did Miss Lyon attach to the word *rest* from what is generally understood! Her views, I apprehend, approximated to what the Bible calls rest in heaven, viz., a state of intense activity in the service of God.

TO MRS. BANISTER.

"March 20, 1843.

"When I last wrote to you, I engaged to address you again very soon. I have been very sick for a week, or I should have written some days sooner.

"In my last, I requested a special interest in your prayers until you heard from us again. I communicated also something respecting our religious state. Just at that time, I felt that we were in a very trying, critical condition. I had been absent three Sabbaths. After spending another Sabbath here, and becoming more acquainted with the state of things, I began to feel 'surely the Lord is in this place, and I knew it not.' In all seasons of religious interest in this house the Lord has ever delighted to own and bless the holy Sabbath. For the last week, a work has been going forward with convincing evidence that it is indeed the work of the Lord. I believe I told you in my last that I spent a few days in Boston, that I might have quiet and time to look over our condition, and to seek the right way. The state of our school in general has been unusually encouraging this year. There has been a very sweet spirit, a pleasant docility, and a consistent deportment. Our evening prayer meetings have been like a connecting artery through which the life-blood flowed. Our semi-monthly missionary meeting has been better attended than ever before, and we have all thought that the missionary spirit was advancing in the seminary. This spirit seemed to receive an impulse by Miss Fisk's leaving us, and devoting herself to this work. I have thought we seemed preparing for every thing else desirable except for the reception of the special influences of the Holy Spirit. To this there seemed some great barrier. This was the great thing to be sought. This we needed to convict and convert sinners, to give that living faith in the great atoning sacrifice without which it is impossible to please God. This we needed to overcome the world, to fix our hopes, to establish our joys, to settle forever our confidence. I returned from Boston not knowing whither I should be led, or whether there was any thing special that could be done. But I felt a trust, and a reliance on an invisible arm, greater and sweeter than I can ever describe. What a privilege it is to walk by faith! What a privilege it is to have no wisdom of our own, to have no plan for the future, that the wisdom of God may be more manifest, and that the indications of Providence and the guidance of the Spirit, day by day, may be more precious! I found, on my return, that a spiritual change was passing over the face of things, that the Spirit of God was gently moving on the face of the waters. The teachers I found more active in gathering up the fragments of time for religious duties and privileges connected with those under their care. Some Christians were becoming deeply interested. Many of the impenitent were in an inquiring state, and some very deeply affected. The work appears now to be going directly forward. Some eight or ten expressed a hope at different times along in the winter. This number is now increased probably to about twenty-five. We are passing a very important time. There are some exceedingly difficult, dark cases. Some have passed through revival after revival, have been deeply affected, indulged a hope once or twice, have made one effort after another, and now, as they suppose, are settled down in a state of disconsolate indifference. May the Lord give you a mind and heart to pray for us! May I not hear from you soon? Let me have a page from your own heart.

"I should love to write you a long letter about my own personal feelings. Some views of truth have of late passed before my mind in an exceedingly interesting manner to myself. With what condescension does God come down in the simplicity of truth to our own personal wants! Let God be honored, let Christ be all and in all, and let every created being be less than nothing and vanity."

At the close of a business letter, dated April 13, 1843, she writes, —

"I hoped I should have quite a large part of this sheet to tell you what the Lord hath wrought for us since I last wrote you. I believe just at the time that I sent my last letter, a cloud of mercy was gathering over our heads, and a few drops had fallen upon us. The cloud had so long been gathering, and so gently, that we scarcely knew it; but soon the windows of heaven were opened, and the blessing descended, so that there was scarcely room in our minds or hearts to receive it. When I returned from Boston, there were a few more than fifty without hope. In about three weeks, all but six expressed some hope that they had found the Savior; in a single week of this time, more than thirty of the number.

"In all my privileged experience connected with the work of the Spirit, this, I think, has been of unparalleled rapidity; and yet I have never witnessed more quietness and stillness than in its progress, or any less of what some call *reaction* to be watched against in the result. It has seemed like a sudden, powerful shower bursting upon us, but descending with so much gentleness that not a leaf or twig among the tender plants is turned out of its place, and then so suddenly giving way to the beautiful sun and refreshing dews. But as teachers, we have a great work to cherish these tender plants. Shall we not have your prayers? O, to follow Christ in the work of cherishing them is what I want. This desire enters almost daily into the very depths of my soul with an untold and unwonted strength."

In the following, reference is made to the "Missionary Offering:" —

"SOUTH HADLEY, June 12, 1843.

"MY DEAR MRS. B.:

"I will just communicate to *you* a secret. I have been employing all the time I could take for the last month in writing an article, which I expect to put into a *very little* book. How much I should value a little of your aid in fitting it for the press! But this cannot be with your health and cares, and with my extreme pressure relative to time. As a mere matter of friendship, however, I should love just to read it to you. If the printers can spare it, I shall take it with me, though there may not be time to read it. It would take about one hour and a half. I am extremely anxious that no one should guess at the writer of this little book."

The following letter was among the last which Miss Lyon wrote: —

"SOUTH HADLEY, January 29, 1849.

"MY DEAR MRS. SAFFORD:

"Our school have just returned after vacation. We know but little of the religious state. The influences of the Holy Spirit in the work of conversion are very often at a close nearly with a vacation. Looking at common influences, and the results, the facts in the case seem to be, that just before a vacation, all who have much interest feel a kind of necessity laid upon them to give their whole attention to the subject. This circumstance is made a means of good in the condescending mercy of God. After the vacation is passed, not many remain with much interest; either they have entered the ark of safety, or have gone back to the world. I do not know how it is now. But will you not pray that this year may be an exception in this particular? Pray that the Spirit may abide with us, not only in the building up of Christians, but in the conviction and conversion of sinners. The grace of our Lord Jesus Christ is rich and boundless, and here is our only hope."

Such a history as the preceding is certainly very instructive as well as interesting to every Christian who loves revivals. It lets us into the true secret of the extraordinary exhibitions of divine grace with which this school, as well as its prototypes, have been favored; and that is, the uniform and systematic fidelity of the instructors. Practically, as well as theoretically, they have given religion the first place in their teachings, and have really felt more solicitous about the eternal than the literary welfare of their pupils; and God has honored those who thus honored Him, by that special influence that subdues and converts the soul. And how free have these seasons been of all extravagance and enthusiasm! Such revivals are not followed by a painful reaction, as in some of the churches where animal feeling has done more than God's Spirit. The very large proportion of converts in these revivals, compared with those in the churches generally, is also a feature very remarkable. Doubtless the thoroughness and adaptation of the means employed have had an important connection with such results. For, in general, God operates according to means; that is, he acts according to certain laws, as really as in the ordinary processes of nature; and, of course, the more appropriate the means, and the more faithfully applied, the more glorious will be the results.

In some subsequent extracts which we shall present, we shall see that the means preparatory to these revivals were not used by Miss Lyon alone, but equally by the other teachers.

Precisely how many revivals Miss Lyon passed through during her life, it may not be possible to state. A friend is confident that Miss L. informed her that the number was about thirty; but some, well qualified to judge, doubt whether this number is not rather too large. But when we recollect that she witnessed eleven at South Hadley, is it not probable that in the thirteen previous years, in which she taught at Ashfield, Buckland, Derry, and Ipswich, and in the previous twenty-four years of her life, she might have passed through as many as twenty more?

In most of these she was a prominent actor, and had agonized in prayer before they came. How few of the ministers of the gospel have had experience half as abundant!

Cultivation of a Benevolent and Missionary Spirit in the Seminary.

Not much was said, in starting this institution, about raising up missionaries. Yet in fact the principles on which it was founded, and the manner in which it has been conducted, could not but lead to such a result. All who engaged in the work of founding and conducting the enterprise were ex pected to do it on the same benevolent principles that form the mainspring of missionary labors. They were not to expect any pecuniary reward, save what was essential to support them by the most economical mode of living. The pupils were taught that they ought to engage in the business of teaching from a sense of duty, and a benevolent desire to do good. And hence they were not to avoid any field of labor because it was hard and uninviting. They were to hold themselves in readiness to go to any part of our own wide country, where Providence should point out the post of duty. And surely some of these posts are quite as repulsive to any thing but benevolence as any foreign missionary field. Indeed, so wide is our country now, that the distinction between home and foreign missions is nearly lost; and when we hear of a person going to Oregon, or California, we hardly know whether to denominate him a domestic or a foreign missionary. Hence those ladies who were made willing to go to any part of our wide territory as teachers (and that was a leading and expressed object of the seminary) would easily be persuaded to go to foreign lands on the same errand of mercy.

But this was not all. For, from the first, I believe, special and systematic efforts were made in the school to excite an interest in foreign missions. A missionary meeting, as it was called, has been held, since the third year, at least as often as once a fortnight, or once a month, with this object specially in view. The result has been, that up to 1850, not less than forty members of the seminary have gone forth to the foreign field of missionary labor; among whom not less than *nine* were teachers at South Hadley. With these, communications are frequent, and their letters give great interest to the missionary meetings. At the seminary a journal has for several years been kept of all the important events there transpiring; and a copy of this is sent to the missionaries;

and thus a mutual interest is inspired between those so widely separated. The correspondence forms galvanic wires, through which the missionary spirit is transmitted backward and forward.

Personal consecration is the strongest evidence of interest in the missionary work that can be given. But contributions in money are also an index of the feelings of the heart. Judged of by this standard, one is struck with the amount contributed by the Holyoke Seminary. A few details on this point will be given in another place; and in general it may be stated, that the annual amount has varied from six hundred to one thousand dollars; and this has been done, it should be recollected, by teachers whose salaries varied from one hundred and twenty-five to two hundred dollars, and by pupils, many of whom are from families of small pecuniary means.

I shall now copy some letters of Miss Lyon relating to the subject of missions, though not exclusively so. From these her deep interest in the subject may be seen. I shall also give a few letters from missionaries, showing their estimate of her missionary character.

Miss Fiske, mentioned in some of the following letters, was once a pupil and teacher in the seminary, and the first, I believe, that left for a foreign mission. Miss Rice was also a pupil. Both of them are now at Ooroomiah, in Persia.

TO REV. JUSTIN PERKINS, D. D., OF OOROOMIAH, PERSIA.

"SOUTH HADLEY, February 6, 1844.

"DEAR SIR:

"Your kind letter, bearing date July 7, I have received, for which please accept my cordial thanks. Perhaps you may occasionally grant me a like favor.

"Your testimony to Miss Fiske's happiness and usefulness is very gratifying. Her own letters, too, are all suited to make her friends happy in having given her up for such a work. It is my opinion that the leadings of Providence should be decisive to justify our encouraging an unmarried female to go on a foreign mission. My impressions on this subject were strengthened as I saw Misses Fiske and Myers bidding farewell to friends and home, and kindred and country. How different was their situation from the rest of the company! Every other missionary had *one* intimate friend, and that one the dearest friend on earth. But Miss Fiske has been admirably prepared by the endowments of nature, by the dealings of Providence, and by the influence of grace, for just such a sacrifice. I rejoice that her heavenly Father has called her to this self-denying work, and that she was not disobedient to the heavenly voice. I rejoice, too, that the finger of Providence pointed her out to go, rather than any other one about whom we had conversation. I doubt not that she will find many ways of doing good besides that of teaching. As you wander along together, a lonely band through this vale of tears, and as you are laboring and suffering for Christ's sake, I doubt not that Miss Fiske will often be able, in her own quiet way, to come to one heart and another as an angel of mercy and kindness. Sometimes she may be able to give to some of her companions in toil a cup of consolation, when others, who would fain enjoy the same privilege, have not the time nor the strength granted them.

"Miss Fiske has been very faithful and successful in writing letters. I think this not among the least of the ways given her to serve the cause.

"You speak with interest of your visit to America, and to our beloved institution. Your remembrance of us is gratifying to our hearts. I rejoice that I was permitted to see so much of you while in this country. I enjoyed your visits here very much, and the memory is still precious. We love to recognize your mission and your name, as well as that of our beloved friend, Miss Fiske. I would rejoice and thank

God in your behalf, that your return, your visitation, and your departure, were attended with so many circumstances, comforting to yourselves and favorable to the cause. Among all the duties that devolve on a missionary, it is far from being the least responsible, to be called in providence to visit his native land, and to meet all the people and all things which he must meet, and to make every where an honest, a faithful, and a salutary impression — an impression worthy of Him who came from heaven to earth on a great mission to save a lost and guilty world.

"Give my very affectionate regards to Mrs. Perkins. May the Lord sustain and comfort her under all her trials. May you both have strength given you, for many years to come, to enjoy the privilege of laboring and suffering for Christ's sake.

"Give my affectionate remembrance to Mar Yohannan. I hope he will live to see many missionaries go from his country to different parts of Asia. My love to Miss Myers."

MISS FIDELIA FISKE TO MISS WHITMAN.

"OOROOMIAH, November 24, 1849.

"MY OWN LOVED SISTER:

"I enclose copies of some letters which Miss Lyon wrote me after leaving America. While they are peculiarly precious to me, I did not think of their being useful in preparing her memoir. But my associates here thought I should by all means copy them, and I have done so. It has been a pleasingly mournful task, and I could hardly restrain my feelings in doing it. But I mourn not for her. She is blest, supremely blest, and we would not recall her from that sweet, heavenly home. I shall await the appearance of her memoir with peculiar interest, as will thousands of others. Who *can* do justice to her memory? I am sure no mortal. But her record is with the Holy One. An angel's pen, directed by the Savior, who was so precious to her in life, and in death has done what those who loved her here, fain would, but cannot do.

"I cannot tell you, my dear sister, how often, nor with how much sympathy, I think of you. Never do I ask my own *daily bread*, without asking it for her so dear to me, and on whom such crushing responsibilities rest. May the Lord sustain you. I rejoice to believe that he will. You serve the same God, and in the same cause, that dear Miss Lyon did, and many are the fervent prayers which go up to heaven for you."

MISS LYON TO MISS FISKE.

"SOUTH HADLEY, March 4, 1844.

"MY DEAR MISS FISKE:

"It is one year this week since we were in Boston together. I have often desired to write you some of the passing events, some of deep and thrilling interest, which have transpired since that time. As the mind and heart have been borne along upon the swelling wave, I have thought of you, and thought, too, that I should love to have you know what was passing among us. But I have almost done writing letters, except on business. I can never again sit down to write what will be worth passing so far by mail. But in this little box I cannot refrain from depositing a note. But what shall I write? Every thing must be told you over and over again, except it may be some of the passing things in my own breast. And first I would thank you sincerely for your faithfulness and promptness in writing to me, and to us all. I believe it is one prominent way offered you of doing good to write to this seminary. I hope you will have a mind, and a heart, and strength, and time to continue to do what you have begun. I shall enjoy, in my turn, receiving an occasional letter, though I may never write you again.

"You remember the state of the school when you left. After you were fairly gone, I had a little time to look at our real condition. It seemed to me very peculiar and critical, and so it now seems to me in review. I can never forget that week in Boston after you left, which I spent there especially to rest, to meditate, and to try to pray; and I never can forget the scenes of the month which followed, and of the unspeakable grace of God then manifested. But Miss Whitman and others have written you all the particulars. I will just pass that over, and not attempt to describe that remarkable chapter in our history. Suffice it to say, that the grace of God was manifested in a wonderful manner. Those I shall ever regard as among the most striking scenes, exhibiting and illustrating the great scheme of salvation.

"I will just take time to describe an incident in the history of my own emotions, which resulted in the little book which I send you with this — the 'Missionary Offering.' You may inquire how I found time to write a letter long enough to make a book. The truth is, that my spirit was so stirred, and my heart so burdened, that I wrote as fast as possible, without inquiring how I wrote, or whether I had time to write. In the month of April, the scenes of the revival, the prospect of our next missionary subscription, the falling off of the missionary receipts, all combined to give me an unusual current of emotions in view of certain subjects. I was preparing a connected series of topics to present to the school, the substance of which you will find, to some extent, in the first three and last two chapters. I had just commenced before the monthly concert in May, to which reference is made. After reading the affecting circular, which I heard with deepest interest, in behalf of all our school, who were present as well as myself, Mr. Condit invited a young minister, just commencing preaching, to make some remarks. To Mr. Condit's disappointment, and to my distress, instead of following out the subject, he just attempted to make some strictures on our missionary operations, alluding to slavery, and speaking of the want of economy at some of our stations. The defect of the young man was more in the head than the heart. All agreed that his remarks were, at least, ill-timed. But, among other results, they gave existence to the little book. It was scarcely two days before most of the materials were gathered together. They soon assumed a visible and tangible form, merely as a relief to the internal spirit. Thus much for this little circumstance, as little things often interest friends more than greater events."

TO MISS FISKE.

"South Hadley, January 15, 1846.

"My dear Miss Fiske:

"This morning, before I went into the hall, Miss Moore announced that Miss Fiske's little box would be closed at the 9¼ bell. Since dinner, I heard of it, and was invited to look at the contents. I did not really think it was finished, as I had nothing in it. For want of something better, I send you a handkerchief, where you can see my name.

"You sympathize in *all* the things which are passing among us, and especially those events which relate to the missionary cause. I know that some of your kind friends will be sure to tell you that Miss Moore is really going. It will surprise you, as it has many here. The first question generally is, 'What does Miss Lyon think of it?' I have nothing to say in all these things, only to ask that the will of the Lord may be done, and to submit to all the dispensations of Providence, whether with means or without means. This is certainly a great event to us, and especially to me. My only wish concerning it is, that it may be for the furtherance of the gospel. We know so little of the great plans of God, that it is wisest, and safest, and sweetest, to leave all with him.

'Much love to Mr. and Mrs. Perkins."

TO MISS FISKE.

"SOUTH HADLEY, June 16, 1847.

"MY DEAR, MY VERY DEAR MISS FISKE:

"How I should love, if I ever did such a thing, to write you a long letter! I would not try to repeat the many passing events which I hope some of your kind friends have continued to tell you. Nor would I tell you any new truth, nor any new duty, nor any new promise, nor any new encouragement, to labor and suffer for Christ's sake. I would not attempt to point out to you any new resting-place for the feet of weary pilgrims on their way to the celestial city. No, I would only repeat, if I could, a few of the many and precious things which you already know, and on which your heart now delights to dwell. I would only, if I could, while I am in this tabernacle, now and then write you a few words, stirring you up by way of remembrance. I would have you after my decease, also, have these things always in remembrance.

"How I should love to tell you how a kind Providence has led me along ever since last we met, and last parted, — how one comfort has been taken away, and another granted, — how good, very good, God has been to us, and how the promise, 'As thy days, so shall thy strength be,' has *never* failed! . . . .

[Here follow some paragraphs which Miss L. herself calls "*confidential*." They refer mostly to Miss Rice's leaving.]

"Finally, I should love to tell you how my heart goes with her, (Miss Rice,) as I seem to send her forth as one of my own children, — how I now commend her to you, — to your acquaintance, — to your love, — to your sympathy, — to your prayers, — to a participation in all your labors, your joys and your sorrows! . . . . May you both live long, together be abundant in labors, earnest in prayer, and rich in faith, and at last may you receive a crown of glory, which shall never fade away.

"My very affectionate regards to Mr. and Mrs. Perkins. Many thanks for what he has written me in days that are past. Will he not write me again? Ask him to be a father to another of my daughters."

TO MISS FISKE.

"MY DEAR MISS FISKE:

"I cannot let the journal go without a line of sympathy for yourself individually. In the trials by persecution you have been passing through, you have had my deepest sympathy, as well as that of hundreds and thousands of other hearts. But you have had other afflictions making their pathway into your hearts. In these you have had my sympathy. I have wept with you, over dear, dear Mrs. Stoddard. I can think how you loved her, and how precious is love in your far distant home. I can imagine the many things, in your peculiar position, which make a warm heart, a kindred spirit, and a sympathizing soul, (not so much for yourself as for your work,) a sister, and more than a sister. Such was dear Mrs. Stoddard."

(The above had no date, but must have been written in January, '49. I did not receive it till after Miss L.'s death. — *F. Fiske.*)

MISS RICE TO MISS WHITMAN.

"OOROOMIAH, November 24, 1849.

"MY VERY DEAR MISS WHITMAN:

"I have been looking over a package of our beloved Miss Lyon's letters this afternoon, and deep and tender emotions have been awakened.

"They almost all relate to the subject of my going to Persia; but they have so much that is of a personal character in them, that I have copied none of them. I send the copy of a note, which I received while in Erzeroom, on my way to O.

"Endearing and touching recollections of the past have

been awakened, and I rejoice that it was my privilege to enjoy the instructions and counsels of the now sainted one. Though dead, she yet speaks to my heart, urging me to labor for the salvation of souls, and honor the Master, who has called me to this part of the vineyard.

"I rejoice to know that you are appointed her successor in the beloved seminary, and that dear Miss Hazen may share your labors. May the mantle of the departed fall upon you; may your strength ever be equal to your day; may divine wisdom teach you, and may Jesus make all grace abound towards you.

"We will not cease to pray for you, and we will not cease to love our Holyoke home. O, give us your prayers; for the blessings that prayer brings are those we most need."

MISS LYON TO MISS RICE.

"SOUTH HADLEY, June 17, 1847.

"MY DEAR MISS RICE: —

"When Miss Fiske shall hand you this little note, you will be far, far away. Kind Providence preserving your life, I trust this will find you in your new, your chosen, your adopted home.

"Your eyes there will look on the same glorious sun, the same beautiful moon, and the same sparkling stars that ours do in your own native land. Will it not be pleasant, when you are removed from all which once met your eyes, to look up to the heavens, and think that the eyes of your father and your mother may be looking at the same things? But nearer than this can we come together, when we approach the mercy seat. You will be no farther from that precious place of resort, no farther from your God, no farther from your last and best home in heaven. My dear, dear friend, be thou faithful unto death, and thou shalt have a crown of life."

TO HON. DANIEL SAFFORD.

"SOUTH HADLEY, December 3, 1846.

"My health is much better. I can now ride, and I am taking this tonic every pleasant day with great advantage. Let me know how dear Mrs. Safford is when you write. When shall I set my eyes on your faces again? Perhaps you know that cousin Lucy Lyon (now Mrs. Lord) is going to China on a mission under the Baptist board. She and her husband are now here, making us their last visit. They sail from New York some time this month. If my health improves, I may go and be with them at the time they sail. Perhaps you will ask why I do not sit for my portrait. I have thought of it, but think I cannot at this time.

"How afflicting is the providence which has taken away one of our secretaries of the Board of Missions! But my mind dwells much on his sudden transition to his eternal home. How must that world of glory have burst on his astonished vision! But we are left to mourn. Yet let us remember that it is no accident which has taken him away. It is a stroke of the divine hand, planned, directed, and executed by infinite wisdom and infinite goodness. May we not yet see, and may he not even now see, how it comes in to forward the great work of saving a lost and dying world? What a place does Christ occupy as an atoning sacrifice in all the great things of divine Providence! What a book is there yet to be opened and read in the glorious doctrine of the atonement!"

TO MRS. SAFFORD.

"SOUTH HADLEY, June 30, 1848.

"I thank you for remembering me at the time of the meeting of the Board of Foreign Missions. Miss Whitman and myself will be very glad to accept of the favor. I hope there will be a spirit of prayer in behalf of that meeting. The associations connected with meetings in Boston are to me very interesting. It seems like a happy, united family circle gathering around the paternal board. They went out by themselves, but they return bringing with them the children whom God has given them. How few of us will live to see another such family gathering in behalf of missions in Boston! I hope that the good people in Boston, who are favored with so many rich feasts, will have a spiritual blessing on this occasion. Do you not think that the repetition of such things has just the opposite effect on different minds? To some, they weary, or become insipid, or too common to have interest. To others, the more common, the more precious; the more frequent the repetition, the more refreshing is the spiritual feast. Just like the face of nature, unseen by some eyes because so common; but to others, rising every morning with new freshness, with more of beauty, and more of God."

The following is Dr. J. Perkins's estimate of Miss Lyon's missionary character: —

TO MISS MARY C. WHITMAN, PRINCIPAL OF MOUNT HOLYOKE SEMINARY.

"OOROOMIAH, December 18, 1849.

"DEAR MADAM:

"I feel a deep interest, as thousands must, in the contemplated memoir of one whose memory is so fragrant, whose name is so widely and sacredly cherished, whose labors of love were so herculean, and whose influence, past and prospective, is so unmeasurable as that of our long revered and now sainted friend. It is a very responsible trust to become the almoner to the churches and the world of so precious a legacy as the biography of Mary Lyon.

"We have all been deeply interested in the notices of our departed friend which have appeared in the public prints. Yet in every one that I have read I have felt a painful disappointment, not so much in the want of fulness in regard to the parts presented, as in the almost entire omission of some of the most important traits of her remarkable and most estimable character. Almost nothing is said of her as a *religious teacher*, or of the many precious revivals that have occurred under her influence. The most extended notice contains *not one word* in regard to her interest and efforts in the cause of foreign missions, nor as a religious instructor. Now, were these cardinal and most important points in her life and character to be overlooked in the memoir, or to be cast into the shade by the acknowledged brightness and grandeur of her almost matchless career as a mere teacher, it were better, in my opinion, that her memoir should never be written. Would not the results of those precious revivals in so many scores and hundreds of living plants of righteousness, introduced into the garden of God by her honored instrumentality, cry out against such injustice to her memory? Would not the four quarters of the globe, blessed with the labors and influence of so many of her missionary daughters, bearing much of her hallowed impress, raise their united remonstrance? And would not that charming and effective little volume, the 'Missionary Offering,' the product of her overflowing heart, breathing so richly the spirit of missions and of heaven, and the *missionary maps*, placed by her in each room in the seminary, to say nothing of her other numberless, nameless, and long-continued efforts in the same cause, deepen and prolong the sad note of disappointment and dissatisfaction at the omission supposed? These are the points in her character and course that looked most directly to eternity; and was it not preëminently for eternity, rather than time, that Miss Lyon lived and toiled?

"I am aware that it is probably impossible to give all the truth, in her case, through the medium of any memoir. Her full record is on high. If, however, the work be well done, as her character was one of the brightest and most remarkable that adorn our age, or any age, I shall confidently expect that her biography will be a volume of corresponding interest and value, through which, though dead, she will effectually speak for ages to come."

The following extract from a published notice of Miss Lyon's death, by Miss H. Lyman, of Montreal, is scarcely more than the literal truth: —

"Is she missed? Scarcely a state in the American Union but contains those she trained. Long ere this, amid the hunting-grounds of the Sioux and the villages of the Cherokees, the tear of the missionary has wet the page which has told of Miss Lyon's departure. The Sandwich Islander will ask why is his white teacher's eye dim, as she reads her American letters. The swarthy African will lament with his sorrowing guide, who cries, 'Help, Lord, for the godly ceaseth.' The cinnamon groves of Ceylon and the palm-trees of India overshadow her early deceased missionary pupils, while those left to bear the burden and heat of the day will wail the saint whose prayers and letters they so prized. Among the Nestorians of Persia and at the base of Mount Olympus will her name be breathed softly, as the household name of one whom God hath taken."

EXTRACTS FROM THE JOURNAL KEPT AT THE HOLYOKE SEMINARY.

For some years past, it has been customary for one of the teachers to keep a journal of the more interesting events occurring at the institution, which is sent to the foreign missionaries who were once its members. Having been permitted to look over that journal for 1846 and 1847, I am constrained to make rather copious extracts. They relate in a great measure, however, to the religious interests and events of the seminary; and I value the descriptions the more because the writer never dreamt of their meeting the public eye; and, therefore, she wrote in an unconstrained manner. Up to May, 1848, this journal was kept by Miss Susan L. Tolman, at which time her successor in this work, Miss Rebecca Fiske, remarks that Miss Tolman had "decided to become a *reader* rather than a *writer* of the Holyoke journal;" that is, she had become herself a missionary to Ceylon.

"*October* 3, 1846. — To-day, the names of those who are professors of religion and those who are not were taken. More than ninety, nearly half of our family, are classed with those who have no hope. May we, as a band of teachers, be faithful to these precious souls.

"*October* 10. — Miss Lyon is taking the Book of Proverbs in course for morning devotions, and has invited all to read it with her. She does not appear to be as well this year as last. Her extra exertion during vacation nearly exhausted her. An infirmity which must be very trying has recently fastened itself upon her, as we fear permanently. She has become so deaf that it is difficult for her to hear ordinary conversation.

"*October* 14. — Our weekly religious meetings commenced this evening. Miss Lyon met with the Christians. She spoke of her deep emotion in looking upon so many *professed* followers of Christ, of the possibility that some might be deceived, and then, in her own earnest, irresistible manner, urged upon each a thorough self-examination.

"*October* 21. — We must again speak of Miss Lyon's failing health. She has taken a severe cold, which has settled upon her lungs. It is with difficulty she can speak for any length of time.

"*November* 12. — To-day, our second missionary meeting was held. It was one of more than ordinary interest. Letters were read from several correspondents on missionary ground. The Nestorian mission was dwelt upon. A young lady was introduced dressed in Persian costume.

"*December* 1. — Rev. Mr. H. conducted our morning

devotions; we hope he will continue to do so until Miss Lyon is able to meet with us.

"*December* 6.—Miss Lyon is so far recovered that she came into the hall this afternoon, and talked to the middle class about light reading. She urged them to lay aside entirely every thing that could be classed under this head. If they had any with them, she wished they would burn it—send it home—or seal it up and put it in the bottom of their trunks, there to remain untouched.

"*December* 9.—To-day Miss Lyon invited to her room those whose hearts were moved by the Spirit's teachings. Nineteen were present—most seemed deeply impressed. We can but feel that God is in our midst. Christians are beginning to pray more earnestly. Many seem prostrate in the dust before the awful presence of Him who searcheth the secrets of every soul.

"*December* 12.—Truly this has been a day of blessing. Eight are now expressing a hope in Christ. The interest appears to be deepening and extending every hour. Thus far, those who have indulged hope have been principally from the middle class. In fact, the interest seemed to commence there with a few praying hearts.

"*December* 14.—Still the interest is increasing. It goes from heart to heart silently, yet powerfully. The whole house is as still as on the Sabbath. Every footstep is light—every voice is hushed. Several have asked to be excused from school exercises, so intense are their feelings. Many in the senior class without hope begin to inquire for Him who is the way, the truth, and the life.

"*December* 15.—There are now more than twenty who hope they have found a Savior precious as he never was before. Five of the number are from the senior class. Some of the most careless are awakened, and anxiously inquire, "What shall I do to be saved?"

"*December* 16.—To-day is recreation day; but it has

seemed more like the Sabbath. We can only say, God is here. There is scarcely an indifferent one.

"*December* 18. — We had a short religious exercise in the hall this afternoon. Miss Lyon's word to us was, 'Say little — pray much.' This evening, thirty-one, who trust that they have recently consecrated themselves upon the altar of their God, met for a prayer-meeting. May the future of their lives prove that this sacrifice is no partial one.

"*December* 25. — We have had sad tidings to-day. Miss B., one of our teachers, who went home a few weeks ago in feeble health, has been summoned to the spirit land. Miss Lyon mourns deeply her early removal. She had anticipated much from her. But with her sweet submission, she says, 'I feel that it is a blessed privilege to fit dear ones for heaven.'

"*December* 30. — The Spirit still abides with us. There have been signal manifestations of God's power in this revival. 'Behold, the Lord hath passed by us, not in the great and strong wind, not in the earthquake, not in the fire, but in the still small voice.'

"*January* 4, 1847. — Day of fasting and prayer for the conversion of the world. Miss Lyon met the whole school in the hall. After some general remarks, she proceeded to suggest subjects of thought and prayer. We trust prevailing prayer has ascended here to-day from many hearts — for ourselves — for you — for our country — for a dying world.

"*January* 28. — Miss Lyon commenced her lectures upon the subject of missions this morning. She read passages of Scripture, and remarked generally upon the duty of Christian benevolence. She then alluded to the reward to be expected in consequence of denying ourselves for Christ's sake: she differed from some who say, one is never poorer for giving to the Lord. 'If,' said she, 'they mean poorer in a *spiritual* point of view, I agree with them, but not when they say poorer in property; for I do believe the Christian ought to give to the Lord, so as really to feel the need of what he gives — a precious reward to suffer for Christ.' She seemed, if possible, more earnest and animated than ever. O that there were many more who would, in like manner, present to Christians the claims resting upon them! who would, at the same time, be themselves examples!

"Our teachers' business meeting was held this evening. Miss Lyon said she had suffered much from want of systematic habits, and urged it upon us that we should accustom ourselves to a systematic division of our time and duties. She knew our interruptions were many. There were many *little* duties to be looked after, and so it must always be with ladies. 'I do really think,' said she, in her humorous way, 'that it requires more discipline of mind to be a lady, than it does to be a gentleman. The latter has little of the minutiæ of every-day life to attend to. He can rise in the morning and drive into his business. But it is not so with the latter, nor would I have it so.'

"*February* 2. — Miss Lyon has continued her remarks upon the subject of missions for several mornings. We will try and give you the mere outline. Your own minds can supply the rest, better than our poor pen.

"*First.* We must do all Christ requires of us; because a reward is promised to him who gives a cup of cold water: if we have the means to do more, we must not think it sufficient to do this, and only this. *Secondly.* We must feel that we are as unworthy to give in the name of Christ as we are to receive. *Thirdly.* When we give the most with the most self-denial, then do we most deeply feel our unworthiness. When we do so contribute for Christ's sake, then are we brought into a blessed sympathy with his *poverty* — his sufferings. 'O wonderful, wonderful,' she exclaimed, 'this work in which we may share! How would angels delight to have a part in it! And shall we hinder it by unwillingness to give?'

"She spoke of the Bible standard of benevolence. Why should we adopt this standard as our own? Because of the infinite value of souls — of the sacrifice of Christ as our example — of our relations to each other — of the unseen cords that bind us to the heathen world — last, though not least, because it is God's appointed means for the conversion of the world.

"Among other things, she remarked, 'I am so thankful I do not have to decide *where* my mite shall go: I do compassionate those who stand at the helm — the officers of our societies, who must say where the money and men must go; whose cry for the bread and water of life shall be heard, and whose unheeded.'

"In a subsequent lecture she said, 'I would not speak to you things that would rouse your feelings merely, but I would awaken your consciences. I would have you consider this subject of an enlarged Christian benevolence in its bearings upon you through life. Take the Bible standard as yours, and cling to it as long as you live.'

"Then commencing with the Jewish economy, that great starting-point, she traced downward, through the several stages of revelation, every thing that bore directly, or by inference, upon the great question before her.

"In conclusion, she said it was impossible for her to tell what duty required of any one. The Spirit alone could direct individuals. She only asked that we would pray over it, and decide as the Spirit should direct.

"*February* 13. — Miss Lyon spoke to the young ladies upon the formation of correct habits. 'I want you, young ladies,' said she, 'to form good habits. You have no time or strength to spare in overcoming bad ones.'

"*February* 15. — At our morning exercises, Miss Lyon addressed those who have no hope of heaven, no place to lay up their treasure. She said she had thought much of the passage, 'I go to prepare a place for you.' 'Yes, there are many, many mansions, but to some of you none of them belong. This work of salvation is an individual work. Each must do it for herself. No friend can enter the strait gate for you. You must not only leave all behind, but enter willing to follow Christ wherever he may lead. "If thy right hand offend thee, cut it off; if thy right eye offend thee, pluck it out."'

"*March* 11. — At our morning exercises, Miss Lyon has commenced the character of Christ, under the several titles applied to him in Scripture. This morning she remarked upon the passage, 'I am the bread of life.'

"*March* 18. — Our spring examinations are closed. They were interesting and well sustained. To-morrow evening we are to have a social party. About fifty are invited from town. A few of Miss Lyon's friends from abroad are here. These with our own family will make quite a gathering.

"*March* 19. — Our invited guests and young ladies assembled in the parlors about seven o'clock this evening, where we had a pleasant, social time. About nine o'clock we repaired to the seminary hall, where we had calisthenics, music, and refreshments. Miss Lyon appeared to enjoy the evening exceedingly.

"*March* 30. — Our missionary contributions were reported to-day. Whole amount, (first contribution of the year,) $649.50.

"*May* 19. — Within a short time letters have been received from correspondents in Persia, India, China, Sandwich Islands, and the far west; all of them full of glad tidings. Could you but witness, dear sisters, how much interest these journals of yours add to our missionary meetings, you would feel yourselves richly rewarded for all the labor they cost you.

"*June* 18. — In our teachers' prayer-meeting this evening, Miss Lyon spoke of a little note received from Mrs. B. She proposed we should mention the names of those who have

31 *

been connected with us, and are now on missionary ground. We each mentioned one or more of them, until all your names were repeated. We then united in prayer in your behalf. Miss Lyon led. In speaking of you afterwards, she said, 'Let us each be faithful, and we may be but a step behind them in heaven.' If *any one* has a bright crown there, it will be our dear Miss Lyon. Numbers in heathen lands will rise up and call her blessed.

"*June* 22. — This afternoon, as well as every Friday afternoon, Miss Lyon claims as hers to address the young ladies upon general themes. Her subject the last time was, simplicity in dress. She spoke of different fashions, and advised that all who would dress simple and in good taste should avoid extremes. She was very animated and interesting. 'Why, young ladies,' said she, 'what would you think to see a gentleman dressed in low neck and short sleeves?' This afternoon, her subject was, true politeness. 'True politeness,' said she, 'consists more in avoiding than in doing many things.' She dwelt particularly upon respect due to the aged.

"*June* 29. — The subject of Miss Lyon's remarks this afternoon was conversation. She dwelt upon the importance of being able to converse with ease and propriety; mentioned some things to be observed, and some others to be avoided. 'Always be observing,' she remarked, 'and you will always have something to say worth the saying.'

"*July* 23. — In the morning Miss Lyon said she addressed many who were soon to go out as teachers, and she did ardently desire that they might carry with them much of the spirit of Christ. 'To have such a spirit,' said she, 'you must have clear views of the plan of salvation, of the worth of souls; must know when to speak and when to forbear.'

"*August* 5. — The scenes of our present school year have to-day closed. The anniversary occasion was one of more than ordinary interest. Nearly forty of the senior class of 1844 and 1845 met here by class appointment and invitation from Miss Lyon. She was delighted to see together so many of her former pupils. After we returned from public exercises in church, she stood in her accustomed place, and gave us a few parting words as a school. A large number of the young ladies' friends from abroad passed the evening with us. Early to-morrow morning our happy family will be scattered, no more to be united.

" *September* 29. — Our school met to-day for the first time. A very large number present. Miss Lyon's subject of remark to them was, regard to absent or deceased friends. She addressed in her own peculiar manner the stranger ones who have come among us. There were many tearful eyes. The examination of our new candidates is progressing rapidly.

" *October* 5. — Miss Lyon regrets very much that our number is so full this year. There are at least two hundred and fifty. She has done all she could to avoid it. She had more than five hundred applicants.

" *October* 12. — Examinations are nearly finished. Six left this forenoon, because they found themselves unprepared. Miss Lyon's health is improving daily. Her soul is full of benevolence. At the close of teachers' meeting to-night she said, 'Let us each be faithful to our precious charge. How many parents' hearts are beating with anxious hope! It is a privilege to labor for them.'

" *December* 14. — At our family meeting this afternoon Miss Lyon made some remarks upon the duty of preserving health. The theme was suggested by one of the notes of criticism, 'wearing thin shoes and cotton hose.' She spoke of the inclemency of a New England climate in comparison with that under a more genial sky, and of the necessity of additional clothing. She then told them that when they became members of this school it was expected they would have maturity of character and moral principle enough to do what was right without a formal command. If they had not, they had better by all means go to a smaller school for younger persons, where they could receive the peculiar care needed by little girls. As she pursued the subject, her vivacity increased, and she said, 'There are two things, young ladies, that we expressly say you must not do. One is, that you must not violate the fire laws, (alluding to several regulations of the family in regard to fire;) the other is, that you must not kill yourselves. If you will persist in killing yourselves by reckless exposure, we are not willing to take the responsibility of the act. We think by all means you had better go home and die in the arms of your dear mothers.' She said such exposures were a direct violation of two commands of God — 'Thou shalt not kill' and 'Thou shalt not steal;' for a violation of the first involved a violation of the second, as by it they robbed the world of the good they ought to do.

"*December* 16. — For a few mornings past, at devotions, Miss Lyon has been dwelling upon the great doctrines of the Bible — total depravity, nature of sin, &c. Then she took up the commandments in their order. This morning, she commenced upon the connection between the law and the gospel. There has been fixed attention.

"*January* 3, 1848. — The fast for the conversion of the world has been observed by nearly all our family. Miss Lyon suggested many subjects for prayer, said much to revive the drooping, dormant graces of professed disciples, and made a touching appeal to the prayerless ones. A deep and general interest upon religious subjects seems to pervade the minds of most of our young ladies.

"*January* 20. — We have received rich spiritual blessings during the closing weeks of this term. A large number are rejoicing in the assurance of hope. The general features of the revival are of much the same character as last year.

"*March* 30. — Miss Lyon commenced remarks this forenoon upon sacred charity; said the highest form of charity is that which goes out of ourselves. In conclusion, she expressed the hope that we should all have our hearts drawn out on this subject, that Christians may take a higher stand, and Christless ones give themselves unto the Lord.

"*March* 31. — Miss Lyon continued her remarks this forenoon by saying there were certain great principles that she should often repeat; among them these: all things planned by God; sacred charity a divine appointment; wonderful though it is, the design of it the benefit of the giver as well as the receiver. She dwelt upon the thought that sacred charity is a pledge of personal consecration, a test to one's self of a willingness to give up all for Christ.

"*April* 7. — Miss Lyon this forenoon dwelt in a most touching manner upon the great principle that Christian charity may be so practised and illustrated as to make us feel what a price was paid for our redemption. She noticed expressions of Scripture like this: 'Ye are bought with a price,' &c. 'Always,' she added, 'remember this when you put your hand to this work.'

"*April* 13. — I wish it were in my power to convey to you all the precious thoughts Miss Lyon has given us upon the subject of Christian charity. Though she has dwelt so many years upon this theme, there is nothing tedious through repetition. She leads us not in the same beaten track of thought. Every year brings out some new thing from the rich treasury of her full soul. In her remarks this forenoon she said the telegraphic wires had been established between us and the heathen; if we do not now send them the gospel they must perish.

"*May* 17. — The teachers' several duties have been arranged. Dear Miss Lyon's duties who can describe? All things which belong to no one else are hers. And this amount is no small fraction of the whole.

"Miss L. remarked to the young ladies this afternoon on the importance of keeping in view the good of the institution in all they do. 'You have all,' she said, 'embarked in *this ship*, and, if the ship sinks, must sink with it.' She warned them against imitating the man who refused to take his turn at the pump to save the vessel, with the excuse, that he had paid his passage, and saw no reason why he should do more.

"*May* 24. — Death has entered our family, and removed one lovely by nature and still more so by grace. She was all ready for the coming of her Savior. She said it was enough for her 'to have some little corner in heaven.' In connection with this event Miss Lyon dwelt upon the great salvation. She spoke of the difficulty she had always had in communicating any just views upon this subject. In her heart she had often been ready to exclaim, 'O that God would speak! And now,' she said, 'God had spoken to us.' She felt it was not so much a voice of warning as an invitation; not a voice from the tomb, but a voice from heaven. God had given us an impressive lesson on his great salvation; and she entreated that we should give heed to the things we have heard, 'lest at any time we should let them slip.'

"*May* 30. — This afternoon Miss Lyon gave us the last chapter upon a subject which she commenced some time before. She dwelt upon the importance of ladies' striving to acquire system, stability, and energy; urged all to follow judgment rather than impulse; said, of all the leading-strings they would find in the world, the last for them to follow should be fancy.

"*July* 4. — In the hall, this afternoon, Miss Lyon amused us with some of her most playful remarks. Miss W. had heard that the village lads were going to have fireworks this evening, and thought it not well that our family should lose their sleep to witness the display. So she remarked upon the probable splendor of the scene with such mock sublimity as to quell every vestige of excitement, had there been any. She then gave all the remarkable permission to look out of their own windows, though not to leave their rooms. Miss Lyon added her contribution of merry words, and all joined in a hearty laugh.

"*July* 11. — Our missionary subscription is completed, and the amount has been stated to the school. Whole amount given to foreign missions, $646·79; home missions, $361·00. Whole amount, $1007·79.

"*August* 29. — You will ask, 'Where is Miss Lyon during the long vacation? Is she also enjoying rest?' We would we could say she is. But she is in South Hadley. Much does her spirit long for rest, and much does she need it. We fear for the next year. Yet I would trust and remember that 'our Father is at the helm.' We, doubting, often ask, 'If she falls, who shall take her place?' We often fear she may fail. Powers of mind and body so hardly tasked cannot always last. We fall back on the assurance, God will provide."

The following is a copy of a letter addressed by Miss Lyon to her pupils now on heathen ground: —

"September 1, 1848.

"My dear Missionary Daughters:

"The journal which you have received through Miss W.'s instrumentality, and so long by dear Miss T.'s pen, who is now to be one of your number, has been a gratification to me. I have enjoyed the thought that you would thus keep along with the little occurrences at your Holyoke home. Often have I desired to beg the privilege of inserting a little note, with the salutation of mine own hand. But communion like this, even, 'with ink and pen,' I seldom can enjoy upon earth. But there is one place of meeting, of sweet communion of spirit, when absent in body. There I love to ask our heavenly Father to bless you all, to bless you individually in your work, to bless the dear companions of your missionary joys and your missionary toils, and to bless, too, the children whom God has given you in the land of your adoption. But there is another and better home than this. There I trust we shall all meet, and hold such communion as earth has never known. May you all have grace to run with patience the race set before you, looking unto Jesus in all your missionary course.

"As you will learn, Miss W. had it in heart to keep the journal for you this year herself. But Providence has otherwise decided. Her health will not allow her even to be an observer of the events at your former happy home. I anticipated much pleasure to herself in writing, and to you in reading from the pen of her whom you all know and love. To supply her place my thoughts have rested on Misses H. and C. as being those whom you all remember. They have consented to take it.

"In this arrangement I am very happy, as you will feel more the link of friendship than if coming from the pen of one whom you have never seen. With some of you they were class-mates, seat-mates, or room-mates. With others of you they were fellow-teachers, striving with you for the upbuilding of Christ's kingdom in this little miniature of a world. You will feel more sure of their personal sympathy, because while writing for you they are writing also for a dear brother and sister far off in India. You will remember that we expect from you a return. We are aware of the effort this must cost you amid all your other cares and abundant labors. But we trust that this effort will not be in vain, as a small item in your missionary work. While I am writing this, I am forcibly reminded of the probability that one of your number will never read it — one dear to my heart, my only sister's own daughter, and to me a daughter indeed, and even more than a daughter. Yes, I think from day to day of dear Mrs. B. as now in heaven; though it is possible, in the events of Providence, that her life is spared. Mrs. W., too, another of our missionary band, has finished her short work, and gone home to her rest. May you who still live work while the day lasts, and may you long be spared, and may you yet gather in many sheaves from the opening fields, which are now white and ready for the harvest. While life and memory are spared you will be remembered and loved by me."

"*October* 25. — Miss Lyon bears the removal of her main dependence, Miss W., with cheerfulness, trustfully looking for brighter days in future. She hopes this year to give more time and energy to the literary department than she has usually done.

"*October* 30. — Knowing what you do of our family arrangements, your first inquiry will be with regard to our spiritual welfare. About one hundred of our pupils are without hope. The fixed and earnest attention of this class to religious instruction is evidence to us that the Spirit is hovering around us, and willing to bless if we are willing to receive. May we have grace given us to sow all the seed and gather all the fruit our heavenly Father would have us.

"*December* 1. — Yesterday was our annual Thanksgiving. All the teachers, and a larger number than usual of the young ladies, remained with us. Invitations were extended to the trustees. Miss Lyon has long been wishing to enlarge the circle of those in town to whom she extends invitations, and she took this opportunity to do it. Between seventy and eighty were invited. The young ladies interested themselves much in preparing. The first part of the evening was spent very socially in the parlors. Afterwards, we had entertainments in Seminary Hall as usual.

"*December* 6. — In accordance with Miss Lyon's proposal, we have this year a regular missionary society formed. The officers are a president and secretary; the terms of membership are, the regular attendance upon the meetings of the society, or, if detained, the rendering of a written note to the secretary before the time of the meeting. Miss Lyon was chosen president. Her duties are to preside in the meetings, appoint the times of the meeting, and direct as to intelligence brought before the society. She is most faithful in these duties. She makes it her object to bring out at each meeting something of profit which shall be remembered.

"*December* 14. — Miss Lyon's theme for remark this afternoon was mutual influence. She observed that she had noticed a few young ladies in the family who were not having the most desirable influence over one another, and remarked that she should probably in a few days speak to them individually. She illustrated her subject by examples from chemistry. She remarked that some of the rankest poisons were made by the union of the most valuable and inoffensive elements; as, for instance, oxygen and nitrogen, whose value and importance were so well known, were a constituent in nearly all of them. So, many young ladies, who were harmless oxygen and nitrogen by themselves, if brought together, would make nicotine or strychnine.

"*December* 28. — A box of curiosities from India was forwarded to us last week. Letters were received from India, China, and Persia.

"*January* 5, 1849. — There has been a good deal of religious interest this year; several conversions, though not so general a revival as last year."

Would that the limits of this work allowed more extended extracts from this journal of the seminary; for, as a whole, it does give such an insight into the manner in which this great family is managed, such an impression of the happy influence of Christian love as the controlling power, and of the happiness which it brings to all who yield to its demands, as cannot but excite the interest and admiration of every pious heart. Perhaps, however, I ought rather to apologize to the seminary for having opened to the public eye so much of their domestic life. If so, my apology is, that the internal operations of the seminary do really afford one of the best developments of Miss Lyon's character, since they have been nearly all contrived and arranged by her judicious and sagacious mind.

Before closing this section, I shall add some of Miss Lyon's correspondence upon several subjects, which shows us that her interest was not confined to the favorite seminary, but that she admitted to a proper share of her regard and attention whatever ought to interest any intelligent Christian woman. Many such letters have been given in the earlier parts of this memoir; but the following, which bear date subsequent to the opening of the new seminary, show that, amid its absorbing cares and duties, other objects did not lose their interest. And yet most of the letters have reference to the seminary.

The following extracts from letters of two of her nieces, who have themselves been distinguished as teachers, and now occupy important spheres of labor, will show Miss Lyon's interest in, and efforts for, her relatives — a subject already referred to more than once.

FROM MRS. BEDORTHA.

"TROY, N. Y., February, 1850.

"I remember how, from early childhood, my mother used to talk of sending myself and sisters to aunt Mary Lyon's school. This idea always afforded us the greatest pleasure. She trained our minds and manners with much care to this end while we were but little girls, and lived in Ohio. Yet we were of sufficient age to understand enough to cause us greatly to wish to attend aunt's school. She used to have conversations of some length with us respecting it, urging us to efforts of improvement to prepare us for that school; and my youngest sister (now a missionary in India) has since told me that it was immediately after one of these conversations that, being sent by my mother, with a little tin pail in her hand, to a rivulet, a few yards from the door, to bring some water, she took great pains to take every step very carefully all the way there and back again, so that she might be nice enough to be sent to aunt's school when she should be of sufficient age. Our mother continued her efforts to obtain this object till the way was prepared, after many hinderances; so that both my sisters found themselves at Ipswich Female Seminary under the immediate instructions of my dear aunt Mary, where their highest anticipations were fully realized, and the most earnest wish of their hearts gratified. With her direction and instruction she enabled them to complete the course of study, and appointed them to places for teaching, till the missionary feeling which my youngest sister had long possessed ripened under such a genial influence, and she sailed as a missionary to India. Providence directed my own way to another school, where I finished a course of study similar to what my sisters had gone through. Yet I could not feel satisfied till I had been to learn what I could from the experience of my dear aunt at Holyoke. Each time when I had spent a season there, I went away feeling that I had reaped a rich and fresh harvest of important information, not only respecting the subject of teaching, but of useful maxims and new thoughts relating to the best manner of managing the practical affairs of life and the most excellent methods of influencing mind. I always felt that hers was an intelligence in which lay a rich mine of experience, and from her lips came the best of wisdom in things pertaining both to the present and future life. I was never in her society even for only a few moments without feeling instructed and wiser by something she uttered. Her influence extended to all her relatives; her example and advice quickened them often in the paths of uprightness; particularly did it stimulate her nephews and nieces to efforts to obtain an education. In her school she educated the daughters of two of her sisters and the daughters of her brother. One of the latter is now a missionary in China. Of her nephews, a part have taken a liberal course of study, and some are in preparation for the gospel ministry. She aided the children of her brother and sisters in obtaining an education, not only by her counsel, but many of them by small sums of money, to make a beginning in their education, and afterwards lending them larger sums, which they were to pay when by teaching they had gained it."

FROM MRS. BURGESS, (FORMERLY MISS MOORE,) MISSIONARY IN INDIA.

"AHMEDNUGGUR, April 13, 1850.

"DR. HITCHCOCK:

"It has given me much pleasure to learn that you have undertaken to prepare the memoirs of my dear aunt. You were her early friend, and have kept up your acquaintance with her almost uninterrupted, so that you are perhaps better able than any one else to describe the circumstances which helped to form her character.

"There was one way her ever-flowing benevolence manifested itself, of which you may not be fully aware. I refer to the pecuniary aid she rendered her younger relatives to obtain an education. This aid, if of much amount, was always in the form of a loan, to be repaid as circumstances would permit. I am one who remember with many emotions of gratitude her timely offer of assistance when I was strongly desiring to enjoy higher opportunities for mental improvement than could be possessed in an academy in a western village. One remark in the letter conveying to me the offer of assistance made a permanent impression on my mind. It was, her expressed hope that I should never forget the injunction 'to do good and *communicate;* forget not, for with such sacrifice God is well pleased.' I feel now, without doubt, the influence of that wish, when I am trying to *communicate* to the school of thirty Hindoo girls under my charge, and a group of women and little children who come more or less under my influence, the truths of the Bible. Many of her younger relatives (who generally possessed more of a desire for knowledge than the means of obtaining it) are much indebted to her for timely assistance. She did very much, also, to inspire love of knowledge and hope of success by her own cheerful temperament and looks of encouragement.

"The aid she rendered was mostly in the form of a loan; but her right hand, prompted by her generous heart, often gave when her left hand knew it not. I well remember the visit of a young nephew, who spent a part of a college vacation with her. His eyes glistened with emotion as he left her room, where he had been to take leave of her. She had slipped into his hand a five dollar bill, saying, 'Take that to help in your college expenses the coming term.'

"This offer of pecuniary assistance was not by any means confined to her relatives. Many young ladies with whom she became acquainted shared largely in her sympathies in this form. But of that I need not speak; it was, as you well know, her abounding desire, always, in every way, to *do good* to others, and to subserve the cause of her Master."

The following, on the same subject, was prepared by Mrs. Cowles, but thought more appropriate for this place in the memoir.

"For a person of her means, Miss Lyon was very generous.

When Dr. Packard, of Shelburne, visited Ipswich, in September, 1834, to confer with her and a few of her friends as to the incipient steps of the enterprise, she paid his travelling expenses, and never repaid herself out of the contingent fund raised soon after. In the following October, a wealthy gentleman was engaged in establishing a female seminary in Bristol county. She visited him, and aided him with her experience in devising measures for its prosperity. While making suggestions as to the ways and means for promoting his object, she also improved the opportunity to spread her own plans before him. As she was departing, he placed a bank note in her hand, doubtless as a remuneration for her time and pains. 'Thank you,' said she; 'this will help towards the thousand dollars we are trying to collect for contingent expenses;' and to that purpose it was faithfully applied. She travelled hundreds of miles, between September, 1834, and November, 1837, in aid of her object, always at her own expense. The old rates of postage then prevailed; and though she made it a rule never to tax a person of whom she solicited a contribution with the postage on a letter, and to prepay a letter whenever she had any doubt on whom the postage ought to fall, the funds of the seminary were never drawn upon to meet any part of the expense of her large correspondence. She engaged a person to assist, at the opening of the school, in getting the domestic department into operation. That person, finding the duties more onerous than she had anticipated, was obliged to withdraw from the undertaking. In addition to her stipulated wages, which were paid from the income of the establishment, Miss Lyon bestowed on her a parting gift, nearly equal to her wages, as some compensation for her disappointment. To an associate teacher, whom she loved, and who, as she thought, had made pecuniary sacrifices for the good of the institution, she gave, the same year, thirty dollars as a bridal gift.

"Such tokens of friendship were not allowed to interfere with her religious charities. She held all she possessed as a steward, and asked not, 'What shall I give to the Lord?' but, 'How much may I take for myself?'

"She endeavored to be careful not to injure character by ill-judged charity. She sought so to help her nephews and nieces as to enable them to help themselves. To several of them, who were making great efforts to obtain an education, she gave twenty-five dollars each in money, and afterwards lent them considerably more, in some cases to the amount of one or two hundred dollars each. All the money thus lent had been paid up before her death, except what was due from one of the last who had been favored in this way. With this aid, some of her relatives have become successful teachers; two of her nieces are now in distant heathen lands. To the only son of her eldest sister, who is preparing for the gospel ministry, she left an annuity, to be continued during his pupilage.

"She felt and taught that it injures the character of a young person to receive gift after gift from a hand on which he has no natural claim. Such benefactions, she was accustomed to say, not only destroyed the independence of a noble spirit, but induced a habit of claiming as a right what is only a favor. 'Gratitude,' she said, 'is often a stranger in the hearts of young persons who are adopted into families, and installed as children. So those who receive their education as a boon from the purse of a stranger are apt to lose more in manly self-dependence than they gain in mental culture.' In the Education Society she admired its plan of lending money to its beneficiaries, because it leaves their native independence uncrushed. Well does the writer know one of Miss Lyon's beloved relatives, whom she conducted from a lowly home, and placed under the eye of Miss Grant till she was qualified to fill a station of responsibility which was offered her. Soon after she entered upon the duties of this station, an accomplished and agreeable gentleman, to this day an able agent in the foreign missionary field, invited her to accomyany him in the journey of life. To her the field was inviting, and she felt also that he was a man whom she could love and esteem. She unhesitatingly declined the invitation, because she had not cancelled the debt due for her education ; and that, too, without consulting her friends, who would generously have made up a purse for her ; without writing to her aunt for advice, who would probably have remitted the debt ; and she did this without telling the servant of the Lord, with whose choice she was honored, the exact obstacle which lay in the way of accepting his proposal.

"Who does not like that spirit of independence, that determination to pay her own debts ? It is not necessary to say whether, when that lady had fully met every demand against her, another opportunity was afforded her to walk a similar path ; whether a beloved and honored wife, happy in a domestic circle of her own, she dwells in the temperate or the tropical regions, in the land of vines or of spices. But she is now, and has been ever since her decision, favored with a position in society and a sphere of usefulness sufficient to satisfy any reasonable woman.

"In the summer of 1841, being persuaded by her friends to journey, Miss Lyon visited some of her near and dear relatives in the western part of New York. They were at the time in distressing straits, and knew not whence help could come. By a series of misfortunes, sicknesses, and losses, they had been driven to mortgage their small farm. They were in anxious conference at the moment of her arrival, because their homestead was soon expected to come under the hammer of the auctioneer. 'Here is Mary ; she will help you,' said her uncle, as she stopped at the door of their humble dwelling. She was the angel of mercy to them in their hour of need. She redeemed the farm, took the deed in her own name, gave them a life lease of the spot, and on their death it is bequeathed by her last will and testament to the American Board of Commissioners for Foreign Missions."

The following incidents, related by Miss Robinson, once a teacher in the seminary, show us Miss Lyon's skill in controlling the conduct of pupils without the direct exercise of authority: —

"It was contrary to the rules of Miss Lyon's establishment that any young lady should absent herself from the regular meals, *sick* or *well*, without permission so to do. 'If *you* are not able to come to me yourself, or some other teacher, send your room-mate,' was ever her injunction. Some young ladies would go to the table without turning their plates. The sick had their particular table, which each could leave for her own room whenever she chose, without waiting for the whole company to rise, as was the rule at the *health* tables. No young lady expected to be a little unwell and stay in her own room during meal-time, and keep it from Miss Lyon's knowledge, without being disappointed. Her Argus eyes saw every thing. Neither would she unnecessarily send an apology for non-appearance more than once or twice. Miss Lyon nipped such things in the bud most effectually. I well remember a case illustrative of this power of hers. A friend of mine, feeling rather indisposed, concluded not to go down to the dining-room to tea one night. I was deputed, as her friend, to report her case to Miss Lyon, at whose table she sat. Through carelessness, I did not speak of my friend's illness till after the family had risen from the meal. Then Miss Lyon was inquiring of another teacher why this young lady absented herself from the supper table. Coming up in the midst of the conversation, I explained the matter, as I thought, most satisfactorily — 'My friend did not feel able to come down to-night.' 'Ah, *sick*, is she?' exclaimed Miss L., fixing her piercing eyes full upon me. 'No, O, no, only a little unwell.' 'Wouldn't she like something in her room?' 'Yes, she commissioned me to carry up to her a cup of tea and cracker.' 'You may go to her now,' replied Miss L.; 'I'll see to that.' I ascended to the fourth story to my companion; I found her very comfortably seated in her rocking-chair by the window, watching a glorious sunset. I placed myself by her side, and soon forgot the tea and cracker and all things pertaining to it. In a few moments, a slight tap was heard at the door. 'Come in,' both exclaimed in one voice. The door slowly opened, and Miss Lyon walked into the room, bearing a waiter, with my friend's tea and cracker. Had a spirit from the unseen world appeared before us, we could not have been more astonished. Our apologies were profuse. My poor friend had no idea of Miss L.'s coming from the basement to the fourth story for her. With perfect kindness, our beloved teacher told us that every one was tired at night, and she could come as well as any other. She made particular inquiries of my friend, who had nothing to say, and then departed. That young lady never remained in her room afterwards, when the bell rang for the dining-room, when she was able to take a little tea and cracker.

"I knew a young lady, at the commencement of the term, arrive rather tired, feel rather selfish and indolent, and fancy refreshments would taste much sweeter in her own room. Accordingly, she sent to the general directress of domestic work, and asked that some young lady might come to such a number, with such and such articles of food. Not long after, the supper came. But Miss L. brought it to the healthy, stout young lady, lounging carelessly upon the bed, detailing the incidents of her recent journey to her social companions. How thankful was I not to meet the calm, kind, half-reproachful glance from the weary eye of Miss Lyon!

"Miss Lyon desired us to be as careful of all the domestic utensils as of the furniture in our own rooms. She had a great aversion to our using dishes appropriated to one particular purpose for several. Of course, laxity on this point would be somewhat prevalent."

When her friends, and especially her relatives, were bereaved or afflicted, Miss Lyon was ever ready with the balm of sympathy for their wounded spirits. We quote only a few examples.

TO MISS SARAH BRIGHAM.

"NORTON, July 24, 1837.

"I have sympathized with you in your late afflictions. I need not tell you that I feel deeply interested in all that relates to yourself and friends, and that my interest in your behalf is now more deeply enlisted than ever. How sweet, though painful, must it be to think of your dear mother! You do not dwell on her image, which is ever before you, with painful emotions and anxious doubt where she now is, and what is now her condition, and what her present employments. You can rest quietly in the belief that she is now with her God, beyond all dangers and all troubles. When you first awake in the morning, do you not think of her for a moment as still alive? But the next moment the painful reality rushes upon you that she is indeed no more; that she has gone, forever gone, and you are all motherless. But the painful truth scarcely finds its way into your wounded heart, when your soul is filled with the sweet consolation that she is happy, forever happy; that she does not lie distressed on that painful couch, where you watched her by day and by night. She has gone to rest — eternal rest. How important that such afflictions should lead us to do with our might what our hands find to do! What have we to do with this world, except as a place to prepare for eternity ourselves, and to seek the same preparation in behalf of others?"

TO HER NIECE, L. MOORE.

"December 9, 1846.

". . . . Write me a long letter, and tell me all about your mother. Dear sister, how my heart has sympathized with her every time I have thought of her trial in Abby's going to India! I hope you will do much to comfort her, and may she ever have a Friend in heaven, who shall be better to her than all the comforts of sons and daughters.

"My health is much improved. I do not speak to the whole school, but hope I shall soon. I have not seen your brother yet, but will ride over to Amherst soon and search him out."

TO HER BROTHER.

"SOUTH HADLEY, December 3, 1840.

"But a few years ago, and we seemed an unbroken circle. Though separated from each other, we seven were all living, and could think and pray for one another from day to day. After the hand of death was laid on our dear father, nearly thirty years passed away before any one of us was called out of time into eternity. Since then, how frequently have we been called to mourning! How great have been the ravages of death! You have heard of sister F.'s departure, and now it becomes my painful duty to tell you that another one is gone. Yes, our dear mother is no more. My dear brother, can you think how lonely it was to me as I followed her dear remains to the grave, with no brother or sister by my side? I felt that indeed our family was but a broken circle. As I passed out of the door where I have often met her gladdened and joyful face, as I went along the way where we have so many times rode together to see sister J., and as I looked on her placid face for the last time, 'Can this be,' thought I, 'my dear mother? and is this my last visit to her solitary home?'"

The death of a niece, who was teaching in Willoughby, Ohio, occasioned the following letter to another of the teachers in that place: —

"SOUTH HADLEY, November 27, 1847.

"MY DEAR MISS T.:

"Your kind letters relative to my dear niece have been received. I feel that I have another precious treasure laid up in heaven. You have my sincere gratitude for your kindness to her, especially during her sickness and her departure to her final home; also for writing in so particular a manner. She was a tender, sensitive plant; and since the death of her own mother and her residence with me, I have watched over her with great interest. I love to think that it has been my privilege to aid in fitting her for her present home. I love to think of her where she now is, with a great circle of my dear family relatives, and many of a long train of ancestors. For some wise reason, I have no doubt she was led far away from home to die. It is gratifying to me that her last associations were so pleasant, and her connection with you and the other dear teachers so desirable. She used to write about you with much affection and confidence. It is also gratifying to me, that she was permitted to enter on a field of usefulness, and one so congenial to her feelings. All the little tokens of respect, affection, and attention shown her while living, and to her memory since her death, I value very much. But of how little consequence is all now, in the light of the countenance of her blessed Savior! She has gone, and, as I trust, has arrived safely home. Please give my kind and grateful acknowledgments to all who nursed her and watched over her in her sickness, to all who have contributed to her comfort, and mingled their sympathies and tears in this dispensation of divine Providence.

"You inquire about her things, because she was in some degree indebted to me. I am anxious that all should go to her near relatives. Please send them to her sister C., and I shall write that all may be settled between her and the other friends. I will authorize you to select some articles as keepsakes for those with whom she was associated in W., &c."

TO MISS GRANT.

"SOUTH HADLEY, April 12, 1839.

"MY DEAR MISS GRANT:

"We have just been passing through a trying scene. Death for the first time has entered our windows, and marked one of our number as his victim. It has been a trying, solemn time. It was a disease of the head, and, as is common in such cases, was very deceitful in developing its true nature till a short time before her death. On this account, none of her friends were here to see her breathe her last. Her sister arrived about two hours after, and her father met the remains a few miles from this place, as they were moving towards her last earthly home. She had been with us about a year, and I trust her being here has been the means of preparing her for heaven.

"She became serious last summer, indulged a hope in the autumn, has been consistent through the winter as a Christian, and has seemed to share deeply in the late revival. She has not been very well through the whole year, and I now think that the causes of her last disease have been long at work in her system. But it seems as if an unseen hand had kept back its progress, that she might repent and believe, and prepare for eternity.

"I will take Rees's Cyclopædia at the price you mention, but I have not the means to purchase the Annals of Education. If you do not wish to sell all together, perhaps 'the Memorandum Society,' in the seminary, may purchase one set. It is now vacation, and those to whom the question would be referred are not here. The leading objects of the society are to preserve a history of its members, and a general history of the seminary. It is designed also to make it a means of individual improvement.

"We are thinking of preparing a written catalogue, with various items attached to each name, as a part of the work of the Memorandum Society."

Such a catalogue was prepared, and a new edition is published once in five years; the last in 1847. That contains five hundred and seventy-nine names; two hundred and ninety-nine of whom had engaged in teaching after leaving the seminary. This, of course, embraces only a part of those connected with the institution.

TO MRS. BRIGGS.

"SOUTH HADLEY, September 1, 1841.

"MY DEAR MRS. BRIGGS:

"I have already sympathized with you in your present trial. May the Lord comfort and sustain you, and give our dear Miss Grant all the strength which she needs. How many changes do we meet, and in how many ways are these changes taking place! How does Providence in wisdom set one thing over against another, so that we need not glory in our own strength, rejoice too much in our own happiness, or sorrow above reason! Scarcely a new cord of affection can be spun, but the materials must be drawn from the shattered fibres of some former attachment. On the other side, scarcely are the firmest bonds broken asunder, but they are followed by some new ones of equal, if not greater interest. My feelings were interested on this subject last winter, when Miss Grant informed me that you appeared near your grave. 'How interesting,' thought I, 'must be your situation, as far as you had power to reflect; at one moment looking with deep sorrow on those many cords which must soon be severed; and the next moment, forward to those new and everlasting bonds in heaven just ready to be bound around your heart!

I love sometimes to lose sight of individuals, in thinking of the bundles of eternal life and happiness that are bound up together in heaven. How delightful will be the joys of that happy place! Edwards's views in his 'History of Redemption,' on God's dealings with his church as a *whole*, are very interesting."

TO MRS. SAFFORD.

"SOUTH HADLEY, September 26, 1843.

"I think I shall like the plan (just detailed) very much, as I am very partial to any thing which will relieve me of care. The thought of giving instruction to so many minds brings with it an increasing anxiety. For this I must reserve all the mental and moral strength which I can. I must not depend on the impulse of the moment, and on the united strength of the occasion, so much as I have done the last six years. When I think of the sudden and strong transitions of mind and heart which I have often been obliged to make, I feel that I can never do it again; and even if I could do it, I could not sustain the shock many times more.

"I have taken a health excursion among the hills about forty miles distant, and just returned quite invigorated. I have a good old aunt among the hills. Her home is in the highest, and wildest, and roughest place which I ever visit. She is the last remnant of the old stock, the liveliest image of my dear mother. I always find the ride to her mountain home, and the communing with her on former days, very sweet."

TO MRS. SAFFORD.

"SOUTH HADLEY, May 1, 1843.

"You express a desire that I should think of Boston. How could I do less, when God has given you a heart for so much interest in our behalf? 'Ye knew what great conflict' I had about the time I was in Boston, and you opened your heart to sympathize with me in behalf of those who had never seen your face in the flesh. I thought I had reason to believe that out of our family no one was like minded with yourselves to care for our souls. How can I but remember you in return, and the desires of your hearts, and the work of your hands? That infantile church has its own place, and a very important place, in the great system of means in Boston, which that favored city should use in the renovation of the world. In bringing that church to occupy just its own place in this blessed work, the labors and responsibilities which Providence has assigned to yourself and husband are by no means small. When I spread out my heart before the mercy seat, I cannot but remember your church, your labors in it, and the labors of your beloved pastor. How much do you all need of heavenly wisdom, of holy love, and of godly zeal. May the Lord give you more than we can ask or think."

ON FORMER ATTACHMENTS. — TO MISS GRANT.

"South Hadley, April 23, 1838.

"Do you now and then like to receive a line from me, or have you so many other cares, that it is a tax on your strength more than it is worth? The intimate communion which continued between us for so many years, I do not, I cannot forget. Sometimes former views, and former intercourse, and former mutual duties and obligations, and mutual kindness and faithfulness, in contrast with the present non-intercourse almost between us, come over me, with an overwhelming power. I know it must be so. I know you cannot come to see me, nor can I go to see you; and if I could, I should not feel at liberty to tax your strength with my visits. The same is true with regard to our writing. I am generally entirely reconciled. But occasionally, when I have heard nothing from you for weeks or months, only as I do by the by, as I do from any of my common acquaintances, I find myself involuntarily saying, Is this that same friend with whom I lived and labored so many years, with whom I had so much intercourse from day to day, and with whom I have exchanged so many letters? This is the changeableness of earth. How transitory is every thing here! It seems as if I could say of nothing that it has long been, but only that it once was; or that it now is, and may be a few days longer. Of all the changes that take place, the changing of friends, of companions, of fellow-laborers, of fellow-travellers through this pilgrimage, is the most painful. Rather let these changes come year by year, and month by month, so that there may be no tender and long-strengthened cords to be torn asunder — that there may be no train of recollection and former communion to add to scenes of desolation."

TO MISS GRANT.

"SOUTH HADLEY, March 14, 1840.

"Saturday is my day for writing letters, and for all business connected with letters. I always on that day think of writing to my dearest friend, who, I fear, may be suffering much, though I hope she may be enjoying as much. But sometimes the vain endeavor to be through with all the business letters that demand my immediate attention, and more, to decide how to answer them, affects my head so that I have but little mind or heart left for friends. Sometimes I fear that a letter of mine, written in my blind hand, may be an unwelcome messenger to one who is seeking for quiet. However, I thank you for your precious letter received the present week, and will most gladly reply.

"*July* 25, 1840. — I love to think of your visit here. I am glad you have seen Deacon and Mrs. P. and their home. To me it has been a sweet home to the wanderer. How kindly have I been taken care of these many years!

"I trust your prayers in our behalf will not be less fervent on account of your visit. The thought has often been very interesting to me, that your prayers could be as effectual now as ever; that they did not depend on health, and that your prayers in our behalf might be answered; though I did not feel at liberty to ask your advice, as I was wont to do in former days."

TO MISS GRANT.

"April 15, 1841.

"MY VERY DEAR FRIEND:

"Your letter mailed yesterday I have just received, informing me of the sickness of dear Mrs. B. I cannot forbear taking my pen immediately and commencing a reply. Few can realize, as I can, the deep waters of affliction through which you are now passing. I need not say, that I sympathize with you most deeply, most tenderly. My heart's desire and prayer is, that you may be sustained and comforted by consolations better than all human sympathies. I know your heart is *now* too full to think much of yourself. The thoughts and feelings are all absorbed in the solemn and interesting events just before her, whom you love as a sister, and more than a sister. It is indeed better for her to depart and be with Christ. May the precious Savior take her by the hand, and lead her gently and peacefully through the dark valley, and give her a home with Him, in whose presence is fulness of joy and pleasures forevermore. If you judge it expedient, I should be gratified to have you give Mrs. B. my love. I love her for her own sake, for my sake, and, more than all, for your sake.

"Dear Mrs. P. is spending several days with us. She sends her love."

TO THE SAME.

"August 13, 1841.

"The kindness of Providence towards us the last year has been very manifest. The breeze has been tempered to the shorn lamb. Will you not pray for us, that as we come together, a preparation of heart may be given to teachers and pupils?"

TO MISS GRANT.

"SOUTH HADLEY, March 8, 1841.

MY DEAR FRIEND:

"I thank you for communicating so much about the health of your body, and the health of your soul. I have long wanted to hear from you, and have often attempted to commend you, with all your unknown state, to our covenant-keeping God. The dealings of divine Providence have been such towards me since I last saw you, as to lead me to think with great tenderness of all my friends, and especially of yourself; and more than all, I hope, of that dearest Friend that sticketh closer than a brother. The hand of God has been laid heavily upon me. I have been led through deep waters, but they have not overflowed me. His good hand has been ever my support.

"You have heard of the sickness and death of my dear pupils during the fall vacation. Last year we took unusual pains about the health of our young ladies; altogether more than ever before. So true is it that *the race is not to the swift, nor the battle to the strong;* and that *it is not in man that watcheth to direct his steps.* None but my heavenly Father knows how great a trial this was to my heart. While others have been inquiring about the natural cause, I have felt that we who were most nearly connected ought particularly to inquire about the moral cause, and to seek to know what the Lord would have us learn from his dealings with us. I hope the affliction has not been altogether lost on myself, but that in the hand of God it has been used in some degree to prepare me for the events that have since followed. You have heard of *these.* I have now no mother or sister whom I can go and see; and alone I followed my dear mother to the grave. Her prayers, which I have daily had for so many years, I shall have no more. She, to whose comfort I have been expecting the pleasant privilege of administering for years to come, as almost the only child left her, will need nothing more. I feel my family loneliness; but with it eternity seems very near, with all its precious privileges, purchased by the blood of our glorious Savior.

"The last stroke touching my health has been to me scarcely a trial. As I have been obliged to give up many labors to other hands, and some weeks nearly all, I have felt that I have nothing to say and scarcely any thing to ask, but that God might be glorified.

"After about a month's active labor in organizing the school, I began to find my strength very weakness. I tried to rest, but all seemed only to reduce me still more. I have had but little disease, but a general prostration. For several weeks I could not read much, nor write, nor think, nor feel, nor talk. For about two months I did not go out to church. Now I can go half a day, and do several things of the lighter sort.

"I want to tell you many things about our school, and how kind Providence has been to us, and how the way was all prepared beforehand for me to be laid aside. But I must wait till I write to you again. The Spirit of God has been evidently with us all the year. About fifteen have expressed hope, and many others have a long time seemed but a step from the kingdom of God."

At a later date, she wrote as follows:—

"I have often thought that I should like to consult you, but I would not tax your strength. I have lately been thinking that you could do one thing as effectually as ever, with only the strength you have to spare. That is, pray for us. I want to tell you something of our state, that you can the better do this; but I cannot now. The gentle dews of heavenly grace have been descending on us, as I hope, all winter, though more at some times than others. All of the school but three now express some hope that they love Christ, though in some this hope is extremely feeble."

The simple and affectionate interest expressed in the

following letter is in reference to an event that changed the address of her friend: —

"SOUTH HADLEY, August 18, 1841.

"MY DEAR MISS GRANT:

"I received yours by last mail. To say that I was so deeply interested in its contents that I could hardly sleep, would be saying but little. I have nothing to say on the subject, either good or bad. I have only to desire that this exceedingly important event may be for your own happiness and usefulness, for the happiness and usefulness of others, and also for the glory of God. I trust I shall be able to be with you on Tuesday, the 7th. My thanks to yourself and Mrs. B. for inviting me to pass Monday night with you. If I am prevented from being with you on the 7th, it will be to me a great trial.

"May the Lord guide, keep, and sustain you, my dear friend. My affectionate regards to Mrs. B."

TO MRS. BANISTER, FORMERLY MISS GRANT.

"SOUTH HADLEY, December —, 1842.

"To say that the death of your niece, Mrs. Burgess,* was sorely felt by many, would be saying but very little. You know I loved her much, and valued her highly. I had the privilege of seeing and knowing much of her, taking together all the time, from my first meeting her at her father's in Colebrook, Connecticut, and my first calling her my pupil in Buckland, to her last, farewell visit here, which I shall always remember. She has gone, but she has left in our hearts a sweet memorial. What a privilege it is so to live as to leave such a sweet savor, such a precious treasure in the hearts of surviving friends!

"We have had a very prosperous year in worldly things. Every thing is systematized, and Miss M. and Miss W. urge

* Missionary in India.

forward the wheels so beautifully that all seems more than ever like clockwork. I enjoy very much having every thing done better by others than it can be by myself. If this pleasure continues to increase as it has done for a year or two, I hope I may be prepared to be happy in being old, and in being laid aside as a useless thing. But in spiritual things we are less favored. There has been less interest than we have had any year since the first. Pray for us, that we may not receive all our good things in this life."

TO MRS. BANISTER.

"July, 1843.

"MY DEAR MRS. B.:

"I have finished my business so as to leave to-morrow. I have given directions to have your thirty-two copies [of the 'Missionary Offering,' probably] sent to you. Will you accompany each copy which you give away with one petition — that, sooner or later, God would honor the exceeding riches of his condescending love in blessing it to the salvation of some souls? I have thought more about the instrumentality of prayer, for a few months past, than ever before in the same time. What a field of usefulness is here opened for all, under all circumstances! What a privilege is it to pray that God may be honored by all our friends, and by ourselves, at all times and in all places; that the interests of immortal souls may be promoted, and Christ's kingdom advanced! It seems to me an infinite privilege to have my friends pray that God may be honored in all I do, compared with their simply praying for my own comfort and happiness."

TO THE SAME.

"SOUTH HADLEY, July, 1844.

"MY DEAR MRS. B.:

"While I have many, very many things to say, I must content myself with a single line. We will receive your niece, and endeavor to meet your wishes on all the points specified in your letter. Miss M. and Miss W. are very faithful in looking after the health and the sleep of the young ladies; so we have been improving and enlarging in this respect from year to year. Now, although we do not actually require *all* to be in bed more than seven or seven and a half hours, yet they need make no exceptions to any family arrangements, if they should add one, two, or three more hours. None need do their domestic work in the ordinary hours for sleep, unless they choose to do so."

TO MRS. BANISTER.

"MONSON, September 3, 1844.

"MY DEAR MRS. B.:

"I am now on my way to Boston, where I shall spend a few days for business, and return to attend the meeting of the Board at Worcester. Mrs. P. sends you her love. Shall we not see you at Worcester? Is it not the duty and privilege of Christians to carry this missionary meeting on their hearts to the throne of grace? Except the Lord build the house, they labor in vain who build it. What a privilege it is to be allowed to coöperate in the least degree in the great work of bringing this world to the love and service of our blessed Redeemer! As we advance in life, may we have a more single eye to the glory of God in all we do, in all we desire, and in all we feel. May we have deeper and more affecting views of the value of the soul, and of the unspeakable and incomprehensible value of the price which has been paid for its ransom. I often feel that my days are rapidly passing, and that I have but a few remaining. But these remaining days are precious days, if they should be spent for the cause of Christ. And what an unspeakable privilege is it to indulge a hope that, when our work is done, through infinite grace, we may be admitted to dwell forever with the Lord!"

TO MRS. BANISTER.

"SOUTH HADLEY, July 9, 1845.

"MY DEAR MRS. B.:

"My mind and heart are full of a thousand things, which I should love to say for friendship's sake. I should love to tell you how much I have sympathized with you in your long-continued and trying sufferings. I should love to tell you of the deep interest I felt in your remarkable escape. O, had you found a watery grave, you would not only have left us all to mourn that we could no more enjoy you on earth, but that we could not even receive your parting blessing at a dying hour. But I have no time. Suffice it to say, that you know full well that the heart cannot always find room and strength to utter its own emotions."

TO THE SAME.

"SOUTH HADLEY, July 23, 1845.

"MY VERY DEAR FRIEND:

"I have allowed your letter to lie by one mail, and if you had been with us yesterday morning, you would not think it strange. About three o'clock in the morning, our building was struck with lightning; but it was saved from a speedy and dreadful destruction. Do you recollect a closet over our ovens for drying towels? The frame to hold the towels was moved on a railway made of iron rails. The electric fluid found its way to these iron rails, and, as I suppose, in a moment every towel was lighted to an intense blaze, and in a few minutes the whole closet was like a burning oven. I think I heard the report when the lightning struck, and in less than five minutes I heard the cry of *fire*. In a few minutes more, I think it would have found its way to the wood-work and doors leading to the stairways, in such a manner that it would have been past control. I have not time to tell you how we were delivered. My mind has been affected by this striking illustration of eternal things, and of our dependence on that unseen hand by which we have been saved from everlasting burning."

TO MRS. BANISTER.

"SOUTH HADLEY, March 25, 1846.

"I wrote to Mrs. Breese, of R., Illinois, last month, making inquiries about her present situation and prospects. She writes, in reply, 'I am now teaching a select school in our own house, sixteen by thirty feet, one story and a half high. We have seventeen scholars, eleven of whom board with us. I sit day after day, with my babe, a large, resolute boy of five and a half months, in my arms, teaching them as well as I can.' Mrs. B. has already sent out a few teachers from her school, and several more are preparing for the same avocation. Most of them could have attended school nowhere else. Such schools as Mrs. B. is teaching must do much for the west. The larger schools cannot meet all their wants; and if such a one as hers could be established wherever pupils could be collected together, or even where the influence of a home missionary is felt, much would be done to bless our nation."

TO THE SAME.

"SOUTH HADLEY, November 27, 1846.

"How I should love to commune with your spirit more frequently than I can! Such communings may be reserved for that 'nobler rest above,' where

'No more fatigue, no more distress,
Nor sin, nor death shall reach the place.'

"I have passed through many scenes, the last year, of deep and tender interest to me, concentrating the feelings of many years into one, and obviously increasing my gray hairs. I feel the loss of my two nieces very much. I feel the loss socially more than in our business, though they were both very important to the school. Mrs. Burgess has gone, and I could not, as I expected, go with her to Boston. It came so near the time of commencing school, that I thought it not prudent to use the extra strength it would require, especially after the excitement and fatigue connected with so great changes in the school. My niece, Miss Lyon, (now Mrs. Lord,) has just come to make us her last visit. She and her husband expect to sail next month from New York for China. I had depended on going to be with her a little while, at the time of her sailing, but my health will not allow."

TO THE SAME.

"South Hadley, April 27, 1848.

"I am glad to know the communings of your spirit with the wise and good. I have read Upham's 'Interior Life' with deep interest and profit. I love to meet with such a heart as is evident in what he writes. It disarms my disposition to criticize. If a sentence does come along, now and then, which might be questioned by the strictest philosophical or theological rules, it is easy to pass it over and gather up the spiritual food.

"In our Sabbath privileges we have had such a constant change of preachers, since our dear Mr. Condit's death, that with my deafness I have gained but little profit. Many things relating to our family and the church and parish render the question of Mr. Condit's successor one of great importance and of deep interest to me. I have enjoyed the privilege of praying that God would send us a man after his own heart, and such a one as he knows us to need.

"We have again received a spiritual blessing in our family according to the riches of the grace of Jesus Christ. During our first term, about fifty expressed hope. During the last term, there has been a continued, gradual, progressive interest. Some one case of hope has occurred nearly every week; still, there are about thirty without hope."

TO MRS. BANISTER.

"SOUTH HADLEY, June 5, 1848.

"Will you not come and make us a visit the week of our anniversary? It happens the first Thursday in August. The examination will occupy two or three days preceding. You have a standing invitation to come, and I enjoy the belief that you always will if you can. I do not know that you can realize what a great pleasure it is to me to have yourself and husband with us on these occasions.

"Our dear Mr. Condit! I am reminded of him every way; I shall be especially at the time of our anniversary. I loved him as a friend on earth; if possible, my spirit loves him more as a friend in heaven. His memory is precious, very precious. But we have another man of God in his stead, (Mr. Laurie.) For this I would thank God. I should love to tell you all about the dealings of my heavenly Father in bringing him here, in helping him along, and the various occurrences, all interesting to my own feelings, connected with his becoming our pastor. But this I must leave till I have the privilege of communing with you face to face.

"I have recently been reading, or, rather, am now reading, McCheyne's 'Life, Letters, and Lectures.' It is just what I need — the sincere milk dealt out in childlike simplicity and godly sincerity. It is just what I need to feed and refresh me when I am so tired that I can do nothing with strong meat. With my feeble strength, and with the burden laid upon me, I feel that henceforth my reading must be mostly for another world. I do want to commune more with your spirit on earth before we go home to our rest in heaven."

TO MRS. BANISTER.

"SOUTH HADLEY, January 9, 1849.

"Our vacation commences this week. I feel compelled to try to flee away from home and find the most quiet retreat I can, partly for my own benefit, and partly to sustain my credit for taking proper care of my unworthy self. Monson will be my principal resting-place; but it is in my heart to take a ride to Newburyport. But whether this plan will exist out of my heart is very uncertain."

Ten days later she writes from Monson,—

"I have been hesitating about the path of duty. But I need two or three days at home before the school begins, which I cannot have if I attempt to visit you. Without being in a hurry to do any thing in particular, I am seeking for rest, which I need most of any thing. This I can best secure by remaining in this place. So I reluctantly give up the prospect of seeing you just at present, a prospect cherished more tenderly in the warmth of my heart than in my judgment. I have some missionary letters, which I would like to read to you. Among others, those relating to the severe sickness of dear Mrs. Burgess. But she is yet to live, as we trust. We have received one letter from her own hand. To me it has peculiar interest. It seems like a voice from the other side of the grave in a most tender, heavenly tone.

"There has been for a few weeks a slow, progressive work of grace among us, and between twenty and thirty have expressed hope in Christ. We greatly fear the effects of vacation. Do pray for us."

TO MISS WHITMAN.

"MONSON, January 22, 1849.

"During two or three years past, I have been trying to mature in the literary department the changes which sprung up in the agitation of the waters on Miss Moore's leaving, and I have been trying to mature things, too, in the domestic department. I had every thing about ready for work this year, without much planning, or agitation, or change. Thus it has come out that this has been the easiest year, in itself considered, we have almost ever had. You know the easy years come along now and then, and now and then the hard years. Now that this easy year should come right along when you are called away in Providence, is surely no planning of mine. So it is. If one thing is made comfortable and easy, we may expect some corresponding trial. If trials and perplexities come, then we may look for some comforting, consoling providence. We may always expect enough of trial and difficulties to make us love to sing, —

'Is this, dear Lord, that thorny road
That leads us to the mount of God?'

and enough of consolation, and support, and blessing, and mercy, to make us feel that Christ's yoke is easy and his burden light.

"I feel rather anxious about you, and shall till I hear again. I shall not send this sheet till I hear from you. My heart's desire and prayer to God is, that you may be kept in the arms of Him who never slumbereth nor sleepeth, and who numbereth the very hairs of our heads. I pray that you may experience much of the grace of God in your body, in your soul, in your spirit. For myself, I always carry about enough of my own self to be a fit occasion for loathing and abhorring myself, for distrusting myself, for casting off all confidence in the flesh. But from day to day, I think I do find crums enough falling from the table to prove the infinite mercy and long-suffering of God, and enough to prove the exceeding grace of the gospel, and enough of strength in the time of extremity to prove that there is an arm on which we may lean with safety. I want to ask you to pray for me in a very special manner about one thing. It is for divine guidance and strength in giving religious instruction. Pray that I may have hid in my own heart all which I attempt to say. Pray that I may speak the words of truth, every jot and tittle — that which God sees and knows to be truth. Pray that hearts may receive the truth in honesty, sincerity, and in faith. Pray that in these seasons God may be magnified, and glorified. We have great reason to fear and tremble about our next term. Vacation came just as the religious interest seemed to be spreading from heart to heart. Miss Hazen will write you all general facts, I suppose. Between twenty and thirty expressed hope. I miss you most of all in the care of souls. But we know not how much you may do by your prayers."

Results of the Experiment.

After these details of the operation of the new seminary through the twelve years after its establishment, in which Miss Lyon lived, it will be interesting to bring the leading results together as to the cost, number of pupils, &c., up to the present time. I am indebted mainly for these statements to the Hon. Andrew W. Porter, the treasurer, and to Miss Mary W. Chapin, who is at present at the head of the institution.

Cost of the buildings and real estate connected with them, ...	$60,000
" of the furniture, ...	6,000
" of the apparatus and library, ...	2,500
Total cost, all obtained by subscription, ...	68,500
The seminary is now out of debt.	
It has funds to the amount of	1800
Whole number of names of pupils on the first fourteen catalogues, ...	2568
Number of different pupils, between . .	1700 and 1800
Completed their course to the close of 1851, . .	415
Number connected with the Memorandum Society to 1847, ...	593

Number who have engaged in teaching, of these 593, ...	279
If one half as large a proportion of the other 1157 pupils, that have been connected with the institution, had engaged in teaching, the whole number of teachers would be . .	551
Number of teachers in the school, ...	55
Amount of private funds expended by Miss Lyon during the three or four years of starting the seminary, ...	$1200 to 1400
Property left by her to the American Board of Foreign Missions, in reversion, excepting about $300, ...	$2000 to 2500

SECTION III.

The Retrospect, the last Visit, the last Instruction, and the Departure.

Thus successfully have we seen the great enterprise to which Miss Lyon had consecrated the vigor of her days carried forward for nearly twelve years, each year exhibiting a nearer approach to perfection in her plans, and a more striking evidence of the wonderful victory she had gained in a most unequal conflict. But the hour of release was at hand, and we cannot but feel a deep interest to witness the close of a life so happy and useful.

It would be strange if a person of Miss Lyon's piety, as she felt from time to time the severe pressure of infirmity, and was conscious that she had seen more than half a century on earth, — it would be strange if she should not often have had solemn impressions of her nearness to eternity. It may be that God does sometimes give special premonitions to his servants of their departure, when about to take them away. Yet it does not appear that Miss Lyon had any such strong presentiment. On the contrary, only a few weeks before her sickness she seems to have felt unusually vigorous, and indulged a hope that her work was not yet done. This feeling appears in her letter to Miss Whitman, at the close of the last section, written from Monson, on the 22d of January, 1849. Still more manifest is it in a letter dated from the same place, only two days earlier, to Mrs. Burgess in India. Yet, as we shall shortly see, God had led her to the place from whence she wrote for the purpose, apparently, of making preparation for her departure. The tone of these letters shows how well she had improved the opportunity, and it must be regarded as great mercy on God's part that he hid his purpose from her till ready to put it into execution. She thought that the opportunity she enjoyed was intended to prepare her for usefulness on earth, but God meant it to fit her for a higher sphere.

TO MRS. BURGESS.

"MONSON, January 20, 1849.

"MY VERY DEAR NIECE:

"Here I am again with my dear Mrs. Porter. She proposes that we should again write a joint letter to comfort you in your pilgrimage and voluntary exile for Christ's sake. This I am very happy to do, though I think it will not take a very large part of the sheet to assure you of my continued remembrance of you and of former scenes. I wrote once before in Mrs. Porter's letter, two years ago. I have scarcely had a vacation of any sort since then. But I am now enjoying an old-fashioned vacation of *real rest* in this sweetest of all resting-places. Miss Hazen proposed to stay and take all the care, and let me go away. I decided to accept. I began a week beforehand to arrange all things.

I had my plans made out in writing, and left all behind me. Here I can quietly read, write letters, ride, and visit, with nothing to annoy me, and with scarcely a thought of home, except as I attempt to send up my feeble petitions, that the Holy Spirit may come down and dwell with us. This is the more remarkable, as Miss Whitman is away. But one providence meets another. I had many things planned and arranged last year for this, so that this proves one of the *easiest* years. Such years come along now and then.

"My health has been unusually good this year, thus far. So unlike has it been to the winter after you left us, that I have great cause for gratitude. But at all times, whether I have more or less strength, I feel that I am fast hastening to my eternal home, my home of rest in the bosom of my God, as I hope. Still, I trust I may have a little more work to do on earth, and that little may I do faithfully. By grace I am the little that I am, and by grace alone would I do the little that I hope to do. The doctrine of grace, in all its aspects and relations, is more and more precious here; and what will it be hereafter, when we shall be permited to join in that song of Moses and the Lamb to Him who has redeemed us, and washed our robes, and made them white in his own blood! By grace we are redeemed, by grace we are saved, by grace we are received and sanctified, by grace we have our work given us, and by grace strength and a heart to do it.

"My work is made up, as you know, of an endless number of duties, of nameless littleness, interwoven if not confused together. But still my work is a good work. By the enduring grace of God am I permitted to enjoy such a goodly heritage of toil and labor. Every hour I feel not only need of divine aid to lead me, but of an internal, divine power, carrying me along in the right path. It is ever a pathway of grace, unmerited grace. When I am about my work, sometimes called unexpectedly and suddenly from one thing to another, I whisper in my heart, 'Lord, help me to be patient, help me to remember, and help me to be faithful. Lord, enable me to do all for Christ's sake, and to go forward, leaning on the bosom of his infinite grace.' How amazing is that goodness that allows us to do all for Christ's sake, and always to pray in his name! May you experience largely of that grace which alone can make your spared life a blessing.

"Much love to Mr. Burgess, Mr. and Mrs. Hazen, Mrs. Wilder and Fairbanks, and Mrs. Ballentine. The thought is pleasant to me that an early friend of mine is your fellow-laborer."

On the 15th of February, only about three weeks before her death, Miss Lyon addressed another letter to Miss Whitman, in which she spoke of her plans for the next autumnal vacation. Suggesting a course for Miss Whitman, during the summer, in her feeble state of health, she says, "During the vacation, (in the autumn,) I thought I might meet you to journey together, or visit and read together, or both, somewhere among the mountains and in the quiet valleys of New England. So you see that I am calculating on quite a resting time next autumn myself."

And, indeed, she has found that "resting time," but not on earth. It was among celestial scenery that her autumn and her eternity were to be spent, and in sweet converse with her Savior and some of the spirits whom she had been instrumental of guiding to that blessed world. Often had her thoughts turned to that better land with strong desire; but it is obvious she did not deem it so near. One week previous she had said in a note to Miss Whitman, "I often feel a longing of heart to sit down and tell you some of my joys, or sorrows, or anxieties. Then I feel that you are absent, indeed. But I get along. Sometimes I make a substitute of Miss ———, sometimes I ponder all in my own heart alone, and always I endeavor to go to Him who can be touched with the feeling of our infirmities. This world is to be used faithfully and diligently, but only as a waymark to that better home, where, I trust, we shall rejoice together over many dear ones gathered into our Father's house."

As the letter to Miss Whitman, of the 15th of February, has the latest date of any I am able to present from Miss Lyon, it will be interesting to quote the first part of it, which refers to objects dearest to her heart.

"I need not tell you we were last evening [upon the receipt of a letter from Miss W.] much gratified. First, I thank God for your expressed desires to live for God alone. Next would I thank him for your continued desire to spend your strength for the good of this precious institution, the founding and building up of which I feel more and more to be the handiwork of God. I trust that you will have fifteen years added to your life, if we will all suffer the trial of your taking a thorough rest and recruiting now. I hope fifteen years, too, will be granted to you after I shall cease from my labors."

The Retrospect.

Distinguished individuals, who are incessantly occupied from day to day, and from year to year, in important duties, are not apt to pause often and devote much time to a retrospect of life. Or, rather, if religious persons, they are apt to resolve to set apart some such seasons, and, by the constant pressure of duties, to delay the time till the unexpected summons comes to depart. Knowing the incessant occupation of Miss Lyon, we might presume such would be the case with her. But it was not so; and fortunately some account of that retrospect has been preserved. The following interesting details have been communicated by Mrs. Louisa Russell, wife of Rev. Ezekiel Russell, formerly of Springfield, and now of Weymouth. Mrs. Russell (then

35

Louisa Billings) was one of Miss Lyon's teachers in the Buckland school, and Mrs. Winslow was her pupil, and is now wife of Rev. Miron Winslow, missionary at Madras.

"It was in September, 1848. Miss Lyon was spending the day in Springfield, and while walking the street, she unexpectedly met my sister, Mrs. Winslow, then on the eve of her second departure for India. Perceiving that this was a last occasion for an interview with one of her pupils, she readily accepted an invitation to tea. At the table was a gentleman who attended school with her at the academy in Ashfield. Many years had since passed. The gentleman then was a mere lad; and though a lad, he had a part with her in the dialogue, in which he played the infant in the bulrushes, while she performed the no less important part of the mother. They had not met since. The exhibition had been forgotten, or, if not forgotten, not recalled. But now the scene was revived, with the seeming power of a present sensation, and along with it a whole train of circumstances and events on which her active mind and warm heart expatiated with an interest peculiar to herself. The effect on her was electric; and the whole company at the table felt the power of the current as it passed along the invisible wires of thought and feeling. 'We have here the "eagle's nest,"' said one, 'without Dr. Rush or his patient. This time we can play with Hamlet left out.' And so we did, little thinking that the one then acting was to retire so soon forever from the stage.

"The founder of that school in Ashfield, said she, was a man of genuine benevolence. He was in the habit of visiting the different schools of the town, and when he did, his eye was sure to fix on every promising scholar, and a word was dropped that never failed to awaken brighter hopes and give fresher vigor in the work of acquisition. Perceiving that many were in moderate circumstances, and could not be sent abroad for the purpose of an education, he founded this academy, the genial influences of which, she remarked, first wakened to life her own mental energies, and gave her an impulse that had never ceased to act. 'That institution,' she continued, 'has done an immense amount of good. Many who otherwise would never have had access to any thing worthy the name of literary advantages, received there the first rudiments of an education. In that quiet retreat among the hills, the intellect was stirred, the taste refined, and intensity given to the desire for knowledge. To mind and heart that institution was what the mountain airs are to the physical powers. And I can perceive,' she said, 'that those who have gone forth from it have brightened, and cheered, and blessed the pathways which they have trod.' The obligations to her teacher, Mr. Burritt, she acknowledged with warmth and satisfaction, while she displayed her usual discrimination in the analysis of those mental qualities for which that gentleman was distinguished. It was a sunny scene that opened on her view at the table, and all seemed to share with her in the exhilaration.

"'How thankful ought I to be,' she continued, on returning to the parlor, 'for the incidents that have revived these pleasant portions of my life! This was unexpected. My duties for years have been so urgent, and my cares so pressing, as to shut the past in this sense from my thoughts. But seeing you, Mrs. W., and your sister, brings before me, fresh as yesterday, those winter scenes in my Ashfield and Buckland schools, over which the spirit of the living God hovered, and moved in the bosom of many a pupil, I trust, the pulsations of that life which is spiritual and eternal. And my friend here, Mr. S., once the infant in the bulrushes, has carried me still farther back in my career, and made the morning shine on the noon, or the evening, as I now begin to think it is, of my life. Something of this I have before experienced. Former pupils have often met me, whose countenances had faded from my recollection, when the mention of their names would flash whole trains of delightful associations upon my mind. This, I apprehend, will be one source of our happiness in heaven. As we move to and fro amid the myriads there gathered on the mount of vision, we shall meet one after another, now forgotten, who will bring different portions of our lives to our recollection, filling us with untold wonder and joy. O, I love to think of the joy in reserve for the righteous, and of the various sources of it at the command of the Redeemer, who is himself the crowning attraction of heaven.' Mrs. Winslow replied, 'Your pupils are going up to participate in this joy from all quarters of the globe, and it must be pleasant for you to think of it.' 'Yes,' was her answer, taking my sister's hand, 'I often think of the happiness, through grace, of being permitted to welcome one after another, as they finish the toils of earth, to the rest of heaven.' 'How strange it seems, Miss L.,' said one, 'to hear you speak so freely of heaven! It was always an earnest desire of mine that you should take up the subject that now so fills your thoughts in some of your morning exercises in school. You always spoke then of duty, of action; of *present* duties and of *present* action. You seemed neither to think or speak of any thing else, and appeared to have for it no time.' Smiling, she replied, 'So it was. I had no time. I did what I deemed of the most consequence It was my endeavor to discharge present duties, engage in present action, and leave results more to themselves. But I am changed now. Of my active life I took leave on my fiftieth birthday. It was the most solemn day of my life. I devoted it to reflection and prayer. I felt that half a century had been given me for exertion, that incessant opportunities had been furnished for usefulness in a noble sphere, and my heart went up to God in grateful praise for the vigorous health and disposition that had enabled me to bear such burdens, sustain such toils, and accomplish something, as I devoutly trust, for the good of the world and the cause of Christ. A half a century! The thought all but overwhelmed me. Yet it had been given me, and it was gone, gone with its burdens, its toils, and its scenes of precious, thrilling delight. I was sensible of deficiencies, of great deficiencies. These I regretted.. But I could not regret that the toil of half a century had ended. It was certain that another such period of exertion — of cheerful exertion it had always been to me — would never be allotted on earth. I was certain that before another fifty years should have elapsed I should wake up amid far different scenes, and far other thoughts would fill my mind, and other employments would engage my attention. *I felt it.* There seemed to be no ladder between me and the world above. The gates were opened, and I seemed to stand on the threshold. *It was the most solemn day of my life.* Of my active toils I then took leave. I felt that I could no longer do as I had done. The disposition was not wanting, but waning health forbade the expectation. I felt that the evening of my days had come, that I needed repose. It is evening with me now. I now care for what no one else thinks of doing.' To use her own expression, 'I gather up the odds and ends, and keep the machine in motion. I need rest, and repose is grateful. I have laid aside my armor, and I now think more of results. My day has gone, its evening come, and it has become natural for me to think and speak more of the results of duties discharged, of actions performed, than it once was. I have for it more time, and a setting sun, you know, always invites to different thoughts and inspires far other emotions than when shining upon us with his morning beams, or throwing down upon us his meridian splendors. I feel the change. I think of heaven, and I do love to think of those who, I trust, are gathered there, of their joys, and the sources of it. Christ, of course, is the great object of attraction there; but our mental economy is wonderful, and all its laws will act there in eternal harmony, and add bliss and rapture, as I conceive, to that world. I therefore often think of the happiness of being permitted, through grace, to welcome one after another of my acquaintance and former pupils, who are now toiling in every quarter of the globe in the same glorious work with myself, to the rest of heaven. You, Mrs. W., are to leave children. In a few days, you are to turn your back upon them forever. But it is a sacrifice for Christ. Few make it. Few can make it. Few can conceive of the thing as a free-will offering to God. Most would instinctively shrink from it, and shrink with shuddering. But Christ in such cases has pledged a reward, and a reward proportionably glorious. In heaven, we shall never regret any sacrifice, however painful, or labor, however protracted, made or encountered here for the cause of Christ. It will come back to us in imperishable blessings there.'

"It was on one of the first days of September. It had been a calm and brilliant day. The sun was setting as the interview closed and she arose to take leave. The river, from the abode in which the visit was paid, seemed to sleep. The air was soft and still; and sky and landscape in and around Springfield — always attractive and soothing when the sun sets unclouded in the summer months — for that evening's livery were arrayed in their mildest beauty and glory. The notes of the swan had broken and died away on our ears. It was her last visit."

The first and last Visit.

The pages of this work have shown that perhaps the most attractive of all the retreats to which Miss Lyon occasionally resorted to escape from care and labor, and refresh her weary spirit with heavenly manna, was the house of Hon. Andrew W. Porter, in Monson. Not only did she find there the largest hospitality, but, in her intercourse with Mr. and Mrs. Porter, that religious sympathy and communion which gratified the strongest desires of her heart. Thither did Providence mercifully direct her steps, when he would prepare her for her final departure from the world. I am so fortunate as to be able to present an account of that last visit from the pen of Mrs. Porter. She has prefixed to it a brief statement of Miss Lyon's first visit, which I could not find it in my heart to omit, although not exactly in the right place.

"My first acquaintance with Miss Mary Lyon was in March, 1836. In answering myself to the door bell on a snowy day of that month, a stranger lady stood before me. She introduced herself as Mary Lyon, of Ipswich, and remarked that the gentleman with whom she came had driven round to the carriage-house on account of the storm. I was prepared to give her a cordial reception, having a high regard for Miss Grant and Miss Lyon, as principals of the Ipswich Seminary; but what could have led her there that stormy day I could not think. Soon the Rev. Mr. Tyler, an acquaintance of ours, came in and introduced her, inquiring if Mr. Porter was at home. I replied, 'He is gone to Boston, but we expect him home in this evening's stage.' Some regret was expressed, but Miss L. immediately remarked, 'Providence orders all things right,' and as soon as outside garments were disposed of, with much animation and no less apparent vigor from exposure to the storm, told me in brief their errand. 'You have probably heard,' she says, 'of the contemplated female seminary,' (mentioning its principles.) I told her I had heard something of it, and read some articles in print, in which I was much interested. She proceeded: 'The trustees met yesterday, (at South Hadley, I think.) We have arrived now at a point where we cannot proceed much farther till a gentleman is found to superintend the erection of the building. An act of incorporation has been obtained the past winter, and the town in which it is to be located has been decided on; a gentleman is needed whose business talents have been tested, who has had experience in building, and one in whose integrity the community would have confidence; one, too, who would do it without remuneration, for there are not sufficient funds to devote any to that purpose; and it is all a work of benevolence. Last evening your husband was mentioned to the trustees, as one to whom it was best application should be made. Rev. Messrs. Hawks and Tyler were appointed to wait on him, and I requested to accompany them. Now, do you know of any thing in his business, health, or views, that you would expect would prevent his considering the subject.' I told her he had suffered much the past year from a nervous headache, and had decided on a long journey to the far west as soon as travelling would allow, to try the effect of relaxation from business, and journeying. Aside from that, I should expect he would, at least, consider the subject.

"Mr. Hawks, who had now arrived, Mr. Tyler, and Miss L. held a consultation, and it was decided they should leave to attend to their Sabbath appointments, and Miss L. remain, as I had invited her to do, till the next week. One of the gentlemen was to return on Monday. Miss L. remarked, 'If this enterprise was to go forward, the Lord had some one provided for this service, and it might be Mr. Porter, and it might not.'

"After tea she proposed going to her room, as Mr. Porter would be fatigued when he arrived, and she was up till a late hour the night previous.

"Not a word was named about the proposed seminary till Monday. Some ten or twelve years after, she told me those were nights of prayer with her; and 'the Lord,' said she, 'not only answered my prayer in inclining your husband to engage in the work, but much more than I asked. He gave me in yourself and Mr. P. personal friends, and at your house a home whenever I have needed quiet and rest. O, that first visit,' she remarked, 'and that chamber where I commended anew the enterprise to God, and could finally submit your husband's acceptance and all to him!'

"I have told you of her first visit to our house; I will now tell you of her last.

"When at the seminary on the Thanksgiving occasion previous to her death, I said to Miss L., 'You know an invitation to spend your vacations with us is stereotyped; may we not expect you in the winter vacation?' She replied, 'I think I shall come previous to vacation, and rest, for *circles* are so broken up then, that it is more difficult getting along than in the term time. She came, however, in that vacation; and the first evening after she arrived, she told me, 'that what decided her to come after concluding she should remain at the seminary during vacation was, she had never felt the responsibility of giving religious instruction as this winter. O, when I come before those young immortals to teach them eternal truths, I am borne down with a sense of its importance as never before, and I wanted to come to my *resting-home*,' (as she was wont to call our house,) 'where, in that quiet chamber, I could seek anew for wisdom, grace, and strength for the great work.'

"The teachers, she said, were very urgent she should go to New York to sit for her portrait; so much so, that she was reluctant not to comply with their kind request, and accept of their generous offer to bear all the expense. 'But to me,' she added, 'it seemed of so little consequence to have my picture taken, compared with seeking a better preparation for my important duties, that I could not comply.'

"Every thing in her conversation and appearance indicated a 'fresh anointing.' All business with regard to the seminary was laid aside. Previously, she had invariably come with account books, and a list of various items of business to consult Mr. P. about; and as soon as he came in, business was the theme. Now she introduced no subject of business but twice during her stay, and one of those times said but a few words.

"Mr. Porter said to me on Sabbath eve, (she came the Friday previous,) 'Does not Miss L. seem unusually spiritual?' I replied, 'I think so, evidently; I never saw her so heavenly-minded.' Little did I then think she was pluming her wings for her upward flight. She appeared as well as I ever saw her, and repeatedly spoke with gratitude of her excellent health. At our dinner table, a day or two previous to her leaving, she remarked, playfully, 'Mr. P., you and Mrs. P. have been afraid I should break down at the seminary, but,' (dropping her knife and fork, and straightening up,) 'Do you not think I am in pretty good trim? I have an excellent appetite, I sleep like a child, and have none of that chilliness I have had when rather exhausted with my labors; I feel quite vigorous.' We both told her we thought we had not seen her better, and the conclusion of us all was, that she had as good a prospect of physical ability to labor on at the seminary for ten years to come, as for the past ten years.

"Except coming down to prayers and family worship, she spent the mornings till our hour for dinner in her chamber. I had frequent occasions to go to her room, and always found her with her Bible, Hodge's Way of Life, or Bible History of Prayer, by Goodrich, and the remarks she would make showed an elevated state of devotional feeling.

"One morning, I went soon after breakfast, and found her with a large Bible open at Solomon's Song. She told me she rose very early that morning, and had read through that book, (Solomon's Song.) 'And I think I have never enjoyed it so before, though I have read it often for a few years past. I have been able to drop the figure, and view Christ's strong love to the church. O, how wonderful this love! What infinite condescension, in his exalted state, to leave the realms of purity, and dwell with fallen, polluted man! Yet by it he *lost none of his dignity*.' From this she drew the inference, that when, from the principle of benevolence, we voluntarily dwelt among the wicked, we need not be degraded.

"She seemed, in conversation, to dwell more on the scenes of childhood and youth than I had ever known her. One afternoon, she told us of her maternal grandfather, who was a Baptist clergyman. 'I think,' she says, 'he was a most holy man. When a child, I can remember my conviction that he loved and served God, and was living for *another* world, not *this*. When I was about ten years old, there was what was called *a reformation* among his people, and many were baptized. I should think it was a genuine work of grace. My mind was then much impressed by hearing his conversation with those who came to him *under conviction* for sin, as it was termed, and I never lost those impressions. He was remarkable for praying much for his posterity, that none of them might ever be left to slight the offers of mercy through a Savior. When I last visited my native place, I went with a relative to two graveyards where forty-two of his descendants are buried. I had a delightful view of the faithfulness of God to his believing people. They had all left a comforting evidence they had died in the faith.' She was enthusiastic in talking of him, and said, 'What a blessing to have such a grandfather! how to be prized above all the world calls great.'

"When she left us, I felt, more than ever before, that it was a rare privilege to enjoy her personal friendship, and have her so frequently an inmate of our family. Ever since my first acquaintance with Miss L., I had thought I had never seen the blessed principles and precepts of the gospel of Christ so strikingly exemplified in any of his professed followers. But on account of her active business habits, and constantly planning for improvements in her beloved seminary, I had not seen exhibited that contemplative, devotional state of mind which was developed in this visit. There was evinced an absorbing love to the Lord Jesus; Christ was her theme, and the privilege of laboring for him, and making sacrifices for his cause, dwelt on much. I think I have never witnessed a nearer approach to the mercy seat than was apparent in social prayer just before leaving. It was almost the last sound of her voice I ever heard.

"In the three weeks that intervened between this and her last sickness, she wrote me three or four times. The same spirit was manifest. Just the day that a letter came in the evening's mail informing us of her illness, and desiring to have Mr. P. come to South Hadley, I had been looking over and filing away letters. I was quite unwell, and it affected me with dizziness and faintness, as it usually did. The feeling came over me, Why do I thus retain my letters, and suffer so much in occasionally looking them over? I have now no daughter who might enjoy reviewing them, and in a moment of despondency I put a large quantity into the stove. At night, when a letter from a teacher told us Miss L. was sick, I was filled with regret, for I presume fifty of them were from her. But it was too late; Providence had doubtless some wise design in permitting it. Miss Whitman, who roomed with her, says she wrote more frequently to me, the last three or four years, than to any other individual. Her benevolent, sympathizing heart sought thus to relieve, as much as she could, my loneliness, in my feeble, bereaved state. Some letters, written during seasons of religious interest in the seminary, were exceedingly valuable. I can hardly forgive myself the rash act of destroying them, or account for it either, as it is unlike my disposition or habits."

The last Instruction and the Departure.

It sometimes happens that when the time has come for those greatly beloved, and in stations of great usefulness, to die, Providence commissions the destroyer to execute his work in a sudden and distressing manner. Thus is the anguish of the separation shortened; and though nature may murmur, grace looks upon such a course as an indication of special mercy. Such is the aspect in which we ought to regard the sickness and death of Miss Lyon. They came suddenly and unexpectedly, and reason was taken away also. But before that took place, an opportunity was given for her to leave in the hearts of her pupils some of the noblest sentiments ever uttered by uninspired mortals. These constituted her "Last Instruction." The "Departure," which followed, had nothing in it very peculiar. She sunk rapidly under the power of strong disease, against which her vigorous constitution struggled mightily. Indeed, had there not been an accumulation of circumstances at the time of her sickness, adapted powerfully to disturb her feelings and awaken a morbid excitement in her nervous system, she would doubtless have recovered. But these circumstances, as well as every thing else relating to the event, were ordered by a wise and benevolent Providence; and our proper feeling should be, *The Lord gave, and the Lord hath taken away; blessed be the name of the Lord.*

The details of this trying event, and of the last instruction given by Miss Lyon to the seminary, are contained in the journal kept there for the missionaries; and I have liberty to make the following extracts: —

"*March* 9, 1849. Since our last date, we have been led through scenes of deep, deep affliction. About four weeks ago, one of our young ladies had a severe attack of influenza, with swelling in the throat, somewhat like quinsy. An additional cold brought on erysipelas, and she was quite sick with it. For two or three days, we saw no cause for alarm in her case, as we supposed it to be a common form of the disease; but it proved to be the malignant erysipelas, so prevalent and so fatal in many places four or five years since. On Wednesday, February 21, it became evident that she must die very soon. The disease settled upon the brain, congestion followed, and she lay in a senseless state, from which nothing could arouse her. It was thought she could not live through the night. This was to us all a most unexpected stroke. The painful intelligence must be communicated to her parents in Weare, New Hampshire, who, as yet, knew nothing of her sickness. The brief notice that she was very sick, and could live but a few hours, was sent by private conveyance, telegraph and mail, and reached them in about thirty-six hours. The anxious father, in entire suspense with regard to the circumstances of her sickness, started immediately, and arrived Friday evening, just in season to see her die. She recognized him, but was too far gone to say any thing. There had never been a death here, when the circumstances seemed more trying than in this case. But we knew not that a still heavier affliction awaited us. We thought not that death would very soon come again, and take from us our dearly-loved Miss Lyon. But so it was. For about two weeks before Miss W. was taken down so suddenly, Miss Lyon had had something of the influenza hanging about her, but had not allowed herself to give up to it at all. When the intelligence of Miss W.'s condition was communicated to her, she was in a state to feel most deeply all that was trying in the case. She had just taken more cold, was more fatigued than usual, and had one of her hard headaches coming on. The next day was the annual fast for literary institutions, and she felt much anxiety to have the day blessed to us. The result of all was, such a headache and nervous excitement, that she could not sleep that night, and the next morning she was scarcely able to lift her head from her pillow. She attended devotions, but was able to say only a very few words. We have never seen her appear so sick in the hall as she did that morning. She was kept as quiet as possible during the day, slept well that night, and on Friday seemed better. She went into the hall both in the morning and afternoon. Those who heard her will not soon forget her remarks on that day. Would that we could convey to you her words, her manner, and the impression made upon our minds. But this we cannot do.

"She wished to lead us to turn from the trying circumstances in which we were placed, and follow that dear dying one up to the 'celestial city,' and, as its pearly gates opened to receive her, look in, and catch a glimpse of its glories. She seemed to have a most enrapturing view of heaven, and, with a full heart, exclaimed, 'O, if it were I, how happy I should be to go!' but added, 'Not that I would be unclothed, while I can do any thing for you, my dear children.' She then addressed the impenitent in a most impressive manner, and expressed much gratitude that the dying one was not of their number. A sense of the misery of the lost seemed to come over her, as she said, with much feeling, 'If one of you were on that dying bed, I could not take you by the hand and go with you down to that world of despair. It would be too painful for me. I should feel that I must draw the veil and leave you.' She urged them to enter at once upon the service of Christ, not from fear of death, but from a view of his infinite perfections, and his claims upon them. Miss Wingate's disease was of a form so malignant, and so dreaded, that there was a tendency to excitement. Miss Lyon read to us some passages from the Bible which speak of the fear of God, and made some remarks in connection. She looked upon all anxiety about the future as distrust of God, and asked, 'Shall we fear what he is about to do?' adding, 'There is nothing in the universe that I am afraid of, but that I shall not know and do all my duty.' Miss Wingate died about ten o'clock that evening, and it was important that her father and sister should leave with the remains early the next morning. Of course, there was much to be done to get every thing in readiness. Much effort was made to relieve Miss Lyon entirely from care and anxiety, and every thing was done faithfully and promptly. Still she did not sleep. She had felt a strong desire to have the father arrive before death had done its work, and she said she was 'so filled with gratitude to God for his goodness in this respect, that she could not rest.' The next morning, her whole appearance indicated too plainly that she was suffering from severe headache and intense mental excitement. She slept considerably during the day, and as she seemed quite comfortable, we fondly hoped that, after the rest of the night, she would be quite well; but that evening's mail brought the distressing intelligence of the death of a nephew by suicide while deranged, and without leaving evidence that he was a Christian. With her clear views of what it is for a soul to be lost, and her deep feeling in regard to it, this intelligence, coming when she was in that weak state, was too much for her, and that was not only a sleepless night, but a night of anguish. We could have wished that letter had not come just at that time. Still we know that that, as well as every other circumstance, was ordered in infinite wisdom, and we would not complain. As might be expected after such a night, the morning found her worse. She has had an affection in her head somewhat like scrofula, which has troubled her more or less for years. It has been worse than usual all this winter. In past seasons, when she has had a cold, there has been a swelling of the face connected with this difficulty. On Saturday, there was some swelling, and it increased on the Sabbath, but did not appear like erysipelas till Sabbath evening. Monday morning, her physician pronounced it a mild form of the epidemic erysipelas, — not malignant, like Miss Wingate's. He expressed much fear for the result, not from the disease, but on account of her peculiar temperament, her age, the state of her constitution, her past labors, and the extreme nervous excitement from which she was suffering when taken. We felt exceedingly anxious for her. For a time, every thing seemed encouraging. There was scarcely an unfavorable symptom in her case. The disease seemed to be entirely under control. Wednesday, it reached its crisis, and then the swelling began gradually to disappear where it first appeared. We had looked forward to this turning-point with intense anxiety, as we supposed it to be the critical time with her. When Thursday morning came, the swelling had continued to lessen, and she seemed no worse, and for a little time our anxiety was relieved. But she was not as much better during the day as we hoped she would be. As we have before said, her nervous system was intensely excited when the erysipelas came on, and as the disease left her, the excitement returned. This was the only unfavorable symptom. There was a free circulation, her pulse was good, and her skin seemed in a natural state. Every effort was made to keep her quiet, but all was in vain. That excitement increased until it became insanity; not the delirium frequently attendant upon fever, but real mental derangement. For nearly three days, she talked day and night, without intermission, in a worried, excited manner. This, in her weak state, produced congestion of the brain, of which she died last Monday evening, March 5. During the day, she said very little, and seemed to be in an unconscious state most of the time. Early in the evening, her pastor, Mr. L., called to see her. His voice seemed to recall her to consciousness for a little time. He said to her, 'Christ precious.' She seemed to summon up all her energies to make one great effort, raised both hands and clinched them, lifted her head from her pillow, and exclaimed audibly and with emphasis, 'Yes.' This was the last word she uttered. Short passages of Scripture were repeated, and her countenance showed that she understood and appreciated them. Those which spoke of the glory of

God seemed to interest her most. Mr. L. asked, 'Have you trusted Christ too much?' She made an effort to speak, but had not sufficient strength. Seeing this, he said to her, 'You need not speak; God can be glorified in silence.' As he said this, an indescribable smile came over her countenance. Mr. L., speaking of it, said, 'O, that soul is *full* of the love of the Savior.' This moment of consciousness, this last ray from her setting sun, was very precious to us. In about an hour after, her freed spirit was mingling in the glories of heaven. We thought of those almost 'last words,' 'O, if it was I, how happy I should be to go!' If the *thought* of these glories was so enrapturing to her, what must the *reality* be? Mourn for her we cannot. If there ever was a Christian eminently prepared for heaven, surely she was one. She has been unusually well this winter, and with her increase of physical strength there has been an increase of spiritual strength. We have never known her present the truth in a more clear, impressive manner, or speak more from the fulness of her heart, than she has this winter, especially the few times she has met us this term. Her increased spirituality has manifested itself in her daily familiar intercourse, as well as in her instructions in the hall.

"She spent her last vacation with Deacon and Mrs. P., of Monson," (as already described.) "When she returned to us, she appeared as if she had received anew 'an unction from the Holy One.' There was a vividness in her thoughts, a life and a power in her words, that seemed irresistible. As we were alone with her in her room one day, but a very short time before her sickness, she said to us, familiarly, 'I don't know why it is that my mind is so active. It seems to me, sometimes, as though I am doing my last work.' We thought not then that those were prophetic words. But how soon were we made to feel their truth! We would not recall her from that 'exceeding and eternal weight of glory' which is now hers. We would not have her lay aside her harp of gold, and come back to this sinful, sorrowing world. We would not murmuringly ask, 'Why was she not spared to us a little longer?' Rather would we be grateful to the Giver of all good that we have ever known her, that her light has shone upon us and the world so long and so brilliantly. Still, we may and must weep for our loss. We cannot tell you how dark, how trying these last days have been to us. You can scarcely conceive of the feeling of bereavement, of desolateness, that came over us, when we found she was really gone. It was to us like the blotting of the sun out of the heavens at midday. There is much that is afflictive in the circumstances of her removal. Sometimes, we are almost ready to ask, 'Can it be that every circumstance is ordered in infinite wisdom?' Yet we will not indulge a murmuring thought. It is exceedingly trying to have her taken away so suddenly, so unexpectedly, in Miss W.'s absence, when she seems so essential to us, and just at *this time*, when it appears so desirable that she should make that improvement of Miss Wingate's death which she so well knew how to make. It is trying beyond measure to have the light of her last days obscured by such a dark cloud. Yet can we not see wisdom in this seemingly mysterious providence? For, if hers had been such a triumphant death bed as we would have asked for her, might we not have been tempted to look more at that, and less at her *bright example*? O, what are a thousand *death beds* to such a *life* as hers!

"The funeral was on Thursday, March 8, at two o'clock, P. M. Previously, the corpse had been kept in the little room adjoining the seminary hall on the south side. It has been used for a similar purpose several times before. When Miss Wingate was laid there, Miss Lyon spoke of it as 'that sacred little room.' It is doubly sacred now. The young ladies took their last look of that loved countenance before going to church. There was a peaceful, pleasant, natural expression, that we scarcely dared to hope for. This was a great comfort to us, for during her sickness she looked so unlike herself, that friends would not have recognized her. After prayer in the seminary hall, by Mr. Laurie, we walked in procession to the church. There were only three relatives present — Mr. Wing, her brother-in-law, his son, and Mrs. Burgess's brother. These walked next to the coffin; then, in order, the trustees of the institution, the teachers, the senior class, the remainder of the school, and friends with us from abroad. We were forcibly reminded of those anniversary occasions, when we have so many times walked in procession and taken our seats in church in a similar manner; and the thought that we were for the last time following that dear one who had always been with us was almost overwhelming.

"All the services in church were impressive. Prayers were offered by two of the trustees, Rev. Mr. Harris, of Conway, and Rev. Mr. Swift, of Northampton. The sermon was preached by Rev. Dr. Humphrey, from the texts, 'The path of the just is as the shining light, that shineth more and more unto the perfect day,' 'The memory of the just is blessed.' They were afflicted in our affliction, and knew how to guide our thoughts and lead us to the throne of grace. The hymns sung were those commencing, 'God moves in a mysterious way,' 'Servant of Christ, well done,' and 'Why do we mourn departing friends?' We were interested in having this last one sung, because it was the one our dear Miss Lyon read to us as expressive of her feelings, when we were assembled in the hall just before Mr. Wingate left us with the remains of his daughter. This was the last time we heard her voice in that hall. We have mentioned that the evening before, which was the last time she met us at the table, she read the fifth chapter of 2 Corinthians.

MONUMENT TO MARY LYON.

"From church the procession moved to the grave. This is on seminary ground, a little south of the orchard. It can be distinctly seen from most of the rooms on that side of the building. It is a sacred spot, and many will love to visit it. As we gathered around the grave, the school sung the words set to the tune 'Mount Vernon,' altering them a little to make them appropriate. Mr. L. did not, as is usual, return the thanks of the mourners for the sympathy manifested; 'for,' said he, 'we are *all* mourners;' but he made a few impressive remarks, designed to lead us all to a suitable improvement of the event. We need not tell you how sad our hearts were as we returned from that grave to this desolate house. All the trustees, and nearly all of their wives, were here yesterday. Deacon P. was with us about half the time during Miss Lyon's sickness, and after her death. It was very gratifying to our feelings to have him here so much. The trustees all cheered and comforted us by their sympathizing and prayerful spirit. Last evening, their wives and the teachers had a precious little prayer meeting. They pledged us a daily remembrance at the throne of grace. It encourages us very much to know that others are seeking divine strength and divine guidance for us. The trustees wish us to go on, and carry out as fully as possible all Miss Lyon's principles and plans; and we feel strongly that there is a sacred obligation resting upon us to do this as far as is in our power."

Over the grave of Miss Lyon a beautiful monument of white Italian marble was erected a few months after her burial. This is defended by an iron railing about thirty feet square. The monument is a single square column, resting on a pedestal of granite. But the annexed sketch renders description unnecessary. The inscriptions on the four sides are as follows: —

On the west side.

MARY LYON,
The Founder of
Mount Holyoke Female Seminary,
and for twelve years
its Principal;
a Teacher
for thirty-five years,
and of more than
three thousand pupils.
Born February 28, 1797.
Died March 5, 1849.

On the north side.

"Give her of the fruits of her hands, and let her own works praise her in the gates."

On the south side.

"Servant of God, well done;
Rest from thy loved employ;
The battle fought, the victory won,
Enter thy Master's joy."

On the east side will soon be placed the memorable sentence which Miss Lyon uttered in the last instruction she gave to her school, as related on the preceding pages, viz.: —

"THERE IS NOTHING IN THE UNIVERSE THAT I FEAR BUT THAT I SHALL NOT KNOW ALL MY DUTY, OR SHALL FAIL TO DO IT."

The following lines on the death of Miss Lyon, by Miss Mary Esther Graves, a former pupil, were sung at the twelfth anniversary of the Mount Holyoke Female Seminary: —

"O sisters, in our souls may well be grieving,
For this cold world now holds one noble soul the less;
And God hath left to us, by this bereaving,
An empty blank where was her boundless tenderness.

"Great heart laid low! what tears were shed for thee,
When thou, so loved, to death's dark vale descended!
O'er earth's proud ones no grief like ours shall be,
E'en though by costly rites and honors high attended.

"In distant lands thy children scattered wide
With sorrow shall lament thee, and with tears recall
The memory of that wondrous wealth of love
Which could with equal warmth embrace and cherish all; —

"The largeness of thy soul, that made for thee
Great things most possible and easily achieved,
Thy energy of will to do or bear,
And work out all the plans thy noble heart conceived; —

"They shall remember every word and tone,
The solemn, earnest prayer, at twilight hours most sweet;
When thou wast fain to bear up with thine own
Our stubborn souls, and lay them weeping at Christ's feet.

"We know thou art not dead, not silent sleeping,
But only gone where nobler work than this is planned;
Thou'lt reap the harvest sown with care and weeping,
And we — God grant we meet thee there, at his right hand."

SECTION IV.

Estimate of Miss Lyon's Character and Labors.

It has been an object with the compilers of this work, as far as possible, so to present the correspondence and other papers of Miss Lyon as to impress upon our readers the leading features of her character, and the development of its traits, without much of formal statement on our part. At first, we feared this would be impossible, both because Miss Lyon, with a single exception, to be soon noticed, has left no private journal, and because her reference to her own feelings in her letters was only incidental, and generally formed an appendix to some letter on business. Of all the letters inserted in this volume, as remarked on a previous page, probably not one was written with the remotest idea on her part that it would ever appear in print; and her friends can easily conceive with what energy and earnestness, were she now alive, she would lift her hands, and open her large eyes, and exclaim against the use we have ventured to make of letters written under such circumstances. We do in fact value them so much the more, because they were all called forth by the feelings of personal friendship. Had we been copying from any private diary, we could not be sure that the writer, as she indited some beautiful sentiment, was not thinking that possibly that sentence might one day see the light, and, therefore, must be carefully adjusted and trimmed. But now we are sure that every sentence is an exact picture of Miss Lyon's feelings at the time she wrote. And if I mistake not, we have been able to present enough of such correspondence to give the attentive reader a fair impression of the sentiments and character of this lady, and of their gradual development. It may be, however, that those but slightly acquainted with her history will not derive from the details we have given correct notions of her character and progress; and, therefore, a brief analysis of it may be desirable. That may be important, too, as a means of deriving from her history those practical lessons which it is adapted to teach.

I propose, in the first place, to present the general features of Miss Lyon's character, and then refer to some characteristics more in detail.

General Characteristics.

This part of the subject I shall present in language used by myself in my anniversary address after her decease, and in the language of Dr. Humphrey in his sermon at her funeral.

In my address I remark, —

"We will first consider Miss Lyon's physical adaptation to the work assigned her.

"God gave her a vigorous and well-balanced physical constitution. Her stature was at a medium; the muscular powers were displayed in great strength and vigor; the vital apparatus was very strong, so as to give a full development to the whole system, and impart great tenacity of life. The brain was largely developed, and in proper proportion to produce a symmetrical character. The nervous system was full, yet free from that morbid condition which in so many produces irritation, dejection, or unhealthy buoyancy of the spirits, and irregular action of the mind. In short, all the essential corporeal powers were developed in harmonious proportion. You could not say that any of the marked temperaments were exhibited, but there was rather a blending of them all.

"Now, just such a physical system seemed essential to the part in life for which this lady was destined. Many, indeed, have been distinguished as instructors of youth whose constitutions were frail, and whose shattered nerves thrilled and vibrated in every exigency. But Miss Lyon had another office besides teaching to execute, which demanded unshrinking nerves and great power of endurance. In building up a new seminary, not conformed in many respects to the prevailing opinions, she could not but meet many things most trying to persons of extreme sensibility, and needing an iron constitution to breast and overcome.

"We will consider, secondly, Miss Lyon's intellectual adaptation to the work assigned her.

"And it gives a just view of the character of her mind to say, that it corresponded to that of her body; that is, there was a full development of all the powers, with no undue predominance to any one of them. It were easy to find individuals more distinguished by particular characteristics, but not easy to find one where the powers were more harmoniously balanced, and where, as a whole, the mind would operate with more energy and efficiency. She did, how ever, exhibit some mental characteristics, either original or acquired, more or less peculiar. It was, for example, the great features of a subject which her mind always seized upon first. And when she had got a clear conception of these, she took less interest in minute details; or, rather, her mind seemed better adapted to master fundamental principles than to trace out minute differences. Just as the conqueror of a country does not think it necessary, after he has mastered all its strongholds, to enter every habitation, to see if some private door is not barred against him, so she felt confident of victory when she had been able to grasp and understand the principles on which a subject rested. Her mind would work like a giant when tracing out the history of redemption with Edwards, or the analogies of nature to religion with Butler, or the great truths of Theism with Chalmers; but it would nod over the pages of the metaphysical quibbler, as if conscious that it had a higher destiny. And yet this did not result from an inability to descend to the details of a science when necessary.

"The inventive faculties were also very fully developed in our friend. It was not the creations of fancy merely, such as form the poet, but the power of finding means to accomplish important ends. Nor was it invention unbalanced by judgment, such as leads many to attempt schemes impracticable and quixotic. For rarely did she attempt any thing in which she did not succeed; nor did she undertake it till her clear judgment told her that it would succeed. Then it mattered little who or what opposed. At first, she hesitated; especially when any plan was under consideration that would not be generally approved; but when, upon careful examination, she saw clearly its practicability and importance, she nailed the colors to the mast, and, though the enemy's fire might be terrific, she stood calmly at her post, and usually saw her opposers lower their flag. She possessed, in an eminent degree, that most striking of all the characteristics of a great mind, viz., perseverance under difficulties. When thoroughly convinced that she had truth on her side, she did not fear to stand alone and act alone; patiently waiting for the hour when others would see the subject as she did. This was firmness, not obstinacy; for no one was more open to conviction than she; but her conversion must result from stronger arguments, not from fear, or the authority of names. Had she not possessed this feature of character, Mount Holyoke Seminary never would have existed, at least not on its present plan. But its triumphant success for one third of a generation is a striking illustration of the far-reaching sagacity and accurate judgment of its originator.

"Besides this seminary, the most striking example of the inventive powers of our friend is that only volume which she has left us, — I mean the 'Missionary Offering,' — called forth by an exigency in a cause which she dearly loved, and whose most striking characteristic is its missionary spirit. Yet it is, in fact, a well-sustained allegory, demanding for its composition no mean powers of invention and imagination.

"Miss Lyon possessed, also, the power of concentrating the attention and enduring long-continued mental labor in an extraordinary degree. When once fairly engaged in any important subject, literary, scientific, theological, or economical, there seemed to be no irritated nerves or truant thoughts to intrude, nor could the external world break up her almost mesmeric abstraction.

"Another mental characteristic of our friend was her great power to control the minds of others. And it was done, too, without their suspecting it; nay, in opposition often to strong prejudice. Before you were aware, her well-woven net of argument was over you, and so soft were its silken meshes that you did not feel them. One reason was, that you soon learnt that the fingers of love and knowledge had unitedly formed the web and woof of that net. You saw that she knew more than you did about the subject; that she had thrown her whole soul into it; that in urging it upon you, she was actuated by benevolent motives, and was anxious for your good; and that it was hazardous for you to resist so much light and love. And thus it was that many a refractory pupil was subdued, and many an individual brought to aid a cause to which he was before indifferent or opposed.

"Finally, I must not omit to mention her great mental energy and invincible perseverance. That energy was a quiet power, but you saw that it had giant strength. It might fail of success to-day, but in that case it calmly waited till to-morrow. Nay, a score of failures seemed only to rouse the inventive faculty to devise new modes of operation; nor would the story of the ant that fell backward sixty-nine times in attempting to climb a wall, and succeeded only upon the seventieth trial, be an exaggerated representation of her perseverance. Had she lacked this energy and perseverance, she might have been distinguished in something else, but she never would have been the founder of Mount Holyoke Female Seminary.

"But I hasten, thirdly, to speak of her religious adaptation to the work assigned her.

"And it is in her religious character, and there alone, that we shall find the secret and the powerful spring of all the efforts of her life which she would wish to have remembered. But I approach this part of her character with a kind of awe, as if I were on holy ground, and were attempting to lay open that which she would wish never revealed.

In her ordinary intercourse, so full was she of suggestions and plans on the subject of education, and of her new seminary, that you would not suspect how deep and pure was the fountain of piety in her heart, nor that from thence the waters flowed in which all her plans and efforts were baptized and devoted to God. But as accidentally, for the last thirty years, the motives of her actions have been brought to light, I have been every year more deeply impressed with their Christian disinterestedness, and with the entireness of her consecration to God. Without a knowledge of this fact, a stranger would mistake for selfishness the earnestness and exclusiveness with which she often urged the interests of her seminary. But in the light of this knowledge, the apparent selfishness is transmuted into sacred Christian love. Her whole life, indeed, for many years past, has seemed to me to be only a bright example of missionary devotedness and missionary labor. I have never met with the individual who seemed to me more ready to sacrifice even life in a good cause than she was; and had that sacrifice been necessary for securing the establishment of her favorite seminary, cheerfully, and without a moment's hesitation, do I believe, she would have laid down her life. I would, indeed, by no means represent her as an example of Christian perfection. I could not do so great injustice to her own convictions. But since her death, I have looked back over the whole of my long acquaintance with her in almost every variety of circumstance, to see if I could recollect an instance in which she spoke of any individual in such a way as to indicate feelings not perfectly Christian; or if I could discover any lurkings of inordinate worldly ambition, or traces of sinful pride, or envy, or undue excitement, or disposition to shrink from duty, or of unwillingness to make any sacrifices which God demanded; and I confess that the tablet of memory furnishes not a single example. What I considered errors of judgment I can indeed remember; but not any moral obliquity in feeling or action. They doubtless existed, but it needed nicer moral vision than I possess to discover them.

"I ought to add that this eminence of Christian character was founded upon a clear apprehension of biblical principles. She thoroughly understood and cordially embraced the doctrines of the Puritans, just as they lie in their massive strength in the Bible; not as they often come forth, alloyed and weakened, from the moulds of a self-confident philosophy. To study these truths was her delight. To explain them to her pupils was one of her most successful efforts as a teacher. Would that I could present on canvas the picture of Miss Lyon, as it lies in my memory, when she was engaged on the Sabbath in the study of Christian truth. I have frequently seen individuals in the somnambulic and mesmeric state, but none of them apparently more unconscious to external scenes than she was when thus absorbed in the contemplation of divine truth.

"There were two religious principles which exerted an overmastering influence upon Miss Lyon's character. One was, a sense of personal responsibility; the other, trust in an overruling Providence. As the Savior, when he went up to Jerusalem for the last time, with all his sufferings full in view, advanced before his disciples, as if in haste to suffer, so did she, when duty called, never wait for others, but was ever ready to precede them, and measure the amount of her sacrifices, donations, and efforts by her sense of duty rather than by the example of others. And it was this sense of personal responsibility which she urged always upon her pupils, and with great success. So strong, too, was her faith in a special providence, that delay and discomfiture in the execution of her favorite plans produced little or no discouragement, but led her merely to inquire more carefully whether there was not something wrong in her, or her plans, which occasioned the delay; and, having done all she could, she would wait long and cheerfully for the divine manifestation. And so often had she witnessed interpositions in her behalf almost miraculous, that her faith might often be seen steady and buoyant when that of others had yielded to appalling difficulties and dangers."

In his sermon Dr. Humphrey says, —

"In glancing at Miss Lyon's character, taken all in all, I hardly dare to express the high estimation which my long acquaintance constrains me to cherish, lest I should seem to exaggerate. I certainly should not express it but in the presence of those who have enjoyed equal or better opportunities for marking her radiant and upward course. I do not say that in her intellectual endowments she was superior to many other females, nor that she attained to the first rank in external graces and accomplishments; but this I do say, that, so far as I can remember, I have never known so much physical, intellectual, and moral power all combined in any one female as in our departed friend. Such labors as she performed would have broken down almost any other constitution years and years ago. Such constitutional energy as she possessed, always in action, often intense, would have shattered any ordinary framework long ere the meridian of life. Such tasks as she imposed upon her brain, especially during the three years which she spent in planning the seminary and enlisting the necessary agencies for getting it up, would have disorganized almost any other. How, under such extreme tension, the 'thousand strings' held together, and 'kept in tune so long,' was a wonder to all her acquaintances.

"Miss Lyon's mind was of a high order, clear, strong, active, well balanced, inventive, which no discouragement could depress, no obstacle daunt. It is very rare, indeed, to find such mental strength and such quenchless ardor controlled by the soundest discretion and the best 'round-about common sense.' One of the strong proofs of Miss Lyon's intellectual superiority, which must have struck all who knew her, was the power which she had to influence other minds. As a teacher and governess of a great school, few have equalled her in this respect. It might be difficult to show exactly wherein her great skill and success lay; but no scholar, I believe, was ever long under her care without feeling herself in a sort of enchanted circle, held there by invisible attractions which it was hard to resist, and from which very few wished to be released. Nor was it the young alone whom she had the power to influence. The maturest minds felt it when she needed their aid; and but for this, she could never have enlisted so many heads, and hearts, and hands as were necessary to build and establish this noble seminary.

"But it was the moral and religious in Miss Lyon's character which eclipsed all her other endowments, and in which her great strength lay. And the most prominent feature was *benevolence*. To do the greatest possible good to the greatest number was her study and delight. I feel that on this point there is hardly any danger of using too strong language. To say that she was preëminently benevolent is not strong enough. In humble imitation of her Savior, she seemed, wherever she went, and in all her relations, to be the very embodiment of love and good will to men, and never to have thought of herself, of her own ease, advantage, or convenience. It was enough for her that others were made wiser, and better, and happier, at whatever cost of toil or sacrifice to herself. She seemed scarcely to know that she had any personal interests to care for. If it were not a solecism in terms, I should say that Miss Lyon *lived out of herself;* and I do say, and I appeal to all who marked her beneficent course from early life, that she lived incomparably more for others, for her pupils, for the church, and for the world, than for herself. I do not believe that an instance can be recollected by any human being, since she entered on her bright career of usefulness, in which she appeared to be actuated in the slightest degree by selfishness. Mistakes she undoubtedly made, for who does not? but all the thousands who knew her might be challenged to show that she ever, by word or deed, appeared to prefer her own advantage to the good of others."

INDIVIDUAL TRAITS OF CHARACTER.

Power of continued Application.

The ability to fix the mind upon a particular subject for a long period depends upon the state of health, the interest taken in the subject, and the previous discipline to which the mind has been subjected. In all these respects Miss Lyon possessed unusual preparation. Her health was usually firm, her nerves not easily ruffled, her interest intense and absorbing in any important object in which she was engaged, and she had early learned to school all her powers into complete subjection to the will. Hence in study, in teaching, and in benevolent effort, many a fellow-laborer has given out exhausted while she was yet fresh, unfatigued, and vigorous. In the responsible and difficult circumstances in which she was often placed, this power of concentration and endurance was of great benefit, indispensable, indeed, to eminent success. I do not doubt that such extraordinary drafts upon her constitution exhausted the powers of life earlier than if she had been more sparing of her strength. But in the great labors of her life, her grand inquiry was, not how to preserve life, but how to use its energies to the best advantage. A few years more or less in this world were a matter of small importance compared with success in her projects.

Power of Attention to Details as well as great Principles.

No one acquainted with this lady will doubt that her mind more naturally seized upon the great principles than upon the details of a subject. Such minds usually find it hard to descend to particulars. Hers was not of this character. At least, the circumstances in which she was called to act rendered attention to minute details indispensable, and her powers were compelled to yield to the necessity with so good a grace that they seemed to be following a natural instinct. In the earlier schools which she taught, peculiar in many respects, no one could arrange the details but herself. Especially was this indispensable when she engaged in the manipulations of a chemical laboratory. In these she was very successful — a thing impossible without scrupulous attention to every item of preparation. So, too, did she keep her eye upon every detail of the new seminary. Scarcely was a brick laid or a nail driven without her cognizance and direction. Every part of the building was planned by herself; as it must have been to meet her views. In like manner did the arrangement and execution of the domestic work demand intense attention to details. And I have no doubt that the planning of the seminary, and the invention of a system by which the domestic labors could be performed without interference with the studies, were two of the severest mental efforts which she ever made, and probably cost her more sleepless nights than any other events.

Accuracy of Judgment.

What a vast amount of labor in this world is lost for the want of an accurate judgment to direct it! Indeed, a sound judgment is a rare acquisition, even among the ablest individuals. But so thoroughly did Miss Lyon study every subject in which she heartily engaged, and so accurately could she weigh every consideration, that rarely was there any waste of labor upon visionary or ill-arranged projects.

The accuracy of her judgment was sometimes put to the severest test. For in some of her noblest enterprises she had to go contrary to the judgment of some of the wisest and best men in New England. They did not dare to give their names and influence to aid in starting the new seminary on the plan she proposed, because they thought many of her views visionary and impracticable. With her great candor and confidence in the opinions of friends, it was a severe trial to go forward in opposition to their deliberate conclusions. But so long and carefully, as well as prayerfully, had she surveyed the whole ground, that the whole path through it was radiant with light in her eye, although to others covered with fog; and she could not refuse to go forward without doing violence to the strongest convictions. She triumphed; and it is but justice to say, that most of those who at first opposed her views were led ultimately to acknowledge the superior accuracy and sagacity of her judgment, and to help forward her enterprise.

The two points on which she differed from judicious friends were, first, attempting to obtain funds for the seminary by appealing solely to the benevolent principle, and offering no hope of pecuniary profit; and, secondly, venturing to leave the domestic labors of the institution to be performed by the pupils alone. The attempt made on the selfish principle to endow the Ipswich Seminary had entirely failed. For a time she seems to have been quite discouraged. But as she mused upon the two points above specified, a new hope insensibly took root in her mind; and, although in her correspondence she rarely speaks of them, there is no doubt but that they were intently examined again and again; for otherwise she could not have acquired so firm a conviction of their soundness as to venture her all upon their operation, in spite of the objections of wise friends and the ridicule of sagacious enemies. They proved, however, to be the grand means of success. The principal agent in obtaining the funds, who stood almost alone with Miss Lyon in maintaining these principles, is decidedly of opinion that without them he never could have obtained the money. I ought also to name a third principle, equally efficacious in securing aid from

Christians of moderate pecuniary means; and that is, the proposal to conduct the institution on such a plan that the expenses should be comparatively small. One or more of this trio of principles had the power to reach the heart and open the purse of a large proportion of the benevolent in the middle ranks of society, and of some among the wealthy; and therefore the enterprise succeeded.

Knowledge of Character.

It ought likewise to be added to what has been said, that Miss Lyon's familiar acquaintance with the principles, feelings, and whole character of the middling classes of society in New England, enabled her to judge with accuracy by what means they would be influenced, far better than others who had never themselves been familiar with that character. And here the wisdom of Providence was manifested, in taking her from the lower ranks of society, and causing all the early part of her life to be spent among those classes upon whom she was to operate, and for whose special benefit she was afterwards to labor. She thus learnt how to sympathize with their principles and feelings, and to meet their idiosyncrasies and prejudices. Had her early days been spent among the wealthy and fashionable, she never could have so wisely adapted means to ends, and her efforts would have probably ended in merely beating the air; and she would have concluded that the public were too ignorant, or too selfish, to found a permanent female seminary; whereas the only difficulty would have been in her ignorance of human nature. How many instances of such failures do we yearly witness! while the self-satisfied, though, it may be, benevolent authors of the enterprises, never once suspect that the sole difficulty lies in their ignorance of the human character.

It was not, however, in respect to one particular portion of society that Miss Lyon understood their character. She had great skill in reading human character generally from its casual and external manifestations. There was nothing in her intercourse, as is sometimes the case, which seemed to say to the visitor, "Now I mean to find out all about you;" but while there was a seeming indifference as to your character, there was a keen eye and a cool judgment, which together made out its general lineaments from your casual expressions, associations, likes and dislikes. Hence it was that, in selecting agents and others to aid her in her seminary project, experience, almost without exception, showed the judiciousness of her choice. And so, in respect to the numerous teachers she was called to select to aid her in her many schools, how almost universally (quite so for any thing that I know) has the selection been happy! Wherever I have seen Miss Lyon in the midst of coadjutors, it has always seemed to me as if Providence had sent her just the right sort of persons. I do not doubt that it was Providence; and yet the instrumentality has been her unusual power of reading human character by its usual manifestations.

Power of influencing others.

I refer chiefly to moral influences; for rarely in her schools, and certainly nowhere else, did Miss Lyon resort to any other. Yet her principle was, that the rules of a school must be enforced, and if any extremely refractory pupil should resist every other kind of influence, she had no conscientious scruples against physical compulsion; and, according to Mrs. Cowles, she did once resort to that kind of influence in enforcing a rule of the school. But, almost without exception, she knew how to concentrate and combine moral influences, before which none but the desperately depraved could stand; and such she took care to get rid of as soon as discovered. She was always careful never to promulgate any rule that had not good reasons for its observance, nor until she felt morally certain that it could be carried into execution by moral means. She took special care to avoid a predicament, into which less sagacious and less experienced teachers are sometimes brought, of being obliged to enforce rules for no other reason save that of sustaining the authority of the school and the dignity of the instructors. She did not waste her strength in fighting such battles, where common sense is on the side of the enemy, and the victory can be gained only by strangling that stern leader with the cord of authority.

The two principles which Miss Lyon found of mighty efficacy in enforcing her rules were, first, their reasonableness; and, secondly, the demands of benevolence. Many rules in a school are inconvenient and troublesome to conscientious, well-disposed adults; but they can see how necessary they are for the welfare of others, and how reasonable, therefore, it is that they should sustain such rules. At any rate, a benevolent regard to the good of the school should lead them to acquiesce in what might require considerable sacrifice on their part. Such appeals Miss Lyon found as powerful in regulating her schools as she did in obtaining funds for the Holyoke Seminary. And it was often amazing to see how triumphantly she would carry through any measure in her school that seemed important. She knew how to form and set in motion a current which made individual opposition as powerless as chaff before the whirlwind.

But this talent was not confined to her schools. Wherever it was necessary or desirable to influence individuals, or collections of men or women, she knew how to spin those silken cords that would lead them where she pleased. Yet she never pleased to lead them where reason, and conscience, and benevolence did not point the way. Generally, too, those who were thus influenced were not aware that the invisible force by which they were gently urged along emanated from her. Like a practised Mesmerist, she had thrown them into a better than somnambulic state, and it needed only her volitions afterwards to determine their movements. Sometimes, indeed, during their hallucination, she contrived to get money out of their pockets; but when they awoke from the dream of benevolence, they were always thankful that they had been robbed, and invited the robber to come again when the cause of education or religion demanded further help.

Ability to estimate and overcome Difficulties.

There is a great difference in the ability of different men, of equal intellectual strength, to estimate the true magnitude of the obstacles in their path, and in devising appropriate means for overcoming them. The principles by which such estimates are made I call *moral dynamics.* And skill in that science is one of the surest marks of mental power, conjoined to a well-balanced judgment. Many men possess a dazzling brilliancy, and can easily propose splendid schemes; but they seem incapable of forming any correct notions of the difficulties in their way, or of inventing means for overcoming them. The result is, that when put to the test of experience, their fine schemes are found impracticable. They try again, and imagination is alike prolific of some brilliant project; but it is alike impracticable. And so life is filled up with fascinating schemes; but, for want of skill in moral dynamics, the individual leaves no trace of his labors among men, and is remembered only as an ingenious dreamer.

On the other hand, the man whose judgment curbs imagination foresees objections and obstacles, and is able to decide whether he shall be able to overcome them. At any rate, he modifies his plans till he is sure they are practicable; and then he does not fear to risk all upon the attempts to carry them into execution. They may seem visionary to the world; but if he can go forward and show that they are mistaken, there is no surer mark of a superior mind.

There are some who have an accurate foresight of the difficulties they will have to encounter, yet they seem to lack the grace of perseverance, and soon become discouraged, when the conflict comes. But, after all, it is in the long and doubtful struggle that precedes the establishment of any new and important plan that we discover the true calibre and composition of the man. It is an ordeal from which very few come forth victors. When, therefore, we see a man, in such a struggle, holding on with the tenacity of desperation to his darling object, trampling down one and another difficulty that lies in his path, inventing new methods of attack and defence if the old ones fail, — in short, meeting every exigency with some new and effectual device, — we see that the root of the matter is in him, and we expect that he will come forth victorious at last.

Now, I hardly need say that the conflict of this sort, through which Miss Lyon passed, was of the most desperate and protracted kind; and yet nobly and triumphantly was she borne through it. The difficulties before her were appalling; yet carefully did she survey and gauge them before she put on her armor. The world, and even many of her best friends, while they admired her object and her spirit, felt sad that she was destined to an almost certain defeat. But they did not know how carefully she had surveyed the whole ground, nor what unconquerable energies she was capable of putting forth, nor how firmly her faith clung to divine help. Probably she had herself but a feeble consciousness of that hidden power she was called to exert. Had she known it, she might have said to every difficulty, *Who art thou, O great mountain? Before Zerubbabel thou shalt become a plain, and he shall bring forth the headstone thereof with shoutings, crying, Grace, grace unto it.*

Executive Power.

Given a definite amount of means, and the circumstances favorable and adverse in which a person is placed, it is required to determine how much he ought to accomplish. Work out this problem, and the results will show you nearly what Miss Lyon did accomplish. For she had a marvellous power of executing whatever she had the means of doing. Her practice trod close upon the heels of theory, and usually was nearly as perfect, like the molecular operations in chemistry and crystallography. Having great skill in estimating the difficulties to be overcome, and in devising adequate means, she also possessed a most unusual power of accomplishing the most by those means. In the large educational establishments with which she was connected, nothing was left at loose ends; no drones were allowed in the hive, unless they came there as guests. She had a remarkable power of keeping every body, pupils and teachers, employed, and the result was order, neatness, and despatch. In this way, too, she easily found time and room for introducing any extra operations that were desirable, and especially those of a benevolent and religious character.

The promptness, too, with which this executive power was manifested, deserves notice. The moment a thing was found to be desirable and practicable, she felt uneasy till it was in a course of execution. She suspected herself, as we shall see farther on, of being too impatient in such cases; but how venial such a fault, compared with the very common habit of procrastination! With her there was no putting off till to-morrow what could be done to-day. For a few years, in consequence of the length of some of the compositions, the public services in the church, on anniversary day, did not commence till half an hour after the appointed time. She was reminded of it as something unusual at the Mount Holyoke Seminary. The next year the public services commenced a quarter of an hour before the time appointed; so fearful was the principal lest the school should get the reputation of not being punctual.*

Administrative Power.

Although intimately connected with, this power is distinct from, executive power; or rather, perhaps, the latter is included in the former. Great energy in accomplishing objects may not always be associated with much wisdom; but this is essential to the management of a large literary institution. Here are numerous and quite diverse elements to be controlled. As to the pupils, it is one important qualification in

* The following statement will show the effect upon my own mind of long familiarity with Miss Lyon's great energy, promptness, and executive power. It is a dream, but such a dream as resulted naturally from the impressions made on the mind in its waking hours.

I had been giving a lecture at the seminary upon galvanism, and while putting up my apparatus, one of the teachers entered the room, and in a very quiet manner requested me to step down stairs because the building was on fire. I was struck with her *sang froid,* and still more so, on descending, to find how quietly Miss Lyon and some twenty others were standing by with pails of water, while a man was cutting a hole in the floor to get access to the fire, which was soon subdued.

A little time afterwards, I dreamed that I was at the seminary on anniversary day, when the examinations were going on before a crowded audience, in the large hall at the south end of the building. Happening to step out the door, I saw that all the north part of the building was on fire, the flames rushing out of the windows with such fury that it seemed impossible to save the edifice. However, every body seemed very quiet, and the examinations were not interrupted; but as I passed along, a window opened, and Miss Lyon appeared with a letter in her hand, which she committed to some one to take to the post-office. I thought it a strange time to be writing letters, but was told that it was a circular, which Miss Lyon was getting out to obtain means for erecting a new building!

a teacher to be able to adapt the means and motives to the peculiarities of character, and opinion, and prejudices, among them. And then, a large corps of teachers must be selected and made to act in unison, or a firebrand will be thrown into the school. Moreover, in most schools in this country, it is necessary that the principal exercise a rigid watchfulness over its pecuniary interests, being cognizant of every expenditure, and of the smallest means of income; the whole demanding no mean financial ability. Still further, in schools dependent on public patronage, the principal is expected to see to it that the public are kept informed of its advantages, and their attention favorably drawn towards it.

Now, to meet successfully these various and complicated duties requires great versatility of powers, and much wisdom founded on experience. Mere knowledge of literature and science in a teacher thus situated is but a small part of his qualifications. He must possess a large share of practical wisdom, to enable him so to choose and apply means as to give energy and success to a complicated system. None acquainted with Miss Lyon will doubt that she was eminently successful in her administration of several admirable schools, of which the Holyoke Seminary was the most extensive; yet was it conducted with wonderful skill and success. My own conviction is, that her talents for administration were decidedly superior to her skill as an instructor in science or literature.

Character as a Teacher of Science and Literature.

I have no doubt that Miss Lyon's mind was better adapted for giving instruction in science than in literature, using the latter term in the sense of belles-lettres, or polite literature; or rather, she could present and illustrate great and demonstrative principles better than the less settled and more tenuous distinctions and features of polite literature. It seemed to make but little difference, however, whether it was physical, intellectual, or theological science, for all these she taught almost equally well.

Perhaps the two subjects which she taught with the most success were chemistry and Butler's Analogy — subjects usually thought to demand talents of quite different order. In almost all her schools she lectured on chemistry, and performed the experiments with much success. To do this well requires qualifications of a rather peculiar kind; and in very few cases do we find these qualifications in persons devoted to polite literature or intellectual and moral science. But whoever has ingenuity, and has been taught in early life how to perform domestic labors with neatness and thoroughness, might hope to be at home in the laboratory.

Miss Lyon, however, possessed great versatility of talent; and in whatever department of literature or science engaged, a looker-on would suppose that to be her favorite pursuit. She was, indeed, deeply interested in every branch of learning that developed new and important principles and facts; and what branch does not develop these? Hence it was, as we have seen, that she entered with keen relish into the dry details even of grammar.

Great was her ability, also, to communicate her own interest and enthusiasm to the minds of her pupils. Indeed, enthusiasm is always contagious, and has ever been one of the grand principles employed by Providence for urging men forward in important and noble labors.

She was distinguished, also, for the thoroughness of her instructions. There was no such thing as a pupil's slurring over a recitation with her. Next to the religious interests of her schools was her anxiety to maintain a high standard of scholarship. Because she had succeeded in making the terms of her new seminary so low that the comparatively poor might come there, she knew that the impression would be created that the course of study would be limited and imperfect; whereas her determination was, that it should be as extensive and thorough, in all the more solid branches of learning, as any female school in the land; and those who have attended the annual examinations of that school must have been convinced of her success.*

As a religious Teacher.

I shall probably express the opinion of all who have been members of her schools when I say that Miss Lyon's superiority as a teacher was nowhere so conspicuous as in her religious instruction. Nowhere else has her death occasioned such a blank. At least five times each week did she feel it her duty to explain and comment upon some portion of Scripture before her school; and the extra occasions for such expositions were numerous. For most of these occasions she made preparation by a careful study of the Bible, and usually by noting down the leading thoughts she wished to present. They were, in fact, skeletons of sermons, though I am not aware that one of the sermons was ever written out. Many of these skeletons are in my hand, and if it were possible, I should add some of them as an appendix to this work, as a sample of her mode of presenting religious truth. Mrs. Cowles, however, has given us, in Part II. of this memoir, some vivid recollections of Miss Lyon's mode of religious teaching, and in Section II. of this part I have quoted from the journal of the institution several descriptions of her religious discourses. They were probably among the most efficient means by which so high a standard of piety was maintained, and so many were converted.

* At one of these examinations, when the senior class had just recited to Miss Lyon in Butler's Analogy, we happened to overhear the conversation between two presidents of colleges who were on the platform. Says one of them, "How is it that these young ladies recite in Butler so much better than our senior classes?" "I do not know," was the reply, "unless it be that they have a better teacher."

A prejudice, certainly not always unreasonable, exists against female preachers. When they address promiscuous audiences of both sexes, it is, perhaps, always of questionable utility. But shall we hence conclude that woman in no circumstances may expound the Scriptures to her own sex? Is it not specially commendable in teachers? Because they take a text, and present the truth, it may be, in as logical, forcible, and impressive a manner as the able male minister of the gospel, is the practice to be condemned? Surely not with reasonable men. I never had an opportunity to hear Miss Lyon sermonize. I presume I should have sought the opportunity in vain. But from the brief outlines of her efforts in this direction which I have looked over, and from the accounts of such efforts by her pupils, I cannot doubt that they were characterized by a logical ability, theological accuracy, biblical knowledge, and evangelical unction, from which many a male minister of the gospel might learn much. She was a diligent student of the Bible, and not only imbibed its spirit deeply, but had a clear conception of its doctrines as a science. Her doctrinal system was that of Calvinism, as explained by the ablest American divines. Her expositions to her school, however, were usually of a character highly practical, and she took no great interest in discussions merely speculative. In the skeletons of her discourses you see but few formal statements and defences of doctrines. But these formed the foundation on which she rested her instructions, and from which she drew her strongest appeals.

An interesting and instructive fact, as to Miss Lyon's feelings about communicating public religious instruction, is given by Mrs. Porter, in her account of Miss Lyon's last visit to her house. It appears that a leading object she had in view, in resorting to that sweet resting-place, was to prepare herself for communicating religious instruction, because she never before had realized so much her responsibility, and she hoped in that quiet chamber to obtain anew the wisdom and grace she needed. For almost thirty years had she been in the habit of dispensing divine truth to her pupils, and, in the estimation of every one but herself, with great skill, and certainly with great success. Yet at that late period did she so shrink from this work that it was only by earnest prayer that she could obtain courage and confidence enough to continue the effort. O, were those of us who preach the gospel more holy, how much more should we tremble when we think what a work is committed to us, and what a high honor and privilege are conferred upon us!

Character as a Writer.

Miss Lyon never wrote but one book, and that a small 18mo. of one hundred and two pages — the "Missionary Offering." This was prepared upon the spur of a special occasion, and in a brief time. Nevertheless, as a literary production it is not devoid of merit. Its plan demands much strength of imagination to raise it above ridicule. We see at once that the writer is rather unaccustomed to the armor she has put on; yet we also see that a little practice only would make it fit quite gracefully. Aside from the imaginative part of the work, it contains some fine descriptions. The account of "the mountain home," in Part I. of this memoir, will be recollected by our readers as one example. One of the concluding paragraphs contains sentiments so admirable, and expressed in language so appropriate, that I give it as a sample of what she might have done as a writer, had duty led her to devote herself to authorship.

"These were the words uttered by the voice of Wisdom, and, as she ceased, my thoughts returned to my own bosom. A sense of my own individual responsibility rested upon me with an indescribable weight. I felt that my duty in my own little sphere, and with my own feeble ability, was more to me in the sight of God than the duty of all the world besides. Could I throw my influence over the whole country, and bring thousands into the treasury of the Lord, it might not be so important a duty for me as to give from my own little purse that last farthing which God requires. Could I make my voice heard from one end of the land to the other, and so plead in behalf of the perishing heathen that all our missionary concerts should be filled with hearts bowing together in the presence of God, it might not be so important a duty for me as to carry my own feeble petition myself to the throne of mercy, and there, in the name of our blessed Redeemer, plead the promises with an earnestness which cannot be denied. While I mused on these things, my heart seemed ready to sink under its load, and I fled away to the cross of Christ, that there my weak and fainting spirit might find support, comfort, and guidance. There I looked up and cried, 'My dear Redeemer, make me *to know the fellowship of thy sufferings;* make me conformable to thy death.' Then under the banner of the Savior's dying love, I felt it to be the most precious privilege in the universe to deny myself, to take up my cross, and to follow the Lamb whithersoever he goeth." — p. 101.

Miss Lyon issued not a few circulars, explanatory of her schools, and often containing important hints upon education; and these, with her letters, as given in this work, are the only other means we possess of learning her character as a writer. The practised author will see at once that, while there is great strength and directness in her style, there is too much diffuseness and repetition. Her mind seemed to be so full of ideas and illustrations that she allowed too many of them to escape from her pen. She seems never to have learnt the most important art, so useful, and yet so seldom practised, of condensing her thoughts as much as possible. To spend a few months in a modern telegraph office would be a most useful discipline for persons whose minds seem to be crowded with thoughts.

Prudence.

Persons of great strength and decision of character, who engage in any new enterprise, which, if successful, will put others into the background, usually raise up not a few enemies. But such was not the case with Miss Lyon. Those who did not like her plans rarely, if ever, thought of censuring her severely. One reason was, that the evidence of sincerity and purity of motives was too palpable to be mistaken. But another reason was, that she put an unusual restraint upon her tongue. She was remarkably fluent in conversation, and often for hours would talk almost constantly; yet I do not remember ever hearing any thing she said quoted as injuring any one's feelings, or of a partisan or sectarian character. She must have been remarkably prudent to talk so much without dropping any thing which even enemies could take hold of. But it hardly needed so much watchfulness over her words as some must exercise, because she had no feelings save those of kindness towards any one. When thwarted or neglected by any one, she felt it keenly; but a few tears and a short prayer usually restored her serenity and kind feeling, and I doubt if any one can recollect severe remarks which she ever made towards others. She had great power in making a thing appear ridiculous, yet she never ridiculed persons, but only opinions.

Social Character.

Her great readiness in conversation and generous warmth of heart adapted her to become the life of a social circle. But so full of labors were her days that she could not devote as much time to social intercourse as she could have wished. Yet wherever known, she was ever a welcome guest; and she always delighted to make those happy with whom she associated. Young children were great favorites, and her influence over them was strong and salutary.

As a Friend.

We suspect that the pages of this memoir have disclosed one trait in this woman which will rather surprise many who had no intimate knowledge of her character. I refer to the great warmth and ardor of her attachment to her confidential friends. It rose in some cases almost to the romantic feelings of what goes by the specific name of love. It shows us how well adapted was her nature for a devoted attachment to a husband and children, and how happy a man must have been who should receive such love from such a heart, had not a sense of duty to higher objects constrained her to lavish that love upon the world rather than an individual.

In addition to the ladies already named to whom Miss Lyon was so ardently attached, she had many highly esteemed friends, with whom she delighted to spend a few hours, or a day, from time to time; and all such found her friendship an unfailing and unchanging spring, from which the waters always gushed forth warm and abundant. Religion was the basis of all her friendships, and hence nothing but your desertion of its principles or spirit could alienate her feelings.

Hospitality.

Herself for so long a wanderer, Miss Lyon knew how sweet to such was a cordial and sincere welcome. Hence, when she had secured a home, its doors were ever wide open to all her friends. Although in that hospitable mansion she was necessarily much occupied, yet you knew that she would do all she could for your happiness.

Cheerfulness.

This trait of character was most remarkably developed in our friend. Never, in the most trying periods of her great struggle, when almost every other heart seemed sad at the prospect of failure — never did I see a cloud over her countenance. But it was always radiant with hope. Through the glass of faith she could look beyond the darkness, and see the sky clear. Doubtless a vigorous state of bodily health contributed very much to this continual sunshine, as an opposite state often does to darkness and despondency; yet faith in God's providence and confidence in her principles were no less necessary to maintain her almost unvarying buoyancy of spirit. And it contributed exceedingly to the pleasure of her social intercourse that she seemed always to be looking at the bright side of objects, and never obtruded her private troubles upon your notice.

Economy and Self-denial.

These two virtues, so intimately related, were by Miss Lyon reduced almost to mathematical rules. As to economy, she did not push it to such extremes as to starve the body or the mind, or to produce noticeable singularity. In respect to dress, while she would have it plain and enduring, she would have it decent and appropriate; not exciting attention, like the inmates of monasteries and nunneries, by its coarseness and peculiar fashion, which say to the beholder, "See how self-denying we are, and how separate from the world!" Rather did she prefer, as far as possible, to conform to the prevailing modes of dress, so as not to excite attention; and moreover all nature taught her that Providence never meant that man should cover himself with garments that make the human form disgusting. On the other hand, if the prevailing fashions required that costly and finical ornaments should be added to garments already comfortable and becoming, she did not hesitate to be singular, because such fashions required sacrifices which she could not make.

As to food and drink, the fundamental principle adopted

at the seminary has been, that such kinds and in such quantity should be used as would give the greatest strength and ability to labor, both bodily and mentally, and secure the best and most permanent health. These objects, according to the established principles of physiology, demand that the solid food, whether vegetable or animal, should be plain, and substantial, and well cooked; and no one who has been a frequent guest at the table of the seminary can doubt that these principles have been substantially carried out there. As to the cooking, I have found it decidedly superior to that met with generally in the larger hotels and boarding-houses in our country. Many probably would miss some delicacies, which a person accustomed to them would deem quite important, but which are, in fact, deleterious. Some, too, doubtless, never get reconciled to the habit of using cold water only at meals, which is used by all save those on the sick list. And by such a practice, many, I doubt not, are saved from that list; for I hesitate not to say that the ablest physiologists in every age are decided in the opinion that water, "unmixed and unspoiled," is the best of all drinks for the young, and that to become strongly attached to other beverages, such as tea and coffee, is an indication of the commencement of a morbid state of the system.

In respect to the above points, and all others, indeed, where economy and retrenchment were practised at the seminary, we may truly say that there was no extravagance of opinion or action; but the rule of the Latin poet, so useful in many of the affairs of this world, was adopted, —

> "Est modus in rebus: sunt certi denique fines,
> Quos ultra citraque nequit consistere rectum." *

There was another class of objects about which Miss

* There is a medium in things; there are certain bounds, beyond which and within which the truth is not found.

Lyon was obliged to have some fixed principles. There was a chord in her soul that responded quickly to whatever in the fine arts or other arts was agreeable to good taste. How far, then, should she go in gratifying a taste for the productions of the artist, the architect, the landscape gardener, &c.? She was sure that the cultivation of such a taste was lawful, even for a religious man, in some circumstances. But such objects were for the most part beyond her pecuniary means, unless she gave up a darling feature in the seminary, and followed the example of too many of our female schools, which put their terms just as high as the public will bear. So far as comfort and respectability of appearance were concerned we have seen that she felt it her duty to go. But all beyond this, unless offered as a gift from her friends, she subjected to the test of its comparative importance. Fine architecture, fine paintings and music, beautiful gardens, with fountains and statuary, &c., are quite desirable. But then, while the world is so full of ignorance, irreligion, and misery as it now is, while the funds of our benevolent and educational institutions are so entirely inadequate to the noble objects they have in view, is it right for the Christian, especially for one of limited means, to indulge in objects of taste, or any superfluities, which, however lawful and desirable in themselves, are certainly far inferior in importance to the renovation of the world? This question Miss Lyon decided in the negative, and acted accordingly. We have seen that she expended from twelve hundred to fifteen hundred dollars, after leaving Ipswich, in getting up the seminary, — probably about all she then possessed, — and that she left to the cause of missions nearly the whole of the property that remained at her death, viz., two thousand dollars. But this was only a small part of her benefactions. I am credibly informed that she expended more for benevolent objects, from year to year, than she used for herself, exclusive of board. How few Christians reach such a standard as this! If they did, what an altered aspect would the world soon exhibit!

Leading Motives of Action.

There are three leading selfish motives which, I fear, will go far, in many cases, to explain the gigantic and self-denying labors men have undergone to found and establish new institutions, economical, educational, and religious. The first is the hope of pecuniary gain; the second, a love of distinction among men; and the third, the hope of posthumous reputation. Let us see whether Miss Lyon could have been influenced by any of these.

It was surely not a love of money; for, by the very constitution of the seminary, both she and all connected with it were cut off from the hope of making money, save so far as to enable them to live in the most economical manner.

As to the two other selfish motives, — the desire of a name before or after death, — what sentence is there, in all her correspondence given in this memoir, that could be construed into such a desire? And had there been any such intimation in her unpublished letters, the compilers would certainly have brought it out. For in their work they have kept a sharper lookout for defects than excellences in her character. They know that in the lives of most persons eminent for benevolence the little imp, selfishness, is not unfrequently seen peeping out from behind the cloak of benevolence; and hence our readers would expect some such development in the case of Miss Lyon. But those most intimate with her were not able to discover it.

But the following extract of a letter to Miss Grant, dated March 1, 1833, just as she was about leaving Ipswich to commence her great enterprise, affords the best development of her motives of action which I have found; and there are in it such marks of verisimilitude as must satisfy any one that she speaks the honest sentiments of her heart. I give it, with some comments, as quoted by me in my address at the anniversary subsequent to her death, although it has already been presented in Part II. p. 178.

"'For myself, if I should separate from you, I have no definite plan; but my thoughts, feelings, and judgment are turned towards the middle classes of society. For this class I want to labor, and for this class I consider myself rather peculiarly fitted to labor. To this class in society would I devote directly all the remainder of my strength, (God permitting;) not to the higher classes, not to the poorer classes. The middle class contains the main springs and main wheels which are to move the world. Whatever field I should occupy, it must be a humble, *laborious* work. How I could get a footing sufficiently firm for my feet to rest upon the remainder of my days, where my hands could work, I know not. But by wandering about a year or two, perhaps Providence might open the door. I should seek for nothing permanent after my decease as to the location of my labors; but I should consider it desirable that I should occupy but one more field, that I should make but one more remove, till I remove into my grave.'

"What a beautiful development of Christian character does this extract present! What a waiting upon God and confidence in his providence! How and where she could get a foothold to labor she knew not; 'but by wandering about a year or two, perhaps Providence might open the door.' How does such faith remind us of that other servant of God, who, 'when he was called to go out into a place, which he should after receive for an inheritance, obeyed; and he went out, not knowing whither he went.' What humility and readiness to labor are here shown! 'Whatever field I should occupy, it must be a humble and *laborious* work.' Yet what holy sagacity is exhibited in strongly desiring to labor for the middle classes, because 'they are the main springs and main wheels to move the world'! That is, she wished to labor where her efforts would do the most good. And finally, what perfect freedom from the ambition of having her name attached to some great institution, by which many have supposed she was actuated in her severe labors! 'I should seek for nothing permanent after my decease as to the location of my labors.' How evident that such a state of mind was just the one that was needed for the herculean task of founding this institution! and how obviously it was the natural result of that long and severe discipline through which she had passed!"

The conclusion to which all the facts lead us, and which accords with the unanimous opinion of all her most intimate friends, is, that the leading motive of her life was the benevolence of the gospel. It was a simple desire to advance God's glory and man's good. These are convertible terms, and whoever promotes the one cannot but advance the other. Hers was a benevolence that embraced every human being, and hence her intense interest in foreign missions. But it did not, therefore, omit to feel a deeper interest in those with whom she was connected by the ties of nature, of friendship, or of proximity. Because God had placed these individuals near to her in order to call forth her special attention, she thought a sufficient reason for laboring and praying more earnestly in their behalf. And still there was room enough in her large heart for all the world beside.

If we look back upon the whole life of Miss Lyon, we can hardly fail to see that the controlling influence of Christian benevolence was the grand secret of her extraordinary success. If we watch the progress of most Christians, we shall see that, although love to God and to man predominates in their lives, the leaven of selfishness is largely mixed with higher motives, sometimes almost to the time when they exchange worlds. But just so soon as Miss Lyon sat down calmly to examine her spiritual condition, — probably when she first went to the school at Byfield, — she seems to have consecrated herself more entirely to the works and principles of benevolence than is scarcely ever witnessed. From that time to the day of her death it is difficult to discover, from any thing she said, or wrote, or did, any mixture of selfishness with benevolence. During her childish days, at the primary school and the academy, it is probable that the pride of superior abilities and the love of distinction were spurs to her efforts; though even then we have testimony that she seemed unconscious of her superiority. But when at Byfield she made up her mind to be a Christian indeed, she put away childish things. The sun, as it rose above the mountains, was a full-orbed circle, and so it continued till it set in glory. Spots there were, undoubtedly, upon its surface, and they seemed to her almost to cover its face. But it needs better glasses than I have found to discover them.

Defects of Character.

The defects of a person's character appear less or greater, according as we agree with or dissent from his opinions and courses of conduct. Now, Miss Lyon's opinions upon education and religion were distinctly marked, and her practice very decided. Those who reject the doctrines of evangelical or orthodox religion, will, of course, regard her tenacious adherence to them and decided inculcation of them as unhappy defects, which more light would have removed. So those who regard revivals of religion as of doubtful utility, or the result of fanaticism, and those who suppose it indelicate for a teacher to make individual appeals to her pupils respecting personal religion, will regard the whole system of means adopted by this lady as improper. Those also who object to a young lady's being obliged to engage in culinary operations while at school will regard the system in operation at South Hadley as a defect in Miss Lyon's judgment. Many also consider the exclusion from that school, to so great a degree, of certain ornamental and fashionable branches, such as painting, music, and dancing, as a most serious defect.

Now, Miss Lyon never expected to please persons who differed from her on such points. While she entertained the kindest feelings towards such, she did not expect their patronage; although, as a matter of fact, many such have sent their daughters to her school; showing, at least, their liberality and confidence in her honesty of intention. Yet, partly from these differences of opinion, and partly from the public life Miss Lyon was obliged to lead for several years, many strange notions concerning her have prevailed in the community.

Not a few, for instance, have looked upon her as a sort of Amazon, of strong mind and inflexible purpose, but wanting in those tender and delicate feelings which are appropriate to woman. But it does seem as if her letters to her intimate friends, given in this volume, ought to remove such an impression, and convince every one that there was a warmth and intensity in her attachments and sympathies, which seems more like the enthusiasm of the devoted lover than the cool, calculating friendship of the stern and the phlegmatic. I fancy that, even to many of her acquaintance, this will be a new feature in her character. For during most of her public life was she obliged to suppress these more tender and delicate feelings, and do the work of a resolute and persevering man.*

* One misrepresentation respecting her school Miss Lyon tried hard to correct, but with indifferent success; for up even to the present time we find her school represented as "a manual labor school." (Dr. Davis's *Half Century*, &c., p. 75.) Certainly Dr. Davis meant to state only the truth of the case; but we have had other proofs that this opinion is widely spread. Yet in the domestic arrangements of the school she never dreamt of any such plan. She introduced this feature into her school because she thought it would contribute to the comfort and independence of the pupils, because she thought it would encourage mothers to teach their daughters domestic work, because she thought it would tend to make such

To those large classes of the community who sympathize with Miss Lyon in her views of religion and domestic economy, the features of her character and policy above referred to, instead of being regarded as defects, are looked upon as her chief glory. Still I do not deny that even in the eyes of such she had defects. I have already intimated that I had not been able to discover any moral defects, though doubtless they existed. Her defects related to matters of less consequence.

Enough, probably, has been said about minor defects in her manners. So often had this subject been brought to her notice in early life by her intimate friends, that she thought her deficiencies were many, and submitted herself to their training. But she never took lessons of the dancing, or the drawing, or the music master; and she found too little interest in the minute rules of polite society to keep her attention much upon them, and so she made up her mind to endeavor to treat all men according to the gospel standard of politeness, and be satisfied. Had she taken the opposite course, I doubt not she would have passed for a fine lady, and been welcome in the saloon, the ball-room, and the pleasure party; but I doubt whether her manners would have been as acceptable to the middling classes of society as they have been; and I am quite sure that this memoir would not have been called for after her death.

The idea that Miss Lyon was gross in her manners, and negligent in her dress, after she became a teacher, is not true. She was unassuming and kind, though frank in her address, hospitable without stint in her seminary, dignified in public, fluent and able in conversation, and ever ready to aid others when in her power. And such politeness she taught

labors respectable, and because she thought that the daughters of the middling and poorer classes, at least, ought not to become wives till they learnt how to take care of a family.

and illustrated in her schools. If any parents wished their daughters to learn the minor graces of manners, she desired them to go somewhere else.* She taught only the great principles of dress and manners, and expressly declared that her school was not intended to give a complete education, but only its essential parts. This whole subject, however, has been so well treated in Part II. of this memoir, that I need not add another word.

I have often thought, without, however, having had much opportunity for personal examination, that Miss Lyon had the defect as a teacher of using too many words. Teachers often use too few; for it is usually important to repeat over again and again the principles of learning, before pupils will get a clear idea of them. But if we undertake to explain them by a multitude of prolix illustrations, we often produce confusion. I have thought often that Miss Lyon erred somewhat in this direction. Yet this defect, if it existed, was so neutralized by the enthusiasm she was able to awaken in her pupils, and by the clearness of her own views of every principle she attempted to explain, that her prolixity was little thought of.

Not a little complaint has been made that Miss Lyon's great power of physical and mental endurance led her to expect too much from her pupils. I cannot doubt that there was some foundation for this complaint; and I believe, that after a time, in consequence of some examples brought before her, she became fully aware of this tendency. She tried, I know, to guard against it, and modified some of her rules. Yet it was not certainly till late in life that she had much experimental knowledge how hard it is for a person in feeble health to do the work of one who is vigorous, or even to do any thing with entire system. It should be added, however, that Miss Lyon did not attempt to educate those of feeble constitution and delicate habits, though willing that others should do it. But she aimed to train up those who might be able to stand in the front rank, in the great battle which learning and religion have to sustain with ignorance and wickedness, and she could not have two sets of rules in the same institution.

Towards the close of life, as age and infirmity began to show their influence, and accustomed as she always had been to bear so many burdens, she seemed anxious to assume too many duties, as if she could do them better than any one else. Doubtless in this she was greatly influenced by a benevolent desire to relieve others; and yet it often embarrassed rather than assisted the other teachers. But an infirmity of advancing age ought hardly to be reckoned a defect of character, but rather as a providential indication that the time for her most active labors was drawing to a close.

This is certainly a meagre list of defects in a character so marked with excellences. A sympathy with her religious, economical, and educational views in general, and personal friendship, may have blinded me to her failings. Yet I have searched for them in all quarters, except where I knew strong prejudice to exist, and quite as diligently as for excellences. I do not doubt that among her pupils, now and then, one might be found who never sympathized at all with her principles of benevolence, of education, or domestic duties, and who yet was forced to conform to rules based on her views. Such individuals, I presume, would feel that the defects of Miss Lyon's character were very glaring; though probably unable to define their objections, unless it were to complain of her unrivalled power of always carrying her point. But until such persons can show that without Miss Lyon's principles and traits of character they can accomplish for the world's good what she has done with them, we must look upon their evidence as suspicious.

That Miss Lyon practised the same rigid scrutiny over her minutest as well as most important actions, we have an interesting evidence. I have remarked that she left no private journal, with one slight exception. That exception consists of the following private paper, on which she noted down some of those minor points on which it became her to exercise a special watchfulness. It shows how rigid was her self-discipline, and that she was not able, any more than those who have gone before her, to reach a high standard of piety without strenuous efforts.

I. *Worldly Intrusion on sacred Time.*

1. In secret prayer.
2. In reading the Bible.
3. In little opportunities for ejaculatory prayer.
4. In family devotions.
5. Sabbath generally.
6. " Hearing the word.
7. " Prayer in sanctuary.
8. " Communion service.
9. " Holy communion with God the Father, Son, and Holy Ghost, and with the disciples of Christ.
10. Longing after the blessings of the Sabbath to be disseminated.

II. *Misspending Time.*

1. Indefinite musings.
2. Anticipating needlessly.
3. Needless speculations.
4. Indulging in reluctance to begin a duty.
5. In doubtful cases not deciding at once.
6. Musing needlessly on what has been said or done, or what may be.
7. Spending time in reverie which should be spent in prayer.

III. *Self-control.*

1. Too ardent in a new thought.
2. Too desirous for immediate execution.

3. Feelings discomposed by opposition.

4. Expressing disagreement, when it would be better to wait a little.

5. Reminding others of their deficiencies, without sufficient object. (Be like Christ. Inquire, before speaking, whether it will do good, whether duty requires; if not, avoid alluding to them.)

6. Referring to mistakes of pupils in little things, family duties, domestic work, &c. (Inquire if they designed to do right; if their mistake involves any general principle; whether there will be any occasion for them to commit the same again.) Be like CHRIST — like CHRIST.

Moral Sublimity of her Course.

If an individual rise out of obscurity, and gradually work his way upward and onward, throwing off a light that cannot but arrest public attention, or sending out an influence that stirs deeply the elements of society, and if to the end of life that individual holds on in a brilliant and undeviating path, the beholder cannot contemplate his course without a feeling of sublimity. And especially if that individual has advanced original opinions, which have stirred up against him the prejudices of the ultra-conservative, but which, nevertheless, have ultimately outlived all prejudice, and triumphed, still grander does his course appear. Yet more magnificent does it become, if it appear that pure benevolence was the controlling motive in this person's heart. Indeed it then constitutes true moral sublimity.

Apply now these statements to the case of Miss Lyon. From the time when she first began to distinguish herself as a teacher, about thirty years ago, she seems to have given herself up to the work of benevolence with an entireness and whole-heartedness unusual with young Christians. Her vigorous physical and intellectual powers were at once brought wholly into the service of God and man. Wherever she went her pathway was radiant with love, though she seemed unconscious of its brightness. It was interesting to see how her course widened and ascended as she went forward. If one plan had to be given up, another more promising succeeded. The world thought her quixotic, and pitied and ridiculed her fanaticism. But with her heart fixed on God and on doing good, she made no reply, or returned only blessing for reproach. Her influence widened ; her plans succeeded ; the world began to applaud, and the wise confessed her superior discernment and wisdom. At her death she had opened a perennial fountain of influence, whose streams had already reached the remotest nations of the earth, and which, through future generations, is destined to do more for the happiness of the world than all the acts of the mightiest queen that ever ruled. Surely the whole picture impresses us forcibly with its moral sublimity ; and we might almost have expected that the chariot and horses of fire would have been granted to close a scene so much like an angel visit.

There were some particular scenes in Miss Lyon's life, from which, as we now see them, we get an impressive lesson of moral grandeur. One was the time when she closed her connection with the Ipswich school, and went forth alone to the great work of founding the new seminary. To accomplish such an object, it would be necessary to enlist a great many hearts and hands ; for some sixty thousand dollars must be provided ; and this she proposed to raise by an appeal to the benevolent principle only. She had seen a seemingly judicious effort to accomplish almost the same object fail in a wealthy, enlightened, and religious part of Massachusetts, although the appeal was made both to the selfish and benevolent principles. Moreover, the plan she now proposed contained some features which were not approved by her most judicious friends. Yet in silence almost, and single-handed, she moved forward to the conflict. Well do I remember the first meeting which she called, of perhaps half a dozen or more of the friends of female education, in the valley of Connecticut River, and which took place at my house. Those friends saw the enterprise to be a noble one; but how could it ever be accomplished? Such, I doubt not, was the secret feeling of almost every one, though not expressed to Miss Lyon. To her we pledged whatever of influence or time we could devote to the work. But little did we know what Providence had in store for her. Little did we imagine that any of us should live to see the work accomplished, and sixteen hundred pupils go forth from the institution into every quarter of the globe. True, it did cost gigantic efforts on Miss Lyon's part, and from those intimately associated with her; for it is a law of the natural and moral government of God, that great objects demand great efforts for their accomplishment. But now that we can compare the magnificent results with the instrumentality, the picture is certainly full of moral grandeur.

Another scene, perhaps equally grand, was the retrospect which she took of her life upon her fiftieth birthday. Previously she seems to have been too busy to pause and look over the way in which the Lord had led her. But now the panorama lay spread out around her. Far off in a quiet mountain spring could she see the feeble beginning of her course; but soon one and another tributary could be observed coming in, till now the current was moving deep and strong, loaded with blessings to the whole human family. Many hundred energetic and devoted women could she see laboring for the world, converted to God through her instrumentality in the numerous revivals through which she passed; and not less than three thousand pupils, scattered through the world, disseminating every where the noble sentiments she had taught them; a mighty leaven spreading through the surface of society to lift it up to the daylight, and fitting it to bring forth an abundant harvest to God's glory and man's good. And when she thought of the permanent character of her new seminary, she could not but see its widening influence upon the world's noblest destinies, down to the time when the earth shall be filled with the knowledge of the Lord as the waters fill the sea. Truly the whole scene must have been one of overwhelming interest, and well calculated to awaken pride in a selfish mind. But in her heart it only roused into intense action a feeling of gratitude to God, who had given her such a noble field of labor, and crowned her efforts with so much success.

One other scene of moral grandeur I must notice. The chariot had come for her removal, though she knew not that it stood by the door. But she had just been down to the banks of Jordan to see one of her beloved pupils pass over; and as she returned, she said to those who survived, "O, if it were I, how happy I should be to go!" She had been called, yet there was one more message for her to deliver — the noblest she ever uttered. Fear and anxiety had begun to spread in the seminary lest a malignant and fatal disease was among them. Under the influence of an excitement almost supernatural, having just been looking, as it were, into heaven, and burning with a desire to lead her pupils to trust Providence, and fear no evil, she appeared before them, and exclaimed, "Shall we fear what God is about to do? There is nothing in the universe that I fear, but that I shall not know and do all my duty."

These two noble sentiments embrace almost the sum and substance of practical religion to him who is supremely devoted to the will of God. He believes that every event of life is embraced in God's providence, and, therefore, he need never be anxious about any of them, after having committed himself unreservedly to the divine disposal. Yet he may still fear that he shall fail either in a knowledge of his duty, or in its performance. Noble sentiments to constitute a Christian teacher's last instruction to her pupils! Appropriate words for the Christian to utter just as she was entering the portals of heaven! Worthy a place on the marble that hands down her memory to posterity!

PRINCIPLES FIRST ESTABLISHED, OR MORE FULLY APPLIED, BY MISS LYON'S EFFORTS IN THE CAUSE OF FEMALE EDUCATION.

1. *Permanence in a Female Seminary.*

Since the funds for the Holyoke Seminary were all contributed on the benevolent principle, they must be entirely used for the good of the school, and never for private emolument. Hence, if funds can make any institution permanent, they will do it here, unless they are grossly neglected or perverted. Teachers and trustees may succeed one another from generation to generation; but there the buildings and their contents will stand, to be used only for the purpose of female education. When Miss Lyon founded the institution, she was not aware that any seminary was in existence, in this country or in Europe, that possessed any such inherent principle of vitality. Hence this experiment introduced a new and most important principle into this department of education. Since that time, I believe the example has been followed in several places; but I have no definite statistics on the subject. That this feature promises much for the education of our daughters, no one will doubt. It cost Miss Lyon much, as we have seen. Let her have the credit of first proving it practicable.

2. *The successful Appeal to the Benevolent Principle for obtaining Funds.*

It is an interesting fact in the history of this enterprise, that when the selfish principle had been tried under favorable auspices and failed, benevolence should have carried the day. It speaks well, indeed, for the moral character of New England. But it shows also how much stronger in the Christian's heart is benevolence than selfishness, and how much more certain one may be of success by an appeal to the former than the latter, if a case can be made out clearly demanding benevolent interposition. Till Miss Lyon made the effort, it was not thought that, to found schools for the education of females was a work of consequence enough to be placed alongside of the missionary enterprise. But she satisfied the church of its vast importance, and thus struck a chord which drew forth pecuniary offerings from benevolent hearts to a greater amount than selfishness had ever bestowed. We trust that a discovery so important will furnish the key for unlocking treasures still more abundant, for raising neglected woman to her true intellectual and moral rank.

3. *Successful Combination of domestic Labors with a high literary Standard.*

Manual labor schools had been in operation before Miss Lyon commenced her efforts; that is, schools where the pupil's labor, a part of the day, for compensation, and thus pay their tuition or board. But their operation has been, for the most part, unsatisfactory. Miss Lyon never had much confidence in them, especially among females; although her plan, as we have seen, was mistaken for a manual labor establishment. There was labor, indeed, in her plan; but undertaken in the way practised at the seminary, it does not interfere with, nay, it probably promotes, attention to study, because it aids the other kinds of exercise in invigorating the physical system. In the manual labor schools it has been found often that the standard of scholarship was lowered by exhausting labors. But at the Holyoke Seminary this evil is avoided. The plan, therefore, is another indication of Miss Lyon's sagacity and accuracy of judgment. Nor should it be forgotten that in this matter she went ahead of her wisest contemporaries, and had to venture almost alone upon an experiment whose failure would have been extremely mortifying.

4. *Union of a high Standard of Study with a high Standard of Piety.*

The grand complaint among Christians in respect to our literary institutions is, that when teachers and pupils become deeply interested in their studies, their piety droops, if it do not die; so that it often becomes true, as Henry Martyn says, that "Christ is crucified between two thieves — classics and mathematics." But no such complaint can be brought against the schools founded and taught by Miss Grant and Miss Lyon; and it is this feature that has endeared them most to the devotedly pious. That the standard of scholarship and of study has always been very high in these schools, no one acquainted with them can doubt. What the standard of piety has been, let the pages of this memoir testify. It is no boast to say that it has been higher than that of the scholarship. Now, this result has been accomplished mainly in two ways. First, by making Christian benevolence the grand motive of all intellectual effort. Under the influence of such a motive, even severe study of literature and science becomes efficient means of growth in grace. With such a motive to stimulate him, Jonathan Edwards could make the solution of a question in metaphysics almost as powerful a means of promoting his piety as prayer.

How controlling the religious sentiment was in Miss Lyon's system of instruction will appear from the following summary of her "excellences as an educator," as put down by Miss Grant (now Mrs. Banister) at my request. They consisted, she says, —

"In her knowledge and love of the character and government of God. In her knowledge of the human mind; its capacities; its destiny; of the effects of habits, and the way to form them aright; of the relation of the human mind to its Creator and to its fellow-creatures, and of the obligations growing out of those relations. In her entire and cordial reception of the Bible as a revelation of God to man; in her knowledge and love of this blessed book. In having the first and second table of the moral law written on her heart; in her peculiar facility in leading others to an intellectual understanding of this law. In her deep appreciation of the gospel as opening a way for the salvation of the lost; her living faith in all its truths, especially in Him who is *the* truth. In her glowing benevolence to all for whom Christ died. In her burning zeal to do all in her power towards extending the knowledge of the Redeemer to every creature. In her understanding and heartfelt sense of the necessity of bringing great and unalterable truths in contact with the human mind in a way suited to produce their legitimate effects. In a practical belief that what ought to be done can be done. In a deep sense that without God's blessing all will be in vain. In an abiding reliance on God, and a cheerful expectation of his blessing."

The second means by which the high standard of scholarship was prevented from lowering the standard of piety was to make instruction in religion as systematic, as thorough, and as personal as instruction in literature and science. The one subject was begun as early as the other, and rarely were the two allowed to interfere. The preference, indeed, was always given to religion; and if, in any emergency, they came into competition, there was no hesitation in deciding whether learning or religion should have the preference. At the commencement of each session it was ascertained who were professors of religion, and who not; who indulged the Christian hope, and who not; and the different classes were put under appropriate instruction. The teachers of the sections made themselves acquainted by kind personal intercourse with the spiritual condition of the pupils under their instruction, and felt a peculiar responsibility for those under their charge. Interesting and peculiar cases were reported at the teachers' prayer meetings, and specially commended to God.

Such systematic and thorough exertions in behalf of their pupils God, as we might expect, was ready to bless; as he did, term after term and year after year; and as he always will do wherever teachers are equally faithful. Let no instructors think strange if they are not thus blessed, if they neglect these most reasonable means of success. And let these ladies have the credit of solving this most important problem, how to combine hard study and successful scholarship with warm-hearted piety.

LESSONS TAUGHT BY MISS LYON'S LIFE AND LABORS.

I can refer here only to the most prominent of these lessons, such as are taught most distinctly.

1. *Motives of Action.*

The grand secret of Miss Lyon's distinguished success lies in the fact that she so early and so fully adopted the benevolence of the gospel as the grand controlling principle of her life. This armed her with a power to labor and suffer to an extent quite amazing to ordinary minds, governed by selfish principles. She felt certain that she meant the good of others, and, therefore, she knew that God approved of her conduct. Hence disappointments, delays, and perplexities could not disturb her equanimity or damp her ardor. She knew nothing of the chagrin and exasperation of disappointed ambition, none of the heartburning and jealousy of wounded pride, and none of the despondency and irresolution of selfishness thwarted in its plans. If not successful at once, she was sure that renewed effort, perhaps a little modified, would be rewarded. Though she labored for man, she did not look for her reward from him, but from God; and, therefore, perverseness and ingratitude only led her into nearer communion with her Father in heaven.

What an example for our imitation! Most of us try for a great many years, even after hopeful conversion, to mix selfishness and benevolence — principles as repellent as oil and water; and the result is, that we are double-minded and vacillating, inconsistent and unhappy. Afraid to leave our cause and our reputation in God's hand, we aspire after human distinction with morbid eagerness, and are unwilling to labor for the good of others unless the world are looking on and shouting approbation. In short, the leaven of selfishness works so powerfully within, that we have little quiet, and because we are striving to build up two incompatible interests, we are apt to fail of both. We do not know where the difficulty lies, and wonder why we do not accomplish more, and why we are so unhappy. Could we, like Miss Lyon, early open our hearts to the full influence of Christian benevolence, we should attain to at least a portion of her success and happiness.

2. *Trust in Providence in the darkest Hour.*

Rarely has God put the faith of his servants to a severer test than Miss Lyon's. Acting from motives of whose purity she was conscious, she, in conjunction with Miss Grant, had labored for years to give permanency to a female seminary. But after being tantalized for a long time with every reasonable prospect of success, one prop after another was struck from beneath their hope, until Miss Lyon, at least, gave it up in seeming despair, concluding that she should never see a permanent female institution. But though she seemed to acquiesce in what appeared to be the will of God, it is clear that a lingering hope still played around her heart, and she watched with intense interest the first indication of an opportunity to throw herself, body and soul, into the work. Delay and discouragement had, in fact, served only to intensify her desire, and make her consecration to the work more entire. So strong was her faith that it needed only the faintest ray of light to make it all sunshine around her. To others she appeared to be walking in darkness, with no star of hope to cheer and guide her steps. But she felt sure that an infinite hand had taken hold of hers, and was leading her forward; and, therefore, she could take step after step in the dark with as much confidence as if she could see before her an iron pavement. To human sagacity the next step might seem to lead over a precipice. But, confident that she was in the path of duty, she was equally sure that God would hold her up. And so he did, at last, plant her feet upon a rock.

What an instructive and animating example of strong faith have we before us! We see that if we can only be sure that we are in the path of duty, we need fear nothing else, but may commit every thing to God, in the certain confidence that the result will be satisfactory and glorious. It is of little consequence how deep is the darkness before us, if we can only feel that our hold is strong upon the divine promise. No one whose motives are not pure, and who has not a spirit of prayer, can have such faith. It was the gift of God in Miss Lyon; it must be his gift in others. May he bestow it abundantly upon the churches!

3. *The true Spirit of Revivals of Religion and the proper Means of securing and promoting them.*

The history presented in this volume seems to me peculiarly instructive on this subject. During the last thirty years, a great deal has been said about spurious revivals of religion, and improper modes of conducting them. But I doubt whether any of the disputants, who are pious men, would hesitate to say that the revivals in the schools of Miss Lyon and her associates were genuine and conducted in a proper manner. They were brought about by earnest prayer and the plain presentation of evangelical truth. They were noiseless and solemn, and did not interrupt the ordinary pursuits of the pupils or teachers. Hence there was little or no reaction, and few of those hopefully converted turned back to the world.

Within a few years past, there have been long and learned discussions in the religious newspapers on the question why the influences of the Spirit had been so generally withdrawn from the churches. How easily might they have solved the question, had they spent a few weeks at the Buckland, Ipswich, Derry, or Holyoke school! Soon after the beginning of the term, could they have looked into Miss Lyon's heart, they would have seen there an anxious fear lest the term would pass without a revival of religion. She feared, too, lest the difficulty lay in her own heart. Perhaps she would leave the seminary for a few days to go into some retreat, where she might examine her heart and seek help from God. Then, as she returned, you would witness a new unction attending all her religious efforts. Teachers would catch the same spirit, and soon the solemn countenance and the tearful eye would show that God had heard prayer, and usually did the work go on till many a heart was melted and subdued.

Now, in such a scene as this, repeated from term to term, might the speculating theologian and editor find enough to solve their doubts about the Spirit's withdrawal, and a rebuke for their want of fidelity. Here they saw no speculative wrangling, but the union of strong and simple faith with earnest labor. The teachers first got their own hearts ready for a visitation of mercy, and then they were prepared to labor for the salvation of others. And if like antecedents are followed by like consequents, the same preparation and fidelity will be followed by like results in all seminaries of learning as well as in the churches.

Why, then, are not such results witnessed? May not the

question be answered by inquiring whether the same antecedents exist? Is it not a fact that, in many of our seminaries of learning that glory in the name of Christian, not only week after week, but term after term, pass away before the teachers take the trouble to inquire into the spiritual condition of their pupils? and often in a four years' course of study does it not happen that not one word is said to individuals respecting their personal religious feelings? In some seminaries, with numerous teachers, should we not inquire in vain even for a weekly private prayer meeting, where the spiritual state of the institution might be learnt and prayed over? And yet you will find teachers in such schools wondering why revivals are few and far between, and quite unable to see why Mount Holyoke Seminary should be so distinguished by their frequency and power.

I must think that in Miss Lyon's history, in connection with revivals, there is valuable instruction, even for the pastors of our churches. Where can they find a better model, as to means and results, of such a work, than was uniformly presented in her schools? Why should even ministers be ashamed to learn wisdom, on a subject so important, from a woman, especially from one so eminent for wisdom and piety, and whose experience in revivals was so extensive?

4. *An elevated Example of Christian Character for Imitation.*

Whatever diversities of opinion there may be as to some minor traits of Miss Lyon's character, all will agree, I doubt not, in regarding her piety as of a very high order, and worthy to be held up as a model for imitation. So deeply rooted was it in the great principles of the gospel; so free from extremes of every sort; so gentle, yet so energetic; so active, yet so contemplative; so keenly alive to the wants of those near at hand, yet so expansive and all-embracing, so full of good works, yet so full of Christ; so weak in itself, yet so strong in the Lord, — in short, so harmonious and full in all its proportions, that every Christian husband and parent would wish that, next to Christ, his wife and daughters might take her as their model. And in an age like the present, many of whose tendencies are adverse to elevated piety, it is well to be able to hold up such a model. How few of us, who profess religion, do not see our deficiencies when we compare our motives and whole character with hers! And when we think what she was and what she did, who of us does not feel desirous of catching at least a portion of her falling mantle?

But I hasten to a close; and I do it in words which I used to terminate an address at the first anniversary of the seminary after her decease.

"Such was Miss Lyon; such the discipline through which she was made to pass to fit her for her work, and such the magnificent results. We are amazed when we look back at the amouut and magnitude of her labors. Very few females have done so much for the world while they lived, or have left so rich a legacy when they died. Nor is the fair picture marred by dark stains, save those of microscopic littleness. From the days of her childhood to the time of her death, all her physical, intellectual, and moral powers were concentrated upon some useful and noble object, while selfishness and self-gratification seem never to have stood at all in the way, or to have retarded the fervid wheels of benevolence. I cannot, therefore, believe that it is the partiality of personal friendship which leads me to place Miss Lyon among the most remarkable women of her generation. Her history, too, shows the guiding hand of special providence almost as strikingly as the miraculous history of Abraham, of Moses, of Elijah, or of Paul. O, it tells us all how blessed it is to trust Providence implicitly when we are trying to do good, though the darkness be so thick around us that we cannot see forward one hand's breadth, and bids us advance with as confident a step as if all were light before us.

"This picture, too, is a complete one. Her life was neither too long nor too short. She died at the right time, with her armor on and yet bright. But her friends saw that, strong as her constitution naturally was, it was giving way under such severe and protracted labor, and the infirmities of declining years beginning to show themselves, even at the age of fifty-two. But with her Savior she could say, 'I have finished the work which thou' (God) 'gavest me to do.' All her important plans had been carried into successful operation, and tested by long experiment; and the institution was in the right condition to be committed to other hands. She had, also, of late been rapidly ripening for another sphere of labor. One of her friends, who had been more intimately connected with her for several years past than any other, when at a distance she heard of her sickness, felt confident that it would be unto death; for she had known how, for some months previous, her friend had been feeding daily on manna, and pluming her wings for her upward flight. Severe, therefore, as her removal seemed when first announced, it happened just at the right time; and I cannot wish to call her back. But I do feel, — and many who hear me I doubt not feel it too, — I do feel a strong desire to be borne upward, on an angel's wing, to the Mount Zion where she now dwells, and to hear her describe, in the glowing language of heaven, the wonders of Providence, as manifested in her own earthly course, as they now appear in the bright transparencies of heaven. Yet further, I long to hear her describe the still wider plans she is now devising and executing for the good of the universe and the glory of God; and how admirably her earthly discipline fitted her for a nobler field of labor above; so that those providences, which appear to us to have been consummated on earth, were, in fact, only a necessary means of adapting her to a work which shall fill and delight all her powers throughout eternal ages. Gladly, too, would I listen to her intensely earnest inquiries respecting her beloved seminary and friends on earth; and learn whether, in some way unknown to us, she may not be still able to administer to their welfare. O, how sweet, too, would it be, could we listen to that rapturous song of praise which ever and anon she would pour forth to her Redeemer, as his glories strike her eye, or his past kindness touches a chord of gratitude in her heart!

"But, alas! how vain are all such aspirations! And yet, my Christian friends, if we are faithful to God and duty as she was, in a very few days all this intercourse and communion will be a reality. Some of us may not, indeed, be able to sound so lofty a note of praise as our glorified friend; but our song and our communion shall nevertheless be the music and the intercourse of heaven; and that will be enough."

"We enter heartily into the spirit of the work, sympathizing in the enthusiastic love betrayed in every comment upon the character, labors, trials, and triumphs of one of the noblest of all New England's daughters. That it will be widely purchased and widely read there is no doubt, and it possesses a double value in giving the history of an institution peculiar and original in its features, which has had, and is still to have, an important influence in shaping the educational systems of the country." — *Springfield Republican.*

INDEX RERUM; or Index of Subjects, intended as a Manual to aid the Student and the Professional Man in preparing himself for Usefulness. With an Introduction, illustrating its Utility and Method of Use. By Rev. JOHN TODD. The plan of this work is very simple, and so exceedingly well adapted to the purpose for which it is intended that it has received the approbation of all who have examined it.

"*It is just the thing.* I have never had a system so complete as yours. I shall take an early opportunity to speak to the whole body of students in regard to it, and shall advise every man to buy a copy." — *From Professor Worcester, of Amherst College.*

"I am happy to say that the plan and execution of the Index Rerum are both such as will fully meet my approbation; and I shall recommend it to my pupils as a valuable auxiliary to their studies." — *From Professor Olmsted, of Yale College.*

"I have no hesitation in saying that the plan of the Index Rerum, by Mr. Todd, is better adapted to the object for which it is intended than any other with which I am acquainted. Its great excellence consists in its simplicity, and this renders its advantages so obvious, that to those who want any thing of the kind an inspection of the work must preclude the necessity of any recommendation. It will give me pleasure to speak well of it here." — *From President M. Hopkins, of Williams College.*

"I fully concur in the favorable opinion expressed of the simple arrangement and utility of the Index Rerum.

"GEORGE BANCROFT."

"Of the necessity of something of the kind to hold fast the thousand important facts and sentiments which refuse to be detained by the slight associations of the moment, I have been fully, painfully sensible. A few years ago, I adopted the plan recommended by Locke, but soon relinquished it, as requiring too much time and labor. I subsequently purchased the Cambridge Theological Common Place Book, but here I found myself embarrassed by a printed index of subjects designed only for professional reading. And it *is only in the plan of the Rev. Mr. Todd's work that I find an arrangement exactly suited to the wants of the professional and literary man.*" — *From Professor M. P. Jewett, of Marietta College, Ohio.*

THE STUDENT'S MANUAL; designed, by specific Directions, to aid in forming and strengthening the intellectual and moral Character and Habits of the Student. By Rev. JOHN TODD.

"I thank you very cordially for your STUDENT'S MANUAL. I have not found time yet to read it through; but I have read a number of chapters, and highly approve of both the design and execution. It cannot fail to do good. It will attract by its manly independence of tone, as well as by the sparkling brilliancy of its thoughts. *Macte virtute!* Persevere in your own advice, and it cannot be that you will not reap a bountiful harvest." — *From Professor Stuart, to the Author.*

"We do not often meet with a book which contains a greater amount of sound counsel and honest sense than this." *Knickerbocker.*

"This book is just what the title intimates. It supplies a vacancy which no other work has filled. It discusses a great variety of subjects, and all with ease, energy, and practical sagacity. No student should fail to possess it and to *use it as a manual.* We recommend it to all young men who are concerned to cultivate their minds and to be respectable and happy in life." — *Recorder, Philadelphia.*

"In our opinion, Mr. Todd has thrown together some of the best practical lessons for students, or for young men generally, that we have ever seen embodied in a single work." — *U. S. Gazette, Philadelphia.*

"We have looked through this volume with more than ordinary care, and certainly with more than ordinary interest. Every student has felt the need of a friend, willing and able to instruct him on the thousand questions which arise in relation to his course of studies, time of labor and exercise, his health, diet, discipline of mind, &c. It will be found a pleasing volume, its lessons being always conveyed in an easy and attractive style, and urged by familiar historical or other illustrations." — *Philadelphia Gazette.*

LECTURES TO CHILDREN; familiarly illustrating important Truth. By Rev. JOHN TODD.

"We take peculiar pleasure in recommending this little book to our youthful readers as an important acquisition to the juvenile literature of our country. The author has succeeded in adapting his style to those for whom he writes. His illustrations are so simple, that we think they cannot fail to bring his subjects down, or rather, to carry them *up*, to the comprehension of the youngest reader. The style of this book is somewhat like that of Abbott's works, yet abounding more in anecdotical illustration, and evidently designed for the youngest readers. The author's points are briefly and simply stated; his illustrations attractive, beautiful, and satisfactory." — *New York Evangelist.*

"This book is, in our opinion, written in the right style, and on the right principles for interesting and benefiting children." — *Abbott's Magazine.*

Extract from a Letter. — "In begging you to express my thanks to —— for the excellent little volume of 'Lectures to Children,' I cannot refrain from mentioning the great delight, and I hope edification, with which my daughter, of five years old, peruses them. I have kept them as a part of her Sunday reading, because they opened such fine subjects of conversation for that sacred day. But this morning she comes to me, and says, fervently, 'Mother, if I get all my lessons perfectly, may I read one of Mr. Todd's sweet sermons?' and by her application to her simple tasks in geography, natural history, and writing, won the desired reward. Such a suffrage from a simple-hearted and intelligent little one weighs more, in my opinion, than the praise of practised critics." — *From Mrs. Sigourney.*

"We very much question whether Mr. Todd *could* have engaged in any labor which would better subserve the great interests of religion — the interests of that blessed kingdom which is most dear to every pious heart — than by writing these Lectures. He has *not descended* from the high and holy work of the ministry by preaching to children or writing for them, as *some* may suppose. He is magnifying his office. When did the Savior appear more divinely glorious than in his exhibitions of affectionate regard for *little* children?" — *Sabbath School Visitor.*

"It is a book which every pastor and every Christian parent should study, in order to learn how to adapt instruction on the most important Christian doctrines to the capacities of a child." — *Boston Recorder.*

THE YOUNG MAN; Hints addressed to the Young Men of the United States. By Rev. JOHN TODD.

"Among all the good books for young men which the present age has produced, we know of none better adapted than this to elevate their character and destiny." — *From Rev. Dr. Sprague, of Albany.*

"To say that this book will bear recommending is saying nothing at all. It will bear *reading*, and that the fiftieth time. It will bear analysis and criticism more rigid than we have time to apply to it." — *Boston Recorder.*

"This 18mo. of 355 pages we wish could be placed in the hands of every young man in our country." — *Philadelphia Gazette.*

"It discusses in an able, earnest, and affectionate manner the subject of character, and its value and foundation; of the temptations of young men, their habits, industry and economy, cultivation of the mind, self-government and religious views; and also the great end of living. This work contains continuous counsel, and will be found a precious friend to those young men who consult its pages and heed its suggestions." — *Bangor (Me.) Whig and Courier.*

"The works of no author at the present day are perused with more interest than those which emanate from the erudite mind of Mr. Todd." — *Northampton Courier.*

TRUTH MADE SIMPLE; being a System of Theology for Children. By Rev. JOHN TODD. 18mo. 424 pages.

"This volume contains eleven lectures on the attributes of God. An address to mothers is prefixed, which is fitted to produce a deep impression. We commend this little volume to parents as one 'which is so plain that children can understand it, so pretty that they will read it, and so good that it will make them good.'" — *Philadelphia North American.*

"The author has succeeded admirably, not only in making truth simple, but exceeding beautiful, even to the comprehension of a child." — *New York Commercial Advertiser.*

"All parents and Sunday school teachers should read this work. Children of every age will be fascinated by it." — *Philadelphia Episcopal Recorder.*

"We know not where to begin or where to end in commending this work to the notice of parents. From the interest manifested by children to hear more, when we have read extracts from the work, either at our quarterly meetings or on the Sabbath, we are led to infer that this is one of those rare productions which children will love to hear read again and again, which, while it engages the attention, cannot fail to enlighten the understanding and favorably impress the heart and conscience." — *Mothers' Magazine.*

THE SHORTER CATECHISM ILLUSTRATED. By Rev. JOHN TODD, With Engravings. Vol. I. 18mo. 246 pages.

"It is entirely new in its design, and, like all the author's works, peculiar in its execution. The design of this work, as expressed by the author, is, 'to aid parents to instruct their children in the great truths of religion.'" — *Philadelphia North American Gazette.*

"This work will be sought after by almost every Christian family, and we doubt not, in the hands of Providence, be the means of much good." — *Pittsfield Eagle.*

"This is one of the very best little books for children we have yet seen." — *New Haven Morning Journal.*

THE SHORTER CATECHISM ILLUSTRATED. By Rev. JOHN TODD, D. D. Vol. II. 293 pages.

"This work is designed to explain and enforce the truths of Scripture in that familiar and attractive style for which the author is so justly celebrated." — *Boston Daily Traveller.*

"A unique work, evincing no ordinary power of invention, and an unrivalled fertility of illustration." — *N. Y. Tribune.*

"We never read a clearer and more satisfactory exposition of 'fixed fate, free will, foreknowledge absolute,' and other as dark and mysterious theories, than in these simple, unpretending stories." — *Weekly Eagle, Brattleboro'.*

THE MORAL INFLUENCE, DANGERS, AND DUTIES CONNECTED WITH GREAT CITIES. By Rev. JOHN TODD.

"A most important object is treated in this little volume. We would that it were in the hands of every young man exposed, or about to be exposed, to the thousand temptations of our large towns. Its hints are also valuable to parents and guardians who send their children into the midst of danger, where so many miserably perish." — *New York Observer.*

"A work replete with important truth and valuable instruction." — *Christian Observer, Philadelphia.*

"It is written in a style of simplicity and force, and should be placed in the hands of every young man about to take up his residence in a 'great city.'" — *Boston Mercantile Journal.*

GOULD'S ADAMS'S LATIN GRAMMAR. — *New edition — fine paper.*

TODD'S WORKS. — The Student's Manual. 12mo. pp. 392. Truth Made Simple. The Young Man. The Lost Sister of Wyoming. Stories on the Shorter Catechism.

"The author of these works is much known in this country and Europe as a man of great ability and distinguished success as a writer. There is a peculiar attraction about his style, a force and vividness in his sentiments and illustrations, which cannot fail to make them popular, and, by their high character and design, and the necessity which calls them forth in the midst of most urgent professional duties, they do equal honor to the author's head and heart." — *Boston American Traveller.*

HISTORY OF A ZOÖLOGICAL TEMPERANCE CONVENTION HELD IN CENTRAL AFRICA. By EDWARD HITCHCOCK, D. D., LL. D., President of Amherst College. Beautifully illustrated.

"Dr. Hitchcock has succeeded in a preëminent degree in combining instruction and amusement, so that the man of science may be edified; while it is adapted to the understanding of the common reader, and will prove a most attractive volume to all classes." — *Star of Temperance, Rochester.*

"It is an admirable *jeu d'esprit,* and will be read with delight by the whole of that immense class who love temperance and fun." — *Puritan Recorder.*

"A charming and instructive fable, and one that will implant good seed in many a youthful mind." — *Philadelphia Paper.*

"A very successful attempt to inculcate the principles of total abstinence by means of allegorical illustrations." — *Burritt's Christian Citizen.*

"President Hitchcock has in this *report* offered one of the most entertaining works of the day. The wit is of the sharpest point — the satire penetrating as a blade. Many a generous laugh will be had over the irresistible pungency and satirical truth of this little volume." — *N. E. Washingtonian.*

www.ingramcontent.com/pod-product-compliance
Lightning Source LLC
LaVergne TN
LVHW010525100826
845148LV00001B/95

* 9 7 8 1 4 2 5 5 9 1 1 3 7 *